The
NAPA & SONOMA
Book

A Complete Guide

THE
NAPA & SONOMA
BOOK
A Complete Guide

TIMOTHY FISH

*with Peg Melnik, Chris Alderman
and Jean Saylor Doppenberg*

Berkshire House, Publishers
Stockbridge, Massachusetts

ON THE COVER AND FRONTISPIECE

Front Cover Landscape — *View of rolling vineyards in the Napa Valley, Faith Echtermeyer; Inset — Wine barrels at Sebastiani Vineyards, Sonoma, courtesy SVVB; Beringer Vineyards chefs demonstrate their skills in the Rhine House's grand hall, St. Helena, courtesy Beringer Vineyards; Balloon flights over Napa Valley, courtesy NVVB.*

Frontispiece — From the top: *V. Sattui Winery, St. Helena, Chris Alderman; Winemaker Mike Grgich in the barrel room of Grgich Hills Cellars, Rutherford, Chris Alderman; Wine tasting at Buena Vista Winery, Sonoma, courtesy SVVB; The Wine Exchange, Sonoma, Chris Alderman.*

Back Cover — *Napa cabernet sauvignon grapes, ready for harvest, courtesy NVVB; Sonoma Mission Inn, Boyes Hot Springs, courtesy SCCVB; Vintage Festival, Sonoma Plaza, courtesy SVVB.*

THE NAPA AND SONOMA BOOK: A COMPLETE GUIDE © 1992 by Berkshire House, Publishers

Photographs © 1992 by Chris Alderman and others (see acknowledgments)

ISBN 0-936399-16-3
ISSN 1056-7968 (Series)

Editors: David Emblidge, Virginia Rowe
Design of original text for Great Destination series: Janice Lindstrom
Cover design: Jane McWhorter

Berkshire House, Publishers
Box 297, Stockbridge, MA 01262
Manufactured in the United States of America

The **GREAT DESTINATIONS** Series

- The Berkshire Book: A Complete Guide
- The Santa Fe & Taos Book: A Complete Guide
- The Napa & Sonoma Book: A Complete Guide
- The Chesapeake Bay Book: A Complete Guide (Spring 1992)
- The Coast of Maine Book: A Complete Guide (Spring 1992)

Contents

Acknowledgments..ix
Introduction...x
The Way This Book Works..xi
Cities in Napa and Sonoma Counties..xi
  Populations of..xiii

CHAPTER ONE
Aged to Perfection
HISTORY
1

CHAPTER TWO
Here, There and Everywhere
TRANSPORTATION
14

CHAPTER THREE
The Keys to Your Room
LODGING
26

CHAPTER FOUR
The Finer Things
CULTURE
77

CHAPTER FIVE
Pleasing the Palate
RESTAURANTS AND FOOD PURVEYORS
112

CHAPTER SIX
Vintage Harvest
WINERIES
169

CHAPTER SEVEN
On the Run
RECREATION
220

CHAPTER EIGHT
An Embarrassment of Riches
SHOPPING
256

CHAPTER NINE
Just the Facts, Ma'am
INFORMATION
276

Index...291
    Lodgings...296
    Restaurants..297
Maps...300

Acknowledgments

Many people made this book possible. Foremost is co-author Peg Melnik, my wife. Her fingerprints are all over this book, from writing the *Information* and *Shopping* chapters to taking the lead on *Restaurants*, to helping guide the tone and style of the writing. Peg never missed a deadline, even after giving birth to our daughter Sophie.

Two others toiled with equal devotion, Chris Alderman and Jean Saylor Doppenberg. Chris was our chief photographer, dashing around Wine Country, camera in hand. She also wrote the *Recreation* chapter. Jean tackled one of the book's toughest assignments, researching and writing the *Lodging* chapter. The phrase "bed & breakfast" makes her downright jumpy by now. Jean also wrote the *Transportation* chapter.

Many thanks, also, to our team of restaurant reviewers, who had the tough job of eating and drinking, with the tab on us. (It's actually harder work than it sounds.) Gourmet researchers and writers included L. Pierce Carson, Mark Cohen, Loren and Jean Doppenberg, Chris Kent, Joan Lisetor, Rosie McDaniel, Diane Peterson, Chris Smith, Mark Sternfield and Betsy Wing.

Another source of comfort was Chris Kent, who not only helped research the *Shopping* chapter but served as fact-checker for the entire book. Thanks to photographer Kris White, as well as Brian Epp for his excellent maps.

Numerous organizations proved to be great resources. The Napa County Historical Society and Sonoma County Museum supplied many of our priceless historic photographs. The chambers of commerce of Calistoga, St. Helena and Napa as well as the Sonoma County Convention and Visitors Bureau and the Sonoma Valley Visitors Bureau provided detailed and valuable information.

Finally, particular thanks to Virginia Rowe, Mary Osak, and David Emblidge at Berkshire House for pulling it all together.

Introduction

In July of 1989, I remember distinctly, my wife Peg and I had two free nights to ourselves. During the other 28 days and nights we were busy tending to the friends and relatives who had descended upon us. Since moving to Sonoma County in March 1989, it sometimes feels like we have become vacation central. When we arrived, a woman from Welcome Wagon came to our door. A comment she made stuck with us: "Living here, you don't really need to get away because every weekend is a vacation."

She was right, of course. Napa and Sonoma counties *are* remarkable. Why else would three million people a year vacation here? Wine, obviously, is the siren call. A few days sampling the cabernet sauvignons, zinfandels and chardonnays, and visiting the wineries—quaint or castlelike—and you may forsake beer forever. But as you read this book you'll see that there's far more to Napa and Sonoma than wine.

I'm continually amazed at the beauty of this place. Merely driving to work remains a treat. There is a sense of mystery and strength in the surrounding mountains. The vineyards and fields take on a vibrant yellow in the spring as the wild mustard arrives with the fog and rain. In the summer, the vines grow bushy and green, weighed down with grapes, and in the fall they take on the delicate reds and yellows of autumn leaves. The hills rolling to the coast assume a shimmering green in the spring, reminding me unmistakably of Ireland. With its cliffs and pounding shore, the coastline is dramatic and jagged. It rivals even the famed Big Sur to the south.

With this Great Outdoors comes a whirl of recreational activities, everything from tennis to tidepooling. For those who prefer pampering to a strenuous hike among redwoods, Napa and Sonoma will indulge. The restaurants of Wine Country insist that you can be healthy and luxurious at the same time, marrying the best of local meats and produce with just the right wine. The inns, bed & breakfasts and spas appeal to every style, from easy country pleasure to posh extravagance. The multicultural, multinational history is reflected today in place names, architecture and cuisine, and the range and quality of shopping opportunities—in wine, art, clothing and gifts—are wide and diverse.

How can you possibly know where to begin? That's where we come in. We've created a book to guide you through Wine Country with a minimum of fuss and a maximum of pleasure. We wish you a congenial and happy stay. Read on and enjoy.

Tim Fish
Petaluma, California

THE WAY THIS BOOK WORKS

This book is divided into nine chapters. Entries within each chapter are first divided into "Napa County" and "Sonoma County," and then each county is broken down geographically, according to the names of cities, moving generally from south to north.

Some entries include specific information, telephone numbers, addresses, business hours and the like, organized for easy reference in blocks in the left-hand column. All information was checked as close to the publication date as possible. Even so, since details can change without warning, it is always wise to call ahead.

For the same reason we have routinely avoided listing specific prices, indicating instead a range. Lodging price codes are based on a per-room rate, double occupancy during summer months. Off-season rates are often cheaper. Motel prices are rated on a separate scale in the *Lodging* chapter. Restaurant price ratings indicate the cost of an individual meal including appetizer, entree and dessert but not cocktails, wine, tax or tip. Restaurants with *prix fixe* menus are noted.

Price Codes

	Lodging	*Dining*
Inexpensive	Up to $75	Up to $10
Moderate	$75 to $125	$10 to $20
Expensive	$125 to $175	$20 to $30
Very Expensive	$175 or more	$30 or more

Credit cards are abbreviated as follows:

AE—American Express	DC—Diner's Club
CB—Carte Blanche	MC—Master Card
D—Discover Card	V—Visa

The *area code* for Napa and Sonoma counties is 707. For all the phone numbers in the 707 area, we cite local exchanges only.

The best sources for year-round tourist information are the **Napa Chamber of Commerce** (226-7455; 1556 First St., Napa, Ca., 94559) and the **Sonoma County Convention and Visitors Bureau** (575-1191; 10 Fourth St., Santa Rosa, Ca., 95401).

CITIES IN NAPA AND SONOMA COUNTIES

Napa and Sonoma counties, you'll discover, resist being broken down into neat geographic areas. Easier to categorize is Napa Valley, with its strip of small towns and villages beginning in the south with the population center, the city of Napa. North from there is Yountville, a popular tourist mecca with numerous shops and restaurants. The vineyard villages of Oakville and Rutherford come next, followed by St. Helena with its lovely downtown storefronts. Finally, at the county's warm northern end is the resort town of Calistoga. Sonoma County is larger and more varied. Sonoma Valley, narrow and somehow separate, is home to the historically interesting city of Sonoma and to the vineyard communities of Kenwood and Glen Ellen at the southern end. In south-central Sonoma County is the river town of Petaluma, bordered on the north by the suburb Cotati, and the ever-growing bedroom community of Rohnert Park. Santa Rosa is Sonoma County's largest city as well as its business and cultural hub. To the north, surrounded by vineyards, is the quiet community of Healdsburg. "West County," as locals call it, has a personality of its own. Its wild terrain makes it part "rugged individualist," but its popularity as an immigration spot for San Francisco's counter-culturalists during the 1960s makes it part "earth child," as well.

CITY POPULATIONS

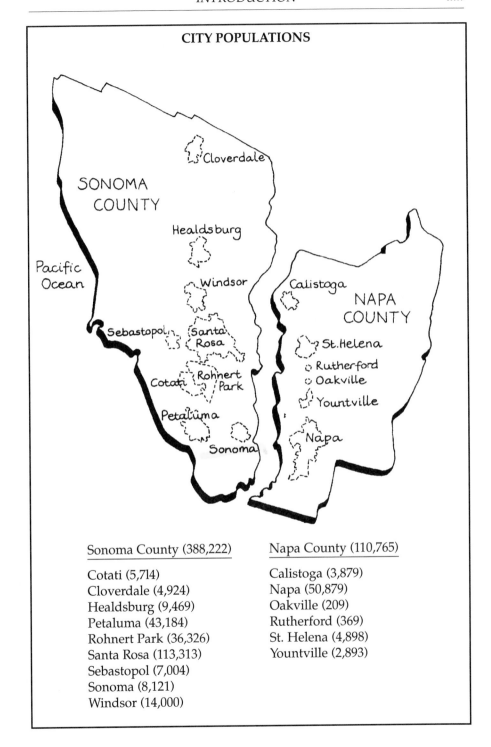

Sonoma County (388,222)

Cotati (5,714)
Cloverdale (4,924)
Healdsburg (9,469)
Petaluma (43,184)
Rohnert Park (36,326)
Santa Rosa (113,313)
Sebastopol (7,004)
Sonoma (8,121)
Windsor (14,000)

Napa County (110,765)

Calistoga (3,879)
Napa (50,879)
Oakville (209)
Rutherford (369)
St. Helena (4,898)
Yountville (2,893)

CHAPTER ONE

Aged To Perfection
HISTORY

History repeats itself; that's the one thing that's wrong with history.

— Clarence Darrow

Courtesy Napa County Historical Society

The Beringer Brothers Winery in the late 1800s.

Why was it back in school that the worst, most monotonous teachers taught history? It didn't take long before all those dates and wars and proclamations made your brain glaze over like an Easter ham. Well, that history won't repeat itself here. It helps of course that Napa and Sonoma counties have a lively past, busy with fascinating people and places — and YES, dates and wars and proclamations, too. From the thunderous tremors that raised the land from a prehistoric sea to the chic winery life of today, Napa and Sonoma counties have been twins, not identical but fraternal. They share similar origins but have grown into distinctly different siblings.

NATURAL HISTORY

A vast inland sea once spanned Napa and Sonoma counties, the salt water over the millennia nourishing the soil. The Mayacamas, coastal and other mountain ranges attest to the land's violent origins. Continental plates have fought for elbow room here for millions of years, colliding and complaining, creating a tectonic furnace of magma and spewing forth volcanos and towering mountain spines that now divide and surround the two counties.

The rolling hills of the Carneros mark the southern borders, where Napa and Sonoma counties meet the San Pablo Bay. Between them looms the Mayacamas range with the peaks of Mt. Veeder and Diamond Mountain. Low

1

NAPA-SONOMA TOPOGRAPHY

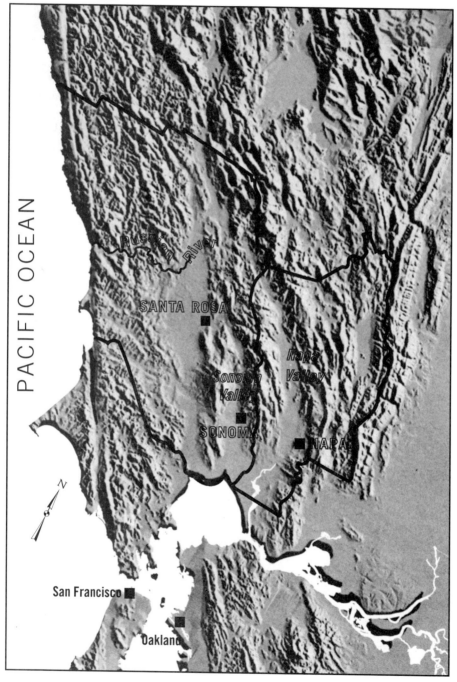

coastal hills border Sonoma on the west and the Blue Ridge shoulders Napa on the east. On the northern edge begins a vast stairstep of ranges that lead to the California border and beyond.

At 4,343 feet, Mt. Saint Helena is the area's tallest remnant of the volcanic area. Today, magma still simmers below the hills, producing the area's powerful geysers and Calistoga's soothing mineral water. Another vivid reminder occurs on occasion: earthquakes. The San Andreas Fault runs up the center of Bodega Head on the coast and the more timid Rodger's Creek fault sits beneath Santa Rosa and Healdsburg.

When the ancient sea receded, it left bays and lagoons that became fertile valleys. The Napa and Russian rivers formed and for eons roamed back and forth over the face of the Napa and Santa Rosa plains, mixing the soil and volcanic ash. Napa Valley, five miles wide and 40 miles long, dominated east of the Mayacamas. The land to the west was more vast, with dozens of smaller valleys: Sonoma the largest and most temperate, the parched Alexander and Dry Creek valleys to north, and near the ocean lay the lush Russian River Valley where Redwoods the width of two-car garages began to grow. All the while the Pacific continued to pound western Sonoma, even today eroding its jagged coastline.

It's hard to imagine a land more made-to-order for wine. The oil is rich with minerals from ancient oceans and volcanic ash, and the rocky nature of the land creates excellent drainage. Cool air masses from the Pacific meet the dry desert air from the east, creating a unique climate. Fog chills the mornings, then burns off as the days turn ideally warm, and as the sun sets the crisp air returns. And perhaps most important — rain. Typically, Napa and Sonoma counties are drenched from December through April, then things dry up until November. In all, a perfect spot for wine.

As humans were entering stage right, Napa and Sonoma counties already pulsed with life. Cougars, lynx, rattlesnakes, wolves, elk, deer roamed along with the mightiest of all, the grizzly bear. Hawks, buzzards, eagles and loons glided the hillsides. Sturgeon and salmon swarmed in the rivers, and along the coast, whales, otters and sea lions prospered and the Great White Shark lurked. Many have survived the arrival of man, though in reduced numbers. Others were not so lucky.

SOCIAL HISTORY

FIRST INHABITANTS

Brave the occasionally harrowing California freeway system and you'll inevitably see this bumper sticker: "California Native." How natives moan about newcomers. It's rather silly, of course, since people are such a recent addition to Northern California — 5,000 years, in the big scheme of things, is hardly enough time to unpack.

The earliest "newcomers" crossed the land bridge that once connected Asia and Alaska and wandered south. The first known inhabitants were the Pomo and Miwok Indians in Sonoma and Wappo who lived in Napa Valley and eastern Sonoma County. It was a plentiful place and allowed the Indians an unhurried way of life, the men hunting and women gathering berries, mussels and other food. They gathered near the streams when salmon returned but were careful because the grizzly bear had a taste for salmon as well. Communities thrived. Most were small but some villages had populations of 1,000 or more. Coastal Miwok used shells as money, and Pomo women achieved great expertise as basket makers. Pomo men lived away from their wives in communal lodges, which also served as ceremonial sweat houses as well as impromptu schools for boys. The Indians gave special names to this land of theirs, names that remain today. Not that historians particularly agree on what the words mean. *Napa*, depending on which story you believe, is Wappo for "grizzly bear" or "fish" or "bountiful place." *Petaluma*, a city in southern Sonoma County, may be Pomo for "flat back" or Miwok for "behind the hill" — both referring to the Sonoma Mountains and the flat Petaluma plain. *Cotati*, another Sonoma County city, sounds poetic but its possible Pomo meaning is anything but romantic: "Punch in the face." One name that didn't stick was *Shabakai* or "Long snake" — that's what natives called the Russian River.

The Sebastopol Indians fashioned their canoes out of tule tied with grape vines.

Courtesy Sonoma County Museum

The first Europeans arrivals were heavily outnumbered. As many as 12,000 Wappo lived between Napa and Clear Lake to the north, and 8,000 Pomo prospered in what are now Sonoma, Lake and Mendocino counties. That would quickly change.

Sonoma County was the first to be explored by the white man, and as explorers often seem to do, they stumbled onto it by accident. Lt. Francisco de Bodega y Cuadro was piloting his Spanish ship the *Sonora* along the coast in search of San Francisco Bay. Startled Indians paddled out in canoes to greet the *Sonora*, presenting the crew with elaborate feather and shell offerings. Rough seas and a damaged skiff prevented Bodega y Cuadro and crew from actually coming ashore but Bodega's name stuck somehow — Bodega Bay.

The first expedition actually to land in Sonoma County came the following year when a small party of Spaniards set out from their military outpost, The Presidio, in San Francisco. Crossing the bay, they entered the mouth of the Petaluma River with the crazy notion that it ended up in Tomales Bay and the vast Pacific. (Always looking for shortcuts, those explorers.) It didn't of course, so Lt. Fernando Quiros and his crew explored the Petaluma plain instead.

Fruit of the Vine — Who's on First

Spanish missionaries are usually credited with bringing the first wine grapes to Sonoma and Napa, but that might not really be the case. Russian colonists at Fort Ross apparently imported vines from Peru as early as 1817, predating the Spanish by a good seven years. But the padres made up for it in volume. Father Jose Altimira, founder of Mission San Francisco Solano in Sonoma, planted 1,000 vines of Mission grape, a rather coarse variety brought north from Mexico for sacramental wine.

Napa's first vineyard was planted in 1838 by Napa's first settler, George Yount. He brought Mission vines east from Sonoma and made wine for his own use. It didn't take long before the entrepreneurial spirit set in, and Gen. Mariano Vallejo of Sonoma was the first to succumb. Vallejo became California's first commercial winemaker in 1841, eventually planting 70,000 vines. His wine sold under the name Lachryma Montis or "Tears of the Mountain" and became the toast of San Francisco. The winery was hardly a chic shop; his cellar, press and sales outlet were housed in an army barracks. As for a tasting room . . .

Russians and not the Spanish, however, were the first to establish an outpost in the area. By the early 1800s, the Russian–American Trading Company, a private entity supported largely by Imperial Russia, was expanding south after the Alaskan fur trade began to play out. In 1809, Ivan Kuskov and crew landed in Bodega Bay and scouted the area. They returned in 1812 and established a colony they called Rumiantsev. Exploring the coastline further, Kuskov selected a blustery bluff a few miles to the north and established Fort Ross the following year. The fort became the hub of Russian activity and Rumiantsev their major port. Though a prime location for fur trade, Fort Ross was not the most habitable place. Even today the bluffs overlooking the Pacific are fogged-in much of the year and the wind and dampness can be severe. One early visitor wrote: "It is so easy to catch cold here that even those inhabitants of Ross who were born here are sick almost every year." Later, ranches were established inland where the climate was more moderate, and the Russians grew much-needed grain and produce for their Alaskan settlements. The slaughter of sea otters, meanwhile, was ruthless and devastating. By 1821, the annual catch had dropped from hundreds to 32.

THIS LAND IS WHOSE LAND?

The Spanish weren't keen on the Russians hanging around just to the north. They were determined that their presidio in San Francisco would be the dominate force in the area. Even when Mexico declared independence from Spain in 1821, that didn't lessen the importance of the land north of San Francisco. California had been largely explored and established through the mission system, which began in 1769 as a way to civilize "heathen" Indians and convert them to Catholicism. It was also a way to establish a Spanish presence, and if successful, a mission could add greatly to the wealth and power of the church.

In 1823, Father Jose Altimira, an ambitious young priest at San Francisco's Mission Dolores, became convinced that a new mission was needed in the northern territory. Church authorities, cautiously considering their waning influence with the new Mexican government, balked, so Altimira turned to Don Luis Arguello, Mexican governor of California. Arguello saw an opportunity to thwart the Russians and approved the idea. Altimira set out that year with a party of 14 soldiers to explore the land north of the bay, from Petaluma to Napa to Suisun. According to legend, he marked his path by sowing mustard seed, which today blooms mint yellow every spring. Altimira was most impressed by Sonoma Valley, its mild climate and tall trees.

On July 7, 1823, with a makeshift redwood cross, Altimira blessed the mission site in what is now the city of Sonoma, and the San Francisco Solano Mission was established. It was California's last mission and the only one established under Mexican rule. In the early years, the mission was a great success, and despite having the reputation of being a harsh taskmaster, Altimira converted more than 700 Indians. In the fall of 1826, Indian laborers had just brought in a bountiful harvest when they staged a violent uprising. The mission was partially burned and Father Altimira fled for his life. He was replaced, the mission rebuilt, and in 1834 the mission was at the height of its

Mission San Francisco Solano in Sonoma, as it may have looked in the late 1820s.

prosperity when the Mexican Congress secularized the mission system and returned the acquired wealth to the people. It was the beginning of a new era.

Lt. Mariano Guadelupe Vallejo was an enterprising 28-year-old officer given the opportunity of a lifetime. The Mexican government sent him to Sonoma to replace the padres and also establish a presidio and thereby thwart Russian expansion. Vallejo's ambitions were far greater than even that; he soon became one of the most powerful and wealthy men in California. As commandant general, Vallejo ruled the territory north of San Francisco and eventually set aside more than 100,000 acres for himself. He laid out the town of Sonoma around an eight acre plaza — the largest in California — and for himself built the imposing Petaluma Adobe in 1836. It would be the largest adobe structure in Northern California and the first crop-producing rancho in the area.

It was Vallejo who pushed for the settlement of Napa and Sonoma counties. He found frontiersman like George Yount. Others had been exploring Napa Valley since 1831, but Yount was the first with the notion of settlement. Befriending the already powerful Vallejo, Yount requested a land grant. Vallejo consented, but only after Yount converted to Catholicism and became a naturalized Mexican citizen. (Zoning laws were *really* tough then.) Yount never became an upstanding Catholic but he did establish the 11,814–acre Rancho Caymus in 1836, now the Yountville area of the central Napa County. About that same time, Vallejo was giving Sonoma land grants to family members, who established the rancho predecessors of Santa Rosa, Kenwood and Healdsburg. Mexican influence continued to expand, particularly after 1839, when the Russians, having wiped out the otter population, gave up and sold Fort Ross.

Otters weren't the only inhabitants facing annihilation. Indian uprisings were not uncommon. Yount's house in Napa Valley was half-home, half-fortress. Vallejo occasionally led campaigns against rebellious Indians, but perhaps the most devastating blow came to the Indians in 1837 when a Mexican corporal inadvertently brought smallpox to Sonoma Valley. The white man's disease all but wiped out Sonoma County's Indian population.

BEAR FLAG REVOLT

Throughout the 1830s and early 1840s, American settlers streamed into California, lured by stories of free land. Mexican rule, however, denied Americans land ownership and this led to confrontations. Tensions peaked in 1846 when rumors spread that Mexico was about to order all Americans out of California. At dawn on June 14, 30 armed horsemen from Sacramento and Napa valleys rode into Sonoma. So began the Bear Flag Revolt, 25 eventful days when Sonoma was the capital of the independent Republic of California. Though significant, it was a revolution of almost comic proportions. Few soldiers still guarded Sonoma when the riders arrived and the insurrectionists captured Sonoma without a single shot. Vallejo was roused from his bed and tied to a chair. One story has it that Vallejo tried sly negotiations with the rebels, freely offering rebel leaders his brandy and getting them drunk. Whether that's truth or folklore, the rebels prevailed. By noon, William Ide was elected leader of the new republic and a makeshift flag was hoisted to the top of a pole in the plaza. Saddlemaker Ben Dewel crafted this makeshift flag for the new government, using a grizzly bear as the chief symbol. (Though some said it looked like a prized pig, not a bear.) The Bear Flag Republic had a short reign. In July, an American navy vessel captured the Mexican stronghold of Monterey and claimed California for itself. The Bear Flag boys immediately threw in with the Americans and four years later, in 1850, California became a state. The Bear Flag was eventually adopted as the state flag, in 1911.

The 1840s and 1850s were formative years for Napa and Sonoma counties. The Gold Rush of 1848 sent Americans by the thousands into the Sierras. The once powerful Sonoma almost became a ghost town, as residents left to pan gold and San Francisco achieved new significance. Other towns were born of miner commerce, the river ports of Napa and Petaluma for example.

Loggers felling a giant redwood near Guerneville around 1880.

Courtesy Sonoma County Museum

A FIRST GLASS OF WINE

During this time, California's wine industry was conceived. Oats and wheat had been the primary crops of Sonoma and Napa counties, and sheep and cattle were also dominant. Vallejo and Yount grew the crude Mission grapes brought north by the priests for sacramental wine, but it wasn't until 1856, when a Hungarian aristocrat named Agoston Haraszthy arrived in Sonoma that the idea of a wine industry first took root. Haraszthy had attempted vineyards in San Diego and San Mateo and immediately recognized potential in the soil and climate of Sonoma and Napa valleys. Purchasing land and a winery northeast of the Plaza, Haraszthy established Buena Vista, "Beautiful View."

By 1858, Haraszthy had already surpassed Vallejo's accomplishments as a winemaker and even inspired a German apprentice named Charles Krug, who founded Napa Valley's first winery in 1861. That same year, convinced that the Mission grape wasn't the only variety that would thrive in California, Haraszthy toured the wine regions of Europe and returned with cuttings from 300 classic varieties. It was his experimentations with these grapes that brought Haraszthy fame and earned him the title "Father of the California Wine Industry." Wineries began to spring up throughout Napa and Sonoma counties, spawning wine dynasties such as Beringer and Inglenook that still live today.

The later part of the century was a boom period. Between 1850 and 1860, Napa county's population grew from 400 to almost 5,000. By 1869, Sonoma county's residents numbered 19,000. Petaluma, its largest city, was on its way to becoming the egg capital of the world. The burgeoning city of Santa Rosa had snatched the county seat from Sonoma in 1854, and with the completion of the San Francisco and North Pacific train line in 1870, its destiny as the North Bay's largest city was established. It was the era of the highwaymen, as the legendary Black Bart and others robbed stage coaches around the North Bay. It was an era of genius. Calling the area a "chosen spot," horticulturist Luther Burbank created varieties of fruit trees that brought the curious from around the country. It was a time of pleasure. The resort town of Calistoga, founded by California's first millionaire, Sam Brannan, had become a vacation mecca. It was a time of creativity. Robert Louis Stevenson was inspired by a stay in Napa Valley and called its wine "bottled poetry."

The wine industry was small but growing in the late 1800s, though it shared the land with other important crops: hops, timber and apples in Sonoma and wheat in Napa. Wine making and drinking in those days was anything but the chic activity it is today. Wine was sold almost exclusively in bulk, and often wasn't even blended until it reached its selling point. It was sold from barrels in saloons and stores with customers usually bringing their own containers. Gustave Niebaum of Inglenook and the old Fountaingrove Winery in Santa Rosa were among the first to bottle their own wine. Niebaum was also the first to use vintage dates on his wine and to promote "Napa Valley" on his labels.

Winemaking received two blows late in the century: the depression of the 1870s and phylloxera. The wine industry somehow weathered the economic hard times, though people like Haraszthy were not so lucky. His winery failed and business setbacks forced him to pursue dealings in Central America, where he met his death. Accounts say he was devoured by an alligator while crossing a Nicaraguan river. As for Phylloxera, it attacked the vineyards of Sonoma and Napa counties with equal fervor.

Phylloxera, a microscopic voracious aphid that infests vine roots, first appeared in Europe in the 1860s, devastating the vineyards of Chateau Margaux and Chateau Lafitte and others. Only by grafting their vines to American root stock, were the Europeans able to save their classic wines. While the European wine industry recovered, California wine began to receive its first

*Three renowned Americans
meet in Santa Rosa in 1915:
Thomas Edison, Luther
Burbank and Henry Ford.*

Courtesy Sonoma County Museum

world notice. Sonoma County — not Napa — had been the undisputed capital
of California wine, but fate and phylloxera would change all that. Phylloxera
surfaced first in Sonoma Valley in 1875, and it slowly spread north to the Russian River. By 1889, Sonoma County's vineyards were in ruin when the French
invited American wines to compete in the World's Fair. Napa Valley's wines
scored well, raising Napa from obscurity to fame. Although phylloxera later
came to Napa, the crown had been snatched. Growers tried everything to kill
the bug, from chemicals to flooding their fields, but nothing worked. Eventually most were forced to pull out their vines. Some planted again, using resis-
tant stock. Others gave up and planted fruit trees.

Not long after that, just after the turn of the century, famed writer Jack London began buying property in Glen Ellen. Saying he was tired of cities and
people, he retired to the mountain retreat he called "Beauty Ranch," becoming
the first of a long line of celebrities drawn to life in Wine Country.

A COMPLAINT FROM MOTHER NATURE

A new century brought new tragedy. Downtown Calistoga was leveled by a
fire in 1901, and on April 18, 1906 what became known as the San Francisco Earthquake was equally as devastating in Sonoma County, particularly
in Santa Rosa. Built on the loose foundation between two creek beds, Santa
Rosa shimmied like gelatin, laying waste to downtown and killing 100 people.
(It didn't help that the brick buildings were poorly constructed.) Three large
downtown hotels, one reporter wrote "fell as if constructed of playing cards."
It would be years before Calistoga and Santa Rosa recovered. San Francisco, of
course, was destroyed, but a fact not often reported was the impact that event
had on the California wine business. Many of the wineries stored their wine in

the cooler climate of San Francisco and the quake destroyed almost two-thirds of the state's wine supply. The castlelike wineries of Napa County — Greystone Cellars, Beringer, Inglenook and the others that harkened to the grandeur of Bordeaux — were spared the earthquake. But something called Prohibition loomed more dangerously on the horizon.

Prohibition had been a growing movement in the United States since the turn of the century and by 1917, a majority of states had outlawed alcohol. The United States Congress cinched it with the Volstead Act, and on January 1, 1920, Prohibition began. In Sonoma County alone, it left three million useless gallons of wine aging in vats. Sebastiani in Sonoma, Beaulieu in Rutherford and a handful of others survived by making religious wine and medicinal spirits. Most wineries closed, almost 130 alone in Sonoma County and more than 120 in Napa Valley. By the time Prohibition was repealed in 1933, the Great Depression was on, followed by World War II. Recovery took time.

In 1937, the opening of a single bridge would forever change Sonoma County. It wasn't just any bridge, mind you, but the Golden Gate, spanning the mouth of the San Francisco Bay. Sonoma County became a thoroughfare in California's major north–south corridor, the Redwood Highway. And Sonoma County became its own destination — for example, the Russian River area, already a popular resort spot for San Franciscans, boomed.

After World War II, the vineyards of Europe were once again devastated and with the flow from Europe cut off, America turned to its own wine. The end of the war began the slow rebirth of the wine industry, and Napa and Sonoma began prospering in the 1950s and 1960s. By the early 1970s, a small tourist industry began forming around the wineries. Tourists were drawn to free wine tastings; restaurants and hotels began to appear. When corporations began eyeing the family-owned wineries, there was no question that Napa and Sonoma were ripe with potential *and profit*. Inglenook was the first to go

Effect of the 1906 earthquake on the dome of the Sonoma County Court House.

Courtesy Sonoma County Museum

*A 400-year-old carved oak cask
at Inglenook Vineyard
Company.*

Courtesy Napa County Historical Society.

corporate when United Vintners bought it in 1964, Beaulieu and others followed. In Napa Valley, new wineries began opening, some small operations called "boutiques" in industry lingo, others more dramatic such as Sterling, a towering white villa perched on a hill south of Calistoga. Brash young winemakers like Robert Mondavi promoted California wine like no one had in the past. By the 1970s, even the French, who so often had turned up their nose at California wine, saw California's potential particularly for sparkling wine. Moet–Hennessy was the first to arrive, building Domaine Chandon in Yountville in 1975. Others were to follow.

Sonoma and Napa counties also became a favorite location of film makers. Alfred Hitchcock immortalized Bodega Bay in *The Birds*; thousands stop each year for a photo of one of Sonoma County's most-recognizable landmark, the Bodega School. Later, wine life at its most ruthless was portrayed in "Falcon Crest," which used Spring Mountain Vineyards in Saint Helena as a backdrop.

Wine Country's greatest achievement and the final turning point for Napa and Sonoma came in the summer of 1976. At the now infamous Paris tasting (see page 13), French wine experts for the first time picked several California wines over the classic wines of Bordeaux and Burgundy in a blind tasting. History was made, and Napa and Sonoma counties' prominence in the world of wine was set.

Today, Napa and Sonoma county continue to grow, much to the chagrin of old residents. Three million tourists arrive each year, drawn increasingly by wine, landscape and climate. Santa Rosa is a small but blossoming metropolis of suburbs. Highway 29, the main road through Napa Valley, pulses with activity. How different it is from the days of grizzly bears and Wappo, yet Napa and Sonoma remain strikingly beautiful places.

Upstaging the French

California and French wine lovers have a longstanding love–hate relationship — California loves French wine and France hates California's. We exaggerate, but only somewhat. California winemakers have always aspired to the quality and reputation of Bordeaux and Burgundy wines, while French enthusiasts ignored California. That is, until May 24, 1976.

It began with British wine merchant Stephen Spurrier, who had a taste for California wine but had a difficult time convincing his English and European customers. Spurrier hit upon the idea of staging a blind tasting of California and French wine, using the nine greatest palates of France. It was unheard of. California had beaten French wines in past tastings, but the judges were always American, and what did they know.

Judges knew they were sampling both French and American wines, though the bottles were masked. As the tasting progressed, the tasters began to point out the wines they believed were Californian and their comments about them grew increasingly patronizing. When the sacks were removed, the judges were mortified: the wines they thought classic Bordeaux or Burgundy were in reality Californian. Six of the 11 highest rated wines, in fact, were from California, almost entirely from Napa. The 1973 Stag Leap's Cabernet beat 1970 vintages of Chateau Mouton–Rothschild and Chateau Haut–Brion, and a 1973 Chateau Montelena bested Burgundy's finest whites. France contested the findings, of course, but it was too late. California, particularly Napa, earned it's place on the international wine map.

CHAPTER TWO
Here, There and Everywhere
TRANSPORTATION

Courtesy Sonoma County Museum

The Redwood Highway through downtown Santa Rosa in the Early '30s — the major north-south route until 1949 when the Highway 101 bypass was built, also lined with redwoods.

Back when gridlock was considered an overturned ox cart and three gawking by-standers, Napa and Sonoma counties were easy places to get around. Not that the terrain doesn't conspire against smooth travel. Almost any approach requires at least a minor mountain expedition.

Perhaps that's why the earliest explorers came by way of water in the late 1700s. The Sonoma coast was the area's first highway marker. As sailing ships from around the globe plotted the New World, the Napa and Petaluma rivers, which connect to San Francisco Bay, allowed early settlers a fast way inland.

By the mid-1800s, trails from the central valley would take travelers along Clear Lake to Bodega Bay, as well as south and east along the Bay to Benicia. Carts and stagecoaches brought folks along primitive roads, stirring dust in the summer and wading through mud in the winter.

By the 1860s, steam ships were chugging up and down Napa and Petaluma rivers, going as far north as those two cities, bringing in new settlers and taking the abundant produce of the two counties to San Francisco and beyond. Railroads steamed into the scene in the 1870s with names like "Southern Pacific" and "San Francisco North Pacific," and they connected the towns of the two budding counties to Oakland and the East Bay.

The automobile changed everything, for better or for worse. Of course Sonoma County remained somewhat innocently isolated from San Francisco — it's a long loop around that Bay — until the big day in May 1937. That's when the Golden Gate Bridge opened a speedier route north, and Sonoma and Napa counties became one of *the* travel destinations for San Francisco, and for the world.

14

GETTING TO NAPA & SONOMA

BY CAR

Although planes and trains will bring you to the threshold of Wine Country, the vast landscapes and the romance of the region are best appreciated by automobile. There's no substitute for the convenience of having your own wheels so you can explore at your own pace. "Explore" is the operative word when traveling by car through this region. Your wanderings may be rewarded when you "discover" an off-the-road, up-and-coming winery or stumble upon a roadside diner with heavenly home-cooking.

From Eureka/Seattle: Travelers from the north can reach Wine Country via two major roadways — Hwy. 101 or I-5.

Hwy. 101 brings visitors into the heart of Sonoma County. Several exits allow for exploring the beauty of the Alexander Valley, where some of California's most sought-after premium wines are produced. One of the back roads not to be missed, especially if your destination is Napa Valley, is Hwy. 128 East, just north of Geyserville. To reach central Sonoma County, stay on Hwy. 101 southbound.

Travelers using I-505 will exit at Hwy. 128 in Winters. Follow it west to Rutherford, through the beautiful Howell Mountains, catching a panorama view of the valley. If the city of Napa is your destination, connect with Hwy. 121 from 128, and travel south.

From the South: Like visitors from the north, drivers arriving from southern California can choose between Hwy. 101 or I-5.

Traveling Hwy. 101 brings you through San Jose to the heart of San Francisco. Stay alert — 101 empties onto the streets of the city and can be a bit confusing. Carrying a detailed map of San Francisco streets is a good idea. Continue across the spectacular Golden Gate Bridge, through the striking hills of Marin County. To reach central Sonoma County, continue north on 101. To reach the city of Sonoma or Napa Valley, exit to Hwy. 37 in Novato and connect with Hwy. 121.

If speed is a concern, and you want to avoid San Francisco, try I-5. Follow I-5 north through the Central Valley, then connect with I-580 and continue into downtown Oakland and connect with northbound I-80. Cross the Carquinez Bridge into Vallejo and exit to Hwy. 29 north and continue into Napa. To reach Sonoma County, connect with Hwy. 12 west just south of Napa.

From the East: Wine Country is an easy jaunt from Sacramento or Reno. From I-80, connect with Hwy. 12 west. Once off the interstate, it's a scenic 15-minute drive to the junction of Hwy. 29, the main thoroughfare running the length of Napa Valley. After crossing the Napa River bridge, make the broad turn northward and continue into the town of Napa, or turn left at the junction of Hwy. 12 if your destination is Sonoma.

NAPA AND SONOMA ACCESS

Approximate mileage and times between towns and cities:

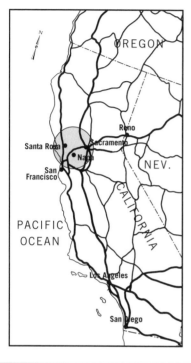

Napa County	Time	Miles
Napa (the city) to:		
Eureka	4 hrs.	255
Los Angeles	8 hrs.	439
Oakland	¾ hr.	46
Reno	3½ hrs.	200
Sacramento	1 hr.	61
San Francisco	1 hr.	56
San Diego	11 hrs.	600

Sonoma County	Time	Miles
Santa Rosa to:		
Eureka	4 hrs.	219
Los Angeles	8 hrs.	431
Oakland	1 hr.	60
Reno	4 hrs.	229
Sacramento	2 hr.	97
San Francisco	1 hr.	56
San Diego	11 hrs.	600

BY BUS

In 1990, Greyhound bus service was scaled back nationwide because of the company's ongoing labor problems. As a result, very limited Greyhound is currently available (mid-1991) directly to Sonoma and Napa counties. It is possible to ride Greyhound to San Francisco, then make connections on Golden Gate Transit to reach Wine Country. (See "Getting Around Napa & Sonoma" in this chapter.) A travel agent will have the most up-to-date information on Greyhound schedules and connections. **Greyhound** in San Francisco: 415-495-1569

Golden Gate Transit (for travel between San Francisco and Sonoma County): 415-332-6600; one-way fare from San Francisco to Santa Rosa in 1991 was $3.70.

WITHIN WINE COUNTRY

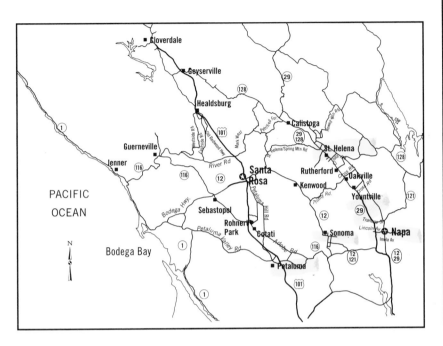

	Time	Miles		Time	Miles
Napa (the city) to:			**Santa Rosa to:**		
Calistoga	½ hr.	25	Bodega Bay	¾ hr.	22
St. Helena	15 min.	18	Geyserville	25 min.	21
Rutherford	10 min.	11	Healdsburg	15 min.	15
Sonoma	15 min.	12	Jenner	¾ hr.	32
Santa Rosa	¾ hr.	36	Petaluma	20 min.	16
Yountville	10 min.	8			

Moving north or south in Napa and Sonoma counties is easy going. Highway 29, Napa Valley's Main Street, cuts a straight path from the San Pablo Bay north to Lake County. Most of Napa's wineries are along this often crowded two-lane road; Silverado Trail to the east is a quieter two-lane, and has its share of wineries also. In Sonoma County, Highway 101 travels north and south at interstate speeds. Moving between Napa and Sonoma, Highway 12 offers the smoothest path, through winding hills. The Oakville Grade/Trinity Road is a roller coaster around Mt. Veeder, offering some of the best views of both counties. Petrified Forest and Spring Mountain roads scale the northern Mayacamas Mountains, and at the top merge with Calistoga Road from Santa Rosa.

BY TRAIN

A mtrak's westbound *California Zephyr* and north-to-south *Coastal Starlight* trains drop off Napa County-bound passengers in the city of Martinez, about 40 miles south of Napa. Amtrak has continuing ground transportation that delivers passengers directly to Napa, but not Sonoma.

Amtrak: 800-872-7245 for information and reservations. It is advisable to consult a travel agent for assistance in booking on Amtrak.

BY AIR

A ir travelers bound for wine country can arrive and depart from one of three major airports handling numerous domestic and international airlines.

San Francisco International, Oakland International, and Sacramento Metropolitan are all within easy driving distance of Napa and Sonoma counties. United Airlines' Express service operates commuter/connecting flights six times daily between San Francisco and Sonoma County Airport. Currently, there are no commuter services or connecting flights in or out of the Napa airport.

If you're piloting your own small plane or arriving by chartered plane, wing directly into Sonoma County Airport northwest of Santa Rosa or into Napa County Airport, six miles south of the town of Napa. Several private charter services are based at both county airports, primarily offering sightseeing flights but also providing for-hire transportation to and from Bay Area airports and beyond.

United Airlines Express: 800-241-6522 for information and reservations.

BY AIRPORT RENTAL CAR

T his is the way most people from afar get to Napa and Sonoma. Highways in the Bay Area are well marked for the benefit of visitors in rented cars, but a good Wine Country road map is essential. Rental companies are usually helpful in plotting routes and will often supply drivers with basic maps to reach their destinations.

In Sonoma County, an automobile is almost a necessity for moving between city and coast and from winery to winery. In Napa Valley, however, many wineries, restaurants and bed & breakfast inns are located conveniently along the 28-mile length of Hwy. 29. Unfortunately, heavy traffic is common on Saturday and Sunday and during peak summer months, so an ambitious itinerary can be cut short by gridlock. A word of advice: Visit Napa Valley, if you can, on weekdays when traffic is usually lighter, and on weekends tour and taste at the star-attraction wineries along Hwy. 29 before noon or after 3 p.m.

(Distances following are approximate; travel times depend upon traffic conditions and time of day. Refer to "Arriving by Automobile" in this chapter for further details.)

From San Francisco International Airport: Take Hwy. 101 northbound and into San Francisco. The highway empties onto the streets, so watch the signs. Continue through the city and across the Golden Gate Bridge. Head north through Marin County on 101 to arrive in Sonoma County. To reach the town of Sonoma or to continue eastward to Napa Valley, take Hwy. 37 in Novato and connect with Hwy. 121.
Miles: 72 to Santa Rosa; 68 to Napa.
Time: 75 to 90 minutes to Santa Rosa; 2 hours to Napa.

From Oakland International Airport: To reach Napa County directly, take I-80 north through Oakland, continue north past the city of Berkeley, then follow the signs for Vallejo and Sacramento. Cross the Carquinez Bridge into Vallejo, and connect with Hwy. 29 north bound to Napa.
Miles: 46.
Time: One hour.

To reach Sonoma County, take I-80 North to Oakland, connect with I-580 to Richmond, and cross San Pablo Bay by way of the Richmond-San Rafael Bridge. Once across the bridge, connect with Hwy. 101 north in Marin County and continue north to Sonoma County.
Miles: 82.
Time: 75 minutes to 2 hours.

From Sacramento Metropolitan Airport: Take I-5 South and connect with the I-80 West bypass, and follow the signs to San Francisco. Then take the Hwy. 12 and connect with Hwy. 29 north. Cross the Napa River bridge and continue north into the town of Napa. To reach Sonoma, turn left on Hwy. 12 at the junction.
Miles: 61 miles to Napa; 97 miles to Santa Rosa.
Time: 90 minutes to Napa; 2 to 2½ hours to Santa Rosa.

BY AIRPORT SHUTTLE

Reasonably-priced express shuttle buses and vans operate between SF Airport and Santa Rosa or Sonoma Valley, and from SF Airport to Napa. A similar shuttle runs between Oakland Airport and Napa. These comfortable vehicles operate from 16 to 20 hours a day, seven days a week. Shuttles depart from SF Airport (outside the baggage area on the lower level) about every 60 minutes to two hours, depending on the operator, and deliver passengers to selected drop-off points in Wine Country, such as the Flamingo Hotel in Santa Rosa. Your travel agent can arrange a car rental for you in Napa or Sonoma counties. (See "By Rental Car" in this chapter.)

To reach Napa from Oakland Airport, *Grapevine Airport Service* operates 14-passenger buses daily. Departures from Oakland (Terminal 1 information desk and Terminal 2 baggage pick-up area) between 6:15 a.m. and 10:30 p.m. Passengers are delivered to limited stops in Vallejo, Napa and Yountville.

One-way fares (cash only) range from $13 to $25, depending on the operator, the drop-off point, and any excess luggage requirements. Children usually ride free or at half-fare. Reservations are required by most shuttle services at least 24 hours in advance; *Santa Rosa's Airporter* and *Airport Express* shuttles recommend reservations but also take walk-ons if space permits. Schedules fluctuate, so it's smart to reserve shuttle services in advance through a travel agent. (Some operators suspend service on major holidays; others offer a limited number of trips on holidays and weekends.)

Airport Express,
  SF Airport to Santa Rosa: 707-584-4400
Evans Airport Service,
  SF Airport to Napa: 707-255-1559
                                     707-944-2025
                                     707-643-8432

Grapevine Airport Service,
  Oakland to Napa   707-253-9093
Sonoma Airporter,
  SF Airport to the town of Sonoma   707-938-4246
Santa Rosa Airporter,
  SF Airport to Santa Rosa   707-545-8015

GETTING AROUND NAPA & SONOMA

BY RENTAL CAR

It is common for most visitors to Wine Country who arrive by air to rent cars at the metro airports. But rental cars are also available upon arrival in Wine Country; local information and reservation numbers are listed below. Passengers are picked up from airport shuttle stops, or from Sonoma and Napa county airports, then delivered to the agency's office to finalize the paperwork. Reservations up to a week in advance are recommended, especially if you prefer a particular make and model or visit in the high season.

Per-day charges may vary significantly between the big names and the bargain-basement agencies based in Wine Country. Renting a mid-size vehicle, for example, can range from $23.95 daily with unlimited mileage (Action Auto Rentals in Santa Rosa) to $48 daily, unlimited mileage (Hertz in Napa). Most companies allow 100 to 150 free miles daily, or up to 1,000 free miles weekly. (All prices quoted are current in mid-1991.)

Napa County

Napa	Budget Rent-A-Car	224-7845
	Enterprise Rent-A-Car	253-8000
	Hertz	226-2037 or 800-654-3131
	U-Save Auto Rental	258-0711

Sonoma County

Santa Rosa	Action Auto Rentals	575-8717
	Agency Rent-A-Car	575-1180
	Bay Area Rentals	575-1600
	Budget Rent-A-Car	545-8013
	Encore Rent-A-Car	586-0727
	Enterprise Rent-A-Car	575-6800
	U-Save Auto Rental	575-4334
Sonoma County Airport	Avis	571-0465
	Hertz	528-0834

BY BUS

Public bus service is available within Sonoma County from *Sonoma County Transit* and between cities in Sonoma County and San Francisco on the *Golden Gate Transit System*. Commuter bus service was scheduled to begin in mid-1991 in Napa Valley, with pick-up and drop-off points in Calistoga, St. Helena, Yountville, and Napa. Riders are to be dropped off in Vallejo, where they may connect with the trans-bay ferry service or take the *Bay Area Rapid Transit* (the "BART") system to reach San Francisco.

Commuter buses are precisely that — vehicles designed to shuttle daily commuters in and out of San Francisco and between North Bay cities and towns. But this method of travel could be indispensable for the Wine Country visitor on a tight budget. One drawback: bus stops, which can be few and far between, are usually not close to wineries and other tourist attractions.

One-way fares average from $3.70 for the Santa Rosa to San Francisco run (Golden Gate Transit) to $1.40 to reach Glen Ellen from Santa Rosa (Sonoma County Transit). Because these buses are basically people-movers for Monday-though-Friday commuting, weekend service is scaled down considerably.

If buses will be your primary form of transportation, it may be essential to gather together the most current timetables and route maps, which are updated frequently. *Golden Gate Transit, Sonoma County Transit* and *Napa County Rideline* will mail detailed maps and up-to-the-minute schedules at your request.

The cities of Santa Rosa, Napa, Healdsburg and Petaluma also offer bus service within those city boundaries.

Napa County

Napa Valley Rideline (launching mid-1991 for travel along Hwy. 29 between Calistoga and Vallejo, with bus and ferry connections to and from San Francisco): 800-696-6443 or 255-7631

The V.I.N.E. (Napa city bus): 255-7631

Intercity Van-Go Up-Valley (limited hours of service between the Napa Valley towns of St. Helena, Calistoga and Angwin): 963-4222 or 252-2600

The opening of the Golden Gate Bridge in 1937 linked Napa and Sonoma counties with San Francisco, opening them up as travel destinations.

Courtesy Sonoma County Museum

Sonoma County

Golden Gate Transit (for travel between San Francisco and Sonoma County): 415-332-6600

Sonoma County Transit (for travel within Sonoma County): 576-RIDE
Santa Rosa Transit (city bus): 524-5306 or 524-5238
Petaluma Transit (city bus): 778-4460
Healdsburg In-City Transit (city bus): 431-3309

BY TRAIN

The Napa Valley Wine Train, with luxurious Pullman dining cars, travels the 36 miles round-trip between the towns of Napa and St. Helena. It is actually a gourmet restaurant on rails and not a true form of transportation. (See *Restaurants,* Chapter Five.)

BY LIMOUSINE

The ultimate in personal transportation is the limousine, and for many visitors to Wine Country, chauffeured travel goes hand-in-hand with wine tasting. For others, the pricey three-hour ride to the Sonoma Coast can be a romantic and unforgettable luxury.

Both Napa Valley and Sonoma County have an abundance of professional limousine services that will map out wine-tasting itineraries for the novice or deliver connoisseurs to wineries of their choosing. Most also offer day-long, fixed-rate touring packages with extras, such as gourmet picnic lunches or evening dining, included in the price. Per-hour rates range from $30 on weekdays to $60 on weekends, not including taxes, driver gratuities, parking fees or bridge tolls. A three- or four-hour minimum is standard, and complimentary champagne is often served. Reservations are required at least two or three days in advance, and as much as a week in advance during peak vacationing months. Some recommend booking at least a month ahead of time. (Prices quoted are current at mid-1991.)

For your added safety, the limousine service you engage should be both licensed and insured. Ask your hotel concierge to recommend a service or talk to your travel agent. Listed below are some of Wine Country's most popular limousine services. Companies may be based in one county, but they frequently take passengers all over Wine Country and beyond.

Napa County

Chardonnay Limousine	944-1194
Crown Limousine	226-9500
Limousine D'Elegance	255-1557
Reliable Limousine	258-2229

Sonoma County

A Perfect Experience Limousine	585-1320
Advantage Limousine	762-1724
All Occasions Limousine	584-0701
Diamond Star Limousine	579-3561
Four Star Limousine	545-4442, 415-952-6810
Lap of Luxury Limousine	579-0433
Lon's Limo Service	539-5466
North Bay Limousine	578-4777
Pacific Limousine	664-0362
Royal Coach Limousine	944-2566
Touch of Class Limousine	526-4869

BY TAXI

When buses are too inconvenient and limousines too expensive, call for an old standby: the taxicab. The companies below are on duty 24 hours a day, seven days a week. Per-mile fares range from $1.60 to $2.

Napa County

Napa	Napa Yellow Cab	226-3731
	Napa Valley Cab	257-6444
St. Helena	Taxi Cabernet Tours	963-2620

Sonoma County

Guerneville	Bill's Taxi Service	869-2177
Santa Rosa	Blue Cab	575-5100
	Country Cab	546-0370
	George's Taxi Yellow Cab	546-3322 or 544-4444
Sonoma	Checker Cab/Yellow Cab	996-6733

NEIGHBORS ALL AROUND

TO THE SOUTH

The striking countryside and tony hamlets of Marin County are directly south. In San Rafael, just east of Hwy. 101, don't miss the dramatic Marin Civic Center, one of the last buildings designed by Frank Lloyd Wright. If you're not in a hurry, consider trekking north or south on Hwy. 1, the winding two-lane that hugs the rugged coastline. It will take you by Muir Woods, home to some of the tallest redwoods north of the Bay, and also the majestic Mount Tamalpais. Drive to its 3,000-foot summit for a spectacular view of San Francisco (clear weather permitting, that is). Point Reyes Lighthouse is also worth a stop 20 miles west of Hwy. 1, as well as the many oyster farms near Marshall.

Farther south is one of the most intriguing, romantic, and ethnically diverse cities in America: San Francisco. It's just a one-hour drive from Wine Country. Ride a cable car, snack on scrumptious dim sum in Chinatown, gorge on culture and shopping or just admire the view. (See "Neighbors All Around" in *Culture,* Chapter Four, for more suggestions.) Across the Bay is Oakland and the ever-eclectic Berkeley, both stops worth making.

TO THE EAST

While motoring your way to Sacramento along I-80, your thoughts may turn to . . . onions. The aroma of onions and other commercially-grown produce fills the air in fertile Sacramento Valley, where fruits and vegetables are tended in endless, flat fields. The city of Sacramento, the state capital and once a major hub for rail and river transportation, is proud of its historical center of Old Town, a faithful recreation of the city's original town center with a multitude of shops, restaurants and museums.

TO THE NORTH

Not to be outdone by Napa and Sonoma, Mendocino County is also a major player in the game of fine wine, with several premium wineries along Hwy. 101 open daily for tasting and tours. The coastal hamlet of Mendocino, one of Hollywood's favorite movie locations, is also a treasure trove for shoppers. Its art galleries, antiques shops and fine dining, and its New England-like atmosphere, make it a popular second destination for Wine Country visitors.

CHAPTER THREE
The Keys to Your Room
LODGING

Chris Alderman

A hotel with a past. Each room is sumptuously appointed with antiques amid old oak and stained glass.

Following the Gold Rush of 1849, adventurers with gold dust in their pockets drifted into Napa and Sonoma counties looking for cheap land and ways to invest their new-found wealth. Further riches came from silver mining in Napa County and from the booming timber industry in Sonoma County. By the time the railroads laid their tracks in the region in the 1870s, prosperity had firmly taken hold and building flourished, creating a curious hodge-podge of stately homes and hotels.

This late 19th-century mixture of quasi-Victorian architectural styles (Queen Anne, Italianate and Eastlake Stick, among others) has been described as "buildings that came to pass not by blueprint but by whim." Unlike their more plain Midwestern counterparts, Northern California farm homes and lodges were sprinkled generously with gingerbread outside and swathed in mahogany and marble inside. Some began life as stagecoach stops, railroad inns and even distilleries; others entered the 20th century as a schoolhouse, hospital or general store. Not only are they still standing, but they have been lovingly and authentically renovated into showplace bed & breakfast inns.

Just 12 years ago, only 50 bed & breakfast establishments were operating in

California; today there are 800-plus and more open for business every year. (Most have from three to 10 guest rooms; others have 20 rooms or more.) One of the largest concentrations of B&Bs in the state is in Wine Country, and many are housed in structures rich in history.

A map of B&Bs in Napa Valley, in fact, looks like a game of connect-the-dots. This increased competition has redefined service in the industry, so innkeepers are always searching for new ways to satisfy guests and perhaps one-up the inn down the road. For example, the morning meal has evolved from once-standard "light continental" fare. Today's breakfast is a gourmand's delight, often served buffet- or family-style and including, but not limited to, creative egg entrees, quiche, Yountville or Sonoma sausages, waffles or pancakes, oven-fresh breads with homemade jams, farm-fresh fruit and champagne, a feast from which you may sample as little or as much as you like. Additionally, *prix fixe* gourmet dinners whipped up by local chefs one or two nights a week are now *de rigueur* at many Sonoma County B&Bs.

What separates Wine Country inns and B&Bs from larger motels and hotels are scenic, off-the-beaten-path locations and, above all, *personal service.* Innkeepers have a great fondness for people; they wouldn't be in this type of business otherwise. So expect to be pampered at intimate inns, where the price of your room may include the use of plush terrycloth robes or an in-room piano and hors d'oeuvres and wine at twilight.

The list of amenities goes on: Private balconies and decks overlooking vineyards or oak groves. Saturday evening wine tastings with award-winning vintners. Complimentary bottles of premium wine. Home-baked chocolate chip cookies at your bedside. Private baths are not only standard these days, but many are equipped with whirlpool tubs for two. Air-conditioned B&Bs are common in Napa Valley, where temperatures can rise significantly on sunny summer days.

In Sonoma County the cool ocean breezes help to temper the summer heat, so air conditioning is usually not necessary. Perhaps the most striking difference in B&Bs between the two regions is the hospitality of innkeepers. Sonoma County literally oozes with laid-back proprietors who tend to welcome strangers like one of the family, while those in Napa Valley, though friendly, are generally more reserved. The exception may be in Calistoga, a burg that rubs shoulders with Sonoma County's Petrified Forest. By virtue of its county fairgrounds, hot springs and a funky, fickle geyser, Calistoga has the most rural and "down home" atmosphere you'll find in Napa Valley.

Don't expect a B&B to be less expensive than a conventional hotel or motel. Unlike its budget-wise British cousin, the Wine Country B&B is an intimate, serene and pricey luxury accommodation and almost always worth it.

A majority of the accommodations described in this chapter are bed & breakfast inns and hotels, the lodging of choice for visitors seeking a romantic getaway enhanced by premium wine, fine food, walks on the beach and rejuvenating mud baths. The balance are elegant resorts, business-class or historic hotels and motels with exceptional facilities. We have elected to spotlight establishments that enjoy excellent reputations for hospitality, ambience and location, while giving an honest appraisal of their facilities. (Keep in mind that over time, policies, amenities and even furnishings may change at some inns, as will the complimentary goodies.)

If you're more at ease staying with a familiar motel chain where there are few surprises, or you must have a room phone and TV, or budget is your first consideration, Wine Country offers many delightful options. A hand-picked selection of the region's best-priced and most strategically located motels is included near the end of this chapter. Additionally, we've listed campgrounds that are popular for their locations and facilities.

NAPA AND SONOMA LODGING NOTES

Rates

High season for Wine Country innkeepers is generally from April to October; off-season runs November to March. A few inns, however, make no distinction between the seasons and may charge the same rate year-round. At those that do recognize off-season, expect to pay 20% to 30% less. Likewise, mid-week rates may be significantly less than weekend rates.

The following price codes are based on per-room, double-occupancy, high-season weekend rates at B&Bs and the better lodgings.

Inexpensive	Up to $75
Moderate	$75 to $125
Expensive	$125 to $175
Very Expensive	Over $175

These rates exclude local taxes and any service charges that may be added to your bill.

Minimum Stay

A majority of inns and B&Bs require a two-night minimum on weekends; a three-night minimum is the norm on holiday weekends. (Virtually all inns and B&Bs are open year-round in Wine Country.) Hotels and motels are usually not picky about your length of stay.

Deposit/Cancellation

It's advisable to make reservations at popular inns and hotels several weeks in advance, as most fill up on weekends even in the off-season. There is sometimes a small fee to request a specific room at a B&B; always ask about any extra charges. A deposit by credit card for the first night is usually required.

Because small inns rely on keeping rooms booked, strict cancellation policies can apply. A $10 to $15 handling fee deducted from your deposit is standard if you cancel from seven days to 48 hours in advance of your reservation. With less notice, the inn will usually keep the deposit in full, but only if they can't rebook the room.

Restrictions

Smoking is not permitted inside smaller inns and B&Bs, and pets are prohibited almost unanimously. As a general rule, children under 10 or 12 are discouraged, but some inns welcome kids and infants with open arms. In-room telephones and televisions are not usually furnished at B&Bs; likewise, room service is not provided. To avoid any surprises or disappointments, always inquire in advance about the inn's current policies and list of amenities. Hotels and motels generally have designated smoking/non-smoking rooms and children are welcome. Pets are accepted at the manager's discretion; always inquire before booking.

Information

Many of these services will arrange accommodations in both Napa Valley and Sonoma County. Some can also make reservations for balloon rides, visits to spas, wine tours, and catering services.

Accommodations Referral Hotel Hotline	963-8466
Bed & Breakfast Almanac/	
Wine Country Cottages	963-0852
Bed & Breakfast Exchange	942-5900
Bed & Breakfast Inns of Sonoma County	433-4667
Bed & Breakfast Inns of Sonoma Valley	996-4667
Hotel Connections	763-2208
Napa Valley's Finest Lodgings	224-4667
	or 257-1051
Napa Valley Reservations Unlimited	252-1985
Napa Valley Tourist Bureau	944-1557
Tourist Information Tower and	253-2929
Self-Guided Tours	or 800-FOR-NAPA
Wine Country B&B Reservations	257-7757
	or 944-1222
Wine Country Tourist Bureau	252-3130

COASTAL RENTALS

There is probably no place more wild and beautiful in Northern California than the rugged Sonoma Coast. Fortunately, there are scores of rental homes and cottages where vacationers who wish to extend their Wine Country visit may enjoy the splendor of the coast in private seaside hideaways.

The coastal community of Sea Ranch, at the north end of the county, is a popular destination for a relaxing vacation, with Mendocino Coast attractions just a short drive away. It is affectionately known as the "Banana Belt" because of a warmer, less foggy climate than is typically encountered on the north coast. Farther south, Bodega Bay offers excellent rental properties, easy accessibility to Sonoma County's premium wineries, and is also convenient for day trips to San Francisco.

Most of the rentals are privately-owned cottages and homes with fully equipped kitchens, fireplaces or woodstoves, hot tubs, washers and dryers, dishwashers, TVs and stereos. Many have full ocean views, but some are nestled further off the shoreline in forests and meadows. Bed linens, towels and maid service are usually not provided, but may be rented in advance. Rental conditions are similar to B&Bs, with a two-night minimum the norm (a week minimum in high season) and comparable cancellation terms. A deposit of at least $100 is typically required and held as a damage and cleaning deposit. Additionally, the full rental amount is usually due prior to your arrival. Rental fees vary greatly, depending on the number of occupants, the location of the home, the amenities and the season.

Listed below are property management and realty companies that arrange home and condo rentals on the Sonoma Coast.

Bodega Bay Vacation Rentals	875-4000 or 800-548-7631
Don Berard Associates	884-3211
Ocean View Properties	884-3539
Rams Head Realty and Rentals	785-2427
Sea Ranch Vacation Homes	884-4235

LODGING IN NAPA COUNTY

Napa

ARBOR GUEST HOUSE
Innkeepers: Rosemary and
  Bruce Logan.
252-8144.
1436 G St., Napa, CA
  94559.
Lincoln Ave. exit E. off
  Hwy. 29, R. on Marin St.
  to G St.

Built just after the 1906 earthquake by a San Francisco craftsman appropriately named Rumble, this inn is reminiscent of grandmother's Midwestern farmhouse. There are five guest rooms in the main house and carriage house, all remodeled and restored by the current owner, a contractor by trade. A two-person whirlpool tub near the fireplace makes the Winter Haven room popular, and Rose's Bower, the top floor of the carriage house, is requested often. The Napa Valley Wine Train station is just a mile away.

BEAZLEY HOUSE
Innkeepers: Jim and Carol Beazley.
257-1649.
1910 First St., Napa, CA 94559.
First St. exit E. off Hwy. 29 near Jefferson St.
Price: Moderate to Expensive.
Credit cards: MC, V.

Bright blue and white awnings make this 10-room mansion easy to spot. The home, built in 1902, was one of Napa's first B&Bs. The rooms are equally divided between the main house and the refurbished carriage house. All are warm and comfortable, but the carriage house may be the most desirable — a fireplace and two-person spa is standard in each of its five rooms. A full breakfast is served in the home's dining room, and guests may take tea in the afternoon in the spacious living room.

BROOKSIDE VINEYARD
Innkeepers: Tom and Susan Ridley.
944-1661.
3194 Redwood Rd., Napa, CA 94558.
Off Hwy. 29, 1 mi. W. on Redwood Rd.
Price: Moderate.
Credit Cards: None.
Special Features: Pool.

One of the best B&B bargains in the valley, Brookside Vineyard is also as hands-on to a working vineyard as you're likely to get on a visit to Wine Country. During the pre-harvest season, the innkeeper, who is also a winemaker, welcomes early risers to help him collect grapes for testing and crushing. In autumn, you may want to gather grapevines for making wreaths. Regardless of the season, Tom Ridley will gladly share his grape growing and winemaking expertise over afternoon vino. The home's creekside setting lends a romantic touch to the three guest rooms furnished in Laura Ashley prints. This property is also home to a fruit orchard, gazebo, and a holiday bonus — a Christmas tree farm.

CANDLELIGHT INN
Innkeepers: Joe and Carol Farace.
257-3717.
1045 Easum Dr., Napa, CA 94558.
1st St. exit W. off Hwy. 29 to Easum Dr.
Price: Expensive.
Credit Cards: MC, V.
Handicap. Access: Yes.

On a parklike city acre in Napa, this 1929 English Tudor mansion has three romantic suites with private baths and one with private sauna. Lovely gardens surround the house.

Price: Moderate.
Credit cards: MC, V.
Handicap. Access: Yes.

CHURCHILL MANOR
Innkeeper: Joanna Guidotti.
253-773-3485 Brown St.,
  Napa, CA 94559.
1st St. exit E. of Hwy. 29, R.
  on Coombs St., L. on Oak
  St., R. on Brown St.
Price: Moderate to
  Expensive.
Credit Cards: AE, MC, V.
Special Features: Bicycles;
  croquet.

From the moment you spy Churchill Manor, you know it's special. The inn, a National Historic Landmark built in 1889 with Greek Revival columns, has the wraparound verandas and grand parlors of days gone by. The eight guest rooms are situated on the second and third floors of this graceful mansion, and all have private baths and queen- or king-size beds. Handpainted Delft tiles, 24-carat gold trim and an antique beaded opera gown are among the rich details in the rooms. The tariff includes a generous buffet-style breakfast served in the sunroom, where regional varietal wines are enjoyed in the evening.

COUNTRY GARDEN INN
Innkeepers: Lisa and
  George Smith.
255-1197.
1815 Silverado Trail, Napa,
  CA 94558.
Imola Ave. exit E. of Hwy.
  29, 1½ mi. N. on
  Silverado Trail.
Price: Moderate to
  Expensive.
Credit Cards: AE, MC, V.

The Silverado Trail is the alternative route of travel through Napa Valley, and it's easy to see why with charming roadside B&Bs like this one. There are eight guest rooms in all at this wooded riverside property — one is its own cottage with a fireplace and deck. Rooms have an elegant and refined Old World atmosphere. A shaded rose garden with lily pond and fountain completes the picture. Your British-bred hosts serve a change-of-pace English breakfast complete with grilled sausages and tomatoes, and you'll be treated to yummy dessert treats when you return from an evening out.

CROSS ROADS INN
Innkeepers: Sam and
  Nancy Scott.
944-0646.
6380 Silverado Trail, Napa,
  CA 94558.
Intersection of Yountville
  Cross Rd. and Silverado
  Trail E. of Yountville.
Price: Expensive to Very
  Expensive.
Credit Cards: MC, V.
Special Features: Exercise
  equipment

Stunning valley views are just one of the attractions at Cross Roads Inn, which, despite its Napa mailing address, is actually near Yountville. The three-story chalet on 23 mountainous acres is surrounded by oak trees and wildflowers, and the unusual circular fireplace in the lounge is one-of-a-kind, rising 20 feet into the ceiling. The four guest rooms, some with whirlpool spas, are named after Beatrix Potter characters, and each is situated in a separate wing of the house. All have private baths and decks. High tea and sherry in the dining room cap off a day of wine touring.

ELM HOUSE INN

Innkeepers: David and
  Betsy McCracken.
255-1831.
800 California Blvd., Napa,
  CA 94559.
1st St. exit E. to California
  Blvd.
Price: Moderate.
Credit Cards: AE, MC, V.
Handicap. Access: Yes.
Special Features:
  Whirlpool.

This village inn has Italian marble fireplaces in many of its 16 rooms (all with private baths), and is sheltered by three huge, historic elm trees. The rooms are sound insulated for ultimate privacy, and also have individual temperature controls, TVs, phones and stocked refrigerators. There's also a honeymoon suite with high ceilings, chandelier and its own whirlpool. Expect a delicious complimentary breakfast each morning. Located just blocks from shopping and dining.

HENNESSEY HOUSE

Innkeepers: Lauriann
  Zemann and Andrea
  Weinstein.
226-3774.
1727 Main St., Napa, CA
  94558.
Lincoln Ave. exit E. of
  Hwy. 29, R. on Main St.
Price: Expensive.
Credit Cards: MC, V.
Special Features: Sauna.

This home on the National Register of Historic Places is a stunning example of a perfectly restored 1889 Eastlake Queen Anne residence and carriage house. Inside the 10 guest rooms are feather beds, private baths and whirlpools, fireplaces and air conditioning. A full breakfast is served in the dining room, where the restored handpainted and stamped tin ceiling is the focal

Hennessey House, a Queen Anne residence, is listed on the National Register of Historic Places.

Chris Alderman

point. There's also an evening wine hour for guests. Guests here, however, may be left wanting for friendlier hosts.

INN AT NAPA VALLEY
Manager: William Stadler.
253-9540 or 800-433-4600.
1075 California Blvd.,
  Napa, CA 94559.
1st St. exit E. of Hwy. 29 to
  California Blvd.
Price: Expensive.
Credit Cards: AE, CB, D,
  DC, MC, V.
Handicap. Access: Yes.
Special Features: Indoor
  and outdoor pools;
  sauna; spa; restaurant
  and lounge.

All 205 rooms in this hotel are two-room suites with French country furnishings and are equipped for light cooking with mini-refrigerators, coffeemakers and microwave ovens. In addition, all rooms have wet bars, phones and TVs. Daily complimentary full breakfast is cooked to order, and two hours of complimentary cocktails are served each evening. Outside there's a pond with swans and ducks, and a tropical atrium with a skylight for dining. This is an elegant business-class hotel — formerly Sterling Suites Hotel — that's also ideal for leisure travelers. Restaurant Caffe 1991 is a pleasant place, too. (See Chapter Five, *Restaurants*.)

JOHN MUIR INN
Manager: Joan Shelsta.
257-7220 or 800-522-8999
  (in CA).
1998 Trower Ave., Napa,
  CA 94558.
Hwy. 29 at Trower Ave.
Price: Moderate to
  Expensive.
Credit Cards: AE, D, DC,
  MC, V.
Handicap. Access: Yes.
Special Features: Pool; spa.

A 60-room, better-than-average motel on the north side of Napa for easier access to up-valley wineries and restaurants. The spacious rooms and suites are tastefully furnished, and many have wet bars and kitchenettes. Continental breakfast is included in the tariff.

LA BELLE EPOQUE
Innkeepers: Merlin and
  Claudia Wedepohl.
257-2161.
1386 Calistoga Ave., Napa,
  CA 94558.
1st St. exit E. of Hwy. 29,
  N. on Jefferson St. to
  Calistoga Ave.
Price: Moderate to
  Expensive.
Credit Cards: AE, MC, V.

The stained glass windows and fine Victorian-era furniture at this six-room inn will transport you to another time and place. Family heirloom antiques and collectibles are scattered throughout the guest rooms and the common parlor. There's also a remodeled wine cellar and tasting room, open every afternoon for guests to try complimentary Napa Valley wines. It's just a short walk to the Napa Valley Wine Train station.

An old water wheel and duck pond at the Inn at Napa Valley.

Chris Alderman

LA RESIDENCE COUNTRY INN

Innkeepers: Craig Claussen and David Jackson.
253-0337.
4066 Hwy 29, Napa, CA 94558.
First R. turn N. of Salvador Ave., S. on Byway East frontage road.
Price: Inexpensive to Expensive.
Credit Cards: MC, V.
Handicap. Access: Yes.
Special Features: Pool; whirlpool.

Built by a New Orleans riverboat pilot who arrived in San Francisco during the Gold Rush, this 20-room inn still has the flavor of the Old South in its plantation shutters and parklike setting. The pace is slow-and-easy, with lots of porches and decks and a jogging and bicycling trail that stretches all the way to Yountville.The rooms are also designed for relaxation — each has a sitting area, and many have fireplaces and air conditioning.

NAPA INN

Innkeepers: Doug and Carol Morales.
257-1444.
1137 Warren St., Napa, CA 94559.
1st St. exit E. of Hwy. 29 to Warren St. near Clay St.
Price: Moderate to Expensive.
Credit Cards: MC, V.

Music plays a starring role at this unique Victorian-era inn. The parlor is filled with antique instruments, from the player piano to the accordion, violin and music box. There's also a collection of antique clocks and a Thomas Edison talking machine. Upstairs, the finest of the five guest rooms is the Grand Suite. Encompassing the entire third floor of the house, it has a sitting and dressing area, and boasts a private balcony as well. Complimentary breakfast, of course, is served in the dining room.

Chris Alderman

Many pro-am golf tournaments are held at the Silverado Country Club.

SILVERADO COUNTRY CLUB

Manager: Kirk Candland.
257-0200.
1600 Atlas Peak Rd., Napa, CA 94558.
Silverado Trail at Atlas Peak Rd., 1 mi. NE of Napa.
Price: Very Expensive.
Credit Cards: AE, CB, D, DC, MC, V.
Special Features: Two 18-hole golf courses; 8 pools; 20 tennis courts; 3 restaurants; 3 lounges; room service.

Golf is king at Silverado. Its two challenging 18-hole courses designed in 1966 are among the finest in the country, and many celebrity pro-am tournaments are held here. With more than 1,000 regular members, the area is constantly bustling with activity. President Theodore Roosevelt and General John J. Pershing once stayed in the main house of this 1,220-acre estate well before it was a country club.

Today there are 280 rooms scattered over the property ranging in size from studios to three-bedroom suites. The units are individually owned by members, but rented out like hotel rooms. (The Oak Creek East area is the most secluded; the Clubhouse side is convenient to the tennis courts and golf courses.) All rooms are comfortably furnished to feel like home, and the kitchenettes have just about everything you need to do light cooking. Barbecue grills may also be rented.

Golf isn't the only attraction at Silverado, however. The concierge staff is probably the best in the valley. These helpful, longtime residents are fully trained to help sort out the who, what, when and where of just about everything going on in Wine Country.

STAHLECKER HOUSE

Innkeepers: Ron and Ethel Stahlecker.
257-1588.
1042 Easum Dr., Napa, CA 94558.
1st St. exit W. off Hwy. 29 to Easum Dr.
Price: Moderate to Expensive.
Credit Cards: MC, V.

In a newer home than most B&Bs, this 1948 ranch-style has appealing guest rooms with canopy beds, antique furniture and private baths. Relax on the immense sundeck surrounded by oak and laurel trees, or read in the living room. Your hosts (a race car driver and an artist) serve a gourmet candlelight breakfast in the dining room and complimentary beverages around the clock.

Yountville

BORDEAUX HOUSE

Innkeeper: Mohammad Daeabhoai.
944-2855.
6600 Washington St., P.O. Box 3274, Yountville, CA 94599.
Off Hwy. 9 at Washington St.
Price: Moderate.
Credit Cards: AE, MC, V.

The six guest rooms in this Mobil-rated 4-star inn are furnished in Italian contemporary style. Each room has a fireplace and private bath; most have balconies or patios. Continental breakfast is served in the common room.

BURGUNDY HOUSE

944-0889.
6711 Washington St., P.O. Box 3156, Yountville, CA 94599.
Washington St. exit off Hwy. 29, L. 1/2 mi.
Price: Moderate.
Credit Cards: None.

A brandy distillery in 1874, this charming two-story structure is now a five-room inn. Antique furniture and period pieces are at home amidst the 22-inch-thick walls of rugged fieldstone and river rock masonry. A decanter of Napa Valley wine helps visitors settle in, and a full breakfast is served in the garden or inside. All rooms have private baths. Innkeeper hospitality is not what it could be.

Rugged fieldstone and river rock masonry walls characterize Burgundy House, once a brandy distillery.

Chris Alderman

MAGNOLIA HOTEL
Managers: Bruce and
  Bonnie Locken.
944-2056.
6529 Yount St., Yountville,
  CA 94599.
One block E. of
  Washington St.
Price: Moderate to
  Expensive.
Credit Cards: None.
Special features: Pool;
  whirlpool.

**NAPA VALLEY LODGE,
  BEST WESTERN**
Manager: Erika Cimpher.
944-2468 or 800-368-2468.
Hwy. 29 at Madison St.,
  Yountville, CA 94599.
Price: Moderate to
  Expensive.
Credit Cards: AE, D, DC,
  MC, V.
Handicap. Access: Yes.
Special Features: Pool; spa;
  sauna; exercise room.

**NAPA VALLEY
  RAILWAY INN**
Innkeeper: Hazel Boll.
944-2000.
6503 Washington St.,
  Yountville, CA 94599.
Off Hwy. 29 to Washington
  St.
Price: Moderate.
Credit Cards: MC, V.
Handicap. Access: Yes.

OAK KNOLL INN
Innkeepers: Jan and Tom
  Bird.
255-2200.
2200 E. Oak Knoll Ave.,
  Napa, CA 94558.
3 mi. S. of Yountville, Oak
  Knoll Ave. to Big Ranch
  Rd., L., then R. 4/10 mi.

Many of Napa Valley's old hotels are steeped in history, and the Magnolia Hotel is also blessed with a colorful past. The 12-room structure built in 1873 has been a bordello, a home for farm laborers, a 4-H headquarters and a speakeasy, among other things. It is now renovated and its guest rooms are furnished with antiques. The extensive wine cellar is worth exploring, and the pool and whirlpool offer relaxation in a private setting. Full breakfast is included, served family-style in the fireside dining room.

With all the amenities of an exceptional hotel, Napa Valley Lodge enjoys the AAA 4-Diamond rating. The 52 luxurious and spacious rooms with private balconies or terraces with postcard views of the valley are furnished with airy wicker and tropical plants. In-room coffeemakers and cooler/refrigerators are provided, and a continental buffet breakfast is served. This is a restful location surrounded by ripening grapes in the vineyards, and it's an easy walk to Washington Square shops and the Vintage 1870 complex, a former winery converted to shops and restaurants. (See Chapter Eight, *Shopping*.)

Take a step back to the time the railroad reigned — stay in one of nine turn-of-the-century railroad cars (three cabooses and six rail cars) completely refurbished into luxurious suites. Period furniture and decor help guests relive the past glory of rail travel. A brass bed, sitting room with loveseat and a full bath complete each room. Next door is shopping and dining at Vintage 1870. (See Chapter Eight, *Shopping*.)

Tall French windows, rustic stone walls and vaulted ceilings distinguish the four guest suites at this luxurious inn set well off the bustle of Hwy. 29 and surrounded by 600 acres of Chardonnay vineyards. The rooms have king-size brass beds, Italian marble fireplaces, private baths and sitting areas with overstuffed chairs and sofas. A full breakfast (served at your leisure in your room

Price: Expensive to Very
Expensive.
Credit Cards: MC, V.
Special Features: Pool;
whirlpool; croquet;
bicycles.

OLEANDER HOUSE BED & BREAKFAST INN

Innkeepers: John and
Louise Packard.
944-8315.
7433 St. Helena Hwy.,
Yountville, CA 94599.
3 mi. N. of Yountville on
Hwy. 29.
Price: Moderate to
Expensive.
Credit Cards: MC, V.
Special Features: Spa.

VINTAGE INN

Manager: Nancy
Lockmann.
944-1112, 800-351-1133 (in
CA) or 800-9-VALLEY.
6541 Washington St.,
Yountville, CA 94599.
Washington St. exit off
Hwy. 29.

or on the veranda) and complimentary wine are included in the tariff. This is a peaceful setting with magnificent views, and unpretentious innkeepers to boot.

A contemporary two-story house with four guest rooms decorated in homey fabrics makes this a comfortable base for a Wine Country stay. The high-ceiling rooms have private baths, private balconies, woodburning fireplaces and spectacular views of the valley. The queen-size beds and windows are decorated with Laura Ashley prints. A gourmet breakfast starts your day; at dinner time, Mustard's Grill, one of Napa Valley's premier restaurants, is just a few steps away. (See Chapter Five, *Restaurants.*)

This is an exceptional inn designed with villa-style units clustered around a common waterway. The 80 spacious and beautifully decorated rooms have oversized beds, whirlpool spa tubs, ceiling fans, in-room coffeemakers and refrigerators, private verandas and woodburning fireplaces. Second-story rooms cost a little more but the views are worth it. Smoking or non-smoking rooms are available, as is room service. California

A tiny canal with fountains laces the cluster of villa-style units at the Vintage Inn.

Chris Alderman

Price: Expensive to Very Expensive.
Credit Cards: AE, D, DC, MC, V.
Handicap. Access: Yes.
Special Features: Pool; spa; tennis courts; bicycle rentals; children welcome.

THE WEBBER PLACE
Innkeeper: Diane Bartholomew.
944-8384.
6610 Webber, Yountville, CA 94599.
Just off Washington St.
Price: Inexpensive to Moderate.
Credit Cards: AE, MC, V.

champagne is served with the continental breakfast. Shopping, art galleries and dining at the Vintage 1870 complex next door. (See Chapter Eight, *Shopping*.)

Located in the section of town called "Old Yountville," this red farmhouse with a white picket fence was built in 1850 and now has four comfy guest rooms. After awakening in iron and brass beds, guests enjoy breakfast complete with biscuits. Two rooms have private baths with old-fashioned tubs. The Veranda Suite, the largest room, is complete with its own featherbed, private entrance and veranda with hammock. Plans are in the works for a croquet court. The inn is walking distance to all of Yountville's shopping and dining attractions.

Rutherford

AUBERGE DU SOLEIL
Manager: George Goeggel.
963-1211.
180 Rutherford Hill Rd., Rutherford, CA 94573.
Hwy. 29 to Hwy. 128 to Silverado Trail to Rutherford Hill Rd.
Price: Very Expensive.
Credit Cards: AE, MC, V.
Handicap. Access: Yes.
Special Features: Pool; spa with staff masseuse; tennis courts with staff pro; golf privileges; children welcome.

In just 10 years, the restaurant at Auberge du Soleil achieved status as one of Napa Valley's not-to-be-missed dining experiences. (See Chapter Five, *Restaurants*.) In the mid-1980s, luxurious lodgings (nine maisonette units) were added near the restaurant on this remote 33-acre hillside resort reminiscent of the south of France. It is now one of the valley's most elegant and popular places to stay, and one of the most pricey as well.

Privacy is perhaps the greatest asset of the resort perched above the valley east of Rutherford. Each of the 48 bedrooms and suites has its own entrance and private veranda. The rooms and suites are styled to feel like Provençal farmhouses, with deep-set windows with wood shutters and doors. Terra cotta tiling is used generously throughout on floors and countertops, helping to keep rooms cool during Napa Valley's toasty summer days. The rooms range from standard bedroom and bath to deluxe bedroom and bath, one- and two-bedroom suites, and deluxe suites. The most luxurious are the deluxe bedrooms, with fireplaces and whirlpool baths. Terrycloth robes, wet bars and refrigerators are standard in all rooms.

RANCHO CAYMUS INN
Manager: Mary Tilden Morton.
963-1777.
P.O. Box 78, Rutherford, CA 94573.
4 mi. N. of Yountville at junction of Hwys. 29 and 128.
Price: Moderate to Very Expensive.
Credit Cards: MC, V.
Special Features: Restaurant; room service.

Local craftspeople and the inn's owner and designer, Mary Tilden Morton, can take credit for creating a striking, arts-inspired, Spanish-style lodge. Throughout its 26 rooms are stained glass windows, hand-thrown stoneware and tooled wooden lamps, all made by regional artists. Ecuadorian and Guadalajaran craftsmen also contributed to the colorful furnishings. The modern conveniences in each room are further enhanced by private balconies, wet bars and refrigerators and air conditioning. The four suites have whirlpools, full kitchens, fireplaces and large balconies. Breakfast is served from 7 to 10:30 a.m. (convenient for early risers), in your room or in the gardens.

St. Helena

AMBROSE BIERCE HOUSE
Innkeeper: Jane Hutchings.
963-3003.
1515 Main St., St. Helena, CA 94574.
On Main St. (Hwy. 29) between Madrona and Adams Sts.
Price: Moderate to Expensive.
Credit Cards: None.
Special Features: Children accepted by prior arrangement.

You can't miss the two oversized "1515" signs on the front of this home announcing you've found the Ambrose Bierce House. The renowned writer and curmudgeon philosopher (*The Devil's Dictionary*), lived here before vanishing to Mexico in 1913. (*Old Gringo*, the 1989 film starring Jane Fonda and Gregory Peck as Bierce, suggested one scenario of what may have become of the adventure-seeker in Mexico.) The mystique of his life and work surrounds guests in distinctive air-conditioned suites decorated with antiques, queen-size brass beds and armoires. Guests in street-front rooms may suffer the consequences of steady Main Street traffic (the house is located between St. Helena's two traffic lights), so ask for a room in back.

CHESTELSON HOUSE
Innkeeper: Jackie Sweet.
963-2238.
1417 Kearney St., St. Helena, CA 94574.
1 block off Main St. at Adams St.
Price: Moderate.
Credit Cards: None.

A sun-soaked porch at this small Victorian inn offers relaxation after a day of shopping and wine tasting in the valley. The three guest rooms are spacious and filled with light, and the home is located next door to another B&B and just a block from St. Helena's main street.

CINNAMON BEAR INN
Innkeeper: Genny Jenkins.
963-4653.
1407 Kearney St., St.
  Helena, CA 94574.
1 block off Main St. at
  Adams St.
Price: Moderate to
  Expensive.
Credit Cards: AE, D, MC,
  V.
Special Features: Children
  by arrangement.

Once the home of St. Helena's mayor, this converted B&B is where innkeeper Jenkins raised her three children. The inn's warm atmosphere surrounds you the moment you walk in the door. Lace curtains and multicolored quilts add to the comfortable feel of the guest suites, and the stuffed bears in each room have lent the inn its name. (The teddy bear motif is not as saccharine as it might be; the bears are kept to a subtle but sweet minimum.) The wraparound porch with its peeled willow furniture is great for reading. The inn is located on a quiet residential street with a school (and another B&B) next door, and it's just a block to Main Street shops and restaurants.

EL BONITA MOTEL
Manager: Philippe
  Pierrette.
963-3216 or 800-541-3284.
195 Main St., St. Helena,
  CA 94574.
S. of St. Helena on Hwy.
  29.
Price: Inexpensive to
  Moderate.
Credit Cards: AE, MC, V.
Special Features: Pool.

"An impeccable 1980s version of the brighter side of the 1930s," is how one writer summed up this inviting motel. Perhaps Napa Valley's only art deco motel, the pastel-decorated rooms are clean and cheery. French louvered windows and lots of fuchsia and aqua neon accent the 16 poolside and six bungalow units with kitchenettes. Trees and hedges help cushion the steady hum of Hwy. 29 traffic.

THE FARMHOUSE
Innkeepers: Ron and
  Hannah Nunn.
963-3431.
300 Taplin Rd., St. Helena,
  CA 94574.
SE of St. Helena off
  Silverado Trail.
Price: Moderate to
  Expensive.
Credit Cards: None.
Special Features: Pool

"A home away from home" may be the best way to describe the Farmhouse. Its three comfortable guest rooms are decorated in an understated country style in keeping with its rural setting among the vineyards. Natural wood-frame beds with duvets and the Southwestern-inspired color schemes add comfort and warmth. All baths are private, and the Blue Room is air conditioned. The inn is framed by fruit trees and built around a courtyard that was once the foundation of a Victorian home lost to fire decades ago.

FOREST MANOR
Innkeeper: Coralene
  Lambath.
965-3538.
415 Cold Springs Rd.,
  Angwin, CA 94508.

At this secluded 20-acre English Tudor estate, now a country inn with a honeymoon suite among its three guest rooms, there are vineyards and forest trails to explore. The three-story manor has vaulted ceilings, fireplaces, verandas and spas,

Silverado Trail to Deer Park Rd., to Las Posadas Rd. to Cold Springs Rd.
Price: Moderate to Expensive.
Credit Cards: MC, V.
Special Features: Pool.

and the rooms have private baths, refrigerators, coffeemakers and oversized beds. There's also a whirlpool in the honeymoon suite. About five miles from Hwy. 29, and above St. Helena in the community of Angwin, this friendly inn is a romantic getaway from the bustle of Napa Valley's busy towns.

Chris Alderman

The Harvest Inn calls up another time, another place.

HARVEST INN
Manager: Steacy Drew.
963-9463 or 800-950-8466.
One Main St., St. Helena, CA 94574.
On Hwy. 29 S. of St. Helena near Sulphur Springs Rd.
Price: Moderate to very expensive.
Credit Cards: AE, D, MC, V.
Special Features: Two pools; spas.

There's a bit of Old England in Napa Valley — the Harvest Inn, a stately English Tudor lodge with 55 guest rooms. Most rooms have king-size beds, brick fireplaces, wet bars and refrigerators, and all are furnished in antiques and reproductions. The lush landscaping also helps to create the aura of another time and place. The inn's Harvest Centre has a great room, wine bar and dance floor, and complimentary continental breakfast is served in the dining hall. Overlooking a 14-acre working vineyard, the inn is within strolling distance of many wineries.

HOTEL ST. HELENA
Innkeepers: Athena Martin and Edmond Reynolds.
963-4388.
1309 Main St., St. Helena, CA 94574.
On Main St. near Adams St.
Price: Moderate to Expensive.
Credit Cards: AE, MC, V.

In the thick of St. Helena's shopping and dining, this 18-room hotel on the town's Main Street is richly furnished with antiques. Its turn-of-the-century charm makes it especially homey. There's a wine bar, and continental breakfast is served every morning. Some baths are shared.

INK HOUSE BED & BREAKFAST
Innkeepers: Ernie Veniegas and Jim Annis.
963-3890.
1575 St. Helena Hwy., St. Helena, CA 94574.
1 mi. N. of Rutherford at White Hall Ln.
Price: Moderate to Expensive.
Credit Cards: None

A glass-enclosed, rooftop observatory with a 360-degree view of vineyards distinguishes this 1884 Italianate Victorian listed on the National Register of Historic Places. Each of the four second-story guest rooms has a vineyard view, and period furnishings and private baths round out the room amenities. Just for fun, take a lesson on the antique pump organ in the parlor. This is an exceptional location and setting, and the innkeepers couldn't be friendlier.

MEADOWOOD
Manager: Maurice Nayrolles.
963-3646 or 800-458-8080 (in CA).
900 Meadowood Ln., St. Helena, CA 94574.
E. of St. Helena to Silverado Trail, to Howell Mtn. Rd. to Meadowood Ln.
Price: Very Expensive.
Credit Cards: AE, DC, MC, V.
Handicap. Access: Yes.
Special Features: World-class croquet courts; acclaimed restaurant; golf course with pro; pool; tennis; wine school; children welcome.

M eadowood never falters in its interpretation of luxury. Originally designed as an elegant country club for Napa Valley's well-to-do families, Meadowood was rebuilt after a 1984 fire, then reopened as both a resort hotel and country club.

Reminiscent of New England's turn-of-the-century cottages, the main lodge and 10 smaller lodges scattered around the 250-acre property are tiered with gabled windows and porches, all trimmed in white. Most of the resort's 70 rooms and suites have skylights, ceiling fans and air conditioning for Napa Valley's warmest summer days. (Rooms range in size from one-room studios with fireplaces to one-bedroom suites with sitting rooms.) Each room has a wraparound porch with a view of pine trees and gardens, and queen- or king-size bed with goosedown comforters. Additionally, terrycloth robes, wet bars, refrigerators, coffeemakers, toasters and television are standard in all rooms.

Breakfast is not included in the tariff but a continental feast will be delivered to your door. The Fairway Lodge restaurant is for casual breakfast and luncheon dining; the Starmont Restaurant in the main lodge is reserved weeks ahead in high season. (See Chapter Five, *Restaurants*.) Informal wine tastings on Friday nights are led by the wine school instructor.

The Old World-style croquet courts are reputed to be among the finest in the world (private lessons are available), and the nine-hole members- and guests-only executive golf course is a challenge for even the best players. The Napa Valley Vintners Association has its headquarters here, so you might tee off with some of America's most celebrated vintners who come for golf and lunch.

Wraparound porches at Meadowood provide outdoor dining with garden views.

Courtesy Meadowood

OLIVER HOUSE COUNTRY INN
Innkeepers: Richard and Clara Oliver.
963-4089.
2970 Silverado Trail N., St. Helena, CA 94574.
¾ mi. N. of Deer Park Rd. on Silverado Trail.
Price: Moderate to Very Expensive.
Credit Cards: MC, V.

If Victorian architecture and museum-grade furnishings aren't your cup of tea, visit Switzerland instead. Tucked away in St. Helena on a four-acre estate overlooking the valley, Oliver House, a chalet-style inn, is a slice of Old Europe on Silverado Trail. Four guest rooms (three with French doors) are lavishly appointed with antiques (a 120-year-old Scottish brass bed, for example, and an armoire born in Salzberg the same year as Mozart), and one room has a stone fireplace. (Incidentally, the beds at this inn are rumored to be among the most comfortable in the valley.) Hold out for the top-floor suite, with an open-beam ceiling, Bavarian antiques and balcony. All rooms have private baths.

ROSE GARDEN INN
Innkeepers: Joanne and Tom Contreras.
963-4417.
1277 St. Helena Hwy. S., St. Helena, CA 94574.
S. of St. Helena on Hwy. 29 between Milat Vineyards and Zinfandel Ln.
Price: Moderate.
Credit Cards: None.

Once a ranch foreman's home, this comfy inn is located on three acres surrounded by vineyards, and now houses three spacious and comfortable guest rooms with queen-size iron beds and private baths. The shade of its century-old trees invites reading and relaxing.

**SHADY OAKS
COUNTRY INN**
Innkeepers: Lisa Wild-
Runnells and Jon
Runnells.
963-1190.
399 Zinfandel Ln., St.
Helena, CA 94574.
2 mi. S. of St. Helena, E. on
Zinfandel Ln.
Price: Moderate.
Credit Cards: None.
Handicap. Access: Yes.

**WHITE SULPHUR
SPRINGS RESORT**
Innkeepers: Buzz and Betty
Foote.
963-8588.
3100 White Sulphur
Springs Rd., St. Helena,
CA 94574.
W. on Spring St. from
Hwy. 29.
Price: Inexpensive to
Moderate.
Credit Cards: MC, V.
Special Features: Sulphur
pool.

WINE COUNTRY INN
Innkeeper: Jim Smith.
963-7077.
1152 Lodi Ln., St. Helena,
CA 94574.
Hwy. 29 N. of St. Helena,
E. on Lodi Ln.
Price: Moderate to
Expensive.
Credit Cards: MC, V.
Special Features: Pool; spa.

ZINFANDEL INN
Innkeepers: Diane Blake
and Jerry Payton.
963-3512.
800 Zinfandel Ln., St.
Helena, CA 94574.

Oak and walnut trees surround this friendly country inn with four guest rooms. The antique-furnished rooms have private baths. A full gourmet champagne breakfast and complimentary wine and refreshments in the evening round out each day of your stay.

Established in 1852, White Sulphur Springs holds the distinction of being California's first resort. A rustic, Old World retreat only three miles west in a canyon above St. Helena, it is situated amid 330 acres of redwood, fir and madrone and has hiking trails and waterfalls. The resort is made up of two small inns and eight cottages; most have private baths. The large cottages have kitchenettes, and the sleeping cottages and private rooms have kitchen privileges. Continental breakfast is served daily. The sulphur spring that gave the resort its name more than a century ago still flows out of the mountain and into an outdoor soaking pool at a maintained temperature between 85 and 87 degrees.

A friendly place to unwind in the country, this 25-room guest house is patterned after New England inns. All rooms are furnished with antiques, many have alcove beds and balconies or decks and all have private baths. Those requiring a king-size bed will be out of luck here — most are double or queen-size. Fireplaces are standard in most rooms but are inoperable from mid-April to mid-October. A buffet breakfast is served daily.

A striking example of an English estate planted in the heart of Wine Country. Just three guest rooms, named after varietal grapes, make this a luxury getaway. The Chardonnay Suite may be the most elegant with its stone fireplace, king-size bed

1 mi. S. of St. Helena on
Hwy. 29, E. on Zinfandel
Ln.
Price: Moderate to
Expensive.
Credit Cards: AE, MC, V.
Special Features: Gazebo;
bird aviary.

Calistoga

BRANNAN COTTAGE INN
Innkeeper: Jack Osborn.
942-4200.
109 Wapoo Ave., Calistoga,
CA 94515.
Just off Hwy. 29 (Lincoln
Ave.) near Brannan St.
Price: Moderate to
Expensive.
Credit Cards: MC, V.
Handicap. Access: Yes.
Special Features: Children
welcome, pets
considered.

in a bay window and private entrance. The Zinfandel Room has stained glass accents, private deck and whirlpool tub.

Built around 1860 by Calistoga founder, Sam Brannan, this inn is listed on the National Register of Historic Places as the only guest house constructed for Brannan's Hot Springs Resort that still stands on its original site. Not surprisingly, it's also the oldest building in town. Restoration got under way in the 1980s; reconstruction of the gingerbread gable was based on enlarged vintage photographs.

Today, an eclectic collection of furnishings, including plush and comfortable antiques, furnish the six guest rooms. All have private baths, private entrances and air conditioning. A generous gourmet breakfast (ask Jack to whip up his apple-and-brie omelet with sausages simmered in wine) may be served in the courtyard under lemon trees. The breakfasts are homemade, and Jack ensures that no visitor will be served the same meal twice during their stay.

The house is surrounded by gardens, so guests can always find a private, quiet spot to read and relax, and the sunny courtyard beckons after a day of "spa-ing." Just a minute on foot to tennis courts and three major spas, the inn is only a five-minute walk to shopping and restaurants. In addition, there's a complete concierge desk, so guests' wants and needs inside and outside the inn are cheerfully arranged. Very friendly hospitality.

BRANNAN COTTAGE INN

BRANNAN'S LOFT
Innkeeper: Inge Meinzer.
963-2181.
1436 Lincoln Ave.,
    Calistoga, CA 94515.
On Hwy. 29 (Lincoln Ave.)
    downtown.
Price: Moderate.
Credit Cards: MC, V.

Above the Cinnabar Restaurant in a historic building on the main business thoroughfare, this three-unit inn may be ideal for budget-conscious couples traveling together — one room has an extra sofa bed. In the thick of Calistoga shopping and dining, each unit is equipped with clean and modern kitchenettes, oak furnishings and ceiling fans, and the two larger rooms have furnished private balconies. Better for midweek stays; the hustle and bustle down on the street intensifies on weekends.

CALISTOGA INN
Innkeeper: Rose Dunsford.
942-4101.
1250 Lincoln Ave.,
    Calistoga, CA 94515.
On Hwy. 29 (Lincoln Ave.)
    near Cedar St.
Price: Inexpensive.
Credit Cards: MC, V.
Special Features: On-site
    brewpub, beer garden
    and restaurant.

Wine isn't the only beverage in this neck of the woods. A brewery, Napa Valley Brewing Co. (the first in the valley since Prohibition), makes its home in the old water tower next to Calistoga Inn. (See Chapter Five, *Restaurants*.) The 17 guest rooms (with shared baths) are clean and basic. Complimentary wine and beer is served, as is a light continental breakfast. The inn, about a block from the main highway, is walking distance to spas and dining.

CULVER'S COUNTRY INN
Innkeepers: Meg and Tony
    Wheatley.
942-4535.
1805 Foothill Blvd.,
    Calistoga, CA 94515.
On Hwy. 128 (Foothill
    Blvd.) between Lincoln
    Ave. and Petrified Forest
    Rd.
Price: Moderate.
Credit Cards: None.
Special Features: Pool;
    indoor sauna; spa.

A registered historical landmark, circa 1875, this special inn operated by British-born hosts has six guest rooms decorated with Victorian furniture. The inn is an easy walk to Calistoga's main street dining and shopping. Centrally air conditioned.

FOOTHILL HOUSE
Innkeepers: Michael and
    Susan Clow.
942-6933.
3037 Foothill Blvd.,
    Calistoga, CA 94515.

Set just north of Calistoga near Tubbs Lane, Foothill House offers four elegant suites and a private cottage. All have private baths (two with whirlpool tubs), private patio door entrances, refrigerators and woodburning stove or fireplace.

Between Petrified Forest
Rd. and Tubbs Ln. on
Hwy. 128 (Foothill Blvd.)
Price: Moderate to Very
Expensive.
Credit Cards: MC, V.

Antiques furnish the rooms, including queen or king-size four-poster beds. Two distinctive rooms are the Evergreen Suite and the Quail's Roost. Continental breakfast is served. Although this inn has received accolades in Frommer's guidebook as one of the top 100 B&Bs in the United States, the hospitality could be warmer. Watch closely for their small sign on the road — it's easy to miss.

**HIDEWAWAY
   COTTAGES**
Manager: Ole Yearian.
942-4108.
1412 Fairway, Calistoga,
   CA 94515.
Just off Hwy. 29 (Lincoln
   Ave.).
Price: Inexpensive to
   moderate.
Credit Cards: AE, MC, V.
Handicap. Access: Yes.
Special Features: Two
   outdoor pools.

These 17 cottages (some with kitchenettes and all with air conditioning and television) are adjacent to Dr. Wilkinson's Hot Springs Resort. It is situated on a quiet residential street close to Lincoln Avenue restaurants and shops.

**LARKMEAD COUNTRY
   INN**
Innkeepers: Gene and Joan
   Garbarino.
942-5360.
1103 Larkmead Ln.,
   Calistoga, CA 94515.
South of Calistoga off
   Hwy. 29 at Larkmead
   Ln.
Price: Moderate.
Credit Cards: None.
Handicap. Access: Yes.
Special Features: Smoking
   permitted.

Built on land once owned by flamboyant San Francisco heiress Lillie Coit in the late 1880s, this inn was originally part of Larkmead Winery, as was Hanns Kornell Champagne Cellars next door. It is located in the heart of a vineyard and was built by an Italian-Swiss family before Prohibition. The Palladian architecture is unique to the area; the main part of the house is upstairs, the better to oversee work in the vineyards and catch afternoon breezes.

Four guest rooms, all with private baths, are situated along a hallway in one wing of the house. The king bed in the Chardonnay Room was made from two brass beds salvaged from a Paris hotel. Persian rugs, wicker and colorful fabrics add to the homey feel. In a spectacular setting with sweeping views of Mount St. Helena and Sterling Winery to the north, the inn is well away from Hwy. 29 traffic.

MOUNT VIEW HOTEL
Manager: Renee Hines.
942-6877.
1457 Lincoln Ave.,
    Calistoga, CA 94515.
Center of downtown.
Price: Inexpensive to
    Expensive.
Credit Cards: D, MC, V.
Special Features: Pool;
    whirlpool; restaurant
    and lounge.

Restored in art deco style and on the National Register of Historic Places, this elegant lodge was originally a European-style hotel built in 1917. There are 34 units, including nine luxurious suites furnished in deco period pieces. In the heart of Calistoga shopping and dining, with major spas just steps away.

THE PINK MANSION
Innkeeper: Jeff Seyfried.
942-0558.
1415 Foothill Blvd.,
    Calistoga, CA 94515.
On Foothill Blvd. (Hwy.
    128) near Hwy. 29.
Price: Inexpensive to
    Expensive.
Credit Cards: MC, V.
Special Features: Indoor
    pool.

Postcard views of Napa Valley and lush forests await visitors who stay at this 1875 Victorian. The home's pink exterior may grab your attention, while the flowers, rare plants and exotic palms will hold your interest. All five guest rooms have private baths and queen-size beds. (The Angel Room also has a treasured family collection of angels; the Forest Room is decorated in green.) Innkeeper Seyfried was once a professional chef, so expect a unique full breakfast each morning. Wine and cheese cap off the afternoon. Three acres of landscaped gardens surround the estate, which is a short walk to downtown Calistoga spas and restaurants.

**QUAIL MOUNTAIN BED
   & BREAKFAST**
Innkeepers: Don and Alma
    Swiers.
942-0316.
4455 N. St. Helena Hwy.,
    Calistoga, CA 94515.
W. of Hwy. 29 at Scott Way
    near Dunaweal Ln.
Price: Moderate.
Credit Cards: None.
Special Features: Pool.

Off the beaten track and 300 feet above the din of valley traffic, Quail Mountain B&B sits on 26 acres of forested mountain. It is a secluded, romantic retreat with three guest rooms. Lots of floor-to-ceiling glass, skylights and a solarium will have you believing you're lodging in an elegant tree house, and the white wicker furniture adds to the illusion.

King-size beds, decks and private baths round out the room amenities. (The Fern Room is the most popular with a sitting area, oak floor and outdoor-inspired mural.) Complimentary wine and full breakfast featuring fruit from the inn's orchards is served in the solarium, by the pool or on the front deck.

Originally built in 1917, Mount View Hotel is on the National Register of Historic Places.

Chris Alderman

SILVER ROSE INN
Innkeepers: J-Paul and
   Sally Dumont.
942-9581.
351 Rosedale Rd.,
   Calistoga, CA 94515.
Just off Silverado Trail, S.
   of Hwy. 29.
Price: Moderate to
   Expensive.
Credit Cards: DC, MC, V.
Special Features: Pool;
   gym; whirlpool.

Perched on a rocky outcropping and surrounded by ancient oak trees, this unique retreat has sweeping views of upper Napa Valley and Mount St. Helena. At check-in, guests receive a bottle of the innkeeper's private label Chardonnay, and so begins your first encounter with J-Paul Dumont's wine challenge. Mr. Dumont invites guests to peruse his wine cellar, then challenges them to scour the valley for a bottle of wine that will top the same vintage from his own cellar. At other times it may be a vertical tasting or a blind tasting. In any case, it's all in unpretentious good fun.

The five guest rooms with queen-size beds are comfortably furnished and all have private baths; three have balconies. The Oriental Room is the most requested — its Asian rugs, rattan furniture, shoji screens and bonsai help transport the lodger to the Orient while watching the sunrise each morning over the valley.

Calistoga Spas with Lodgings

Not just motels, and certainly nothing like traditional B&Bs, resort spas are in a class by themselves. It is the full-service spa, not room amenities or decor, that is the star attraction at these predominantly couples-oriented facilities. (See "Spas" in Chapter Seven, *Recreation*.) Many spas offer lodging/spa treatment discount packages. Most have a two-night weekend minimum; some may prohibit children under 12 on weekends and holidays.

CALISTOGA SPA HOT SPRINGS
Manager: Skye O'Byrne.
942-6269.
1006 Washington Ave.,
  Calistoga, CA 94515.
Just off Hwy. 29 at
  Washington St.
Price: Inexpensive to
  Moderate.
Credit Cards: MC, V.
Handicap. Access: Yes.
Special Features: Weight
  and aerobics rooms; four
  outdoor mineral pools;
  children welcome.

Relaxed and unpretentious, this motel/spa has all the amenities of a resort but at budget prices. All 57 family-oriented units have kitchenettes, air conditioning, TVs and telephones. Close to downtown shopping and dining.

DR. WILKINSON'S HOT SPRINGS
Manager: Mark Wilkinson.
942-4102.
1507 Lincoln Ave.,
  Calistoga, Ca 94515.
On Hwy. 29 (Lincoln Ave.)
Price: Inexpensive to
  Moderate.
Credit Cards: AE, MC, V.
Handicap. Access: Yes.

This spa has 42 spacious and functional motel-like rooms, many with kitchenettes. (Rooms in the adjoining Victorian House cost slightly more.) Shopping and dining is within walking distance.

GOLDEN HAVEN HOT SPRINGS AND RESORT
Manager: Lea Kendall.
942-6793.
1713 Lake St., Calistoga,
  CA 94515.
Off Hwy. 29 near
  intersection of Lake and
  Grant Sts.
Price: Inexpensive to
  Moderate.
Credit Cards: AE, MC, V.

Amid towering oak trees and immaculate gardens, this 30-room spa offers many rooms with kitchenettes and all with refrigerators. Rooms with whirlpools, saunas or waterbeds are also available.

INDIAN SPRINGS SPA AND RESORT

Managers: Gary
  Watcherman and
  Shannon Meli.
942-4913.
1712 Lincoln Ave.,
  Calistoga, CA 94515.
On Hwy. 29 (Lincoln Ave.)
  near Brannan St.
Price: Moderate to
  expensive.
Credit Cards: MC, V.
Special Features: Pool.

Sixteen whitewashed bungalow-style cott
overlook 16 acres of palm trees and views o
Mount St. Helena. An easy walk to downtown
shopping and dining.

PINE STREET INN & EUROSPA

Managers: Tom and Jean
  Lunney.
942-6829.
1202 Pine St., Calistoga, CA
  94515.
Just off Hwy. 29 on Pine St.
Price: Inexpensive to
  Moderate.
Credit Cards: MC, V.

Theme decor brings a special enchantment to
the 16 rooms at this older inn and spa. One
plus: it's only two blocks from downtown shops
and restaurants, yet it's away from the main street
bustle.

ROMAN SPA

Manager: Carl Teuscher.
942-4441.
1300 Washington St.,
  Calistoga, CA 94515.
One block off Hwy. 29 at
  First St.
Price: Inexpensive to
  Moderate.
Credit Cards: AE, MC, V.
Handicap. Access: Yes.

Beautifully landscaped gardens surround this
60-room resort. Most units have kitchenettes.
Additional spa services are available next door at
International Spa.

VILLAGE INN & SPA

Manager: Bill Fox.
942-0991 or 800-543-1094
  (northern CA).
1880 Lincoln Ave.,
  Calistoga, CA 94515.
Hwy. 29 at Silverado Trail.
Price: Inexpensive to Very
  Expensive.
Credit Cards: AE, MC, V.
Handicap. Access: Yes.
Special Features:
  Restaurant.

An older but well-kept 43-unit motel situated
close to Silverado Trail and further from
downtown congestion, Village Inn has all ground-
floor units, most with panoramic views of Mount
St. Helena. No minimum stay, and smoking/non-
smoking rooms are available.

y

EL DC᷍ ᷍HOTEL
Manager: C᷍ ᷍g Clark.
996-3030 or 800-289-3031.
405 First St. W., Sonoma,
    CA 95476.
On the downtown Plaza.
Price: Expensive.
Credit Cards: AE, MC, V.
Handicap. Access: Yes.
Special Features:
    Restaurant; pool.

The El Dorado is a very special hotel. Newly restored to its original elegance, the 27 rooms all have private baths. French windows and terraces offer views of the hotel's Spanish courtyard or the historic Plaza. Breakfast is included in the tariff, as is a complimentary bottle of wine. Ristorante Piatti serves regional Italian cuisine.

GAIGE HOUSE INN
Innkeepers: Michol and
    Steve Salvo.
935-0237.
13540 Arnold Dr., Glen
    Ellen, CA 95442.
Off Hwy. 12 on Arnold Dr.
    to Glen Ellen.
Price: Moderate to Expensive.
Credit Cards: MC, V.
Special Features: Pool.

This inn is an Italian Gothic Victorian built in the 1880s and recently restored with five pleasant guest rooms, all with private baths and air conditioning. Full breakfast is served. Well located for wine touring and Sonoma dining.

GLENELLY INN
Innkeeper: Kristi
    Hallamore Grove.
996-6720.
5131 Warm Springs Rd.,
    Glen Ellen, CA 95442.
Off Hwy. 12 at Arnold Dr.,
    R. 1/3 mi. on Warm
    Springs Rd.
Price: Moderate.
Credit Cards: MC, V.

Glenelly Inn was originally established in 1916 as a railroad inn. Today, it's an eight-room B&B with country furnishings, goosedown comforters and clawfoot tubs with showers in all rooms. One room holds a personal collection of hats; the Vallejo Suite features mementos of local figure of note, Gen. Mariano Vallejo. All rooms open to the veranda or garden in this quiet, wooded setting with nearby wineries and restaurants.

HIDDEN OAK
Innkeeper: Catherine
    Cotchett.
996-9863.
214 E. Napa, Sonoma, CA
    95476.
1 block E. of the Plaza.
Price: Moderate.
Credit Cards: AE.
Special Features: Bicycles.

Park your car and put on your walking shoes. Everything you desire for a relaxing visit to Sonoma is just a stroll away from this homey inn a block off the Plaza. The house is a Craftsman Bungalow built in 1913; the three guest rooms all have private baths. A full breakfast and afternoon refreshments are served daily.

JACK LONDON LODGE
Manager: Dale Bedard.
938-8510.
13740 Arnold Dr., Glen
Ellen, CA 95442.
Corner of Arnold Dr. and
London Ranch Rd.
Price: Inexpensive.
Credit Cards: MC, V.
Special Features: Pool;
restaurant and lounge.

Appropriately named for the author who lived just up the road, this small (22-unit) motel is situated on Sonoma Creek in the town of Glen Ellen. Continental breakfast is included in the tariff; it is served weekends and holidays during the off-season and daily from June to September. Don't miss Jack London State Park with its fascinating museum of London memorabilia, hiking trails and horseback riding and Glen Ellen Winery — both are nearby on London Ranch Road, a steep but invigorating walk.

MAGLIULO'S PENSIONE
Innkeepers: The Magliulo
Family.
996-1031.
691 Broadway, Sonoma,
CA 95476.
2½ bl. S. of the Plaza on
Hwy. 12 (Broadway).
Price: Inexpensive to
Moderate.
Credit Cards: MC, V.
Handicap. Access: Yes.
Special Features:
Restaurant and lounge.

Fresh flowers, antique quilts, ceiling fans and an outdoor cabana add warmth to your stay. There are five guest rooms, two with private baths; the remaining three rooms share bath facilities. Continental breakfast is served daily in the dining room. The Pensione is within easy walking distance of historic Sonoma Plaza.

SONOMA HOTEL
Manager: Dorene and John
Musilli.
996-2996.
110 W. Spain St., Sonoma,
CA 95476.
Just off the Plaza on Spain
St.
Price: Inexpensive to
Moderate.
Credit Cards: AE, MC, V.
Special Features:
Restaurant; children
accommodated.

Many of the 17 rooms in this hotel share bath facilities; some rooms are designated for smoking. Regardless, each room is sumptuously appointed in antiques, and old oak and stained glass accents abound. Complimentary continental breakfast is served.

SONOMA MISSION INN AND SPA

Manager: Peter Henry.
938-9000, 800-862-4945 (in CA), 800-358-9022.
18140 Hwy. 12, Boyes Hot Springs, CA 95416.
Just N. of Sonoma.
Price: Very Expensive.
Credit Cards: AE, CB, DC, MC, V.
Handicap. Access: Yes.
Special Features: Complete spa; tennis courts; pool; exercise rooms; restaurants; lounge; wine-tasting room.

"**A** hotel should be no place like home," one hotelier was fond of saying. He could have been referring to Sonoma Mission Inn and Spa, renowned for its luxurious accommodations, coed spa services and two critically-acclaimed restaurants. At the turn of the century, well-to-do San Franciscans began arriving at the first hotel on the site, the Boyes Hot Springs Hotel, to "take the waters" and bake in medicinal mud from the hot springs running beneath the property. Later destroyed by fire, the hotel was rebuilt in 1927 and renamed Sonoma Mission Inn. During the '50s and '60s, several professional sports teams used the inn as their training headquarters.

The world-class spa was opened in 1981 and an extensive renovation of the facility was undertaken in 1985. The natural sparkling mineral water still flows underground and is bottled for guests' consumption, and plans are under way to bring to the surface those same hot waters so revered by the original Indian settlers.

With more than 170 luxurious rooms of many grades and locations around the facility, tariffs are widely varied, and numerous accommodation/spa packages are also available. This is a luxury spa getaway for those who wish to pamper themselves — and can afford to.

SONOMA VALLEY INN, BEST WESTERN

Manager: Aaron Krug.
938-9200 or 800-334-KRUG (in CA.)
550 Second St. W., Sonoma, CA 95476.
One block W. from the Plaza off Hwy. 12.
Price: Moderate to Expensive.
Credit Cards: AE, CB, D, DC, MC, V.
Handicap. Access: Yes.
Special Features: Pool; spa.

An "intimate motel" may be the best way to describe this exceptional lodge just a block from Sonoma Plaza. Rooms and furnishings are well above average for a motel — most are equipped with kitchenettes, wet bars, whirlpools or fireplaces. Complimentary continental breakfast and a bottle of wine are included in the tariff. Special golf packages are also available.

THISTLE DEW INN

Innkeepers: Larry and Norma Barnett.
938-2909.
117 W. Spain St., Sonoma, CA 95476.

This inn is decorated throughout with 1910 vintage Mission furniture. Each of the six guest rooms (two in the main house and four in the adjacent cottage) are complete with private bath, air conditioning, and ceiling fans; one room opens to

½ block off the town Plaza.
Price: Moderate.
Credit Cards: AE, MC, V.
Handicap. Access: Yes.
Special Features:
  Whirlpool; bicycles.

TROJAN HORSE INN
Innkeepers: Susan and
  Brian Scott.
996-2430.
19455 Hwy. 12, Sonoma,
  CA 95476.
Near Spain St.
Price: Moderate to
  expensive.
Credit Cards: AE, MC, V.
Handicap. Access: Yes.
Special Features:
  Whirlpool; bicycles.

VINEYARD INN
Innkeeper: Vicki Garver.
938-2350.
23000 Arnold Dr., Sonoma,
  CA 95476.
S. of Sonoma at junction of
  Hwys. 12 and 121.
Price: Inexpensive to
  Expensive.
Credit Cards: MC, V.
Handicap. Access: Yes.

Rohnert Park

RED LION HOTEL
Manager: Nabih Geha.
584-5466 or 800-547-8010.
1 Red Lion Dr., Rohnert
  Park, CA 94928.
Just off Hwy. 101 at
  Wilfred Ave./Golf
  Course Dr. exit.
Price: Moderate to Very
  Expensive.
Credit Cards: AE, MC, V.
Handicap. Access: Yes.
Special Features: Two
  restaurants; two lounges;
  pool and spa; exercise
  room; gift shop.

a deck. A full gourmet breakfast is served in the dining room or on the deck. This is a charming inn, reasonably priced and in an excellent location for strolling to all of Sonoma's finest.

This turn-of-the-century B&B inn was originally the home of one of Sonoma's pioneer families. The six guest rooms, all with private baths, are lavishly furnished with antiques and modern conveniences. To its credit, the inn is located close to restaurants, wine tasting and shopping. On the down side, there is busy daytime traffic along Hwy. 12; request rooms away the street.

This California Mission-style establishment was once a popular stopover for motorists traveling between San Rafael and Sacramento. Today it is thoroughly remodeled and lavishly redecorated but still reminiscent of those 1950s-era side-of-the-highway motels. The 12 bungalows are furnished with queen or twin-size beds; there are also two-room suites with wet bars and refrigerators. Continental breakfast is served on weekends. Perhaps the most striking feature of this inn is its gardens, created by a landscape designer for Disneyland.

A Mission-style hotel surrounded by two 18-hole golf courses, the Red Lion is popular primarily for its conference and banquet facilities. Leisure travelers will also appreciate its full-service hotel amenities. There are 245 rooms, including six suites. The rooms are decorated with standard hotel furnishings; the suites with French country-inspired furniture. If you're looking for an intimate getaway, steer clear of this first-class, but sprawling, hotel.

Santa Rosa

DOUBLETREE HOTEL
Manager: Bruce Wenger.
523-7555 or 800-528-0444.
3555 Round Barn Blvd.,
   Santa Rosa, CA 95403.
Off Hwy. 101 at Old
   Redwood Hwy. exit,
   4/10 mi. E. on
   Fountaingrove Pkwy.
Price: Moderate to
   expensive.
Credit Cards: AE, D, MC,
   V.
Handicap. Access: Yes.
Special Features: Pool;
   jogging path; restaurant
   and lounge; airport
   shuttle; guest privileges
   at nearby golf and tennis
   facilities.

Luxurious accommodations on a hillside overlooking the city of Santa Rosa with easy access to Hwy. 101. There are 252 spacious, above-average guest rooms and suites scattered over several acres. Caters to business travelers; all rooms have telephone-equipped desks. There are full hotel services and a fine restaurant. Ask for a room with a view when making your reservation.

**FLAMINGO RESORT
   HOTEL**
Manager: Floriann Bynum.
545-8530 or 800-848-8300.
2777 Fourth St., Santa Rosa,
   CA 95405.
Farmers Ln. at 4th St.
Price: Inexpensive to
   Expensive.
Credit Cards: AE, CB, DC,
   MC, V.
Handicap. Access: Yes.
Special Features: Pool;
   whirlpool; tennis courts;
   fitness center; restaurant
   and lounge.

French country furnishings and lush landscaping makes this resort hotel friendly and comfortable. Sonoma Valley's premium wineries are just minutes east on Hwy. 12. Guests have access to an adjacent fitness center, and specialty shops and excellent restaurants are located just blocks away on Farmers Lane. Popular with both business travelers and tourists; continuous shuttle bus service is provided to and from San Francisco International Airport.

FOUNTAINGROVE INN
Manager: Dieter Meier.
578-6101 or 800-222-6101
   (in CA.)
101 Fountaingrove Pkwy.,
   Santa Rosa, Ca 95403.
Off Hwy. 101 at Old
   Redwood
   Hwy./Mendocino Ave.
   exit.

The redwood and stone exterior of this luxury hotel blends harmoniously with the landscape, and the deliberately low sweep of the architecture affords an unobstructed view of the Round Barn historical landmark just up the hill. The rooms are elegantly simple and decorated with tasteful furnishings. Continental breakfast is included in the tariff, and standard hotel services are available. Equus Restaurant is popular for lunch among local business people.

Price: Inexpensive to
  Expensive.
Credit Cards: AE, CB, D,
  DC, MC, V.
Handicap. Access: Yes.
Special Features: Pool;
  whirlpool; restaurant.

THE GABLES
Innkeepers: Michael and
  Judy Ogne.
585-7777.
4257 Petaluma Hill Rd.,
  Santa Rosa, CA 95404.
Rohnert Park Expressway
  E. exit off Hwy. 101 to
  Petaluma Hill Rd.
Price: Moderate to
  Expensive.
Credit Cards: AE, MC, V.

The 15 gables above unique keyhole-shaped windows lend their name to this 1877 High Victorian Gothic Revival inn with mahogany staircase and Italian marble fireplaces. The five spacious guest rooms and adjacent cottage (furnished with a kitchenette and wood stove) have private baths with clawfoot tubs. Full gourmet breakfast and afternoon snacks are included.

MELITTA STATION INN
Innkeepers: Diane and Vic
  Crandon.
538-7712.
5850 Melita Rd., Santa
  Rosa, CA 95409.
5 mi. E. of downtown on
  Hwy. 12, 1 mi. S. on
  Melita Rd.
Price: Moderate.
Credit Cards: MC, V.

At the north end of the Valley of the Moon (and just minutes from Santa Rosa dining), this home was once a busy railroad station, general store and post office. Today it's a warm inn with six guest rooms furnished in antiques and collectibles. Five rooms have private bath. An ample breakfast is served in the large sitting room or on the balcony.

PYGMALION HOUSE
Innkeeper: Lola L. Wright.
526-3407.
331 Orange St., Santa Rosa,
  CA 95407.
Downtown exit off Hwy.
  101 to 3rd St., to Wilson
  St., 1 block on Laurel St.
  to Orange St.
Price: Inexpensive.
Credit Cards: AE, MC, V.

A restored Queen Anne Victorian home near the historic Railroad Square district, Pygmalion House is a five-room inn serving hearty full breakfasts and complimentary afternoon refreshments. Near shopping and dining in Railroad Square and at Santa Rosa Plaza, the downtown mall. All rooms have private baths with showers and/or clawfoot tubs.

VINTNERS INN
Innkeepers: John and
  Francisca Duffy.
575-7350 or 800-421-2584
  (in CA.)
4350 Barnes Rd., Santa
  Rosa, CA 95403.

Surrounded by a 45-acre vineyard planted in Sauvignon Blanc wine grapes, Vintners Inn is one of Sonoma County's finest establishments. It's a European-style hotel with an Old World atmosphere, from its French country decor to the central plaza with a fountain. The 44 guest rooms are

One of Vintners Inn's over-sized Provençal-inspired guest rooms.

Chris Alderman

W. on River Rd. off Hwy. 101.
Price: Moderate to Very Expensive.
Credit Cards: AE, DC, MC, V.
Handicap. Access: Yes.
Special Features: Spa; adjacent to nationally-acclaimed restaurant.

separated into four buildings that ring the courtyard.

Climbing the staircase in each building is akin to going upstairs to bedrooms in a friendly farmhouse. Many of the oversized rooms in this Provençal-influenced inn have fireplaces, beamed ceilings and pine furniture, some dating back to the turn of the century. All rooms are furnished with telephones, TVs and large tub/shower combination baths. Ground floor rooms have patios; second floor suites have balconies with vineyard or courtyard views. Deluxe suites have sitting areas, wet bars and refrigerators.

Continental breakfast is included in the tariff; room service is also available. The inn is ideally located for convenient access to both Sonoma and Napa Valley wineries. Next door is the superb John Ash & Co. restaurant. (See Chapter Five, *Restaurants*.)

Windsor

COUNTRY MEADOW INN

Innkeepers: Sandy Benson-Weber and Barry Weber.
431-1276.
11360 Old Redwood Hwy., Windsor, CA 95492.
2 mi. S. of Healdsburg off Hwy. 101.
Price: Moderate.
Credit Cards: MC, V.
Handicap. Access: Yes.
Special Features: Pool.

A restored 1890 Victorian home, this inn is set amid rolling hills and peaceful meadows, and is within minutes of Sonoma County's finest wineries. The five guest rooms are romantically decorated and include private baths. Some rooms have fireplaces and whirlpool tubs for two. Gourmet breakfast and evening refreshments are included.

Healdsburg

BELLE DE JOUR INN

Innkeepers: Tom and
  Brenda Hearn.
433-7892.
16276 Healdsburg Ave.,
  Healdsburg, CA 95448.
1 mi. N. of Dry Creek Rd.
  on Healdsburg Ave.
Price: Moderate to
  Expensive.
Credit Cards: D, MC, V.
Special Features: Winery
  tours.

Probably the most private and peaceful bed and breakfast inn in Healdsburg, Belle de Jour is set on a tranquil six-acre hilltop with spectacular views of rolling hills and distant mountains. The main farmhouse, an Italianate built around 1873, is where the innkeepers live and prepare scrumptious breakfasts.

The four guest suites, all decorated with French country-inspired furniture and sun-dried linens, are set behind the main house. Two of the rooms have private patios and whirlpool tubs for two. The Terrace Room may be the most luxurious — you may never want to leave the intimate whirlpool tub with its views of the unspoiled countryside. The Caretaker's Suite has a king-size canopy bed and French doors leading to a trellised deck.

The Hearns' 1923 antique touring car is available for personally escorted wine-tasting tours capped by a gourmet lunch. Another bonus: Simi Winery's tasting room is directly across Healdsburg Avenue from the inn. Belle de Jour Inn is elegance and hospitality at its finest.

CAMELLIA INN

Innkeepers: Ray and Del
  Lewand.
433-8182.
211 North St., Healdsburg,
  CA 95448.
2 blocks E. of Healdsburg
  Ave. on North St.
Price: Inexpensive to
  Moderate.
Credit Cards: D, MC, V.
Special Features: Pool.

This 1869 Italianate Victorian home entered the turn of the century as Healdsburg's first hospital. It is now a magnificent inn with nine guest rooms, and still has many of its original and unique architectural details, including the twin marble fireplaces in the double parlor. The rooms are furnished with antiques and accented with chandeliers and Oriental rugs. Located on a quiet residential street just two blocks from Plaza shopping and dining, the inn is named for the 30-some varieties of camellias that landscape its gardens. Very friendly innkeepers.

DRY CREEK INN, BEST WESTERN

Manager: Aaron Krug.
433-0300 or 800-222-KRUG
  (in CA.)
198 Dry Creek Rd.,
  Healdsburg, CA 95448.
Off Hwy. 101 at Dry Creek
  Rd. exit.
Price: Inexpensive.

This motel is distinguished by its outstanding location for wine touring. There is fairly standard motel decor throughout, but a spectacular view of Dry Creek Valley is the payoff in many rooms. Well situated for a day of wine tasting followed by dining downtown on the Plaza, this Best Western is also a popular business meeting facility. Direct bus service to San Francisco Airport is also a plus.

Credit Cards: AE, CB, DC,
  MC, V.
Handicap. Access: Yes.
Special Features: Pool; spa;
  restaurant.

FRAMPTON HOUSE
Innkeeper: Paula Bogle.
433-5084.
489 Powell Ave.,
  Healdsburg, CA 95448.
4/10 mi. S. of Dry Creek
  Rd., 1/2 mi. E. of
  Healdsburg Ave. Price:
  Inexpensive to moderate.
Credit Cards: MC, V.
Special Features: Pool;
  sauna; bicycles.

GRAPE LEAF INN
Innkeepers: Karen and
  Terry Sweet.
433-8140.
539 Johnson St.,
  Healdsburg, CA 95448.
2 blocks E. of Healdsburg
  Ave. near Piper St.
Price: Inexpensive to
  moderate.
Credit Cards: MC, V.

HAYDON HOUSE
Innkeepers: Richard and
  Joanne Claus.
433-5228.
321 Haydon St.,
  Healdsburg, CA 95448.
Off Hwy. 101 at Central
  Healdsburg exit, N. to
  Matheson St., E. to Fitch
  St., S. to Haydon St.
Price: Moderate to
  Expensive.
Credit Cards: MC, V.

Just three guest rooms, all with private baths, offers the right balance of service and privacy in this stately Victorian inn. Two rooms are upstairs; the third is in an adjacent cottage with private deck. French windows and skylights are among the amenities. A generous breakfast is served in the sunroom.

The seven elegant guest rooms in this 1900 Queen Anne Victorian are lushly furnished with iron beds, armoires and warm oak accents, and are all named after grape varietals. The four rooms upstairs all have skylights and tubs for two; the Chardonnay Suite is the most luxurious with its four skylights, separate sitting room and whirlpool tub for two. The quiet porch is perfect for unwinding after a day of wine touring. A full country breakfast is served in the dining room. On Saturday nights, guest vintners bring along their outstanding wines for private tastings. Within walking distance is Healdsburg's historic downtown Plaza.

Located in a quiet, residential area and surrounded by trees, this Queen Anne Victorian is now a four-room inn with an adjacent two-room cottage. It's a short walk to Healdsburg's Plaza for shopping and dining.

HEALDSBURG INN ON THE PLAZA

Innkeeper: Genny Jenkins.
433-6991.
116 Matheson St.,
  Healdsburg, CA 95448.
Matheson St. off
  Healdsburg Ave.
Price: Expensive.
Credit Cards: D, MC, V.
Special Features: Art
  gallery; bakery; gift shop.

Situated directly on Healdsburg's delightful Plaza Park (the town square), guests enter this nine-room inn through the main floor art gallery. Four rooms (most have fireplaces) overlook the Plaza with its bevy of shops, restaurants and tasting rooms. The solarium and roof garden is the common area where guests take breakfast and afternoon refreshments. In-room TVs and phones are available on request. All rooms have private baths, some with old-fashioned tubs. Luxurious.

MADRONA MANOR

Innkeepers: John and Carol
  Muir.
433-4231 or 800-258-4003.
1001 Westside Rd.,
  Healdsburg CA 95448.
From U.S. 101, Central
  Healdsburg exit, W. 1
  mi.
Price: Expensive to Very
  Expensive.
Credit Cards: AE, CB, D,
  DC, MC, V.
Handicap. Access: Yes.
Special Features: Pool

Surrounded by a forest of trees and lush flower gardens, Madrona Manor is a country inn with 18 rooms and three suites in the main mansion, carriage house, the Garden Suite and Meadowoods, all snuggled together on an eight-acre kingdom. Several rooms in the mansion are furnished with the antiques of the original owner, and most have elegant chaises and writing desks. Some of the 18 fireplaces are graced with delicate handpainted borders, and eight of the rooms have balconies or decks. All rooms are air-conditioned and include private baths. Full breakfast is included in the tariff.

Choosing whether to stay in the mansion or the carriage house may be tough: A mansion room

One of the Victorian "grande dames" in the National Register historic district, Madrona Manor presides over beautiful gardens.

Courtesy Sonoma County Visitors Bureau

guarantees sensational kitchen aromas wafting daily up the grand staircase, while a room in the carriage house (ask about Suite 400) away from the restaurant traffic may be a bit more tranquil. Well off the main road, a stay at Madrona Manor is guaranteed to be unhurried, a throwback to the slower pace of the home's Victorian-era heyday. The opportunity to dine daily at the nationally acclaimed restaurant may be reason enough to unpack your bags at Madrona Manor. (See Chapter Five, *Restaurants*.)

RAFORD HOUSE INN
Innkeepers: Gina and Vince
  Villeneuve.
887-9573.
10630 Wohler Rd.,
  Healdsburg, CA 95448.
River Rd. W. to Wohler
  Rd., N. 1/4 mi.
Price: Moderate.
Credit Cards: MC, V.

Situated conveniently near many of Sonoma County's most friendly premium wineries, Raford House is an attraction in itself. Sitting on a verdant hillside where its century-old windows oversee the tending and harvesting of hundreds of acres of premium vineyards, it is one of Sonoma County's oldest Victorian homes and a favorite of visitors searching for an authentic Wine Country atmosphere. Each of the seven guest rooms is decorated in a dominant color; the Blue Room is furnished with a four-poster bed and armoire. Stately palm trees stand as sentinels on the front lawn, though the gardens and the landscaping in general are in need of a loving hand.

Cloverdale

VINTAGE TOWERS
Innkeepers: Garrett Hall
  and Jim Mees.
894-4535.
302 North Main St.,
  Cloverdale, CA 95425.
One block E. of Hwy. 101.
Price: Inexpensive to
  Moderate.
Credit Cards: AE, D, MC,
  V.
Special Features: Bicycles,
  including a tandem.

This Queen Anne Victorian is listed on the National Register of Historic Places. Each of the seven guest rooms is unique, decorated with period antiques and unusual collectibles. Three of the rooms are tower suites. A four-course breakfast is served inside or outside in the gazebo.

Geyserville

CAMPBELL RANCH INN
Innkeepers: Mary Jane and
  Jerry Campbell.
857-3476.
1475 Canyon Road,
  Geyserville, CA 95441.

This ranch-style home sits atop a quiet hill with vistas of vineyards and mountains. Although the furnishings in the five guest rooms are more traditional than antique, all rooms have king-size beds, fresh flower accents and private baths. The countryside is excellent for biking.

Hwy. 101 Canyon Road
exit, 1½ mi. W.
Price: Moderate.
Credit Cards: D, MC, V.
Special Features: Pool;
tennis court; bicycles.

HOPE-MERRILL HOUSE
Innkeepers: Bob and
Rosalie Hope.
857-3356 or 800-825-4BED.
21253 Geyserville Ave.,
Geyserville, CA 95441.
Off Hwy. 101 at
Geyserville exit, 1 mi. N.
Price: Moderate.
Credit Cards: MC, V.
Handicap. Access: Yes.
Special Features: Pool.

A stagecoach stop circa 1870, Hope-Merrill House is listed on the Sonoma County Landmarks Register. A striking example of the 19th-century Eastlake Stick style of Victorian architecture, the home was built entirely of redwood. Aficionados of architectural details will enjoy the historical significance of the structure. It is now an enchanting inn with seven rooms, all with private baths and two with whirlpools. (The Peacock Room is wheelchair accessible.) A full breakfast is served in the dining room, and gourmet picnic lunches in baskets are prepared for daytrippers.

West County

BODEGA BAY LODGE, BEST WESTERN
Manager: Ralph Woellner.
875-3525 or 800-368-2468.
Hwy. 1, Bodega Bay, CA
94923.
Price: Moderate to
Expensive.
Credit Cards: AE, D, DC,
MC, V.
Handicap. Access: Yes.
Special Features: Restaurant;
spa; exercise room; sauna;
pool; bicycles.

Luxurious and more intimate than a standard Best Western hotel, this seaside lodge is sheltered from coastal winds but close enough to hear the surf. All rooms have ocean or bay views and private balconies, and many feature fireplaces, vaulted ceilings, spa baths, wine cooler/refrigerators, wet bars and in-room coffeemakers. Complimentary continental breakfast is provided.

THE ESTATE INN
Innkeepers: Jim Caron and
Darryl Notter.
869-9093.
13555 Hwy. 116,
Guerneville, CA 95446.
1/4 mi. S. of Guerneville
on Hwy. 116.
Price: Moderate to
Expensive.
Credit Cards: AE, MC, V.
Handicap. Access: Yes.

This 1920s Mission-style mansion in a redwood stand has been transformed into a luxurious country inn with 10 guest rooms. No stuffy Victorian museum furnishings here — the rooms have been deliberately decorated to feel like a private home, blending antiques with contemporary pieces and family heirlooms. Rich fabrics drape windows and upholstered furniture, and beds are dressed in fine pastel linens. All rooms have private baths, TVs and phones.

Nestled on a hillside, the many-windowed Estate Inn looks out on a stand of towering redwoods.

Kris White

A solarium with wicker furniture and huge stone fireplace shares the common area with a cozy dining room where the full breakfast is served overlooking a terraced backyard and vineyard. The pool is an added attraction. *Prix fixe* gourmet meals are served three nights a week, including Saturday. Extremely quiet and tranquil, this inn is popular with visiting celebrities.

THE FARMHOUSE INN
Innkeeper: Rebecca Smith.
887-3300 or 800-464-6642.
7871 River Road,
   Forestville, CA 95436.
9 1/2 mi. W. of Hwy. 101
   on River Rd.
Price: Moderate to
   Expensive.
Credit Cards: MC, V.
Handicap. Access: Yes.
Special Features: Pool; in-
   room saunas; croquet.

Eight guest rooms, all newly restored and freshly painted in a pleasing pale yellow, are designed to resemble English country row cottages. Each room has a king- or queen-sized bed (one has twin beds), greenhouse window, fireplace and private sauna. The adjacent turn-of-the-century farmhouse, renovated and updated with custom-made Shaker-style furniture, is where guests take their breakfast and borrow books from the library. *Prix fixe* dinners are offered on Saturday nights. The din of daytime traffic on River Road may jangle some nerves; ask for cottages 7 or 8 to be further from the noise. Exceptionally friendly innkeeper and staff.

GRAVENSTEIN INN
Innkeepers: Jacque and
   Don Mielke.
829-0493.
3160 Hicks Rd., Sebastopol,
   CA 95472.
3.5 mi. N. of Sebastopol on
   Hwy. 116, L. on Graton
   Rd., R. on Hicks Rd.
Price: Inexpensive to
   Moderate.
Credit Cards: None.

Located on six acres amid a Gravenstein apple orchard, this delightful three-story inn has four guest rooms, two with a shared bath. The Bavarian Suite is the most luxurious with a fireplace, private bath and summer porch. A pool is on the grounds. The location is quiet, the atmosphere unhurried, with fine restaurants in Santa Rosa and Sebastopol only minutes away.

HEART'S DESIRE INN
Innkeepers: Howard and
  Justina Selinger.
874-1311.
3657 Church St., P.O. Box
  857, Occidental, CA
  95465.
One block off Hwy. 116.
Price: Moderate to
  Expensive.
Credit Cards: MC, V.
Handicap. Access: Yes.

Perched on a hill overlooking the quiet village of Occidental, this comfortable two-story Victorian inn is surrounded by fruit trees and a courtyard garden with fountain, and is only steps from shopping and restaurants. The eight rooms with private baths are decorated with antique pine furniture, goosedown comforters and fresh flowers. A wraparound covered porch with wicker furniture adds to the relaxation.

The Inn at the Tides
B O D E G A   B A Y

INN AT THE TIDES
Manager: Carlo Galazzo.
875-2751 or 800-541-7788
  (in CA).
800 Hwy. 1, Bodega Bay,
  CA 94923.
Price: Moderate to
  Expensive.
Credit Cards: AE, MC, V.
Handicap. Access: Yes.
Special Features:
  Indoor/outdoor pool;
  whirlpool; sauna.

Six coastal acres with natural landscaping surround this quality inn, which is actually 12 separate lodges. Most rooms have fireplaces and bay or ocean views. Sonoma County's renowned Winemaker Dinner series is held here monthly during spring — if interested, inquire when making your spring reservations. Continental breakfast is served.

**RIDENHOUR RANCH
  HOUSE INN**
Innkeepers: Diane and
  Fritz Rechberger.
887-1033.
12850 River Rd.,
  Guerneville, CA 95446.
12 mi. W. of Hwy. 101. on
  River Rd.
Price: Inexpensive to
  Moderate.
Credit Cards: MC, V.

Within walking distance (500 yards) of Korbel Champagne Cellars, the inn, nearly a century old, is conveniently located for visiting additional wineries and the coast. The eight guest rooms, some with forest or rose garden views, are decorated with English and American antiques. Full gourmet breakfast is served, and there is a nightly *prix fixe* dinner. Transportation is furnished to and from Sonoma County Airport.

Almost 100 years after it was built in 1873, the Potter School starred in Alfred Hitchcock's movie, The Birds. *Today it's the Schoolhouse Inn.*

Kris White

SCHOOLHOUSE INN
Innkeeper: Tom Taylor.
876-3257.
P.O. Box 136, Bodega, CA 94922.
Hwy. 12 to Bodega.
Price: Inexpensive to moderate.
Credit Cards: MC, V.

If you've seen Alfred Hitchcock's movie, *The Birds*, you will appreciate the significance of staying in the schoolhouse that had starred in the 1963 classic. Fans will recognize its familiar exterior when entering town, but the only birds you're likely to notice are a few seagulls — the inn is just two miles from the coast. The former Potter School was built in 1873, and in 1987 the original classrooms were remodeled into four comfortable guest rooms, each with private bath. A light breakfast is served upstairs in the common room. This is an extremely tranquil setting with rolling hills all around, and Bodega Bay is only a five-minute drive away. Yes, that's a silhouette of Hitchcock haunting the upstairs window.

SEA RANCH LODGE
Manager: Chris Cochrane.
785-2371 or 800-842-3270.
P.O. Box 44, Sea Ranch, CA 95497.
29 mi. N. of Jenner on Coast Hwy. 1.
Price: Expensive.
Credit Cards: AE, MC, V.
Special Features: Restaurant and lounge.

An intimate seaside hotel (just 20 units) with a solarium lounge and an excellent restaurant. Rooms have country-style furnishings, knotty pine accents, and all have spectacular views. Some rooms also have fireplaces and private hot tubs. This is a remote location directly on the coast yet easily accessible. Tennis and golf are nearby.

TIMBERHILL RANCH

Innkeepers: Barbara Farrell, Tarran McDaid, Michael Riordan, and Frank Watson.
847-3258.
35755 Hauser Bridge Rd., Cazadero, CA 95421.
Hwy. 1 N. of Jenner to Meyers Grade Rd., to Hauser Bridge Rd.
Price: Very Expensive.
Credit Cards: MC, V.
Handicap. Access: Yes.
Special Features: Pool; tennis court; restaurant for guests only.

The quintessential luxury getaway for solitude, Timberhill Ranch is a past winner of *Country Inns* magazine's "Inn of the Year" award and a member of the prestigious Relais & Chateaux. The 80-acre resort is made up of 15 rustic but elegantly appointed cedar cottages and a main lodge for dining and mingling with other guests. It is located inland from the coast on a remote and sunny ridge. Despite its mailing address, it is closer to Salt Point and Kruse Rhododendron Reserve on the coast than it is to Cazadero.

The cottages, each with a deck overlooking trees and hills, are very private and magnificently furnished with overstuffed chairs, handmade quilts, fresh flowers, fireplaces and mini-bars and refrigerators stocked with refreshments. Breakfast is delivered to your doorstep, and six-course gourmet dinners served with fine wines can be enjoyed in an intimate setting in the main lodge. (Meals are included in the tariff.) Tennis courts, a 40-foot heated pool and a whirlpool offer relaxation, and hiking trails weave in and out of the adjacent 6,000 acres of wilderness.

Petaluma

CAVANAGH INN

Innkeeper: Billie Erkel.
765-4657.
8 Keller St., Petaluma, CA 94952.
Petaluma Blvd. S. exit from Hwy. 101, to Western Ave., to Keller St.
Price: Inexpensive to Moderate.
Credit Cards: AE, MC, V.
Special Features: Children accommodated.

A short walk to downtown Petaluma, the inn was that city's first bed & breakfast establishment. Seven rooms, most with private baths (one is shared) welcome guests, who are served a full breakfast with eggs and fruit from neighboring farms. The English garden is a tranquil rest stop after a day of antiquing downtown.

SEVENTH STREET INN

Innkeepers: Mark and Terry Antell.
769-0480.
525 Seventh St., Petaluma, CA 94952.
Between G and H Sts. on 7th St.
Price: Inexpensive to Moderate.
Credit Cards: MC, V.

One of the first farmhouses in the area, this Victorian home is now a friendly inn with four antique-furnished guest rooms. The detached carriage house is a loft suite, and the original water tower for the main house is now a two-story suite with circular staircase and antique tin bath tub. Children are accommodated here.

MOTELS

The following price codes are based on double-occupancy, per-room weekend rates during high season. These rates exclude local taxes and any service charges that may be added to your bill.

Inexpensive: Up to $50
Moderate: $50 to $75
Expensive: $75 to $100
Very Expensive: Over $100

Napa Valley

Napa

BEST WESTERN INN NAPA (Manager: Tyler Cudd; 257-1930 or 800-528-1234; 101 Soscol Ave., Napa, CA 94558; Hwy. 12/29 at E. Imola Ave. in Napa) Price: Expensive to Very Expensive. AE, CB, D, DC, MC, V. 68 rooms, some wheelchair access. Heated pool and spa, restaurant, loft suites available.

CHABLIS MOTEL (Manager: Ken Patel; 257-1944 or 800-443-3490; 3360 Solano Ave., Napa, CA 94558; Hwy. 29 at Redwood Rd. in Napa) Price: Expensive to Very Expensive. AE, MC, V. Basic 34-unit motel; some units have wet bars, refrigerators, private spas or whirlpools.

CHATEAU HOTEL (Manager: Melanie Su; 253-9300 or 800-253-NAPA in CA; 4195 Solano Ave., Napa, CA 94558) Price: Expensive to Very Expensive. AE, D, DC, MC, V. Heated pool and spa. 115 rooms. Complimentary buffet-style breakfast and social hour. Some rooms have refrigerators.

CLARION INN NAPA VALLEY (Manager: Thomas Veihdeffer; 253-7433 or 800-252-7466; 3425 Solano Ave., Napa, CA 94558; Hwy. 29 at Redwood Rd. in Napa) Price: Expensive to Very Expensive. AE, CB, D, DC, MC, V. One of the largest motels in the valley with 191 rooms. Pool, tennis courts, restaurant and lounge. Some wheelchair rooms.

MOTEL 6 (Manager: Mr. Dickey; 257-6111; 3380 Solano Ave., Napa, CA 94558; Hwy. 29 at Redwood Rd., W. 1 block to Solano Ave.) Price: Inexpensive. AE, CB, D, DC, MC, V. 58 units with a pool. Restaurant next door.

NAPA VALLEY TRAVELODGE (Manager: Don Sweatman; 226-1871 or 800-255-3050; 853 Coombs St., Napa, CA 94558) Price: Moderate. AE, D, DC, MC, V. 44 rooms. Pool, non-smoking rooms available. Complimentary coffee; restaurant next door.

SILVERADO MOTEL (Manager: Andy Patel; 253-0892; 500 Silverado Trail, Napa, CA 94558) Price: Inexpensive. AE, MC, V. 15 rooms recently remodeled, some with kitchenettes.

WINE VALLEY LODGE (Managers: Eugene and Joan Quirk; 224-7911; 200 S. Coombs St., Napa, CA 94558) Price: Moderate to Expensive. AE, D, MC, V. 54 rooms and suites. Pool. Restaurants nearby.

Calistoga

COMFORT INN NAPA VALLEY NORTH (Managers: Don Wood and Charles McCurdy; 942-9400 or 800-228-5150; 1865 Lincoln Ave., Calistoga, CA 94515) Price: Expensive to Very Expensive. AE, CB, D, DC, MC, V. Surrounded by spas, shops, and restaurants. 54 rooms; swimming pool, whirlpool, sauna, continental breakfast. Non-smoking and wheelchair rooms available. Above average.

Sonoma County

Sonoma

EL PUEBLO MOTEL (Manager: Sylvia Cruz; 996-3651; 896 W. Napa St., Sonoma, CA, 95476) Price: Moderate. AE, MC, V. 38-room motel with pool. Restaurants nearby.

Santa Rosa

BEST WESTERN GARDEN INN (Manager: Doris Warner; 546-4031 or 800-528-1234; 1500 Santa Rosa Ave., 95407; 8 blocks S. of downtown) Price: Moderate. AE, CB, D, DC, MC, V. Two pools, coffee shop; 78 rooms. Wheelchair and non-smoking rooms. Guest laundry. Nicely landscaped.

BEST WESTERN HILLSIDE INN (Manager: Robert Coombs; 546-9353 or 800-528-1234; 2901 Fourth St., Santa Rosa, CA 95405; near intersection of Farmers Ln. and Fourth St.) Price: Inexpensive. AE, CB, D, DC, MC, V. Tree-surrounded setting with 35 units, pool, sauna, restaurant and lounge. Kitchenettes available.

DAYS INN (Manager: Robert Chown; 573-9000 or 800-325-2525; 175 Railroad St., 95401; Downtown exit off Hwy. 101 to Third St.) Price: Expensive to Very Expensive. AE, CB, D, DC, MC, V. 140 rooms and suites. Swimming pool, spa, non-smoking rooms, cafe, lounge, room service. Handicap. access. Children stay and eat free. Close to downtown eateries and shopping; walking distance to Railroad Square attractions. (At press time, this lodge was facing the possibility of foreclosure.)

ECONO LODGE (Manager: Anil Kumar; 523-3480 or 800-55-ECONO; 1800 Santa Rosa Ave., 95407; Santa Rosa Ave. exit off Hwy. 101) Price: Moderate. AE, MC, V. 43-room motel with restaurants nearby. Close to downtown shopping and dining.

EL RANCHO TROPICANA (Manager: Lloyd Webb; 542-3655 or 800-248-4747; 2200 Santa Rosa Ave., 95407; Santa Rosa Ave. exit off Hwy. 101) Price: Moderate. AE, CB, D, DC, MC, V. Large (300 rooms) motel and conference center. Restaurant, lounge, and 24-hour coffee shop, plus swimming pools and tennis courts. Wheelchair rooms available. The Airporter, an airport shuttle service to and from San Francisco International, is based here.

HERITAGE INN (Manager: Joyce Wardrop; 545-9000 or 800-533-1255; 870 Hopper Ave., 95403; Hopper Ave./Mendocino Ave. exit off Hwy. 101) Price: Inexpensive. AE, MC, V. 96-room motel convenient to Healdsburg area wine touring. In-room refrigerators; five suites have whirlpools. 24-hour restaurant, fine dining, and fast food nearby. Heated outdoor pool. Handicapped and non-smoking rooms.

HOLIDAY INN SONOMA COUNTY (Manager: Mike Koleszar; 579-3000 or 800-HOLIDAY; 3345 Santa Rosa Ave., 95407; Santa Rosa Ave. exit off Hwy. 101, S. 1 mi.) Price: Moderate. AE, CB, D, DC, MC, V. On-site fitness center, tennis courts, restaurant and lounge, room service. 101 rooms, some wheelchair accessible. Children under 16 stay free.

LOS ROBLES LODGE (Manager: Claus Neumann; 545-6330 or 800-552-1001; 925 Edwards Ave., 95401; College Ave. exit off Hwy. 101, N. on Cleveland Ave. to Edwards) Price: Moderate to Expensive. AE, CB, D, DC, MC, V. Hot tub, pool, restaurant; 105 rooms.

MOTEL 6 (Manager: Linda Latorre; 546-1500; 2760 Cleveland Ave., 95403; Guerneville Rd. exit off Hwy. 101, N. on Cleveland Ave.) Price: Inexpensive. AE, D, MC, V. 100-unit motel sandwiched between Hwy. 101 and Cleveland Ave. Pool.

SANDMAN MOTEL (Manager: John Duncan; 544-8570; 3421 Cleveland Ave., 95403; Old Redwood Hwy./Mendocino Ave. exit off Hwy. 101, S. on Cleveland Ave.) Price: Inexpensive. AE, CB, D, DC, MC, V. Pool, whirlpool, non-smoking rooms available; 24-hour restaurant next door; other eateries nearby. 112 rooms.

SUPER 8 LODGE (Manager: Doug Newman; 542-5544; 2632 Cleveland Ave., 95401; Steele Ln. exit, N. of Cleveland) Price: Inexpensive. AE, CB, DC, MC, V. Close to mall shopping; a variety of restaurants are also nearby.

Healdsburg

FAIRVIEW MOTEL (Manager: Nick Patel; 433-5548; 74 Healdsburg Ave., Healdsburg, CA 95448) Price: Inexpensive to Moderate. AE, CB, D, DC, MC, V. Pool, whirlpool, complimentary coffee. Restaurants nearby.

L&M MOTEL (Manager: Jerry Brester; 433-6528 or 800-922-7117; 70 Healdsburg Ave., Healdsburg, CA 95448) Price: Inexpensive. AE, MC, V. Small 18-unit motel close to Russian River Beach; four units have kitchenettes. Indoor pool, whirlpool, sauna.

West County

BODEGA COAST INN (Manager: Hamish Scott Knight; 875-2217 or 800-346-6999; P.O. Box 55, 521 Coast Hwy. 1, Bodega Bay, 94923) Price: Very Expensive. AE, CB, D, DC, MC, V. 45 elegant rooms with bay and ocean views, some with fireplaces and vaulted ceilings. Restaurant and spa. Two-night minimum over holidays. An exceptional lodging.

BODEGA HARBOR INN (Managers: Elda and Bill; 875-3594; Bodega Ave. at Hwy. 1, Bodega Bay, 94923) Price: Inexpensive to Moderate. MC, V. Rooms, suites, cottages, and rental homes, some with ocean views, decks, hot tubs, fireplaces, and kitchens.

RIVERS END (Manager: Wolfgang Gramatzki; 865-2484 or 869-3252; 11051 Hwy. 1, Jenner, CA 95450; on Hwy. 1 at top of hill in Jenner) Price: Expensive to Very Expensive. MC, V. Just 8 units on a sheer cliff overlooking the ocean, some with wheelchair access. Restaurant and lounge.

SALT POINT LODGE (Managers: Bill and Arlene Pryor; 847-3234; 23255 Coast Hwy. 1, Jenner, CA 95450; 17 mi. N. of Jenner on Hwy. 1) Price: Inexpensive to Expensive. MC, V. Just 16 rooms. Restaurant and lounge, hot tub, sauna, sun deck, some ocean-view rooms. Seaside state park and marine reserve nearby.

An ocean view from one of the balconies of the Timber Cove Inn.

Courtesy Timber Cove Inn

TIMBER COVE INN (Manager: Fred Monighetti; 847-3231; 21780 N. Coast Hwy. 1, Jenner, CA 95450; 25 mi. N. of Bodega Bay on Hwy. 1) Price: Expensive. AE, MC, V. A breathtaking location perched on a rocky cliff overlooking the ocean. Many of the 49 rooms have ocean views, and some have fireplaces, private hot tubs, or sunken tubs. Restaurant and lounge. Two-night minimum on weekends.

UNION MOTEL (Managers: Ralph and Sue Haner; 823-1717 or 874-3555; P.O.Box 427, Main St., Occidental, CA 95465) Price: Inexpensive. AE, MC, V. Pool. Small, no-frills motel that's part of a family-operated restaurant, espresso bar/cafe and lounge complex on Occidental's main street. Close to Bodega Bay and the Russian River.

CAMPGROUNDS

Stoking the morning fire under oak trees in the Wine Country.

Kris White

Wine Country campgrounds and RV parks are plentiful for the adventurous who prefer to "rough it" outdoors in the region's natural areas. To avoid disappointment, however, reservations should always be made in advance, especially for summer and holiday camping. Reservations are mandatory at most California state parks and beaches and are accepted up to eight weeks in advance or as late as 48 hours prior to the first day of the reservation, if space is available. State campgrounds are noted with an asterisk (*) in the listing.

Camping fees in Wine Country state parks vary with the season and the park. (Fees in mid-1991 ranged from $12 to $19 per night per campsite.) As a general rule, developed campgrounds are those with flush toilets, hot showers, drinking water, improved roads and campsites with a table and stove or fire ring. Primitive campsites usually have chemical or pit toilets, tables and a central water supply. Environmental campsites are primitive sites in undisturbed natural settings. En route campsites are day-use parking areas where self-contained trailers, campers, and motor homes may park overnight

To make reservations in state campgrounds, call **MISTIX** at 800-444-7275 (in California) or 916-452-1950 (out of state). Mastercard, Visa, or American Express will hold your campsite; there is a $3.95 service fee for making reservations.

Fees at privately-operated parks and resorts are generally from $6 to $10 per night for tent camping, and from $10 to $15 per night for RV sites with hookups.

Napa Valley

*BOTHE-NAPA VALLEY STATE PARK (942-4575; 3801 St. Helena Hwy. N., Calistoga, CA 94515; midway between St. Helena and Calistoga off Hwy. 29) This 1,920-acre state park has 48 developed campsites. Campers up to 31 ft. and trailers to 24 ft. can be accommodated; a sanitation station is provided. Horseback riding trails, hiking, swimming pool, picnic area, and exhibits. Handicapped accessible in all areas.

CALISTOGA RANCH CAMPGROUND (942-6565; 580 Lommel Rd., Calistoga, CA 94515; SE. of Calistoga off Silverado Trail on Lommel Rd.) A 167-acre park with 150 campsites for tents, RVs (full hookups), and trailers. Olympic-size swimming pool, fishing lake, hiking trails, picnic areas, restrooms with showers, laundry, and snack bar.

NAPA COUNTY FAIRGROUNDS (942-5111; 1435 Oak St., Calistoga, CA 94515) Camping, showers, RV hookups, dump station.

NAPA TOWN & COUNTRY FAIRGROUNDS (253-4900; 575 Third St., Napa, CA 94558) RV parking with full hookups and dump station.

NAPA VALLEY RV RESORT (252-7777; 500 Lincoln Ave., Napa, CA 94558; 1.4 mi. E. of Hwy. 29 on Lincoln Ave. in Napa) Dubbed "a luxurious RV park," this paved resort open year-round has 145 pull-through and back-in spaces, all with full hookups. Laundromat, mini-mart, snack bar, jogging paths.

RANCHO MONTICELLO RESORT (966-2188; 6590 Knoxville Rd., Napa, CA 94558; on Knoxville Rd. about 4 1/2 mi. off Hwy. 128) Travel trailer and camping sites with RV hookups. Restaurant, beer garden, fishing boat rentals, grocery, snack bar.

SPANISH FLAT RESORT (966-2101, 800-822-CAMP in California, 800-824-CAMP out of state; P.O. Box 9116, Napa, CA 94558; Hwy. 128 to Knoxville Rd., Lake Berryessa) 120 lakeside tent and RV sites, sanitation station, restroom with showers, convenience store, and snack bar.

Sonoma County

*AUSTIN CREEK STATE RECREATION AREA (869-2015 or 865-3483; Armstrong Woods Rd., Guerneville, CA 95446; 3 mi. N. of Guerneville) A rugged, natural setting of 4,230 acres with just 24 primitive hike-in campsites. Trailers and campers over 20 ft. prohibited.

BRIDGEHAVEN CAMPGROUND (865-2473; P.O. Box 56, Jenner, CA 95450; S. of Jenner on Hwy. 1) On the Russian River near the coast. 41 tent, trailer, and RV sites in a quiet setting. Just off River Rd., with easy access to both wineries and coastal attractions.

CASINI RANCH FAMILY CAMPGROUND (865-2255; P.O. Box 22, Duncans Mills, CA 95430; 22855 Moscow Rd., off Hwy. 116 at Duncans Mills, 1/2 mi.

E. on Moscow Rd.) A family campground on the Russian River with 225 pull-through spaces, many riverfront sites. Boat and canoe rentals, fishing, swimming, playground, general store, laundry.

KOA SAN FRANCISCO NORTH (763-1492; 20 Rainsville Rd., Petaluma, CA 94952; Old Redwood Hwy. exit off Hwy. 101, W. to Stony Point Rd., N. to Rainsville Rd.) A 60-acre rural farm setting with 312 tent and RV sites with full hookups. Swimming pool, hot tub, convenience store, laundromats, playground, camping cabins.

RIVER BEND RV & CAMPGROUND (887-7662; 11820 River Rd., Forestville, CA 95436; about 10 mi. W. of Hwy. 101 on River Road) Full-service with hookups, general store, canoe rentals; 24-hour on-site security.

*SONOMA COAST STATE BEACH (This state beach encompasses 5,000 acres total, with two campgrounds: Bodega Dunes and Wrights Beach.) *Bodega Dunes Campground* (875-3483 or 865-2391; Bodega Bay, CA 94923; 1/2 mi. N. of Bodega Bay on Hwy. 1.) The larger of the two state beach campgrounds with 98 developed campsites. Trailers and campers up to 31 ft.; a sanitation station is provided. Picnicking, hiking, fishing, horseback riding, and exhibits. Most facilities wheelchair accessible. *Wrights Beach Campground* (875-3483 or 865-2391; Bodega Bay, CA 94923; 6 mi. N. of Bodega Bay on Hwy. 1) Thirty developed campsites; 11 environmental campsites; trailers to 24 ft. and campers to 27 ft. allowed. Picnicking, hiking, fishing, horseback riding, and exhibits. No showers. Some facilities wheelchair accessible.

*SALT POINT STATE PARK (865-2391 or 847-3221; 25050 Coast Hwy. 1, Jenner, CA 95450; 20 mi. N. of Jenner on Hwy. 1) 130 developed campsites (no showers); 10 hike-in tent sites, and 30 en route sites on 5,970 acres. Trailers and campers over 31 ft. prohibited.

SONOMA COUNTY FAIRGROUNDS (545-4200; 1350 Bennett Valley Rd., Santa Rosa, CA 95401; at intersection of Hwy. 101 and Hwy. 12 E.) Full hookups for RVs; tent campers welcome. Restrooms, showers, picnic areas. In the heart of town near freeway; traffic noise could be disruptive.

*SUGARLOAF RIDGE STATE PARK (833-5712 or 938-1519; 2605 Adobe Canyon Rd., Kenwood, CA 95452; 7 mi. E. of Santa Rosa on Hwy. 12, N. on Adobe Canyon Rd.) A 2,500-acre park with 50 developed campsites, nature trail, hiking, horseback riding trails, and exhibits. Trailers and campers to 22 ft.

THUNDERBIRD RANCH FAMILY CAMPGROUNDS (433-3729; 9455 Hwy. 128, Healdsburg, CA 95448) On a family-owned property, this small campground has a pool, ping-pong, and horseshoes. The shaded campsites have a central water supply; RVs welcome. Bath house with showers. Closed July and August.

CHAPTER FOUR
The Finer Things
CULTURE

Tim Fish

One of the few grand old movie houses still standing.

A mere 30 years ago, Napa and Sonoma were still certifiably in the boonies. (And they still are, if you ask some city dwellers to the south.) With the exception of Calistoga's popularity as a resort for the rich and famous during the late 1800s, Napa and Sonoma had always been known as sleepy farming and fishing communities. Sonoma, in particular, was a world away from San Francisco until the Golden Gate Bridge opened in 1937.

Writer Robert Lewis Stevenson brought a touch of civilization to St. Helena in the 1880s, and later Jack London, author of *The Call of the Wild*, retired to Glen Ellen and became a gen-

tleman farmer. Historical sites, such as Sonoma's Mission San Francisco Solano built in 1825, are reminders of a tradition of appreciation for the finer things.

Music, as it always seems to, helped lead the way. The Santa Rosa Symphony was the first to be organized in 1927, followed a few years later by the Napa Valley Symphony. As the communities began to grow after World War II, and with the renewal of the wine industry in the 1960s, Napa and Sonoma's cultural landscape began to flourish as well.

Artists weary of the city and drawn to the beauty of Wine Country began moving north, making Napa and Sonoma the popular artistic havens they are today. Art galleries appeared and wineries began to display art in their tasting rooms. The first theater companies formed in the early 1970s and theaters have proliferated to become the dominant force in the local arts. More recently, dance and opera companies have been established. Wineries have played a special role in this expansion of the arts, promoting them as one of life's necessities as well as the perfect accompaniment to wine.

The following pages will give you some idea of the arts and entertainment possibilities in Napa and Sonoma. The best place to find the latest happenings are the entertainment pages of the *Napa Register* and Santa Rosa's *Press Democrat*. The **Arts Councils** of both counties are also good sources of information. For Napa, phone 257-2117 and for Sonoma, phone 579-2787.

ARCHITECTURE

While Napa and Sonoma may not have the strong architectural traditions found in the East and Midwest, Wine Country has its own grand style. Plain and practical dried brick buildings called adobes ruled until the first buildings of European–style were built in the 1860s, and many of those — particularly in Sonoma County — were lost in the earthquake of 1906. Architectural gems remain, however, and newer ones have been added.

The most obvious treasures are the castlelike wineries of Napa Valley. There is Beringer's stately, German–styled mansion called Rhine House built in the late 1800s; the Gothic fortress of Greystone Cellars built in 1889 and now home to Christian Brothers and Inglenook's Gothic chateau built in 1887. In Sonoma, Hop Kiln Winery along the Russian River is inside a towering and historic hop kiln built in 1880. The building with three tall spires was used to dry beer hops, back when the area was a center for growing that commodity. There are also newer winery wonders. Most striking is white hilltop villa south of Calistoga called Sterling Vineyards. Nearby is the postmodern temple to wine and art, Clos Pegase, designed by Princeton architect Michael Graves. Across Napa Valley is the distinctive shake–roofed Rutherford Hill Winery, which recalls an early Wine Country barn. The chateaus of Domaine Carneros near Napa and Jordan in Sonoma's Alexander Valley are extravagant reminders of France.

The oldest city in the area, Sonoma, also has many of the oldest buildings, including adobes like the Sonoma Mission. The cities of Napa and Petaluma offer walking tours of downtown Victorian neighborhoods. (Check at visitor centers for maps.)

Napa's tour includes the Napa Opera House, 1018 Main St., an Italianate beauty built in 1879 and now being refurbished. There's also the First Presbyterian Church, corner of Third and Randolph streets, a Victorian Gothic built in 1874. Walking tour maps are available at the **Napa Chamber of Commerce** (226-7455; 1556 1st St.).

A thriving river port in the 1870s, Petaluma has retained many of the beautiful homes and buildings from its early years. Whether it's a peek at the majestic Queen Anne styling of the old Gilger house at 111 6th St., or the intricately ornate Spanish Colonial at 47 6th St., Petaluma is worth a leisurely walking tour. Maps are available at the *Petaluma Area Chamber of Commerce* (762-2785; 215 Howard St.).

Many of Santa Rosa's great buildings were lost in the earthquakes of 1906, though McDonald Avenue on the west edge of downtown has survived. It's a wide road of proud homes and tall trees. The centerpiece is Mableton at 1015 McDonald. Built in 1878, it was inspired by the plantation homes of Mississippi.

CINEMA

Although few of Napa's or Sonoma's grand old movie houses still stand — blame it on urban renewal or earthquake — movie–going remains an ardent passion. *The Wine Country Film Festival*, a two-week celebration of the latest foreign and art films, is small but well-respected. The Sonoma Film Institute, staged in a classroom at Sonoma State University but open to the public, is low on atmosphere but high on quality. Finally, Sonoma and Napa are home to many top–name stars, and the two counties' landscapes are cinema stars in their own right. Both are favorite locations for Hollywood feature films and commercials.

THE RAVEN

Easily the finest movie house in Wine Country. The downtown Healdsburg theater was meticulously restored a few years back by owner Don Hyde. The projection and sound equipment is state-of-the-art and the theater is roomy, as a movie house should be. First-run and art movies dominate in the summer, with popular films playing a week or two and smaller ones only a couple of days. Hyde also mixes in a few classics and even brings in live music on occasion. *The Raven*: 433-5448; 115 North St., Healdsburg, CA 95448.

LIBERTY THEATER

A charming theater in downtown St. Helena showing first-run films, though, as you might expect for a small town, a few weeks after release. Mostly American fare, though occasional art and foreign films come for a stay. *Liberty Theatre*: 963-5813; 1340 Main St., St. Helena, CA 94574.

VISTA CINEMA

Another pleasant place for munching popcorn in the dark, this small theater in central Calistoga plays delayed first-run movies and the occasional art film. *Vista Cinema*: 942-5743; 1330 Lincoln Ave., Calistoga, CA 94515.

Seeing Stars

Hollywood seems enamored with Wine Country, Sonoma County in particular. Look close and you'll recognize more than a few famous movie and TV sites. The most famous is perhaps the old Bodega School in Bodega, immortalized by Alfred Hitchcock in *The Birds*. It's a bed and breakfast now (dare you stay?) and an easy stop for snap shots. It's just off Bodega Highway, a few miles inland from Bodega Bay. Another familiar spot is downtown Petaluma, used for the cruising scenes in *American Graffiti*. Soap opera fans, of course, will recognize Spring Mountain Winery in St. Helena as the back drop for "Falcon Crest."

More than a few celebrities call Napa and Sonoma home, at least part time. "Peanuts" creator Charles Schulz is Santa Rosa's most famous denizen. Robin Williams owns a mountain-top ranch between Napa and Sonoma counties. Raymond "Perry Mason" Burr is a well-known Healdsburg resident. Other high-profiles include: winery owners Pat Paulsen and Tommy Smothers, Gene Hackman, Shelley Long and musician-actor Tom Waits.

OTHER CINEMA

Napa County

Cinedome (257-7700; 1175 West St., Napa). Modern seven–theater multiplex showing first-runs in downtown.

Uptown Cinemas (224-7977; 3rd and Franklin Sts., Napa). A downtown four-plex showing first-runs and discount double feature second runs.

Sonoma County

Coddingtown Cinemas (544 1970; 1630 Range Ave., Santa Rosa). A four-theater complex showing first-runs.

Empire Cinemas (584-0123; 6470 Redwood Drive, Rohnert Park). Four theaters showing second-run movies at bargain rates.

Lakeside 5 Cinemas (538-7469; 551 Summerfield Rd., Santa Rosa). First-run American foreign films. A former skating rink and it feels like it.

Pacific's Petaluma Cinema (769-0700; North McDowell Blvd., Petaluma). So much room and style, you forget it's a multiplex. Eight theaters, two quite large and with state-of-the-art equipment.

Sebastiani Theatre (996-2020; 476 First St., Sonoma). A delightful old theater in dire need of refurbishing. Shows late first-run films.

United Artists Cinema 5 (528-7200; 547 Mendocino Ave., Santa Rosa). Compact little multiplex hidden away in downtown. Don't blink or you'll drive right past. First-run films.

United Artists Cinema 6 (528-8770; 620 Third St., Santa Rosa). Ditto Cinema 5.

Sonoma Film Institute. If you can overlook the classroom atmosphere, the Institute is a great place to catch classics and art films. Whether you prefer the Marx Brothers in *Duck Soup* or the latest Kurosawa, the Friday and Saturday night double-features are a great bargain at $3.50. *Sonoma Film Institute:* 664-2606; Sonoma State University, Darwin Theater, Rohnert Park, CA 94928.

Wine Country Film Festival. This annual July event is a fast-paced potpourri of movie screenings, workshops and parties. It spans two-weeks and events arespread throughout Napa and Sonoma counties. Some of the movies that made their debut at WCFF include *sex, lies and videotape* and *When Harry Met Sally*. Stars are usually on hand to schmooze, including Dennis Hopper, Dudley Moore and Michael York. Caution: the films are excellent, but the festival has a reputation for organizational problems. *Wine Country Film Festival*: 996-2536; 12000 Henno Rd., Glen Ellen, CA 95442.

DANCE

Dance is still in its infancy in Sonoma and Napa counties. Sonoma has two nascent ballet companies, while Napa is still waiting for its first. Both Sonoma companies are inconsistent and neither offer the dazzle of San Francisco and other big city ballets. But the potential is there. Also, professional dancers from San Francisco and beyond are frequent guest soloists.

BJ Martin and Jeff Fulton in "Romantic Interlude" at the Redwood Empire Ballet.

Ed Aiona

REDWOOD EMPIRE BALLET

Sonoma County's first ballet, Redwood Empire, dates from 1978. Its company is young, mostly students of Redwood Empire's ballet school. They perform two or three times a year at the Luther Burbank Center for the Arts in Santa Rosa. They mix classic with modern dance, and of course revisit the "Nutcracker" every December. Director Keith Martin is a recent addition and hints of great promise. A former dancer with London's Royal Ballet, Martin also has led the San Diego and Phoenix ballet companies and is a respected choreographer. *Redwood Empire Ballet*: 523-3046; 709 Davis St., Santa Rosa, CA 95401.

NORTH COAST BALLET

The resident company at the new Spreckels Performing Arts Center in Rohnert Park, North Coast performs on Wine Country's most impressive stage. The $8 million facility provides a 40-by-40-foot stage and Deborah Palesch and company put it to fine use. "I feel very fortunate having a place like this to work out of," Palesch says. "The theater is beautiful and the floor is gorgeous for dancers to work on." Dancers come largely from Palesch's dance school, though increasingly professional dancers are participating as well. The repertoire includes classic ballet and modern dance, and "Nutcracker" is a new December addition. *North Coast Ballet*: 584-1700; Spreckels Performing Arts Center, 5409 Snyder Ln., Rohnert Park, CA 94928.

GALLERIES

Whether your thing is abstract expressionism or dolphins jumping through rainbows, there's an art gallery for you somewhere in Napa and Sonoma counties. A new gallery seems to open every weekend. The hills of Northern California shelter some of the finest artists in the country. Best known perhaps is Richard Diebenkorn, a Healdsburg painter of international fame. You won't see his paintings on display in any of local galleries, but you will see the work of many of his colleagues.

Each of the galleries has its own specialty. Some galleries are cooperatives, owned and operated by local artists. Others specialize in ceramics or offer paintings and prints of nationally known artists. Vineyards and seascapes, of course, are the dominate themes. ARTrails is perhaps the most intimate of galleries. Artists open their own studios to the public for two weekends every October in Sonoma.

Napa County

THE HESS COLLECTION
255-1144.
4411 Redwood Rd., Napa,
  CA 94558.
Open: 10–4 daily.
Fee: None.

If there's a gallery in Wine Country that deserves the title, "museum," it's the Hess Collection. Swiss entrepreneur Donald Hess transformed the old Mont La Salle Winery into an ultra-modern showcase for his two great passions: art and wine. Built on the rugged slopes of Mount Veeder, the Hess Collection opened to the public in 1989.

The entrance opens onto a dramatic three-story staircase. The 130-piece collection spans the upper two floors and features the works of internationally known artists such as Francis Bacon, Robert Motherwell and Frank Stella. A mix of painting and sculptures, the works are provocative and often haunting, though humor plays a role, too. And, of course, a taste of wine is available for $2.50. (The Hess Cabernet is dynamite!)

The ultra-modern Hess Collection features internationally known artists along with fine wines.

Chris Alderman

JESSEL GALLERY
257-2350.
1019 Atlas Peak Rd., Napa,
  CA 94558.
Open: 10–5 Tues.–Sun.
Fee: None.

Jessel is the essence of what Northern California galleries are all about. The art is not particularly challenging but lovely nonetheless and the atmosphere is laid back, almost meditative. If you're weary of the bustle of Hwy. 29, Napa's main drag, make a detour to this delightful gallery.

Jessel, a noted artist who prefers just the one name, opened the gallery in 1987 just south of the Silverado Country Club. The gallery shows the work of Jessel and 35 emerging artists from around the country. Offerings include gorgeous pastels and watercolors, as well as jewelry and ceramics.

The vine-covered wooden deck out front also is particularly inviting. Rest your feet at one of the tables and take in the shade from the tall pines as the wind chimes soothe the soul.

Sonoma County

CALIFORNIA MUSEUM OF ART
527-0297.
Luther Burbank Center for the Arts, Mark West Springs Rd., Santa Rosa, CA 95403.
Open: 11–5 Wed.–Sun.
Fee: None.

A museum only in name, the gallery-sized California Museum of Art has nonetheless become one of Sonoma County's most important art spaces. While it may be small in size, it earns the name "museum" in the way it displays art. The emphasis is not on money, but artists — Sonoma artists in particular. The art may be for sale, but this isn't a showroom. Paintings don't fight for wall space, sculptures aren't crowded onto tables with postcards, T-shirts and earrings. And rather than displaying whatever art is handy for quick showings, exhibits pride themselves on quality and linger six to eight weeks. The museum offers two distinct galleries. Occasionally the work of a single artist is featured; more usually, two people or groups share the space.

Sonoma is blessed with more than its share of excellent artists, so the quality is usually high, though the occasional show isn't up to par. The art is serious in nature, few happy landscapes and frolicking sea lions here. Some of the better artists who have displayed include: Zak Zaikane, Gerald Huth and Ellen Koment.

J. NOBLETT GALLERY
996-2416.
22 Boyes Blvd., Boyes Hot Springs, CA 95416.
Open: 10–6 daily.
Fee: None.

The art world's cutting edge gets a bit dull by the time you reach tiny Boyes Hot Springs, north of Sonoma. Or so you might think. In a cul-de-sac off Hwy. 12, J. Noblett is challenging the notion that dynamic art sells only in New York and San Francisco. Of course it helps when New York and San Francisco come to you. J. Noblett is directly across from the posh Sonoma Mission Inn, a big cosmopolitan draw.

Only the Hess Collection in Napa displays art with more style than Noblett. Paintings are given room to breathe and prices aren't posted. One large gallery is devoted to a single artist — the shows change every six weeks — and two other rooms show works by a number of Noblett regulars.

Owner Rusty Schwartz has an exceptional eye. "When I look at a piece of art, I'm not just looking at it with my eyes. I'm looking at it with my head, my heart and my gut," Schwartz said. His tastes lean toward the abstract, whether the slender treelike bronze sculptures of Jack Zajac or the striking colors of painter Kazuko Watanabe. Many of the artists are from the Bay Area, though Schwartz doesn't limit himself geographically. A regular on Noblett walls is the extraordinary Swiss expressionist Robert Indermaur. His paintings have an almost mesmerizing quality.

OTHER GALLERIES

Napa County

Clos Pegase Winery (942-4981; 1060 Dunaweal Lane, Calistoga) A work of art in itself, this winery — designed by the award-winning architect Michael Graves — looks like a post-modern Babylonian temple. A free guided tour of the winery's impressive art collection is offered at 10 a.m. Mon. to Fri.

The Depot Gallery (944-2044; 6526 Washington St., Yountville) If you want to see what Napa artists are up to, check out this cooperative gallery. Offering a potpourri of styles, this is a warm and homey gallery.

Donlee Gallery of Fine Arts (942-0585; 1316 Lincoln Ave. Calistoga) Southwest art from nationally known artists; oils, watercolors, metal and wood sculpture.

The Gallery on Main Street (963-3350; 1359 Main St., St. Helena) Paintings and prints by Northern California artists; vineyards and other landscapes a specialty; oils, acrylics, watercolors.

The Lawrence Gallery (944-1800; Washington Square, Yountville) Specializes in pleasant prints, pastel and watercolors of vineyards and other landscapes.

Napa Valley Opera House (226-7372; 1144 Main St., Napa) This burgeoning arts center will feature in May of 1992 the impressive collection of Rodin sculptures from San Francisco's California Palace of the Legion of Honor.

Robert Mondavi Winery (963-9611; 7801 Hwy. 29, Oakville) One of the first wineries to show art; rotating shows on display in the Vineyard Room.

SoCo Gallery (224-8176; 101 S. Coombs St., Napa) Located in an old tannery building, this is a delightful space to view local art.

The William Gallery (963-8800; 1235 Main St., St. Helena) Contemporary paintings by local and regional artists; the neon-colored abstractions by Jerry Cook and Rod Knutson's almost photojournalistic figurative paintings are highlights.

Sonoma County

Arts Guild of Sonoma (996-3115; 460 First St. E, Sonoma) A cooperative of 45 Sonoma County artists. The front room displays a potpourri of artists, from color vineyard landscapes to playful ceramic figures; the rear gallery offers a rotating exhibit devoted to a single artist or theme.

Bodega Landmark Studio (876-3477; 17255 Bodega Highway, Bodega) West county artists a specialty; oils, watercolors, ceramics.

A display of pots at the Ren Brown Collection in Bodega Bay.

Bodega Bay Photography; courtesy Ren Brown

Buena Vista Winery (963-9630; 18000 Old Winery Rd., Sonoma) Rotating exhibits in the loft of the historic Press House tasting room; artist-in-residence program during the summer, allowing visitors to watch art in action.

Cro-Magnon (433-1415; 132 Matheson St., Healdsburg) Primitive art, artifacts and replicas from around the world.

Matanzas Creek Winery (528-6464; 6097 Bennett Valley Rd., Santa Rosa) Standing exhibit of lovely pastel landscapes by artist-in-residence Mary Silverwood.

Quicksilver Mine Co. (869-9357; 14028 Armstrong Woods Rd., Guerneville) A gift and wine shop, with a small gallery in the back offering rotating exhibits.

Ren Brown Collection (875-2922; 1781 Hwy. 1, Bodega Bay) Modern Japanese prints are the focus of this gallery.

Santa Rosa Junior College Gallery (527-4298; 1501 Mendocino Ave., Santa Rosa) Group shows by faculty and students.

Snoopy Gallery (546-3385; 1667 W. Steele Ln., Santa Rosa) More of a museum and gift shop than gallery, but worth checking out if you're a "Peanuts" fan. Creator Charles Schulz is a local and many of his originals are on display.

Sonoma State University Gallery (664-2295; East Cotati Ave., Rohnert Park) Traveling exhibits of nationally known painters and sculptors, as well as student and faculty group shows.

Vigil's Native American Galleries (996-3763; 452-A First St. E., Sonoma) Art by and about Native Americans a specialty.

ARTrails

A Sonoma County tradition every October. For two weekends, dozens of artists open their studios to the public. It's rare chance to see artists in their natural habitat, not to mention an opportunity for a bargain since there's no art gallery middleman. Sponsored by the Cultural Arts Council of Sonoma County; handy tour maps are available. For more information, phone 579-ARTS.

HISTORIC PLACES

Napa County

BALE GRIST MILL
963-2236.
3 mi. N. of St. Helena on Hwy. 29.
Open 10–5 daily.
Fee: $2 adults, $1 children.
Gift shop.

Just think, if wheat had caught on in Napa Valley, you might be cruising Hwy. 29 in search of the perfect loaf of bread. When settlers first began arriving in Napa in the 1830s and '40s, wheat, corn and wild oats — not grapes — were the crops of choice. Mills, of course, were a necessity, not only as places to grind grain into meal and flour, but also as social centers for the community. Edward Turner Bale's grist mill, built in 1846, was one of three in Napa and the only that survives.

If traffic or the glitz of wineries are getting on your nerves, take an hour for a quiet getaway at the Bale Grist Mill State Historic Park. It seems miles and generations away.

The mill is at the end of a short path, a refreshing walk through dense woods and across a lively brook. The first thing you'll notice is the 36-foot-high wooden water wheel, rolling at a leisurely pace, water trickling down its curved steps. Inside the three-story wood mill house, a woman in a bonnet and period dress greets visitors. She might even offer you a slice of dense bread, made on-site with grain from the mill. The miller may actually crank up the giant millstones and grind flour.

The mill has a colorful past. Its builder, Dr. E.T. Bale, had a reputation as a

Bale Grist Mill, with its 36-foot-high water wheel, is the only one in Napa that has survived the years since it was built in 1846.

Chris Alderman

rogue and scoundrel. He was fond of the bottle and refused to pay his debts. Jailed on a number of occasions, he was publicly whipped and once nearly lynched for shooting a relative of the important Gen. Mariano Vallejo. Finally, Bale settled down and built the mill. It became the gathering spot for the north valley, where friends could exchange gossip and even stage dances. In those days, a miller was a leading citizen in the community and his counsel in business matters was highly respected.

With the coming of new technology at the turn of the century, the mill fell into neglect. It was restored by the Native Sons of the Golden West in 1925 and then again in 1967. It became a state historic park in 1974.

Sonoma County

FORT ROSS
847-3286.
12 mi. N. of Jenner on
  Hwy. 1.
Open 10–4:30 daily.
Fee: $5 per car.
Picnic area; gift shop;
  camping.

A quick history quiz. Who were Sonoma's first settlers (besides the Indians, of course)? If you said the Spanish, you're wrong. It was actually the Russians who established Fort Ross, predating the Sonoma Mission by 11 years.

The Russian American Trading Company, a firm controlled largely by the Imperial Russia government, came to California to escape the cruel winters of Alaska and to hunt for valuable sea otters. They landed south in Bodega Bay, which they called "Rumiantsev," and explored to the north. On a bluff overlooking the Pacific, they built their fort and community, now the centerpiece of Fort Ross State Historic Park.

Under the Russians, the fort thrived for 30 years as a major trading center for trappers and explorers. The Spanish and later, the Mexican settlement of Napa and Sonoma was largely to thwart Russian presence at Fort Ross. By 1830, the sea otter population was decimated and Fort Ross fell into decline. The Russians sold Fort Ross in 1839. It's certainly off the beaten path, miles from the nearest winery, but history buffs won't want to miss it and the drive along Hwy. 1 is spectacular.

Fort Ross, built by the Russians in 1813 on a windy bluff in Bodega Bay.

One structure built by the Russians still stands: the Commandant's House. The two blockhouses, the stockade and the Russian Orthodox Chapel have been carefully rebuilt. The visitors center and museum offer a look at the fort's past, as well as a peek at Russian and Indian artifacts.

LUTHER BURBANK HOME AND GARDEN
576-5115.
Corner of Santa Rosa and Sonoma aves. in Santa Rosa.
Season: Home is open mid–Apr.– mid–Oct., 10–3:30 Wed.–Sun.; garden open year-round 8–7.
Fee: Docent-led house tour is $1 for adults, free to children under 12; no fee for garden.
Gift shop.

Plant genius Luther Burbank remains Santa Rosa's favorite son. Sixty-five years after his death, buildings and businesses bear his name. At the turn of the century his fame was international. Burbank arrived from his native Massachusetts in 1877. In a letter home he wrote — and Santa Rosans love to quote this — "I firmly believe . . . this is the chosen spot of all this earth as far as nature is concerned."

From his Santa Rosa garden, Burbank developed more than 800 new strains of fruits, flowers, vegetables and grasses. Burbank, along with other geniuses like George Washington Carver, transformed plant breeding into a modern science. So great was Burbank's fame by 1900 that 50 people a day came to see the man and his garden. Among his visitors one day in 1915, were Thomas Edison, Henry Ford and Harvey Firestone.

A three-year renovation of the home and gardens will continue through 1993, but that shouldn't hamper visitors. The house was built about 1870 and is rather small, a modified Greek revival cottage. Burbank lived there from 1884 to 1906, when the earthquake damaged the house and Burbank moved. When Burbank died in 1926, his wife Elizabeth returned to the cottage. The property was designated a National Historic Landmark in 1964, and upon Elizabeth's death in 1977, the house and garden became city property.

The half-hour tour of the house is full of facts and artifacts and includes a glimpse inside one of Burbank's original greenhouses. The garden, as you might expect, abounds in Burbank creations, particularly the Paradox Walnut Tree and the Burbank Rose.

MISSION SAN FRANCISCO SOLANO
938-1519.
Corner of Spain St. and 1st St. E., Sonoma Plaza, Sonoma.
Open: 10–5 daily.
Fee: $2 for adults and $1 children under 12; admission good toward entry to Petaluma Adobe and Vallejo House.

This is where European settlement really began. Sure, technically, the Russians established the first outpost at Fort Ross, but the true origins of Napa and Sonoma lie at Sonoma's Mission San Francisco Solano. The white adobe mission with a red tile roof is probably the most popular historic attraction in Wine Country.

To appreciate its significance, it helps to understand the history of California's mission system. The Spanish government and Catholic Church began establishing California missions in 1769,

Sonoma's classic, whitewashed mission, founded in 1823.

both as a way of converting "heathen" Indians and claiming land for Spain. There were already 20 missions when the young and ambitious Father Jose Altimira received permission from the Mexican governor of California to establish a new one north of the San Francisco Bay. On July 4, 1823, Altimira celebrated Mass with a makeshift redwood cross and blessed the site.

The Sonoma Mission was the last to be established, and the mission system was dissolved in 1833. It became a center of religion and culture under Gen. Mariano Vallejo's rule, but was sold by the church in 1881. Used variously as a blacksmith shop and hay barn, the mission was nearly lost until the state stepped in in 1906; restoration began three years later.

Today, only the long, low building to the east of the present chapel is original, although the current chapel was only built a few years later, in 1841. Displays explain how adobe buildings are constructed and how the mission was restored. The chapel is decorated with 14 stations of the cross, authentic relics of the mission period. The chapel decor is patterned after mission interiors of the period, highly stylized primitive renderings by Christianized Indians.

PETALUMA ADOBE
762-4871.
Adobe and Casa Grande
    rds., 3 mi. E. of
    Petaluma.
Open: 10–5 daily.
Fee: $2 for adults and $1
    children under 12;
    admission also good
    toward entry to Mission
    San Francisco Solano
    and Vallejo House.
Picnic tables.

Once the heart of Gen. Mariano Vallejo's sprawling 100-square-mile rancho, the Petaluma Adobe is the area's most meticulously restored adobe. The commanding two-story house was built in 1836 and has three-feet-thick mud walls and a redwood veranda all around.

Authentic is the key word here. The rooms are furnished to the period and goats and chickens roam the outdoor corridors. Outdoor displays include working replicas of a forge and a large oven for baking bread.

The tour is self-guided; the museum details the history of the adobe and how it was restored.

GENERAL VALLEJO HOME

938-1578.
West Spain St., ½ mi. W. of Sonoma Plaza, Sonoma.
Open: 10–5 daily.
Fee: $2 for adults and $1 children under 12; admission also good toward entry to Mission San Francisco Solano and Petaluma Adobe.
Picnic tables.

Gen. Mariano Vallejo may have been the most powerful man in Northern California in the 1850s, but he had a sense of poetry about him when he named his house *Lachryma Montis*. Latin for "Tears of the Mountain," the name was derived from a mountain spring on the property.

Vallejo was born in Monterey in 1807, his father was a Spanish soldier. Following his father into the military, Vallejo was commander of the *Presidio*, the Spanish fort and settlement in San Francisco, when he was sent north in 1834. He commanded the northern frontier for 14 years and was largely responsible for encouraging the settlement of both Sonoma and Napa counties.

Vallejo's home, finished in 1852, reflects his embrace of the American culture. Instead of an adobe house, he built a two-story Gothic Victorian. The house was prefabricated, designed and built on the east coast and shipped around the Horn. Vallejo and family lived in the house for 35 years; the state bought the property in 1933.

The house and grounds are gorgeous, a quiet stop if you need relief from the bustle of Sonoma Plaza. The long driveway is flanked by tall cottonwood trees and the gardens and vineyards are carefully tended. The self-guided tour begins in a large warehouse, where displays detail Vallejo's life and the history of the house. One detraction: instead of tasteful ropes in the doorways guarding the rooms as most historic homes do, ugly white metal bars and cages have been installed to protect the considerable collection of artifacts and personal effects on display.

JACK LONDON STATE HISTORIC PARK

938-5216.
London Ranch Rd., Glen Ellen.
Open: Park open 8–sunset daily; house open 10–5 daily.
Fee: $5 per car.
Picnic tables; barbecue pits, hiking, horseback riding.

"When I first came here, tired of cities and people," Jack London wrote of Glen Ellen, "I settled down on 130 acres of the most beautiful land to be found in California." The writer famed for *Call of the Wild* and other adventure stories, called his home in the Sonoma Mountains "Beauty Ranch."

Today his ranch is the heart of Wine Country's most beautiful state park, now a vast 880 acres of woodlands, fields and hiking trails. The Wolf House is perhaps the park's most prominent feature. The massive castlelike stone building was four-stories tall; it was the culmination of Jack and Charmian London's dreams. On the night of Aug. 22, 1913, only days before they were to move in,

Jack London in Glen Ellen, where his beloved
"Beauty Ranch" is now an 800-acre state historic park.

Courtesy Jack London Library

Wolf House mysteriously burned. The ruins remain today. London died in 1916, reminding many of words he once said: "The proper function of man is to live, not exist. I shall not waste my days in trying to prolong them. I shall use my time."

London's grave along the half-mile trail to Wolf House is another popular stop. You can also stop in London's ranch house, his stone barn and pig palace. The House of Happy Walls, built by Charmian after London's death, serves as a museum, displaying an 18,000-volume library, original furnishings, memorabilia and the Londons' collection of South Pacific artifacts.

MUSEUMS

Napa County

SHARPSTEEN MUSEUM
942-5911.
1311 Washington St.,
   Calistoga, CA 94515.
Open: Noon–4 (winter);
   10–4 (summer).
Fee: None.

If you want a quick lesson in early Napa life, this quaint museum is the place to go. Ben and Bernice Sharpsteen created the museum almost as a hobby after Ben retired as a producer for Walt Disney and the couple moved to Calistoga. Before long, it became a community project and today it is run by volunteers.

The first section of this museum is devoted to the Sharpsteen themselves and, frankly it's rather dull. But the miniature model of early Calistoga that follows is delightful. The town was founded in 1859 as a resort by the flamboyant Sam Brannan. Brannan was a man of many firsts: California's first newspaper publisher, banker, land developer. He built the first railroad and telegraph. He was also California's first millionaire. His elegant Hot Springs Resort was a gathering point for California's rich and famous, and his vision of Calistoga as a haven of healing waters and relaxation still lives today. Only one tiny Victorian cottage remains from Brannan's resort; it was moved in 1977 and attached to the museum. Step inside the wonderfully ornate cottage and you'll step back into the 1860s.

The museum also details a great deal of Northern California history. One display, a Napa Valley Timeline, is particularly intriguing, dating back to the first explorers and the Sonoma Mission through the turn of the century. There are also lessons about the early stagecoach days — a restored coach is on display — the first railroad, Robert Louis Stevenson's days in Napa and on and on. There are enough old photos, newspapers and artifacts to keep any history buff happy.

SILVERADO MUSEUM
963-3757.
1490 Library Ln., St.
  Helena, CA 94574
Open: Noon–4 daily; closed
  Mon.
Fee: Free.

Writer Robert Louis Stevenson was taken in by Napa Valley. In 1880, the author of *Dr. Jekyll and Mr. Hyde* and *Treasure Island* honeymooned with his wife in a cabin near the old-Silverado Mine. He wrote about the area in *The Silverado Squatters*. He called Napa's wine "bottled poetry" and Mount St. Helena was the inspiration behind Spyglass Hill in *Treasure Island*. Although Stevenson spent only a few months in Napa Valley, he has been accepted as an adopted son.

Part of the St. Helena Library Center, the museum has a feeling of a small chapel. Founded in 1969, on the 75th anniversary of Stevenson's death, Silverado is more a library than a museum. It contains more than 8,000 artifacts, including dozens of paintings and photographs, as well as original Stevenson letters and manuscripts. There are also hundreds of books and first-printings.

Sonoma County

**RIPLEY'S MEMORIAL
  MUSEUM**
524-5233.
492 Sonoma Ave., Santa
  Rosa, CA 95401.
Season: Mar. – Oct.;
  11–4. Wed.–Sun.
Fee: $1.50 adults, $.75
  youths and senior
  citizens.

Robert L. Ripley — Believe It Or Not — was born in Santa Rosa, and if you have a taste for tacky, this is the place for you. It's one of 13 museums devoted to Ripley, who for 30 years was the world's authority on the exotic and unusual, as immortalized in his newspaper comic strip "Ripley's Believe It Or Not."

The museum is almost worth the $1.50 admission for its sheer absurdity. By far the most interesting thing about the museum is the building itself: The Church Built From One Tree. A single tree from the massive redwoods along the Russian River supplied the wood for this 1873 church. It's a noble little red chapel in a quiet neighborhood, a church that Ripley himself attended as a youth.

Few Santa Rosans even remember that Ripley was born there. He was still a student at Santa Rosa High School when he sold his first cartoon to Life maga-

One of Ripley's famous "Believe It or Not" features.

Courtesy Ripley Entertainment, Inc.

zine for $8. A budding sports illustrator for the old *New York Globe*, he created his first "Believe It or Not" cartoon in 1918. Before he died in 1959, he scoured the world for the weird.

The museum includes an unintentionally comical video on Ripley and introduces you to some of his odd friends. There's the man who drives six inch nails into his nose. ("In fact, he claims it cleared up his sinus condition!") Or there's the man who can smoke through his eye. The exhibits are all rather wacky and sometimes lame: a few Ripley originals, a life-sized wax figure of Ripley, a battered suitcase plastered with travel stickers, a stuffed Siamese calf, among others.

SONOMA COUNTY MUSEUM
579-1500.
425 7th St., Santa Rosa, CA 95401.
Hours: 11–4 Wed.– Sun.
Fee: $1 adults; $.50 youths 13 to 18.
Gift Shop.

The Sonoma County Museum building, a classic post office from early in the century, was saved from an insidious fate: progress. Slated for demolition, preservationists prevailed and the building was moved to its present site in 1979. Now on the National Register of Historic places, the structure is beautifully restored. A mix of

Spanish and Roman influences, it is considered one of the few remaining examples of classic Federal period architecture in California. Inside the two-story stucco building is rich oak paneling and marble floors. No better place for a museum.

Lobby displays detail the history of the building and its laborious move two blocks north. The main exhibit room offers rotating displays keyed to Sonoma history. The gallery upstairs offers a crash course in Sonoma's past, from the early Wappo and Pomo Indians to the dawning of the wine industry.

A permanent exhibit at the Sonoma County Museum.

Chris Alderman

OTHER MUSEUMS

Napa County

Napa Valley Historical Society Museum (224-1739; 1219 First St., Napa) A small collection used largely for research.

Napa Valley Museum (963-7411; 473 Main St., St. Helena) Rotating exhibits; no permanent displays.

Veterans Museum (944-4398; California Veteran's Home, Yountville) Military memorabilia.

Sonoma County

Healdsburg Museum (431-3325; 221 Matheson St.) Devoted to early Healdsburg history, including Indian artifacts and 5,000 photographs.

Native American Museum (527-4479; Santa Rosa Junior College) Indian artifacts.

Petaluma Historical Library and Museum (778-4398; 20 4th St.) Devoted to early Petaluma history.

MUSIC

Napa County

**NAPA VALLEY
SYMPHONY**
226-8742.
Lincoln Theater, California
    Veteran's Home,
    Yountville, CA 94599.
Season: Oct. – April; Pops
    concerts June and
    December.
Tickets: $18 and $15 for
    adults; $5 students.

The young Asher Raboy is the new conductor for this symphony that dates back to 1933 when Luigi Catalano first gathered a cadre of amateur and professional musicians. Today there are more than 75 musicians from Napa Valley and the Bay Area in the orchestra.

Each of the season's five concerts features a world-class guest artist performing the greatest music of the classical repertoire. Last season, for example, pianist Philippe Bianconi was acclaimed for his performance of Brahms's "Concerto No. 2," and likewise Nathaniel Rosen for his performance of Elgar's cello concerto.

Each summer since 1969, the lovely Robert Mondavi Winery played host to the symphony's Wine Country Pops, a warm and delightful June day in the sun. Last year's concert featured a tribute to John Philip Sousa.

Sonoma County

BAROQUE SINFONIA
546-4504.
Burbank Center for the
    Arts, Mark West Springs
    Rd., Santa Rosa, CA
    95403.
Season: Oct.– Apr.
Tickets: $8, student
    discounts.

If you're a CPA who finds artistic solace in playing the oboe, then Baroque Sinfonia is the place for you. This 20-year-old chamber orchestra is a more leisurely paced version of the Santa Rosa Symphony. (See below.) The 40 musicians are all volunteers and are led by 70-year-old maestro Eugene Shepherd. They play for sheer pleasure and it shows. Don't expect perfection, but the concerts are warm and user-friendly. Their "Sing-Along Messiah" in December is a particular community favorite.

**ROHNERT PARK
SYMPHONY**
584-1700.
Spreckels Performing Arts
    Center, Snyder Ln.,
    Rohnert Park, CA 94928
Season: Oct.– July.
Tickets: $13.50, $10
    matinees and $11 youths
    and seniors.

Unheard of! Symphony orchestras around the nation are struggling to survive, but this fledgling orchestra is financed by *a city*. They also have the privilege of performing in the best hall in Wine Country, the new Spreckels Performing Arts Center, financed by the very same town, Rohnert Park. Some governments, it seems, have their priorities straight.

Deeply engrossed, a member of the Rohnert Park Symphony bows his cello.

Courtesy Spreckels Performing Arts Center

There is yet another rarity involved here: a female conductor. J. Karla Lemon is knowledgeable and a passionate conductor on stage. The roots of this small orchestra date to 1983, when Lemon led the Sonoma State University Orchestra. When that was discontinued, the city of Rohnert Park took the lead. Many of the musicians play in other Bay Area symphonies and Lemon is also a professor at San Francisco State University.

The 1990-91 season, the symphony's first at Spreckels, was ambitious, and it is only now establishing its credentials with top guest soloists. It is certainly catching on with locals; the 511-seat main hall is often filled to capacity. "It's a bumpy road starting out," Lemon has commented. "I really hoped we would be welcomed, and it's a nice surprise that my hopes are coming true."

**SANTA ROSA
   SYMPHONY**
546-8742.
Burbank Center for the
   Arts, Mark West Springs
   Rd., Santa Rosa, CA
   95403.
Season: Oct. – May.
Tickets: $20.50, $16, $11.50
   and $7.50 youths and
   seniors.

Maestro Corrick Brown has a knack for snar-ing up-and-coming guest soloists. You'd expect to see these talents in New York or San Francisco, not Santa Rosa. Recent guests have included guitarist David Tanenbaum and British pianist Ian Hobson. Paired with the respectable talents of Brown's regular corps of musicians, a concert by the Santa Rosa Symphony is a most pleasurable experience.

The symphony dates from 1927 and Brown has been conductor for the better part of those 35 years. He has a penchant for Mahler, Dvorak and Mozart. His musicians, as with most small sym-phonies in the Bay area, come from around the region. Some are semi-professionals with day jobs; others keep busy roaming from one orchestra to another.

Burbank Center for the Arts, a former church, is a large hall of about 1,500 seats. Acoustics aren't what they might be, but Brown and crew overcome the limitations. The symphony's Redwood Summer Music Festival (see below) is one of the highlight's of Sonoma County's musical year.

OTHER MUSIC

Napa County

Chamber Music in Napa Valley (252-7122; 809 Coombs St., Napa) For the past decade this series has brought in top chamber and solo musicians from around the nation. Annual April concerts inside the caves of S. Anderson Vineyards is a top draw.

Domaine Chandon Music Series (944-8844; just off Hwy. 29, Yountville) From the swamp-beat-boogie of the Sundogs to the classics of the Modern Mandolin Quartet, this sparkling wine facility hosts concerts on its terrace throughout the summer.

Robert Mondavi Summer Music Festival (963-9617; 7801 Hwy. 29, Oakville) A tradition since 1969, these June through August concerts on the lush lawns of Mondavi's winery bring in top names in popular music: Tony Ben-nett, David Benoit and Preservation Hall Jazz Band.

Dixieland Jazz Society (226-8114) These Dixieland jazz lovers stage various concerts throughout Napa Valley all year long.

Sonoma County

Buena Vista Entertainment Series (938-1266; 18000 Old Winery Rd., Sonoma) The beautiful grounds of this historic winery are home to a summer-long series of performances, from concerts by Wynton Marsalis and Spyro Gyra to a Mostly Mozart concert.

Cotati Jazz Festival (795-5478) Jazz lovers hop from nightclub to nightclub listening to the best jazz musicians the Bay Area has to offer. This two-day June event marked its 11th year in 1991.

Petaluma Summermusic Festival (763-8920) Cinnabar Theater's annual ode to music and musical theater. Concerts and performances are staged throughout Petaluma during this three-week event each August.

Redwood Summer Music Festival (546-8742; Burbank Center for the Arts, Santa Rosa) Some of the most beautiful wineries in Sonoma — Chateau St. Jean, Lyeth — play host to this annual series by the Santa Rosa Symphony. Picnickers spend a carefree evening listening to Mozart, Gershwin, Copland and the like.

Russian River Jazz Festival (869-3940; Johnson Beach, Guerneville) Jazz along the lazy Russian River has made this the most popular music festival in Wine Country. For two days every September, music lovers sun on the beach or listen from floating inner tubes. The line-up of jazz greats stretches from morning to evening, and has recently included the likes of Larry Carlton, The Yellowjackets, Chick Corea and Tuck & Patti.

Santa Rosa DixieJazz Festival (542-3315; El Rancho Tropicana Hotel) Santa Rosa swarms with Dixiejazz nuts for one weekend every August. A BIG event, bringing in bands from around the world. Don't ask them to play "When the Saints Go Marching In."

NIGHTLIFE

If you're cruising for a good time in Napa Valley at night, you'll discover quickly that things are rather sleepy. It's the nature of the beast. Napa is largely a haven for visitors seeking quiet and relaxation. Tourists, on the other hand, have less of an impact on Sonoma, which has its own large population to entertain. There's plenty to do after 10 p.m., particularly in Santa Rosa. The Friday edition of Santa Rosa's *Press Democrat* is a good source for what's happening.

Napa County

To best describe how dead Napa is at night, consider this. The night clubs listing of the Yellow Pages has all of three entries. One is in Sonoma, the other is a spot 30 mi. south in Vallejo. The only Napa entry is a pub popular with locals, *O'Sullivan's Club* (224-5612; 359 First St., Napa). It's not in the greatest neighborhood, but there is dancing and live music on weekends. Other popular late-night hang-outs in the city of Napa include *Willett's Brewing Co.* (258-2337; 902 Main St.) and *Brown Street Brewery* (255-6392; 1040 Clinton St.). Neither offers music but at least they make their own beer. (See Chapter Five, *Restaurants and Food Purveyors*, for more details on brewpubs.) In Calistoga, *Silverado Tavern* (942-6725; 1374 Lincoln Ave.) can be a lively spot after dinner. Surprisingly, few of the posh hotels and resorts in Napa Valley offer live music.

Sonoma County

Sonoma's club scene is thriving. Live music can be found *somewhere* every night, and DJs seem to be spinning discs in a corner of every bar.

Santa Rosa is the center of Sonoma County's nightlife, although the outlying areas have a number of fine night spots. Sonoma County's premier stage is **Burbank Center for the Arts** (546-3600; Mark West Springs Rd., Santa Rosa).

The Studio KAFE's owners, John and Randi Duran.

Courtesy Studio KAFE

Once a sprawling church complex, the center's main stage is the largest hall in the area, seating about 1,500 in cushioned pews. Recent headliners include John Hiatt, Robert Cray, Bonnie Raitt, Rodney Crowell, Lyle Lovett and B.B. King. Another hot spot for live music is **The Studio KAFE** (523-1971; 418 Mendocino Ave.), a newly expanded club that seats almost 200 and specializes in roots music: blues, reggae, rock and jazz. Recent acts include Richard Thompson, Jellyfish, The Beat Farmers and Sonoma County's own blues harp master Charlie Musselwhite. Also, Wednesday is comedy night. And get this — the KAFE is also a radio station, available on cable hookups only. Most concerts are aired live. **The Daily Planet** (578-1205; Fifth and Davis sts.) is probably the hottest singles scene in Sonoma County. The dance floor is large, the light show impressive and the DJ spins only the latest dance discs. On weekends, there's dancing until 4 a.m.! Friday is comedy night, with stand-up comics from around the Bay Area and dancing after. Sunday is devoted to country music, with festive dance lessons a regular feature.

Santa Rosa's hotels are another good source for late-night fun. **The Flamingo** (545-8530; Fourth St. and Farmers Lane) offers a piano bar most evenings, followed by a live Top 40 band Thursday through Saturday. **Equus Lounge** of Fountain Grove Inn (578-6101; 101 Fountain Grove Pkwy.) is a cozy spot for late-night easy-listening jazz combos. **Magnolia's** (526-1006; 107 Fourth St.) is a favorite with local rockers, bringing in local and Bay Area metal favorites and also that Olympic stature sport — *ahem* — women's oil wrestling. Three pubs have avid local followings. *Kelmer's Brewhouse* (544-4677; 458 B St.) reminds us of an old college hangout. There are darts, plenty of TVs to watch sports and occasional live music. They also make great beer. Brits rule *The English Rose* (579-9966; Armory Drive) and *The Old Vic* (571-7555; 731 Fourth St.). Both are dark and casual spots offering darts and a fine selection of British beers. The Vic also has live music and dinner theater on weekends. (See Chapter Five, *Restaurants and Food Purveyors*, for more details on these pubs.)

Sonoma Valley offers a few choice night spots. *Cabaret Sauvignon* (996-3600; Sonoma Plaza, Sonoma) is a stylish art deco club above the historic Sebastiani Theater. There's the occasional name act, The Tubes and the like, with live music on weekends and DJ dancing and comedy on other nights. A different crowd entirely hangs out at *Little Switzerland* (938-9990; Grove and Riverside, Sonoma). This place is a kick! Polka is king at Little Switzerland, a club and restaurant that dates from 1906. The crowd is older, largely serious polka dancers, but they don't care if you show up for a kitsch thrill and make a fool of yourself on the dance floor. The place is incredibly tacky, with plastic flowers and Swiss Alp murals and faded red and white checkered tablecloths. There's also a beer garden, of course.

South Sonoma County offer some hot dance tickets. *Cotati Cabaret* (544-2263; 85 La Plaza, Cotati) was long the area's Mecca of live music, but has gone through financial troubles and several owners in the past few years. Too bad; it's a nice club that seats 300 with plenty of room to dance. Some big names have performed at the Cabaret, including Randy Newman, Chris Issak, 2 Live Crew, Neil Young, Todd Rundgren, Damn Yankees and Huey Lewis and the News. *Phoenix Theatre* (762-3565; 201 Washington St., Petaluma) is an old movie theater that doubles occasionally as a concert hall. It wouldn't be our first choice for live music, but they certainly bring in some cutting edge

Comedian Dr. Gonzo at the Daily Planet, Santa Rosa.

Courtesy the Daily Planet

music: The Neville Brothers, Primus, Los Lobos and Red Hot Chili Peppers. *McNear's* (765-2121; 23 Petaluma Blvd. N, Petaluma) is a comfortable gathering spot with video games, pool tables and live music on weekends. It's also one of the few places that serves food late. *Steamer Gold Landing* (763-6876; Petaluma Blvd. N, Petaluma) rivals Santa Rosa's Daily Planet as the busy singles' spot in the county. Steamer Gold, in the restored Great Petaluma Mill, has a warmer atmosphere than the Planet, with brick walls and an exposed rafter ceiling. DJ music on most nights, supplemented by live Top 40 bands on weekends.

There's not much happening in West and North County. If you crave the Texas Two-step, then *Marty's Top 'O the Hill* (823-5987; 8050 Bodega Ave., Sebastopol) is the place for you. Country music lovers head for Marty's on the weekends, where live bands help you dance the night away. It's a lively place, not rowdy, and the long-neck beers are ice cold. *Jasper O'Farrell's* (823-1389; 6957 Sebastopol Ave., Sebastopol) is another pub that makes you feel at home. There's live music almost every night and it's a potpourri: jazz, bluegrass, folk, rock. Darts are also a serious passion at Jasper's.

THEATER

Theater is just taking root in Napa County. There are two community theaters, each under five years old and still looking for stardom. Sonoma, on the other hand, boasts a long tradition of theater. It has one professional company and three highly regarded semi-professional groups. There is also a vastly successful summer stock repertory series that brings in top college talent from around the country every year, as well as numerous community theater companies performing throughout the county. As one local director said of Sonoma theater: "I think there are more people who do theater than see theater."

Sonoma County's premier venue for the performing arts.

Chris Alderman

Sonoma County

ACTORS' THEATRE
523-4185.
Burbank Center for the
    Arts, Mark West Springs
    Rd., Santa Rosa, CA
    95403.
Season: Sept.– July.
Tickets: $8, $10, student
    and senior discounts.

Expect the unexpected from this studio theater, Sonoma County's most respected company. Performing contemporary plays in an intimate 75-seat house, Actors' Theatre isn't afraid to take chances. Usually, they pull it off. The actors, an ensemble of some two dozen, are all talented amateurs, and production values are high.

Artistic director Kathy Juarez can always be counted on to select a provocative season of plays, mixing obscure modern gems with small-scale classics. Highlights have included a dynamic production of John Pielmeier's *Agnes of God* and a little known but powerful historical drama *Kingdom Come*, by Amlin Gray. The 1990-91 season also included winning versions of Marsha Norman's *'night Mother* and Richard Greenberg's *Eastern Standard*, not to mention a wild west version of Shakespeare's *The Taming of the Shrew*. That's right partner!

Actors' Theater was a 1983 spin off from the Santa Rosa Players, the grandfather of local theater. The group was tired of staging yet another version of *Oklahoma*. It began with no audience, no money and no equipment. The lighting system of the first show consisted of a single light switch. The group's fortunes have increased over the years, likewise its following. Consistency remains a minor problem, but the potential is great.

CINNABAR THEATER
763-8920.
3333 Petaluma Blvd. N.,
    Petaluma, CA 94952.
Season: Year round.
Tickets: Various.

Opera is a scary prospect for a lot of people. Perhaps it's the elitist air that surrounds it, the assumption that it's only for the wealthy and educated. Or perhaps singing in a foreign language turns people off. Whatever the reason, Marvin Klebe came to Petaluma 21 years ago to change that notion. From that began Sonoma County's most eclectic and cutting-edge theater. "Our main goals are to explore opera as an immediate and human experience to an audience that is not necessarily highbrow," Cinnabar's Elly Lichenstein commented.

Klebe, a powerful baritone, had been a professional opera singer in San Francisco and was searching for a way to make opera more intimate and experimental. Buying the old Cinnabar School on the northern outskirts of Petaluma, Klebe set about transforming it into a studio theater. (Luckily, he's also a master carpenter.) Soon, others — musicians, dancers, actors, technicians — got involved and Cinnabar became a small, thriving performing arts center.

Ann Woodhead, a professor at nearby Sonoma State University, leads an avant-garde dance company at Cinnabar and Western Union Theatre Co., another talented troupe, calls Cinnabar home most of the time. Nina Shuman, the theater's musical director and conductor, has a taste for the offbeat and has gathered a core of devoted chamber musicians, who supply musical accompaniment for the operas and also perform their own concerts.

The heart of the place is Cinnabar Opera Theater. There's not a more intriguing theater company north of San Francisco. No, you won't find a tenor from San Francisco Opera on stage, but you will see the finest singers hovering on "the outskirts" of Bay Area opera fame. Productions have run the gamut from *Falstaff* and *The Magic Flute* to obscure curiosities such as *The Emperor of Atlantis*. All in English.

FOURTH WALL STAGE COMPANY
544-4236.
Lincoln Arts Center, 709 Davis St., Santa Rosa, CA 95401.
Season: Aug.– June.
Tickets: $9 adults, $8 students.

One of the newest companies in Sonoma, Fourth Wall is also one the most promising. Word still hasn't gotten out about Fourth Wall, so even their tiny 50-seat theater is seldom filled. They deserve better. They've only been performing since 1989, but collectively they're an experienced troupe and it shows. Except for an occasional mediocre performance, Fourth Wall hasn't made a false move.

Highlights so far have included exceptional productions of Tennessee Williams' *A Streetcar Named Desire* and Samuel Beckett's timeless *Waiting For Godot*. As for the theater, Lincoln Arts Center is a bit rundown, but you won't find a more intimate theater space. You feel like you're sharing the set with the actors. You can see every stumble, but there aren't many. Well worth checking out.

PACIFIC ALLIANCE STAGE COMPANY
584-1700.
Spreckels Performing Arts Center, Snyder Ln., Rohnert Park, CA 94928.
Season: Sept.– June.
Tickets: $10 and $12.

The debut of Pacific Alliance in 1990 reminded us of that old theater saying: "Break a leg." We've always been suspicious that there's a double-meaning to that phrase — you know, good luck, but we wouldn't mind if you fell on your face.

Pacific Alliance, to explain, is the county's first professional Actor's Equity company. It brought up, as we saw it, mixed feelings in the Sonoma theater community. While most seemed to like the idea that Sonoma was coming up in the theater world, we suspect they were worried the competition could make them look bad. And yet — hey — maybe they could land a role and earn that Equity card.

Whatever the reaction, Pacific Alliance raised expectations and certainly upped the ante. And after an embarrassingly subpar opening show, the dreadful musical *Two By Two*, Pacific Alliance has quickly lived up to the highest expectations. It helps, of course, that the company has the backing of Spreckels Performing Arts Center, which in turn is backed by the city of Rohnert Park. Artistic Director Michael Grice continues to bring superior

Petrucio confronts Kate in
Kiss Me Kate, *at the Summer*
Repertory Theater.

Courtesy Summer Repertory Theater

talents from around the Bay Area. A few talented local "amateurs" are also earning that all important card.

While acting is approaching the level of San Francisco, production values lag behind. Broadway-quality sets, no doubt, require Broadway-level ticket prices, yet we can't help but expect more. Spreckels is also experimenting with a few offbeat productions in its small studio theater, using talent from Pacific Alliance. It's all very refreshing and offers great promise.

SUMMER REPERTORY THEATER
527-4280.
1501 Mendocino Ave.,
Santa Rosa, CA 95401.
Season: June to Aug.
Tickets: Season tickets
$25–$50, individual
shows $6–$10.

No one has a bigger local following than SRT. Every summer for 20 years, Santa Rosa Junior College has organized this three-ring circus of theater, bringing in talented student actors and technical people from around the country. Opening six major productions in four weeks and performing them in a repertory format packs a year's experience into two months.

Some summers are better than others, of course. It all depends on the show and the talent pool, but SRT is always worth a try. Comedy, musical, drama — SRT has proven its mettle with every genre. Recent highlights have included sparkling productions of *Evita* and *Oliver*, and an electrifying adaptation of Arthur Miller's drama *A View From the Bridge*. Although seasons of late have been rather safe, SRT isn't afraid of being radical. A past production of *Equus* with full nudity is still mentioned on occasion.

One of the great pleasures of SRT is discovering a favorite actor and following him or her through several shows. "OK, she was great in *Evita*, but can she pull off comedy?" There are usually one or two stand-outs in the ensemble of 30 actors. Also, SRT's production values are the highest in Napa and Sonoma counties. Sets are always dynamic, on par with many professional theaters. It's also significant that SRT is one of the few local companies performing in the summer, and thus a perfect choice for tourists looking for a pleasurable evening on the town.

OTHER THEATER

There are more than a dozen other theater companies in Napa and Sonoma. Many are community theaters. We include a selection of the best.

Napa County

Dreamweavers (255-5483; 101 S. Coombs St., Napa) is a five-year-old community theater performing favorites such as *Arsenic and Old Lace* and *Fools*. **Magical Moonshine Theater** (257-8007; Yountville) is an internationally known puppet theater that doesn't have a regular Napa performance space. Look for them locally when they're not away on tour — charming and great for the family. **Napa Valley Opera House** (226-7373; 1144 Main St., Napa) isn't currently staging its own shows, but when restoration of the 112-year-old theater is complete, it will become a center for theater and art. **St. Helena Players** (963-5784; St. Helena High School Auditorium) Since 1989, this company has been staging workshops in the fall and summer, culminating in socially conscious productions such as *The Dining Room* and *Coastal Disturbances*. SHP added a summer repertory of three plays in 1991.

Sonoma County

River Repertory Theater (865-2905; Hwy. 1, Jenner) is the West County's eclectic little showcase. It's part community theater, part experimental studio. A recent production of Havel's *Audience* was riotous. **Odyssey Theatre** (578-5492; Sonoma Valley High School, Sonoma) is an uneven community group in Sonoma Valley that occasionally surprises, including the recently biting *Sister Mary Ignatius Explains It All For You* by Christopher Durang. **Santa Rosa Players** (544-7827; 709 Davis St.) began it all 20 years ago. This community theater is an institution and it has its good runs and bad, but just when you're ready to write them off, they delight you. Not to be outdone by SRJC, **Sonoma State University** (664-2474; Rohnert Park) also has a talented theater department and SSU's new performing arts center has the county's best stage for theater. **Western Union Theatre** (763-8920; Cinnabar Theater, Petaluma) is another of the county's best companies, staging offbeat comedies and dramas, plays most companies have never heard of. "I feel that every play should somehow be life-changing, otherwise, there's no reason for doing it," artistic director Beth Craven commented.

SEASONAL EVENTS

If there's one thing they know how to do in Wine Country, it's throw a party. If you live in Napa or Sonoma counties or are visiting and find that you have an open weekend in the summer, then there maybe something wrong with you. There are enough festivals and fairs to keep you busy all year. We list here some of the most popular seasonal attractions. The agricultural products of the Napa and Sonoma region shine forth at the many county fairs. Wine, of course, is the centerpiece of many festivals; we've included those in a separate section that follows.

Bodega Bay Fisherman's Festival (875-3422) is a 20-year-old tradition for this coast town made famous by Alfred Hitchcock's *The Birds*. This mid-April celebration of things nautical includes bath tub races, a trap shoot, harbor tours, kite flying, a foot race, golf tournament and boat parade. The high point of the weekend is the annual blessing of the fleet.

Calistoga Beer & Sausage Tasting (942-6333; Napa County Fairgrounds, Calistoga) is Napa Valley's way of celebrating Oktoberfest. On tap in mid-October are some of the best beers brewed by area pubs and microbreweries, not to mention tasty tidbits from the region's many sausage specialists. Casual atmosphere; great fun. Fee.

Celebrate Sonoma (546-3600; Burbank Center for the Arts, Santa Rosa) has a little bit of everything: arts and crafts, food, dance, live music and clowns. Much of the fun is outdoors in this annual mid-June weekend.

Gravenstein Apple Fair (544-4728; downtown Sebastopol) is as authentic as fairs come these days. Sebastopol was once the apple capital of the world and today specializes in the distinctive Gravenstein variety. There's a potpourri at this August event: arts and crafts, music, hay rides, storytelling and of course apple treats of all kinds.

Health & Harmony Festival (823-4989; Sonoma County Fairgrounds, Santa Rosa) is an Only-in-California type of event. A celebration of food, music and "lifestyle," this annual June fair includes everything from puppet theater to psychic palm readers.

Hometown Harvest Festival (963-4456; downtown St. Helena) is a rich Napa tradition, celebrating the end of the growing season and the summer's bountiful harvest. One weekend in late October, there's scads of food, arts and crafts, music and even a parade.

Hot Air Balloon Classic (579-9734; Airport Business Center, north of Santa Rosa) is easily the most visually striking event of the year. For two days, 60 colorful balloons take to the skies of Sonoma and race with the wind. Balloon races begin at 5:30 a.m. (that's when the wind is best) and there's also a chili cook-off and a barbecue and hoedown during the three-day June fest. Admission: $5.

Calistoga's main street celebrates one of the fun events of the year.

Penn; courtesy Calistoga Chamber of Commerce

Kenwood Pillow Fights & Fourth of July Celebration (833-2440; Kenwood) is the best excuse we know to have a pillow fight astride a greased pole over a mud pit. So silly it's addicting. A favorite with local celebrities like Tommy Smothers. There's also a parade, live music and fireworks.

Napa County Fair (942-5111; fairgrounds, Calistoga) provides the usual down-home fun, but with a twist of chic Napa style, with social gatherings and wine tastings. The usual rides, animals, produce and music, plus wine, wine, wine. Every July.

Petaluma Butter & Eggs Day (762-9348; downtown Petaluma) marks this south county town's early reputation as "The Egg Basket of the World." Poultry, milk and eggs remain a strong presence in Sonoma. One Sunday every April the town celebrates with a parade, music and food.

Piccola Festa Italiana (963-1228; St. Helena Catholic Church) is Napa's way of reveling in its rich Italian heritage. It's everything Italian: food, dancing, movies, music, wine, even boccie tournaments. Late August.

Sebastopol Apple Blossom Festival (869-9009; downtown Sebastopol) finds the apple trees in striking form. You won't find a more beautiful place than Sebastopol in April. Apples rule, of course. Eat apple fritters, cobbler, pies. Plus music, games and arts and crafts.

Slug Fest (874-2200; downtown Guerneville) is an event you won't believe: a celebration of the banana slug. There's a contest for the fastest slug, the fattest and — blech! — the tastiest. There's even a slug race and culinary competition for best slug recipe. A strong constitution is needed for this one.

Sonoma County Fair (545-4200; fairgrounds, Santa Rosa) Sonoma County practically shuts down for two weeks every July, as thousands pour in from the countryside for food, music, rides, blue-ribbon animals and produce. You can even bet on horse races.

Swinging through the air at the Sonoma County Fair.

Bob Martin; courtesy SCCVB

WINE EVENTS

We're still waiting to see this sign along a Napa or Sonoma road: "Garage Sale & Wine Tasting." Wine events are everywhere and all the time in Napa and Sonoma. Locals would get sick of them if they weren't so darn much fun. Sure, it's charming to drive through the countryside to find that beguiling winery or winning zinfandel, but there's also considerable pleasure in sampling and comparing all sorts of wine in one sitting. Most of the following events are staged outside, which adds to the pleasure, and most also include lots to eat, see and do.

Napa Valley Wine Auction (963-5246; Meadowood Resort, St. Helena) is *the* chic wine outing. This three-day June event is busy with extravagant parties, dances and dinners. Auction tickets cost a fortune but are much in demand. All the big names of the Napa wine industry and otherwise attend, and the auction raises millions for local charities.

Napa Valley Wine Festival (253-3563; Town and Country Fairgrounds) marks the end of the wine season. The November wine tasting, dinner and auction raises money for a local charity. Fee.

Russian River Barrel Tasting (433-6782; countryside surrounding Healdsburg) is always the first event of the wine season, and helps lift wine lovers out of the winter doldrums. Besides, everyone loves a sneak preview. The country roads near Healdsburg are busy the first weekend in March with BMWs and Volvo wagons as the faithful from around the Bay Area swarm to taste wine not even bottled yet. Several participating wineries aren't normally among those open to the public and so they're particularly busy. Best of all — it's free.

Russian River Wine Festival (648-9922; Healdsburg Plaza) offers the wines of 30 wineries in one green and sunny place. One Sunday every May, the fest also includes delights from local restaurants, arts and crafts and live music. A $10 fee includes a souvenir glass and five tastings.

Salute to the Arts (938-1133; Sonoma Plaza) is a showcase for local artists, writers, restaurants and wineries. Roam the beautiful historic square and browse the many booths. Free admission, but fee required for wine and food.

Sonoma County Harvest Fair (545-4203; fairgrounds, Santa Rosa) could easily be listed with the regular seasonal events, but the wine tasting is *the* most important in Sonoma County. The fair brings in top wine experts from around the country. Medals are awarded. Then local wine buffs gather to compare their tastebuds to the judges'. Great fun. But there's more to the Harvest Fair than wine. The Grape Stomping contest is a crazy attraction. Admission plus wine tasting fee; souvenir glass included.

Sonoma County Wine Auction (579-0577; Sonoma Mission Inn, Boyes Hot Springs) is a bit less chi-chi than its Napa counterpart, but remains quite the elegant affair. The four-day gala includes tastings, parties and the auction itself. The event is usually sold-out weeks in advance, despite steep ticket prices.

Sonoma County Wine & Food Series (576-0162) is a long-time favorite with locals. There are seven gatherings at different wineries throughout the summer, each featuring a particular varietal. A recent tasting at Chateau St. Jean, for example, featured the best sparkling and dessert wines of the county. Wine is paired with food from local restaurants and live music is also included. Admission is $22 for each event, with a discount for the series. All to benefit the Sonoma County Farmlands Group.

Wine Festival and Crafts Fair (257-0322; downtown Napa) is a busy event that draws wine as well as arts and crafts buffs from around the county. Every September.

NEIGHBORS

With San Francisco so close, it's impossible to talk of culture without mentioning what that world-class city has to offer.

Museums are one of the most popular excuses for the pleasant hour's drive south. Best known is *The Exploratorium* (415-561-0360; 3601 Lyon St.), a magnetic place for families because of its hands-on science displays. Likewise, The *Natural History Museum* (415-750-7145; Golden Gate Park) is a popular spot for kids and families. Art museums include the cutting edge *San Francisco Museum of Modern Art* (415-863-8800; Van Ness Avenue), *The De Young Memorial Museum* (415-863-3300; Golden Gate Park), and the graceful *Palace of the Legion of Honor* (415-863-3300; Lincoln Park), specializing in Rodin sculpture.

Professional performance art is still another of San Francisco's many lures. *The San Francisco Ballet* (415-621-3838; War Memorial Opera House) is one of the best in the country. *The San Francisco Symphony* (415-431-5400; Davies Symphony Hall) is gaining a national reputation as well, and the *San Francisco Opera* (415-864-3330; War Memorial Opera House) is one of the Bay Area's great artistic traditions. And while San Francisco is hardly Broadway, the theater district around Union Square is a happening place. *The American Conservatory Theater* (415-749-2228; Geary Street) is the city's most respected, and small off-Broadway-style theaters abound.

As for nightlife, San Francisco's South of Market district is the place to be seen, a former industrial area with nightclubs on almost every corner. Hot clubs in the city at this writing include DNA, I-Beam, Palladium, The Edge and X. You might be home in time to see the sun rise.

CHAPTER FIVE
Pleasing the Palate
RESTAURANTS & FOOD PURVEYORS

Chris Alderman

A glimpse of diners through an etched glass window on the sumptuous Napa Valley Wine Train.

If wine is "bottled poetry," as the late novelist Robert Louis Stevenson wrote, then fine dining in Wine Country is its culinary equivalent. Both are indeed an art, with artists — true geniuses, at times — behind them. As wineries have encroached on the farmland of Napa and Sonoma counties, gourmet restaurants have overtaken the burger joints. The urban sprawl of fine dining hasn't upset the natives and certainly not the tourists. Today, Wine Country is widely known as a delectable place to please the palate. Some of the most reputable chefs in the country have come here to debut their entrees and couple their creations with fine wine.

Restaurants run the gamut from posh, palatial chateaus to storefront bistros. There is a wide range of cuisine: French, Italian, Mexican, Chinese, Thai and naturally California. In reviewing restaurants we placed a great deal of emphasis on the *creative art* of fine dining. This has to do with both the way entrees are flavored — the risks chefs take — and the way they are pre-

112

sented. John Ash & Co. and Terra are two favorites that have earned high marks in both respects.

There is more, however, to dining out than just the food. Atmosphere, for one. Did the restaurant set the tone for the meal to come? Was it warm, interesting or unique? Most of all, did it work? Service was also key; after all, you *are* on vacation and deserve to be pampered. We were most interested in knowing how well the servers knew the menu and could make intelligent comments about particular dishes.

Each restaurant is given a price code, signifying the cost of a meal including appetizer, entree and dessert, but not cocktails, wine, tax or tip. Restaurants with a *prix fixe* menu are so noted. Reviews are organized first by county, then by city or region, then alphabetically. Food purveyors are grouped alphabetically by type, then name of establishment. Every restaurant appears in the general index, too.

Bon appetit!

Dining Price Code:	Inexpensive	up to $10
	Moderate	$10 - $20
	Expensive	$20 - $30
	Very Expensive	$30 or more

Credit Cards:	AE - American Express
	CB - Carte Blanche
	D - Discover Card
	DC - Diner's Club
	MC - Master Card
	V - Visa

RESTAURANTS—NAPA COUNTY

Napa

CAFFE 1991
Manager: Michelle Lamey.
226-1990.
1075 California Blvd.,
 Napa.
Price: Expensive.
Credit cards: AE, MC, V.
Cuisine: American,
 California.
Serving: SB, L, D.
Reservations: Accepted.
Special features: Atrium.

The atrium is laced with greenery and goldfish frolic in a nearby pond. Caffe 1991 brings the outdoors in. Located in the Inn at Napa Valley, the restaurant's decor is its strongest asset. The wine list is small and first-rate, but only a few wines are available by the glass. Service was attentive, and we appreciated our waiter's knowledge of the menu.

We applaud the diverse menu, though chef Michael Barker tries to cover a lot of territory. The range of homemade pastas is impressive and includes Napa Valley *Cioppino* over linguine pasta

A goldfish pond and lush greenery grace the atrium of Caffe 1991.

Chris Alderman

with scampi, scallops and fresh fish. The slow-hickory-smoked prime rib and the tenderloin of pork served over a sherry wine vinegar sauce are just two of the seven meat dishes offered. And the mesquite swordfish with kiwi and bell pepper relish is one of six seafood entrees. Barker may be spreading himself too thin and as a result some of the dishes rate and others fall short of the mark.

We began with a house specialty, Killer Bread, a hollowed out Sourdough Loaf with mozzarella, swiss and feta cheeses melted on top. Very good, very filling — four people could have easily shared it. The Autumn Harvest Salad was nothing special, leaves of lettuce with a few cherry tomatoes sprinkled on top and a balsamic vinegar dressing on the side. The tomato basil soup was better, creamy with a distinct, sweet taste of fresh basil. The lobster ravioli was tasty with a light and creamy tomato sauce and fresh vegetables on the side. And the grilled breast of chicken, prepared with lemon pepper and rosemary, was juicy and fairly flavorful, but the vegetables and wild rice were bland.

Eyeing the dessert tray, it was hard to reach a consensus. We passed up the delectable-looking Chocolate Bourbon Cake and the Peach Cobbler but surrendered to the Napoleon, two pastry pillows with layers of cream, raspberries and chocolate mousse in between. Unfortunately it looked better than it tasted. All in all, the dinner was pleasant but nothing to savor.

NAPA VALLEY WINE TRAIN
Manager: Vincent DeDomenico.
253-2111.
1275 McKinstry St., Napa.
Price: Very Expensive.
Credit Cards: AE, MC, V.
Cuisine: California.
Serving: Dinner Tues.-Sun.; Lunch Mon.- Sun.; Brunch Sat. & Sun.
Reservations: Required.
Special features: Train ride through heart of Napa Valley.

No need to wear a trench coat, hide behind dark glasses or look for mist-shrouded platforms when you ride the Napa Valley Wine Train. If you're eager for mystery, read an Agatha Christie novel; if you're in hot pursuit of the best in gourmet dining, make a reservation at Auberge du Soleil. But if you're looking for adventure and a little romance, well, by all means, step aboard.

The Wine Train is a relaxing journey through California's historic and scenic Wine Country. It travels 15 to 25 miles per hour and is a feast for the eyes as it traverses 21 miles of track from Napa to St. Helena and back again. As you dine, you glide past world-famous vineyards, wineries and, yes, several signs that protest the Wine Train's presence.

The train tracks through some unfriendly territory, all right. Many natives fear that the Wine Train could make Napa Valley a Disneyland of sorts with gawking crowds of tourists. The owners had originally hoped riders would be able to stop off at several wineries for tasting. For now, passengers are staying on board. Not a bad proposition when you consider the lush interior, the polished mahogany and brass luggage racks, the velvet swag curtains, the etched glass divider panels, the oval backed chairs and the white table linens set with bone china.

The train offers a champagne brunch, a gourmet lunch and a full course dinner. We opted for the brunch. Our meal began with a festive round of Hanns Kornell sparkling wine and a silver platter of exceptionally delicate pastries. A pianist played Chopin in the background and we toasted the rainy season that had left the mountains and hills an emerald green. An unusual Puff Pastry with Apple and Pear Waldorf Salad came next, the fruit complementing the rich pastry. We were not as enthusiastic about the Lingonberry Griddle Cakes with Applewood Smoked Bacon, however. It was mediocre with fatty bacon. A beautifully-crafted Mushroom and Ham Torta with Lyonnaise Potatoes, however, was rich, light and fluffy in texture.

After a shot of coffee we left our dining car and walked to the lounge car with its brown swivel chairs facing the windows giving superb views of the vineyards. We also stepped outside on the platform for what could be called a Wine Country photo opportunity. People had video cameras and 35mm cameras primed to capture Napa Valley on film. We can't deny that the Napa Valley Wine Train is a tourist attraction, but it's still a rich ride and one we recommend.

ROYAL OAK AT SILVERADO COUNTRY CLUB

Manager: Bassam Moussa.
257-0200.
1600 Atlas Peak Rd., Napa.
Price: Very Expensive.
Credit Cards: AE, CD, MC, V.
Cuisine: American.
Serving: D.
Reservations: Recommended.

Even in health-conscious California where people strive to be cuisine-correct, we sometimes get a hankering for a slab of beef. For thick steaks and chops, this is the place to go in Napa Valley. Swordfish steaks, salmon and lobster try to balance the menu, but the Royal Oak remains a hearty dining experience.

Napa Valley's oldest resort, Silverado's home is a venerable circa 1870 mansion built by Gen. John Miller. The Royal Oak dining room is accented with rustic wood beams, hand-carved tables and gleaming copper, and offers a view of Silverado's stout oaks and lush golf greens. The excellent service heightens the atmosphere.

The menu offers no real surprises, but then that's not why people come here. Appetizers are the standards: shrimp cocktail, fresh oysters, onion soup plus an item that's a bit of an oxymoron, crab fingers. Steak options include New York, thick and petite filet mignon and sirloins, as well as triple-cut lamb chops. Royal Oaks' special crunchy potato skins heaped with crispy onions are a specialty.

We started with another Royal Oaks specialty, Seafood on Silver. It's a massive silver bucket brimming with ice and topped with a fish market of oysters, prawns, crab claws and shrimp meat in a shell server. An impressive sight and a light and refreshing overture to what lies ahead. The kitchen's generosity continued with a hefty Caesar salad, its aromatic dressing prepared with walnut oil. The 10-oz. petite filet mignon would be a full cut at most restaurants. Seasoned with crushed peppercorns and cooked over hardwood charcoal until faintly pink inside, it was consumed greedily. The lamb chops were similarly thick and decadent. Frankly, we hardly noticed, but both entrees came with poached pear, papaya salsa and a sauté of vegetables that included red bell peppers, carrots and asparagus.

Royal Oaks' extensive wine cellar offered several infallible matches, particularly the 1986 Silver Oak Napa Valley Cabernet Sauvignon and the Duckhorn 1988 Merlot. But at $53 for the Silver Oak and $42 for the Duckhorn, be prepared to pay for the fine selection. Dinner ends with a rather mediocre but *complimentary* dessert of fresh fruit and pound cake, accompanied by a warm fondue pot of chocolate. Also included is a selection of 36 cordials that are brought to your table by cart.

Yountville

CALIFORNIA CAFE

Manager: Michael Merriman.
944-2330.
Washington Square, 6795 Washington St., Yountville.

This is a class act where you don't have to act classy. The restaurant may be part of a small chain but we appreciated its unpretentious tone, varied menu and exceptional but gentle service. Located in Yountville's smart little Washington Square shopping complex, California Cafe is a fine

Price: Expensive.
Credit Cards: AE, MC, V.
Cuisine: California
Serving: SB, L, D.
Reservations:
Recommended.
Special features: Outdoor
dining.

choice for a quick lunch while browsing or a more luxurious dinner following a day of wine tasting. Contented diners chatting away make the patio a welcoming sight. Inside, the cafe is warm with peach colors, plants and paintings. A pianist frequently performs but the evening we dined the music was intrusive, not soothing.

As we reviewed the menu, we feasted on a fresh loaf of Acme bread, a local favorite. The menu changes daily, offering a bit of everything. Trying to please the masses is not always a good sign. Can one kitchen prepare five pastas, seven seafood dishes, steaks, chicken, duck and even ribs? We didn't try the lot, of course, but we were pleasantly surprised.

A crisp-crusted Pizzetta set dinner in motion. Sliced in quarters, it included hot coppa, sun-dried tomato sauce, marinated artichoke hearts and Italian cheeses. Each bite brought a new delightful taste or texture. We followed with a mammoth Caesar salad with a zingy dressing. Our main courses were Pasta Jambalaya and Grilled Pork Tenderloin. The Pasta, fettuccine with duck, smoked shrimp and Andouille sausage, was beautifully prepared and tasty but less than adventurous in the seasoning. The pork was perfection, served with tangy whole grain mustard, wild mushroom sauce and — perhaps gratuitous — rosemary crepes.

California Cafe's wine list is worth serious consideration, with a selection of the best from Napa and Sonoma. Current wines carry the standard mark-up, but older vintages are steals. A 1985 Beaulieu Private Reserve is a bargain at $55. Wine by the glass is a sizable list, though pricey at times. Even at $8.95 a glass, however, the 1987 Opus One was too tempting for us to resist. It's not a wine you see often by the glass and besides, it includes a souvenir decanter.

For dessert, we sampled fresh strawberries in Champagne Sabayon. Lovely. We also tried a special dessert, *tiramisu*, lady fingers soaked in a variety of liquors and topped with a rich cream. Killer.

COMPADRES
Manager: Jeff Steen.
944-2406.
6539 Washington St.,
Yountville.
Price: Moderate.
Credit Cards: V, AE, DC,
MC, D.
Cuisine: Mexican.
Serving: L, D, weekend
breakfasts.
Reservations: Accepted.
Special features: Outside
patio, beautiful view.

Compadres is like an empty piñata — festive-looking from a distance but a hollow experience up close. Located amid vineyards and near the shopping mecca, Vintage 1870, it has a lovely outdoor patio and an interior of terra cotta brick, costumed with colorful paintings, piñatas and crafts. Even the varied menu promises a true fiesta.

But the glossy image lost its shine when the entrees were served and every dish was a letdown. The burrito with ground beef and covered with red and green sauce was nothing more than tasteless greasy hamburger stuffed in a damp pastry shell. The tostada, topped with a stingy portion of refried beans and sauteed chicken, was also bland. Finally, the Enchilada Del Mar, seafood wrapped in a corn tortilla, suggested a dethawed frozen dinner parading as a Mexican seafood dish. Strike three.

The wine list was tiny, but selected with Mexican food in mind, playing up gewurztraminers and rosés from wineries that make such things well. We stayed with the sangria, which was fruity and not heavy with alcohol. The beer list offered the usual Mexican options.

The service was shameful, as well, with inexperienced waiters and waitresses who couldn't seem to keep the orders straight. Our waiter was downright curt at times. If you really have the urge for Mexican cuisine, head to Rafa's in Cotati. (See Sonoma County.)

THE DINER
Manager: Barbara Kelly.
944-2626.
6476 Washington St.,
   Yountville.
Closed: Monday.
Price: Moderate.
Credit Cards: Not
   Accepted.
Cuisine: American,
   Mexican.
Serving: B, L, D.
Reservations: Only for
   parties of eight or more.

Take a detour, travel back to the '50s via the Diner and taste a Buttermilk Shake, a thick swirl dubbed liquid cheesecake. You may be tempted to use a fork.

The Diner is a good place to stop off for breakfast, lunch, a light snack or a full-blown dinner. The menu is eclectic, mostly Mexican and Mexican-inspired dishes, but it includes a full selection of burgers, sandwiches and soda fountain fare. The restaurant offers a modestly-priced wine list as well as Mexican, American and European beers.

During a quiet moment, which is rare, you might hear strains of a Bach cello suite coming from the stereo. But don't be dismayed, the Diner *is authentic*. In fact the restaurant used to be a Greyhound Bus Station & Diner in the '50s and it still has a strong, soda fountain flavor. Don't expect the glare of neon. This a homier sort of diner. Booths wind their way around the restaurant, while the counter takes the center

A real, honest-to-goodness 1950s diner, still going strong.

Chris Alderman

stage. A large collection of brightly-colored Fiestaware is displayed over the soda fountain, along with vintage gadgets and a newfangled espresso machine.

The food is as varied and fun as the decor. One very un-Mexican house specialty is the German Potato Pancakes, mildly flavored shredded potatoes seasoned with onions, garlic and herbs in a light egg batter and served with applesauce and a slice of homemade sausage. There's also the Humdinger, a quarter-pound ground chuck burger with red onions, and the Paul Bunyon, a six-ounce burger for those with a bigger appetite. We enjoyed the soup special, a spicy white bean concoction, thick and hot with the rich sweetness of onions, carrots and basil. The daily enchilada special, however, lacked verve. The breads, house-baked from organic flours and natural ingredients, are excellent, especially the walnut-raisin and the cottage dill.

The Diner, off Hwy. 29, is just a jog from Vintage 1870, a brick shopping plaza converted from the old Groezinger Winery. After you've given Vintage 1870 the once-over, head over here, slip off your shoes and order up a Buttermilk Shake. In fact, make a meal out of it. The waitress will plop the metal blender cup on the counter in front of you and it's bound to be good for another pour or two.

DOMAINE CHANDON
Manager: Daniel Shanks.
944-2892.
California Dr. at Hwy. 29,
   Yountville.
Closed: Mon. and Tues.
   dinner.
Price: Very Expensive.
Credit cards: AE, MC, V.
Cuisine: French, California.
Serving: L, D.
Reservations:
   Recommended.

If you wear Birkenstock sandals, tie-dyed shirts and live for the Grateful Dead you probably won't go for Domaine Chandon. You might not even if you wear smart suits and adore Frank Sinatra. We find ourselves somewhere in between and while we enjoyed the food here, the pretense and price left a bitter aftertaste.

Housed in a modern, curved concrete building with terrace views of the landscaped grounds, the setting is *très élégante*. An appendage of the Domaine Chandon winery, the emphasis is naturally on sparkling wine. Philippe Jeanty has been Chef de Cuisine at Domaine Chandon since 1978. Trained at the Reims Culinary Academy in the heart of Champagne, he says he features entrees compatible with champagne that combine California innovation with the great traditions of French cooking.

You can choose from a wide range of appetizers including Home Smoked Red Trout Filet, Duck and Goat Cheese Rillettes or a Pizzetta with home smoked salmon. Entrees include Spicy Lobster Risotto, Mesquite Grilled Veal Rack and the Dry-Aged Sirloin of Beef. We started our Sunday lunch with a delicious Quail au Pain accompanied by a tasty and interesting Frisée Bacon Salad. Unfortunately, our Roasted Swordfish was much too dry and tasteless. The accompanying rich caramelized onion-cider vinegar sauce, wilted brussels sprout leaves and apple smoked bacon simply couldn't revive it.

Service was slow and careless. Our waitress made little effort to put us at ease and we had to ask for water refills and for more bread. Be aware that the dinner and lunch menus are almost identical, except the dinner prices are much higher. You may prefer to simply tour the winery. Domaine Chandon, after all, is historic. Moet–Hennessy's investment in the Napa Valley in 1973 established a precedent and led to the migration of foreign sparkling wine producers to the vineyards of California.

THE FRENCH LAUNDRY
Manager: Don Schmitt.
944-2380.
6640 Washington St.,
   Yountville.
Closed: Monday and
   Tuesday.
Prix-fixe: $46.
Credit Cards: None.
Serving: D.
Reservations: Required.
Special features: Garden
   and fireplace.

It's a good thing Bar and Brothel didn't catch on, because a restaurant as romantic as the French Laundry needs a name to match. The grand stone house, built in the 1890s, was indeed a bar and brothel, B.P. (Before Prohibition). Later it became a French laundry, for 30 years catering to wineries and restaurants, keeping their beautiful tablecloths pristine. "We couldn't have called it anything else. Everybody knows it as the French Laundry," says owner Don Schmitt.

The restaurant's checkered past makes dining here quite an adventure. The food is almost incidental. Almost. Approaching the restaurant, tucked in a neighborhood of elegant homes, you feel as though you're on the way to a friend's house for dinner. Inside, a fireplace blazes with the handful of tables scattered between two floors. There is only one seating each night staggered from 7 to 8:30 p.m., so you have the table all evening. We took a decadent three hours. Schmitt encourages diners to roam around the house, wine glass in hand, perhaps even stopping in to see the chef, his wife Sally. In the summer the itch to roam can extend to a lush garden where the Schmitts grow herbs and flowers for the restaurant.

Unfortunately, the dinner wasn't able to match the spectacular setting. At $46 prix-fixe, we expected to be more impressed. Perhaps we visited on an off-night, for the food, though well-crafted, was unimaginative. The prix-fixe is a blessing for those who suffer from chronic indecisiveness. Soup, salad and entree are set, leaving guests to select an appetizer and dessert from a short list. An outstanding list of Napa wines is available at outrageously low prices, about $4 over retail. A Grgich Hills '88 Chardonnay was $26 and even the prized '86 Heitz Martha's Vineyard Cabernet was $64. Unheard of. Two wines were also available by the glass.

The appetizers were a mixed bag. Gingered Shrimp with mustard and chutney was outstanding, warm and succulent and the sauce not too sweet; the '88 St. Andrews Chardonnay was a pleasant match. Smoked Trout with red onions and horseradish cream, on the other hand, looked impressive but tasted like pickled herring. Fennel and Potato soup was rich but too subtle. Our leg of lamb entree was perhaps the biggest disappointment: perfectly cooked, pink and juicy, but impersonating roast beef. The '87 Rutherford Hill Merlot we selected to go with it was still rough around the edges, but enjoyable. Dessert ended things on a high note, however. You won't go wrong with either Strawberries in a Chocolate Meringue or Rhubarb Shortcake.

MUSTARDS GRILL
Manager: Michael Ouellet.
944-2424.
7399 Hwy. 29, Yountville.
Price: Moderate.
Credit Cards: MC, V.
Cuisine: California.
Serving: L, D.
Reservations:
    Recommended.

Highly hyped among Napa Valley's eateries, Mustards Grill actually lives up to its reputation. Opened in 1984, Mustards was the earliest player in Napa's burgeoning restaurant boom. The owners also run Tra Vigne and San Francisco's hot Fog City Diner, but Mustards was one of their first successes. Mustards' secret isn't really a secret at all — hearty bistro food prepared with style, at a moderate price and in a lively atmosphere.

The open kitchen takes center stage, dominating an interior rich with dark wood, black-and-white tile and broad open windows. The tables are rather close, but since the din becomes so loud, it almost lends an air of privacy. While our server seemed harried, he was friendly and took time to answer questions.

Many bistros will attempt too much, offering a potpourri of pasta, Mexican food, steaks and fish. Mustards' menu is varied, but it never spreads itself too thin. It's comfort food with flair. Chicken, duck, rabbit, ribs and a small selection of fresh fish are grilled over wood. There are also hamburgers, tempting side dishes like onion rings and roasted garlic, and even an *ahi* tuna sandwich.

Dark wood, black-and-white tile floors and open windows characterize Mustards Grill.

Chris Alderman

The wine list is well-suited, offering an exceptional short list of Napa and Sonoma wines at the usual mark-up. The wine by the glass selection is also first-rate.

Mustards makes a terrific potato pancake appetizer with a tropical fruit flavored dipping sauce. Its huge Caesar salad is classic and tasty. The vegetable soup we sampled was fresh from the garden with *al dente* veggies. For the main course, we tried the calf's liver, served with carmelized onions, bacon, homemade ketchup and polenta. Though we found the pairing with polenta odd, the liver was perfect. The Mongolian Pork Chop with sweet and sour cabbage and mashed potatoes was also a hit. The chop was juicy and tender and the sauce was addictive. The Joseph Phelps 1986 Vin du Mistral Syrah was a fine match for both. We ended with a highball of a dessert named Jack Daniels Cake. Rich, of course, though thankfully it carried nowhere near the kick of its namesake. We left Mustards *very* full and satisfied. Believe the hype.

PIATTI RISTORANTE
Manager: Giovanni Scala.
944-2070.
6480 Washington St.,
    Yountville.
Price: Expensive.
Credit Cards: MC, V.
Cuisine: Italian.
Serving: L, D.
Reservations:
    Recommended.

How many times have you heard this one: "If you have to choose just one place to eat out . . ."? Well, this cliché is a reality with Piatti. Considering everything — food, atmosphere, wine list, price — Piatti is hard to beat. This is one of five Piattis in California. There's another on the Sonoma Plaza, and although it has a different chef, the menu and ambience are similar. Piatti's atmosphere is electric, the hum of diners and of the open kitchen sending quick pulses throughout the airy dining room. Styled like an Italian trattoria, it is comfortable whether you're casual or dressed up. Warmed by terra cotta tiles and counters, white walls brightened by colorful *piatti* (Italian plates) and whimsical frescos of produce, Piatti is rustic and elegant at the same time.

Service was impeccable from the moment we entered. The general manager and some of the servers are Italian and they lend an authentic Mediterranean air. You can empty a glass of wine while slowly savoring the menu. Piatti has a narrow but well defined wine list, emphasizing Napa and Italian wines. Prices are on the high end; the fine 1986 Clos du Val Cabernet Sauvignon, for example, is $34. There's a short list of wines-by-the-glass and, thankfully, an excellent *Chianti* is usually included.

The menu offers the best of Tuscany: pasta, pizzas and grilled meat and fish. We began with a tangy pizza with pesto, goat cheese, tomato slices and mozzarella cheese. The crust was lighter than air and the toppings never overbearing. Next was the house-cured salmon, which came sliced and topped with watercress, red onions, capers and polenta croutons. Delightful. We opted for an unusual salad and were glad. Sliced marinated beets with slices of fresh mozzarella were served with olive oil and oregano dressing over a bed of Bibb lettuce.

Our main courses included a memorable Neapolitan specialty, *Cannelloni Concetta*, creamy pasta stuffed with a mix of minced beef, spinach, ricotta cheese and porcini mushrooms and served in a rich tomato sauce. The Black and White Spaghetti had an engrossing bite to it. It's a peppery dish heaped with mussels and clams, but be prepared to feast — it's big. The cheese-stuffed ravioli with lemon cream sauce was outrageous, but the most unusual surprise was a roasted onion stuffed with spaghetti and tossed with finely diced anchovies, garlic and chili pepper flakes. If you're not in the mood for pasta, perhaps you'll be lucky and the roasted marinated quail will be a special. It was so good we cleaned the tiny bones clean.

Piatti offers a lush range of desserts, from *gelato* and sorbets to a tongue-numbing ricotta cheese cake. One of Napa's best dining experiences.

Oakville/Rutherford

AMBROSE HEATH
Manager: Paul Nicholson.
944-0766.
7845 Hwy. 29, Oakville.
Credit Cards: AE, MC, V.
Price: Moderate.
Serving: B, L, D on summer weekends.
Special Features: Outdoor dining.

You could eat inside Ambrose Heath, but why bother? People rarely do. The patio is where it's at, where the sun greets a leisurely back yard lunch and a view of the Howell Mountains is all the entertainment you'll need. Ambrose Heath has become one of Napa Valley's favorite lunch stops, offering a small menu of creative sandwiches and colorful salads. Bicyclers with spandex shorts and helmets with rear-view mirrors lock their bikes at the back fence and take a break from the road. Once a wooden gas station with an old style carport, the restaurant is right on busy Hwy. 29, but seated on the rear patio, the highway seems a world away.

About a dozen umbrella tables and three fountains create a gentle atmosphere, a sharp contrast with the interior, done in a style we call "funky refined," with bamboo chairs, white table clothes, colorful signs and posters and a 1960s juke box. Weekend summer evenings, Ambrose fires up a barbecue in the back, grilling chicken, ribs and prawns for dinner. Aside from that, it's breakfast and lunch *only*. The lunch menu has five sandwiches and three salads, most are elaborate-sounding concoctions like a sandwich of bay shrimp with fresh guacamole, green peppercorns, cornichons, chives and spinach. Comfort food comes in the form of a wide basket of French fries.

The bay shrimp sandwich came on a small loaf of phenomenal homemade bread with sesame and poppy seeds. The shrimp retained its identity in the melange which was creamy and indulgent. The Fussili Pasta Salad looked so festive, with thick Italian sausage, marinated artichoke hearts, sweet red onions, black olives and pesto dressing. It was tasty enough but the seasoning

*Outdoor dining at Ambrose
Heath offers greenery, fountains
and a view of the Howell
Mountains.*

Chris Alderman

was restrained, so it lacked the zing to match its appearance. As for the fries
— they were typical, perhaps even a bit overcooked.

Adding to the pleasure was attentive service and a wine and beer selection
other restaurants would envy. Beers included two of our local favorites, Red
Tail Ale and Anchor Steam, as well as an eastern standard that you don't see
here much: Rolling Rock. The wine list offered an exceptional cellar of current
Napa wines, and though selection of wine by the glass was rather sparse, bottle prices were temptingly fair. And for a lunch place, Ambrose has an incredible list of older wines from California and Bordeaux. What on Ambrose
Heath's menu would go with a wine like a 1978 Robert Mondavi Reserve
Cabernet Sauvignon? A wine like that, just about anything, we guess.

AUBERGE DU SOLEIL
Manager: George Goeggel.
963-1211.
180 Rutherford Hill Rd.,
    Rutherford.
Credit Cards: MC, V.
Price: Very Expensive.
Serving: SB, L, D.
Reservations: Required.
Special Features:
    Fireplaces; outside deck.

If you want a post card view of the Rutherford
District, a tapestry woven of vineyards, make a
reservation at Auberge du Soleil. Make sure you
slip in early enough to grab a table on the outside
deck. This vista has a price, of course, but the food,
often garnished with flowers, is pleasing to both
the eye and the palate. We found just a few disappointments — but the attentive service took the
edge off that.

As we entered the restaurant a duo played classical music in the lobby, inviting and setting a tone

of casual elegance. The restaurant is a page out of *Metropolitan Home* magazine with room after room decorated in a chic Southwestern adobe style. The bar is particularly striking with a domed ceiling that gives an airy feeling and the decor of pastel wreaths and stacked fire wood hinting of country living. Inside dining is a more formal affair, but the deck is the choice spot even when the day is overcast. Outside, heaters keep customers comfortable. The view is exceptional, a panorama of rolling foothills, olive groves and terraced vineyards.

The brunch menu offers a varied and atypical selection, and is accompanied by a winning list of Napa wines. The entrees included Eggs Benedict, Steelhead Trout, roast strip of Angus and Bouillabaisse. We began with an appetizer of steamed Sonoma White Asparagus with Parma Prosciutto and Mousseline sauce. Outstanding. The rich sauce didn't overplay its hand. Warm crepes with Grand Marnier strawberry compote should have been on the dessert list. Too sweet for a beginning.

For entrees, the Steelhead Trout with fresh tarragon, olive oil and sherry vinegar was exceptional. The fish, nestled atop a bed of fresh greens, was simply marinated — not cooked, just shy of sushi, actually. A pleasant surprise and a natural companion with Auberge du Soleil's own Chardonnay, a crisp little number made by Round Hill Winery. We can never resist Eggs Benedict, but here we were let down. The toasted Brioche was too harsh in both taste and texture and detracted from the light, sweet pepper Hollandaise sauce. The herb crusted roast strip of Angus was fine, though nothing you couldn't make at home on the charcoal grill.

Desserts were inspired. Distracted by the lovely, tiny roses on the dish, we nearly let our vanilla bean ice cream melt into a milky pool beside the Rhubarb Crepes. Garnished with flowers and fresh berries, the Chocolate-Espresso Mousse was a masterpiece. An orange-pistachio sauce gave it a

Auberge du Soleil offers a Southwestern adobe motif for diners.

Tim Fish

lighter, more delicate taste. At \$35 per person plus wine, the check may cause a double-take, but that's all right. This is a place for special occasions, and besides, we drank in the view, as well.

St. Helena

THE ABBEY
Manager: John and Estella
  Pappas.
963-2706.
3020 Hwy. 29, St. Helena.
Closed: Mon. and Tues.
  dinner.
Price: Moderate.
Credit Cards: MC, V.
Cuisine: American.
Serving: L, D.
Reservations: Accepted

Senior citizens invade the Abbey at lunch by the busloads, but the haughtiest of haute cuisiners avoid it with equal passion. While we don't consider ourselves snobs, in this case we feel compelled to defy our elders. A friend described the Abbey as "a truck stop with a wine list." Snide, perhaps, but we have to agree. Our dinner was saved only by the exceptional service of our waiter.

Open for two decades, the Abbey offers some idea of what fine dining used to be like in Wine Country. A dark atmosphere, a small wine list and a surf & turf menu. The restaurant is one large open room, dimly lit by wrought iron chandeliers. While we examined the menu we nibbled on fresh crusty wheat rolls. OK, so our dinner was saved by two things — the rolls *were* delicious. The menu was the same old same old. First course was largely shrimp cocktail, Crab Louie, Caesar salad, french onion soup. Sandwiches included clubs, chicken breast and grilled sirloin, and pastas were typical renditions of linguine with bay shrimp, cannelloni and such. The grill offered no surprises, either — salmon steak, lobster tail, leg of lamb and the New York Steak.

The wine list, considering the restaurant is part of the Freemark Abbey wine complex, was astonishingly lacking. There were good selections — Robert Mondavi Pinot Noir, Mumm Brut — but too few and no vintage dates. A \$20 bottle of cabernet sauvignon was listed simply as Beaulieu Vineyard. Beaulieu makes three cabernets. Which is it? What year? This is Wine Country, after all.

We began dinner with the soup of the day, a shrimp and curry bisque. It was lukewarm and light on the shrimp and the curry. We tried both the mixed green salad and a Caesar salad, and the Caesar in particular was unexciting and tasteless. Maybe someone was running to the store for Parmesan and lemon juice. The main courses were just as uninspired, lacking visual or palatal panache. The prime rib tasted vaguely of meat and the only interesting element to the Linguine California was the cheese topping. That was indeed rich and the only thing on either plate that was remotely warm. We ended with a respectable Amaretto Mousse Cake and decided that the Abbey is best left to the buses.

BRAVA TERRACE
Manager: Fred Halpert.
963-9300.
3010 Hwy. 29, St. Helena.
Closed: Mon. in winter.
Price: Expensive.
Credit Cards: MC, V.
Cuisine: French, California.
Serving: L, D.
Reservations:
  Recommended.
Special features: Fireplace,
  patio dining.

Chef-owner Fred Halpert worked in Southern France and brings a distinct Mediterranean flair to this new restaurant. After making a name for himself as chef at San Francisco restaurants such as Restaurant 101, Halpert opened his own restaurant in the former Knickerbocker's. He's beginning to draw considerable attention with a menu that matches the robustness of country French food to California's more delicate preferences. While the food may derive from Southern France, the interior reflects the north. Styled as a French chalet, the Brava Terrace evokes an airy ski lodge with peaked ceiling, exposed wood beams and fans. The fireplace and wine bar are focal points. When weather invites, the rear terrace offers views of rolling hills and a pond.

The menu is a challenging array of fish, fowl and red meat that requires close study. Luckily, the service staff was patient and helpful and remained so throughout the meal. Leaving a 20% tip was a pleasure. Appetizers ranged from simple Napa and Sonoma greens, to Five-Spice Duck with cucumber and mushroom salad, to Halpert's own cured salmon. We chose a delightful Provençal salad with tangy herb dressing and Sonoma goat cheese. A cold tomato-basil soup offered the fresh essence of a spring garden. Even more divine was the risotto, creamy Arborio rice tossed with caramelized onions, mushrooms, basil, parmesan and Calabrese sausage. If the appetizers sound like tempting main courses, the kitchen will prepare larger portions with no fuss.

The entrees were equally satisfying. Grilled over an outdoor fire, the Veal T-Bone was moist and tender, with a light reduction sauce and grilled potato wedges and onions. The Delta Sturgeon came in two thin, wide filets and was grilled with eggplant slivers and tomatoes. The ripe, rich flavor of the tomato was a winning contrast to the smoky fish. A 1988 Byron Reserve Chardonnay was an exceptional match to the sturgeon. Brava Terrace's wine list, in fact, offered a library of fine combinations, as well as one of the valley's better by-the-glass selections and reasonable prices. The excellent Storybook Mountain 1987 Zinfandel, a fine choice with the veal, was a tempting $20.

We went to extremes of decadence with dessert. The Chocolate Terrine laced with walnuts and English cream was so addictive the DEA should be called in. It's rich, yet not overburdening. The fresh raspberry sorbet may be the best we've tasted. The creamy essence of the raspberry was intense.

**SPRING STREET
RESTAURANT**
Manager: Jim Zimmer.
963-5578.
1245 Spring St., St. Helena.
Price: Moderate.
Credit Cards: MC, V.
Cuisine: California.
Serving: SB, B, L, D.
Reservations:
  Recommended.
Special features: Garden
  and fireplace.

As you approach this pleasant stucco bungalow, you notice the carefully tended garden where pansies and parsley live side-by-side and you know you're in for a treat. Spring Street is a homey restaurant framed by two stately evergreen trees, trim hedges and an ivy fence. You feel as though you are simply stopping in at a neighbor's for tea, until you read the menu. Then you'll see that you're in for a sophisticated repast.

The lunch and dinner menus are large and varied, offering numerous vegetarian choices as well as hearty meat dishes. And there are always desserts to choose from, including a chocoholic's dream, an irresistible concoction that falls somewhere between a brownie and fudge. There is also a children's menu and specially-priced smaller portions for seniors. The wine list is adequate but nothing to boast about, even though it does offer some good Napa reds and whites by the glass. Quality beers are also available.

Guests can eat indoors year-round in a single grand dining room with quilted tablecloths and fresh cut flowers. In warmer months tables are set outdoors around the oval fish pond and fountain in the arbor garden. The restaurant is crowded with regulars, especially at lunch time and on weekend evenings, and with tourists who often learn about the place through local wineries.

Although a family-style restaurant in terms of its varied clientele and relaxed atmosphere, Spring Street has a remarkably innovative menu of fresh, seasonal dishes. We discovered a wonderful and surprisingly peppery cream of cauliflower soup. The Grilled Polenta Platter proved to be an inspired combination of polenta, pepper jack cheese, marinated tomatoes and basil. The dish came with a crunchy tabouleh salad and a slice of fresh pineapple. Even the old standby, tuna salad sandwich, has a novel twist here. Billed as the "Crunchy Tuna Sandwich," the filling turned out to be a mild almond-studded tuna curry with lots of homemade apricot chutney.

Formerly the home of retired opera singer Walter Martin and wife Dionisia, Spring Street is a lovely retreat. We recommend it highly, even if you can only stop in early and take advantage of the espresso bar from 7 a.m. to 11 a.m. The house-baked muffins and other baked goods are delightful and the fresh-ground coffees are bound to get you kicking.

**THE STARMONT AT
MEADOWOOD**
Manager: Stephen
Goldberg.
963-3646.
900 Meadowood Ln., St.
Helena.
Price: Very Expensive.
Credit Cards: AE, DC, MC,
V.
Cuisine: California &
Country French.
Serving: SB, L, D.
Reservations:
Recommended.
Special features: Resort
setting; hiking trails;
croquet available for
restaurant guests.

The Starmont at Meadowood, at the foot of Howell Mountain in St. Helena, is nestled in a bucolic, wooded setting. The restaurant is a drawing card for the Meadowood Resort Hotel, but may be somewhat overrated. The beautifully-crafted entrees simply didn't live up to their promise.

While considering the menu, our expectations naturally were raised after we were served a tasty tapenade, rich with red peppers, capers, black olives and anchovies. The wine list also led us to believe we were in for a treat. The Napa Valley Vintners Association is based at Meadowood and its prestigious Napa Valley Wine Auction is a regular Meadowood event.

An appetizer of Wild Mushroom Soup was rich and woodsy in flavor but lacked sparkle. By contrast, the Sauteed Dungeness Crab Cake proved to outshine our entrees. The large cake was a succulent, delicately seasoned crab in a pool of Lobster Pesto Sauce. It was delicious, although we couldn't detect the lobster. The entrees, however, were a disappointment to put it mildly. The special, Roasted Canterbury Venison on Savoy Cabbage with Huckleberry Coulis, was surprisingly lackluster. And the *Paella Catalan* (Chef Henri Delcros is from Perpignan), was rich with lobster meat, calamari, mussels, monkfish, and chicken but it was too mildly spiced. The mild lamb sausage was a mistake — a spicier chorizo type would have improved its flavor.

You will undoubtedly have room for dessert and we did enjoy the Maple, Pear and Pecan Souffle served with a pitcher of Brandied Creme Anglais. Rich chocolate and lemon petit fours were brought to the table, gratis, with coffee. As we sipped our coffee we surveyed the restaurant's interior, a curious amalgam. Situated in the large clubhouse and conference center, the Starmont's exposed beams and high ceilings give it a rustic, barnlike feel. At the same time the dining room emanates a formal feeling with its linen-covered tables and formal service.

You may want to digest your meal while exploring the lush grounds, or take off on one of the hiking trails or play a little croquet on the impeccably manicured lawns which the restaurant overlooks.

TERRA

Manager: Lissa Doumani.
963-8931.
1345 Railroad Ave., St.
  Helena.
Closed: Tuesday.
Price: Expensive.
Credit Cards: V.
Cuisine: California,
  Japanese.
Serving: D.
Reservations: Required.
Special features: Located in
  the historic Hatchery
  Building.

At Terra, with its stone walls and steep racks of wine, we felt as though we were dining in a wine cellar. Oh, it's not particularly cool and dark, but we could tell the wine is revered as much as the food by the way the racks are displayed in one of the dining rooms.

The wine list is quite good, and it's impossible to resist ordering a bottle, especially since there is plenty to choose from in the $15 to $30 range. Wine by the glass, however, is sorely limited. As for the menu, it's one of the most varied in all of Wine Country: nine appetizers and entrees and six desserts. The range is to be expected from Terra's chef, Hiroyoshi Sone, who has an impressive resumé. Sone was head chef at Wolfgang Puck's Spago in Los Angeles. At Spago, Sone met his wife, Lissa Doumani, then a pastry chef. Sone and Doumani, whose family owns Stag's Leap Wine Cellars, left Spago in 1988 and found their niche in Wine Country. Terra is housed in St. Helena's historic Hatchery Building, vintage 1884. The high ceilings, wooden beams and arched windows create an intimate setting and our service didn't detract from the intimacy. It was attentive without being intrusive, and our waiter was knowledgeable.

A heaping bowl of steamed mussels began our meal, a light white wine sauce, subtly flavored shallots, attractively played up the black shells. It proved the beginning of an outstanding meal. The grilled filet of salmon with Thai red curry and Basmati rice was lightly spiced — exceptional. The salmon sat on a bed of rice with exotic greens, a smattering of peanuts on top. The entree had an interesting texture, lightly crunchy. We made an unusual match with the salmon, a 1987 Buehler Zinfandel. Red wine with salmon? Why not? The lightly peppery zin was a perfect bridge between the grilled fish and Thai spice. We also liked the 12-ounce New York steak aged with *ratatoi*, roasted garlic and fried potatoes, a hearty meal spiced to perfection. The prize, however, was dessert: a Bartlett Pear Tart with ginger and cream. The fruit was sliced and fanned amid a fluffy crisp pastry that simply served to draw attention to the distinctive flavor of the pear. Theatrical. Delicious.

TRA VIGNE

Manager: Kevin Cronin.
963-4444.
1050 Charter Oak Ave., St.
  Helena.
Price: Expensive.
Credit Cards: MC, V.
Cuisine: Italian, California.
Serving: L, D.
Reservations: Required.

Order a bottle of 1987 Valpolicella Classico, sit back in the vine-covered brick courtyard and pretend you're at a private party in a romantic Italian villa. You might call Tra Vigne the "Little Italy" of Napa Valley.

Housed in a landmark stone building, Tra Vigne has a neo-gothic feel, with gilt and modern accents softened with terra cotta and earth tones. The chairs and tables are blond wood and a bar runs along one wall. The interior is subtle but stunning, while the brick courtyard provides a tranquil option for a more intimate evening. Tra Vigne, which roughly means "among the vines," draws a steady pool of regulars as well as tourists, the true test of a fine restaurant. The relatively short wine list is modest in price but manages to include unusual choices, especially among the Italian wines. As for the service, no complaints. Our waiter was extremely attentive and well-versed with the menu.

Food, here, is generally cooked with a fiery passion. Chef Michael Chiarello has described the cuisine as "American food prepared with the heart, hands and eyes of an Italian." Perhaps part of Chiarello's success is the freshness. Everything is made at the restaurant, including prosciutto, breads, pastas, cheeses and gelato.

Tra Vigne is, literally, among the vines.

Tim Fish

The oven-roasted polenta appetizer, bathed in a balsamic vinegar sauce, was unexpected and surprisingly good. We also sampled an interesting salad, a montage of mangos wrapped in slices of pancetta on a bed of mixed greens and candied walnuts, a wild mix of sweet and savory. A main dish, tomato stew served at room temperature, was good but less appealing than the salad. And the *Ravioli di Magro al Burro*, pasta filled with homemade ricotta, spinach and red chard was bland. The *Petto di Pollo aI Ferri*, grilled lemon marinated chicken breast with mascarpone potatoes, was tangy and delicious.

Dessert — in a word — was superb. We shared an order of the warm, creamy and rich *Budino di Cioccolata e Castagne*, chocolate pudding and chestnuts with a tart cherry sauce, only to fight over the last few bites. Some dishes at Tra Vigne linger on the palate while others are mediocre, but the odds are truly in the guests' favor.

TRILOGY
Managers: Tim Mosher,
Don Pariseau.
963-5507.
1234 Main St., St. Helena.
Closed: Sunday, Monday.
Credit Cards: MC, V.
Price: Expensive.
Cuisine: California, French.
Serving: L, D.
Reservations: Required.
Special features: Courtyard
patio.

Strip away the glitz, pare away the avant-garde entrees and the chic crowd and you're left with Trilogy. This storefront restaurant in St. Helena is understated, pleasantly unpretentious and, most importantly, intimate. The dining room has eight to 10 tables. It's the basics, the food and wine list, that are Trilogy's strongest drawing cards.

Chef-owner Diane Pariseau can lavish attention on her entrees and make you feel as though you are attending a fine dinner party at her home. Pariseau is a culinary arts graduate of Johnson & Wales University in Providence, Rhode Island. She apprenticed in classic French cooking, although she favors the simple and natural to heavy foods deluged with cream and butter. Unfortunately her predisposition to simple and natural causes her entrees to lack zeal. As for the wine list, it is exhaustive. Among the best in all of Wine Country, it earned an award from *The Wine Spectator* after the restaurant was in business for only two years — it's that extraordinary. The selection of wines by the glass, however, is simply adequate.

The service was exceptional, aware but not bothersome. Our waiter served the Mumm Blanc de Noirs as if we were royalty. He also brought chilled glasses to the table when he opened a bottle of Evian spring water. A nice touch.

The menu showed quite a range and included appetizers such as grilled eggplant, Belgian Endive and red bell peppers as well as smoked trout and Arugla with Horseradish sauce. We finally settled on the steamed mussels with shallots, white wine, lemon thyme and cream. The mussels in the creamy broth were garnished with tomato and sprigs of green, lovely but the mussels were still a little too subtle. We felt the same way about our entrees. The sauce that accompanied the sauteed breast of Long Island Duck with star anise and dried apricots was too light. The steamed salmon with lemongrass, ginger, garlic and sesame oil was too delicate. The taste of the duck, however, had more vitality when paired with a glass of 1988 Morgan Pinot Noir. Both entrees were moist and tender and exquisitely presented with wonderfully prepared carrots and sauteed zucchini.

While the appetizers and entrees lacked vigor, the desserts were certainly spirited. We ordered Chocolate Decadence, a chocolate wedge in a pool of raspberry sauce with swirls of cream shaped hearts. Wonderful and too rich to finish. The Cherry Tart in a chocolate crust with cream on top had an interesting candylike texture. And just when we thought we had reached the limit, the check came with two tiny chocolate truffles on top.

As we lingered over coffee, we realized the large storefront window looking out onto St. Helena's Main Street gave the restaurant a special charm. Trilogy is elegant with its white linens, lilac flowers and paintings by local artists framed in gold leaf. A fine place to share a bottle of wine.

Calistoga

ALL SEASONS CAFE
Managers: Alex and Mark
Dirkheising and Gayle
Keller.
942-9111.
1400 Lincoln Ave.,
Calistoga.
Closed: Tues. and Wed.
dinner.
Price: Moderate.
Credit Cards: MC, V.
Cuisine: French, California.
Serving: L, D.
Reservations: Accepted.

All Seasons Cafe reminds us of a Greenwich Village bistro. It has an imaginative menu matched with a modest but urbane setting. Ceiling fans spin slowly over stained glass lights, the floor is black and white tile, and through two walls of windows you can watch downtown Calistoga go by. Behind the smooth wooden bar are racks of empty wine glasses, another mood-setter. The wine selection is fabulous. All Seasons, in fact, has a wine shop in back of the restaurant stacked with new and old vintages and all available at your table. It's a kick to actually see the bottle before you order it.

All Seasons' menu is part wine steward as well, offering general matches with each course. Sauvignon blanc, zinfandel and Rhone wines, for example, are suggested with pastas and pizzas. Obvious to wine buffs, but handy for novices. Starters include a plate of warm brie and roasted garlic, as well as a local favorite of chilled Dungeness Crab, the best of which is on par with lobster. Entrees range from simple pizzas to Black Pepper Fettuccine with Braised Rabbit and grilled lamb rib chops.

We selected the soup of the day, a cream of artichoke, as well as a calzone stuffed with smoked Andouille sausage, mushrooms and Provolone cheese. While waiting, we first nibbled then devoured a warm bread made with smoked Gouda cheese and sun-dried tomatoes. We took a few minutes to browse the darkened and cool wine shop. Inside were old treasures from Sterling Vineyards and Bordeaux, which could be taken back to the table for a price just above retail. A steal. New vintages like the 1987 Stag's Leap SLD Cabernet Sauvignon, of course, carried a higher mark-up, but remained fair.

The soup arrived and was thick, rich and subtle. The aftertaste was luscious, and seemed to evolve with each sip. The calzone arrived with our Christopher Creek 1987 Syrah, and it was such a pleasant pairing that we rationed a sip with every bite. The calzone was larger than we expected, its crust lightly golden and hard. Inside, the sausage had a considerable fire to it and the mushrooms retained their fresh snap. It was infinitely agreeable, though we'll admit we had hoped for something more inventive.

Service at All Seasons Cafe was professional and warm. After our meal, we lingered and chatted an hour over another coffee and glass of wine.

BOSKO'S RISTORANTE
Manager: John Seeger.
942-9088.
1403 Lincoln Ave.,
　Calistoga.
Price: Moderate.
Credit Cards: None.
Cuisine: Italian.
Serving: L, D.
Reservations: Not accepted.

If you've soaked all day in a Calistoga mineral bath and feel as warm and droopy as a strand of well-done fettuccine, then Bosko's is the place for dinner. The food is, what else, Italian, hearty and good. With sawdust on the floor, the atmosphere is friendly and casual, and, better still, prices are reasonable. All this adds up to one thing: busy, especially on weekends and in the summer.

Lunch and dinner menus are the same, with a half-order pasta special available for lunch during the week. That's good because portions are generous. Offered is the usual Italian fare. Pastas are made on the premises — the pasta machine is in full view — and range from the basic spaghetti and meatballs to the enjoyable *Piacere*, which is a linguine dish with shrimp and clams in a spicy white wine sauce. There are also sandwiches, Italian Sausage, Capocollo and the like. The *Fettuccine Veneto*, with broccoli, zucchini and mushrooms in a white cream sauce, was outrageously rich, particularly for a vegetarian dish. We repressed our guilt and indulged.

Bosko's Ristorante has sawdust on the floor and a casual, friendly atmosphere.

Chris Alderman

The wine list is adequate and offers a number of good Napa zinfandels. There's also quality beer selection. Service was cordial but not particularly attentive. We had to flag down our waiter to order coffee and dessert. It was worth it, though. A little number called Chocolate Heaven earned its name, and the White Chocolate Cheesecake was a close second. There's also gelato, biscotti and cheesecake. After a night at Bosko's, believe me, you'll have a few more pounds to soak off in the hot tub the next day.

CAFE PACIFICO
Manager: John Seeger.
942-4400.
1237 Lincoln Ave.,
    Calistoga CA.
Price: Moderate.
Credit Cards: MC, V.
Cuisine: Mexican.
Serving: SB, L, D.
Reservations: Accepted.

Margaritas here are knock-outs. Too bad the food doesn't match. It's hearty Mexican fare, well-presented but without authenticity or imagination. Sometimes, frankly, that's enough for us, especially if the margaritas are memorable. A large dining room with adjacent bar, Cafe Pacifico's decor — like its menu — is pleasant but utilitarian South-of-the-Border. On the menu are the usual *quesadillas, burritos* and *tacos*. We opened with an appealing *Ceviche*, fresh calamari and white fish marinated with lime, cilantro and tomato — spicy and warm. But the *Carnitas Empanadas,* a corn tortilla turnover filled with beef, proved too chewy for us to conquer. For entrees, the Grilled Fish Taco had considerable charm, a build-your-own construction of red snapper filets on a bed of pickled cabbage, with three salsas and black beans. The *Pollo Poblano* was satisfactory, a grilled boneless chicken breast served on a bed of corn and sliced red bell peppers. Something you could easily — too easily — make at home.

Cafe Pacifico has a small wine list of local favorites at fair prices, as well as the best Mexican beers, including Tecate and Bohemia. As for margaritas, well, Cafe Pacifico serves up more versions that you can imagine, all tart and tasty and worth a try.

RESTAURANTS — SONOMA COUNTY

Sonoma Valley

THE FEED STORE
Managers: Drake and
  Madeline Dierkhising.
938-2122.
509 First St. West, Sonoma.
Price: Moderate.
Credit Cards: MC, V.
Cuisine: Eclectic.
Serving: SB, L, D.
Reservations: Accepted for
  groups.
Special features: Small
  outdoor dining area;
  bakery.

After a hard stint at winery-hopping, deciding where to eat can be a chore. "Mexican?" "Hmmm, dunno." "This place seems nice." "No, looks too expensive." That's when a place like the Feed Store Cafe & Bakery comes in handy. It serves a bit of this, a little of that, all of it tasty but not fancy or extraordinary.

The name comes from its location, a circa 1921 feed store. A clothing and antique store share the space. Like the menu, the decor is a little this, a little that: exposed pipes give the ceiling that industrial look, a "Don't Tread On Me" flag and other funky items hang on the walls, pastel colors and greenery soften the edge. One of the Feed Store's biggest draws is its bakery counter. Peer through the case and you'll see delectables like pumpkin cheesecake and zinfandel brownies. But we're not carrying out, not today anyway, so we'll save those for later.

The menu begins with *tapas*, a potpourri of appetizers that ranges from french fries and beer-battered onion rings to *pinchitos*, a charbroiled seasoned beef dish of Moorish–Spanish origin. We tried the *quesadilla*, flour tortillas grilled with cheese and topped with salsa, sour cream and *guacamole*. It's a dish that can be too greasy, but these were delicious. For entrees, the Feed Store offers just about everything, which should send up a warning signal. How can a restaurant, particularly a small one, offer pizzas, pasta, hamburgers, sandwiches, salads, steak and even Blackened Red Snapper and do it all well? They can't. The grilled Chicken *Piccata* had some appeal, but the accompanying rice was as bland as gravel. The Fresh Spinach Cheese Ravioli was an improvement, with light pasta dough and a tomato sauce that offered a bit of a kick. The Feed Store has a tiny but well-considered list of Sonoma Valley wines, all offered by the bottle and glass. Prices are super, with a glass of Gloria Ferrer Brut only $4. More impressive is the selection of imported and specialty beers, such as Sierra Nevada Ale and the wonderful Anderson Valley Oatmeal Stout.

For dessert, the Chocolate Decadence Cake should require a prayer. A chocolate cake with raspberry filling and a rich chocolate icing, 50 calories per forkful. Dessert, in many ways, was the highlight of the meal. The bakery case displays its temptations right by the door. It should be against the law.

THE GRILLE AT SONOMA MISSION INN

Manager: Curt Bradford.
938-9000.
18140 Sonoma Hwy., Boyes Hot Springs.
Price: Very Expensive.
Credit Cards: AE, CB, DC, MC, V.
Cuisine: California.
Serving: SB, L, D.
Reservations: Recommended.
Special Features: Outdoor dining; spa menu of lighter dishes; prix-fixe menu with recommended wines by the glass.

Sonoma Mission Inn is among Wine Country's most gracious resorts, drawing guests from around the country with its luxurious rooms, full spa and easy proximity to Sonoma Valley wineries. The Grille is a key ingredient. Both the atmosphere and chef Michael Flynn's menu are elegant yet not the least stuffy. The Grille is one of Sonoma County's most expensive restaurants. Is it worth it? Yes, though Flynn lacks the panache of other Wine Country chefs, his food is winning.

The calming peach tones of its Spanish-California decor makes The Grille a tranquil dining spot, enhanced by the sound of live piano music from the lobby and a view of the sunset through the french doors and stained glass windows. The Grille also has a superb wine list, mostly from California, and offers the best in each category and price range. Considering the breadth of the Grille's cellar, however, the selection of wines by the glass could be much improved.

The menu is tightly selected, beginning with a half dozen first courses, ranging from sweet white corn chowder to fresh oysters to Dungeness crab tortellini. We began with the tortellini. The pasta was wafer thin but the crab was undistinguished and the thyme sauce was rather bland despite the lovely texture added by wild mushrooms and baby leeks. Our spirits were buoyed however by the wonderful 1988 Kenwood Sauvignon Blanc we selected to go with it. Salads were a distinct improvement, particularly the unusual Caesar salad of crisp romaine hearts. Stacked like sculpture, the lettuce was glazed with a light dressing — hinting garlic and Parmesan — and garnished with fresh croutons and bite-sized sheets of mozzarella cheese.

Entrees included four fish selections and one nod each to duck, veal, lamb, pork, chicken, pasta and steak. The fillet of Bodega Bay sturgeon poached with vegetables in parchment paper was delicate and delicious. Two thick grilled lamb chops offered the other extreme, hearty, lightly spiced with orange and mint, and cooked to a perfect pink. A Zinfandel would have been the right choice with the lamb, but 1988 Olivet Lane Pinot Noir did in a pinch. Sauteed vegetables — carrots, green beans, broccoli — made for an adequate side dish.

Desserts were sufficiently lush, particularly considering the Grille's convenient spa setting where you can sweat it off later. Lighter selections included fresh California berries, but we gave in to our weakness and chose the Alpine Chocolate Almond Crunch Cake. The towering wedge was daunting, but slicing through the hard white icing one discovers a layer cake surprisingly light and delicious.

LA CASA
Manager: Melinda Kelley.
938-1866.
121 E. Spain St., Sonoma.
Price: Moderate.
Credit Cards: AE, CB, DC,
    MC, V.
Cuisine: Mexican.
Serving: L, D.
Reservations:
    Recommended.
Special features: Patio
    dining.

The crowds at La Casa might give you the wrong idea. Eat there and you might think we Northern Californians don't know our Mexican food. We do. We simply can't explain why La Casa is so popular. It's not that the food is bad. It's capable but hardly worth the fuss. Location is probably key. Just off Sonoma Plaza, La Casa is across from the Sonoma Mission, a tourist mecca. It looks inviting from the street and the interior offers a touch of Mexico, sombreros and such, without being obnoxious about it. The chunky salsa tastes fresh. Service is accommodating.

But during a recent visit, disappointment arrived quickly. A margarita, billed as "a perfect blend of tequila, Triple Sec and lime juice" tasted like diluted Kool-Aid. The sangria was worse, a blend of club soda and Hawaiian Punch. We switched to Pacifico beer and ordered food. La Casa's menu offers the usual array of enchiladas, tacos and burritos, either a la carte or with beans, rice and cabbage salad. We decided to play it safe and try a beef *chimichanga* and Dave's Special burrito. Evidently Dave's idea of "special" is different from ours. Wading in a pool of red sauce, the beef, cheese and bean burrito was lathered with sour cream. It was agreeable enough but the tastes were lost in the soup. The shell of the *chimichanga*, the menu promised, was "paper thin" but ours was as dense as pie crust. Too bad, because the shredded beef inside was spiced pleasantly with diced red chiles.

Two good points. La Casa's wine list is small but complements the menu and offers the best Sonoma Valley producers such as Kenwood and Gundlach–Bundschu. Likewise modest but congenial is La Casa's patio, which opens into one of Sonoma's lively shopping courtyards.

Santa Rosa

JOHN ASH & CO.
Manager: John P. Duffy.
527-7687.
4330 Barnes Rd., Santa
    Rosa.
Closed: Mon.
Price: Very Expensive.
Credit Cards: AE, MC, V.
Cuisine: California.

Before John Ash pioneered the notion that Northern California had a "cuisine," Wine Country was largely burger joints and Foster Freezes. Ash, who calls himself a refugee from the corporate world, opened his restaurant in 1980. Recognition didn't take long to follow. He has been deemed one of the 25 hot new chefs in America by *Food & Wine* magazine, and in January of 1991, the restaurant was named one of the top 50

Serving: L, D.
Reservations:
  Recommended.
Special features: Patio
  dining; vineyard views.

in America by the influential Conde Nast *Traveler* magazine. John Ash & Co. is singled out in Wine Country for its creativity in developing dishes and displaying them as if on canvas. The menu is a gallery, art for the palate.

Today Ash has little to do with the daily operation of the restaurant. In 1990 he was hired by Fetzer Winery to be its culinary director. But the restaurant's California cuisine remains exceptional with his protegé, Jeff Madura, at the helm. Madura appears to share Ash's philosophy about food: It is a fine art. Madura strives to make each entree a masterpiece by tending to taste, texture, color and design.

The Grilled Radicchio provided an incredible array of tastes and textures — Italian bacon, goat cheese, mustard sauce and beautiful greens. We hated to take the last bite. It matched well with Ash's own Sauvignon blanc, made by Kenwood Vineyards from vines on the restaurant's property. Ash's wine list, one of the best in Napa and Sonoma, offers two thick books, one of recent wines, another of reserves. The by-the-glass selection was narrow but intriguing — how often do you see Duckhorn Merlot?

For entrees, we let our eyes feast first on sauteed Maine sea scallops in a pool of coconut milk sauce. It looked like a fanciful winter landscape. The scallops lay atop tart apples, a delicate and successful pairing of two contrasting tastes. The loin of venison with a blackberry reduction sauce and wild mushrooms was stunning to look at, but it didn't play as well. The sauce detracted from venison's distinct taste and the result was disappointingly bland. Dessert sounded simple enough, Apple Jack Tart with vanilla ice cream, but there was far more to it than that. The apples were warmed in a butter crisp and cooled off with a dollop of ice cream, and the presentation was so lovely our fork hesitated, but only for a moment.

French windows look out on gently rolling vineyards at John Ash & Co.

Chris Alderman

Ash has moved his restaurant from its storefront location in Montgomery Village to its present bucolic site next to Vintners Inn and it was a good move. You can spy gently rolling vineyards through the french windows or from the terrace. The restaurant's Southwest-inspired decor is stunning. But then the food, of course, is what is most striking.

CAFFE PORTOFINO
Manager: Victor Belmonte.
523-1171.
535 Fourth St., Santa Rosa.
Closed: Sun.
Price: Expensive.
Credit Cards: AE, MC, V.
Cuisine: California Italian.
Serving: L, D.
Reservations:
  Recommended.
Special features: European-
  style sidewalk cafe
  tables.

Caffe Portofino is one of the busiest night spots in downtown Santa Rosa and deservedly so. It blends the best of California and Italian cuisine with the allure of a European-styled night club. The rugged red brick building, dating from 1907, has a handsome oak interior with a bar in front and mirrors that give the narrow restaurant the illusion of space. The tables are covered in tidy white linen and a half a dozen are available on the restaurant's front patio for those who want to "do lunch" alfresco.

The menu is extensive, a list of 30 entrees, including meat, fish, and poultry. It also includes about 13 pasta dishes — from a simple pasta with pesto sauce to adventurous fettuccinis. As for antipasto and salads, take your pick from the 17 choices. The restaurant relies on fresh vegetables, delicate sauces and lots of shellfish. Everything is beautifully prepared and presented in the California nouvelle cuisine style. The wine list is as extensive as the menu. It won the 1990 Award of Excellence from *Wine Spectator* magazine, full

A corner of the oak interior of Caffe Portofino.

Chris Alderman

to the brim with California wines coupled with a limited stock of Italian wines priced from moderate to expensive.

We snacked on french bread and olive oil while we waited for our appetizer. Antipasto Portofino was a generous and tasty plate of smoked salmon and marinated calamari presented on leaves of red cabbage with rounds of cucumber, radish and tomato with a mustard-caper dipping sauce. The house salad was also good although nothing out of the ordinary. The Fettuccini Portofino, however, small bites of pork tenderloin and mushrooms in a garlic sauce on a pasta bed, deserved a standing ovation. And the Mahi Mahi di Capri was extraordinary. The fresh fish filet was pan roasted with white wine and garlic and served on top of baked Roma tomatoes and a dollop of rosemary cream sauce. It was especially good with a glass of Matanzas Creek 1988 Chardonnay.

We couldn't bring ourselves to call for the check until we tasted *tiramisu*, rum-soaked lady fingers layered with Mascarpone, a soft Italian cheese. The dessert lacked the authenticity of lady fingers more patiently saturated with rum, but we still somehow managed to finish it. The service was good but it fell short of great because it was apparent how hard the servers were working to cover their territory. We had the feeling they were all about to break into a jog. Of course you can hardly blame them, the influx of traffic never seems to wane. Caffe Portofino is a Grand Central Station of sorts, especially on a Saturday night.

CALIFORNIA THAI
Managers: Justin and
   Pachara Hanley.
573-1441.
522 Seventh St., Santa Rosa.
Price: Moderate.
Credit Cards: MC, V.
Cuisine: Thai, California.
Serving: L, D.
Reservations: Accepted.

As the name implies, this restaurant, open since 1990, serves Thai food with a touch of California cuisine. Or perhaps it's California with a touch of Thai. Either way it makes for a great combination: healthy, fresh, spicy. The restaurant's decor reflects the menu, a few Thai accents and the subtle warmth typical of restaurants serving California cuisine. The menu is typically Thai in its vastness, offering a dozen appetizers plus soups and salads. There are some 20 entrees, with a large selection of seafood and chicken dishes, and a handful of red meats. We especially appreciated the way the menu explained each dish in detail.

We opened the proceedings with an otherworldly chicken soup called *Thom kha gai*, a sublime mix of moist chunks of chicken, coconut milk, lemongrass, *ma-grood* leaves and lime juice. It had a soothing texture and light fire. The green salad with Thai basil, mint and garlic soy sauce was refreshing but a bit heavy on the cilantro for our tastes. For entrees, a special Prawn *Satay* was also exceptional, large grilled prawns spiced moderately and served with al dente asparagus. Equally good was the Beef *Satay*, strips of beef marinated in spicy coconut milk then grilled. Lathered with the special Thai peanut sauce, it was irresistible.

California Thai has a competent wine list, some 14 Napa and Sonoma wines at fair prices. We prefer the silky Thai lager Singha; it seems to have a special knack of soothing the food's heat. We ended with a mainstay: fried ice cream, a delightfully tangy tropical fruit ice cream in a hot, crisp pastry. Despite a busy night, service throughout our meal was efficient though gregarious. As we finished, owner-chef Pachara Hanley was milling among the tables talking to customers. Always a nice touch. California and Thai make a fine marriage.

THE CHINA ROOM
Managers: Peter and
  Joanne Hsian.
539-5570.
500 Mission Blvd., Santa
  Rosa.
Price: Moderate.
Credit Cards: AE, DC, MC,
  V.
Cuisine: Cantonese,
  Hunan, and Szechwan.
Serving: L, D.
Reservations: Accepted.

Sonoma County has more Chinese restaurants than stoplights. Everyone seems to have a favorite, but The China Room would probably top the list of most aficionados. The restaurant is tucked away in a shopping mall, but don't let the suburban surroundings discourage you. Inside you'll find a refined atmosphere. No red-tasseled lamps or calendar placemats. The owners choose a classic decor with art deco accents over gaudy Chinese trinkets. Comfortable, black-lacquered chairs and white table linens fill the dining room.

The best part of this restaurant hideaway is the fresh food, especially the seafood, prepared with great care, no heavy handed sauces. The China Room steers clear of the all-too-common bulk stir-fry method of cooking. The menu includes both the typical, *Mu Shu Pork* and Mongolian Beef, as well as the atypical, Walnut Pineapple Prawns and Mariner's Love Nest. A vegetarian would fare well at The China Room with 10 meatless dishes to choose from.

We began with the seafood vegetable soup and it was a knockout, with a generous serving of prawns, scallops and whitefish and just a hint of smokiness from small bits of oyster. The green onion and seaweed were added for flavor, not as filler. A foil-wrapped chicken dish was a disappointment, however: dry and overcooked with a weak flavor. The South Sea Scallops were more appealing, although a bit soggy. They were lightly breaded and decidedly fresh atop a bed of jade green sweet peas, mushrooms and cashews. The combination of cashews and peas gave this entree its flavor and flair. A generous heap of plump, crisp mushrooms was a pleasing accompaniment. Delicious. The Seafood Delight Iron Hot Plate was brimming with fresh prawns and scallops but unfortunately the chef could have been more bold with the spices. The entree arrived sizzling and the broccoli and carrots were a nice addition, the carrots sweet, crisp and sculpted into interesting shapes.

The China Room has a modest, reasonably priced wine list, and it includes some interesting selections such as Kikkoman Plum Wine. The restaurant also offers Sho Chiku Bai Sake and Chinese beers for those who crave authenticity. The China Room is a great place to relax and revive with lots of greens after a harried day. There is a limited range of desserts, though the bill comes with the proverbial fortune cookies.

Chris Alderman

A romantic restaurant, tucked away in Santa Rosa's historic Railroad Square.

LA GARE
Managers: Jacquelini
    Beazeley and Roger
    Praplan.
528-4355.
208 Wilson St., Santa Rosa.
Closed: Mon.
Price: Moderate.
Credit Cards: AE, DC, MC,
    V.
Cuisine: French.
Serving: D.
Reservations:
    Recommended.

A traditional French restaurant as romantic and genteel as the dining car on the Orient Express, La Gare ("the railway station") is an out-of-the-way restaurant tucked, appropriately enough, along Santa Rosa's historic Railroad Square. If you yearn for adventure, La Gare may be too conservative, but if it's classic French cuisine you're after, then you'll have made a tasteful choice.

The menu includes *Chateaubriand*, veal, sweetbreads and frog legs, as well as the La Gare specialty, fresh filet of salmon served in a butter, white wine, shallots, parsley, lemon sauce. The wine list is *incroyable*, amazingly diverse, albeit heavy on California wines. The list includes moderately-priced bottles, as well as more expensive older vintages. For instance, you can get away with $12 for Krug Chenin Blanc but be prepared to kiss goodbye $175 for 1982 Chateau Margaux.

We debated whether to order the *Escargots de Bourgogne*, but finally settled on *Le Paté en Gelée la française*, a lovely paté served with mustard, gerkin pickles and a basket of bread. The butter lettuce dinner salad with vinaigrette was even better. We also applaud the smooth and delicate cream asparagus soup. The Beef Wellington entree, a choice filet surrounded by paté and spinach, was outstanding. It was tucked in a flaky pastry and served with a medley of fresh vegetables. Veal in Mustard Sauce was savory, creamy and rich but not as tangy as we had hoped. An order of chocolate mousse and two forks capped the evening off. Luscious, rich bites, enough to make you swear to start a diet the morning after.

La Gare was a pioneer of Sonoma County's French Cuisine and while it may not be on the cutting edge of the *nouvelle cuisine*, the food is definitely worth your while. The relaxed atmosphere is bound to lower your blood pressure a notch, although the menu won't help lower your cholesterol. Step through the door and you'll feel far from the busy streets outside. A small water fountain welcomes you into an intimate world of French lace curtains, stained glass and hanging plants. When the Old World beckons like this, it's hard to resist.

LISA HEMENWAY'S
Manager: Lisa Hemenway.
526-5111.
714 Village Court, Santa
   Rosa.
Closed: Mon. Eves., Sun.
Price: Expensive.
Cuisine: California.
Credit Cards: DC, MC, V.
Serving: L, D.
Reservations:
   Recommended.
Special features: Sidewalk
   patio.

Generally speaking, a mall is a mall, but tucked away in Montgomery Village lies a sophisticated restaurant — fine dining, indeed — that makes you forget you're in a shopping mall altogether. Lisa Hemenway's has french doors that open in warm weather for sidewalk dining under wisteria-hung arbors. Inside, the setting is elegant as well, replete with exhibits of paintings and sculptures by local artists. Lisa Hemenway's California cuisine has quite a following. She gained both experience and credibility by working with John Ash (another successful Wine Country restauranteur) as a pastry chef. Her food draws freely from the cuisines of the world and focuses on imaginative combinations of fresh, local ingredients.

The "appetizer/lite meal" specials are wonderful, especially the Three Baked Cheeses featuring separate ramekins filled with cambazola laced with candied walnuts, brie with sundried tomato and mozzarella with herbs. The menu has a large list of daily specials. A different preparation of filet mignon is available every evening. Ours was grilled to perfection, wrapped in bacon and served with roasted red bell peppers and a sundried tomato relish. Another special was prawns served in a delectable cream sauce, redolent of tarragon and mushrooms and full of baby shrimp. Both main courses were served on large dinner plates artistically arranged with perfectly cooked broccoli, beet-dyed onions and a divine baby yellow crooked-neck squash stuffed with spices. The exceptional salad which accompanied the entrees was a mix of tender exotic greens (baby amaranth, totsoy, mustard) from the Ya-Ka-Ama Indian Reservation in nearby Forestville.

Lisa Hemenway's has a good selection of local wines by the bottle, and a monthly list of reasonably priced reds and whites by the glass. Several imported and domestic beers are available. As for dessert, there is a tempting tray of sweets. Try the Lemon Gateau, a layer cake with lemon curd and lots of whipped cream, decorated with a fanciful dragonfly made out of slices of grapes, melon and candied violets. The dessert is served in a pool of creme anglais ribboned with raspberry sauce. The entire meal was well orchestrated. Lisa Hemenway: Bravo.

Chris Alderman

Lisa Hemenway's makes diners forget they're in a mall.

MATISSE
Manager: Diana Immel.
527-9797.
620 Fifth St., Santa Rosa.
Closed: Sat. and Sun.
lunch.
Prix Fixe: $17.50 and $21.
Credit Cards: AE, CB, D,
MC, V.
Cuisine: California &
French.
Serving: L, D.
Reservations:
Recommended.

Matisse, the restaurant, has the imprint of its namesake, direct and vibrant. The small, storefront restaurant in Santa Rosa is decorated with reproductions of Matisse's paintings on the walls and the entrees on the trables are equally colorful. Matisse is an understated version of fine dining in Sonoma County. It is certainly reasonable with a prix fixe of $17.50 for two courses, $21 for three and a wine list that emphasizes value for high quality. On our visit, there were just a few flaws that detracted from an otherwise fine meal. The bread basket on the table was filled with typical sour dough bread, some of which was stale, and our waitress, although efficient, was obviously unfamiliar with the menu. On the whole the restaurant had a lot to offer, namely an intimate dining room with just 13 tables and attention to detail in many respects. The carnation bud on each napkin was an original touch.

We began with a Wild Mushroom and Asparagus Puff Pastry and a French Lentil Salad. The pastry was wonderfully rich, yet light and fluffy. The salad was even better, especially when matched with the tart taste of a 1988 Gary Farrell Sauvignon Blanc. Designed to look like a sunflower, it was crafted out of yellow and red tomatoes, feta cheese, onions, carrots and lentils. Entrees were just as lovely. The Medallion of Veal Tenderloin with tarragon cream sauce was tender and moist and looked sculpted on the plate. The Grilled Ahi with a sun-dried tomato vinaigrette was also pleasing to the eye with the tomatoes draped over the fish. The light, tangy sauce didn't overpower the fish, simply enhanced it. The flavor was further enriched by a glass of 1989 Dehlinger Chardonnay.

We probably should have skipped the apple tart dessert altogether. It failed to bring out the natural taste of the apples and tasted rather starched. Yet, as we sipped our coffee and listened to Beethoven's "Für Elise" in the background, we realized it had still been a lovely meal. We recommend Matisse, if you're not a perfectionist, because it *is* a cozy retreat.

MIXX
Manager: Daniel Berman.
573-1344.
135 Fourth St., Santa Rosa.
Closed: Sun.
Price: Moderate.
Credit Cards: AE, MC, V.
Cuisine: California.
Serving: L, D.
Reservations:
   Recommended.

The historic Railroad Square in Santa Rosa has had its ups and downs over the years, but if you dine at MiXX you'll be convinced the good times are here to stay. Housed in a building known at the turn of the century as the Silver Dollar Saloon, the MiXX has come a long way. The menu and wine list confirm it as a class act. The front of the dining room is dominated by a magnificent, hand-carved Victorian oak back bar with a massive mahogany front bar. Italian blown glass chandeliers provide subdued lighting and there's usually quiet jazz playing in the background. Despite the elegance of its interior, the MiXX is still a casual and relaxed place. For instance there is a charming and inexpensive children's menu and an ever-changing, pithy "Quote du Jour" on a chalkboard near the entrance.

Dan Berman, owner and executive chef, and his wife Kathleen, are both graduates of the California Culinary Academy and have collaborated to design a creative menu. A daily house special is ravioli and several other imaginative pasta dishes appear regularly such as a Basil Fettuccini with pieces of smoked chicken, Niçoise olives, poached garlic and sun-dried tomatoes served in a delectable cream sauce — an inspired combination. The Bermans have also organized an accommodating menu. It notes that "We can customize many of our dishes or design special items for the vegetarian." Our waiter — knowledgeable and attentive without being overbearing — told us that many of the large dishes could be served in smaller portions for a reduced price.

The wine list is surprisingly good with a large selection of choice varietals by the glass. We ordered a 1988 Arrowood Chardonnay, rich and buttery. It gave a new dimension to the grilled fresh salmon entree glazed with Gorgonzola cheese and topped with tomato chutney. A 1987 Murphy Goode Cabernet Sauvignon, full-bodied and complex, proved to be a good match with the grilled loin of Sonoma lamb served in a petite sirah reduction with dried cherries and a dish of potatoes with gingered carrots on the side. The lamb was cooked perfectly to order but it was disappointingly un-lamblike and could have been mistaken for a filet mignon after it was deluged by the strongly flavored sauce. The salmon accompanied by a small plate of locally grown fresh vegetables and rice was quite good. Both entrees were listed on the menu as large dishes but we ordered smaller portions and found they were more than ample.

The menu changes frequently, especially the desserts made by pastry chef, Kathleen. The temptations often include a *Crème Brulée* served with hazelnut butter cookies, and a magical Banana-Poppyseed-Frangelico Ice Cream served in a Florentine Cookie Shell. You might want to book a room at the beautifully restored Hotel La Rose nearby so you won't have to travel far after such a feast.

THE OLD VIC

Manager: Chris Stokeld.
571-7555.
731 Fourth St., Santa Rosa.
Price: Inexpensive.
Credit Cards: MC, V.
Cuisine: British.
Serving: SB, L, D.

The Old Vic reminds us of our favorite jeans. Slip into them after a long day and ahhhhhhh-hhh! Regulars call this easygoing pub in downtown Santa Rosa simply "The Vic." It's a place of many charms: a warm unpretentious atmosphere, a lively clientele that ranges from ranch hands to Yuppies to expatriate Brits, simple but tasty English food and a wide selection of imported beer on tap. "English food — imagine trying to sell that," owner Chris Stokeld says. "During World War II, English food got such a bad name, because there wasn't any." An Old Vic favorite is the traditional Banger on a Bun, lightly spiced pork sausages. It's delicious, but we favor the puff pastry turnover called pasties, particularly the Cornish Pasty. The crust is fluffy and the inside mixture of beef, potatoes and onions is rich without being heavy. Wash it down with a Harp Lager and we're in heaven. On Saturdays and Sundays, the Vic offers a huge traditional English breakfast at a reasonable price and on weekend nights an avant-garde dinner theater takes the stage.

TAJ MAHAL
Manager: Abdus Salam.
579-8471.
335 Ross St., Santa Rosa.
Price: Expensive.
Credit Cards: MC, V.
Cuisine: Indian.
Serving: L, D.
Reservations: Accepted.
Special features: Oriental-
    style fixed menu offered.

Ever since we stumbled onto Little India in New York's East Village, Indian food has been a favorite. American food seems insipid compared to the wonderfully fiery *vindaloos* and rich curry *barani* rice dishes. And the breads! Best of all: it's a bargain. We've found few Indian restaurants in our travels — granted, we haven't been to India — that stack up to New York's. Taj Majal, alas, doesn't either but the food, for the most part, is delicious. West Coast Indian restaurants, for some reason, are a bit more pricey than elsewhere. Taj Mahal is no exception. The interior of Taj Mahal is clean and simple, but only hints of India: pottery, brass urns, plants, sitar music. Waiters were friendly though absent-minded.

The menu offers the usual Indian array: soup and kabobs for starters; *nan*, *paratha* and other breads; side dishes of *saag*, mango chutney and *dall*. Entrees range from the traditional *Tandoori* Chicken to Prawns *Tikka*. We began with the Lamb Shish Kabobs, spicy roasted sausages served on a bed of onions and lettuce. The sausages were flavorful but dry and the dipping sauce with it seemed wrong. (Our server later admitted that he had brought the wrong one. Too late.) A bland lentil and lemon soup followed, but things perked up with the main courses. The Lamb *Kurma* in a creamy coconut and almond sauce was a knockout, and not nearly as sweet as it sounds. The Chicken *Barani* was not as distinctive as our New York favorites, but its mix of rice, chicken, nuts, yellow raisins was addictive. The fragrant warm onion *nan* bread pulled it all together. Taj Mahal has a small wine list, but Indian food demands beer. We tried an Indian lager, Kingfisher, and it proved the perfect way to soothe our flaming taste buds.

Cotati

RAFA'S
Manager: Lurline Caruso.
795-7068.
8230 Old Redwood Hwy.,
    Cotati.
Price: Inexpensive.
Credit Cards: AE, MC, V.
Cuisine: Mexican.
Serving: B, L, D.
Reservations: Not accepted.
Special features: Outdoor
    dining.

The first time we walked into Rafa's, we were stunned by the sight of a burrito a certain fellow was making in the front window. It was immense! The size of a football, easily. When we sat down and spied the $11.25 Rafa's Especial burrito on the menu, we knew we weren't up to the challenge and ordered the Mini Rafa's. The surprise, of course — the man in the window was making a Mini. We gave it our best shot and found that the taste actually matched the size. While Rafa's may not be authentic Mexican, its motto — "Mexican Food: Quality, L.A. Style" — is indeed true. Americanized or not, Rafa's just may be the best Mexican food in Wine Country.

Atmosphere is not Rafa's strength. The restaurant has only nine tables and a long fountain bar where people with carry-out orders cluster. It's funky, the decor is homey, bordering on worn and tacky and the paper menus have salsa stains. Chichi it's not, but it is a dynamic place to eat. There are also a few tables outside that are snatched up quickly on warm evenings. The only real complaint we have, and it's a minor one, is you can't get a margarita here, or not a *real* one anyway. Rafa's doesn't have a hard liquor license, so the margaritas are made with wine. It's not the same. A prime selection of Mexican beers, including Bohemia, Pacifico and Negra Modelo, compensates.

We've never had breakfast at Rafa's but it should be on the agenda. In addition to the usual American necessities such as French toast and omelets, the breakfast menu includes *Huevos Rancheros* and *Chorizo* Eggs, a tempting sauté of Mexican sausage, onions, beans and corn tortillas. The lunch and dinner menu has all the Mexican usuals — burritos, enchiladas, chile rellenos — plus a few authentic surprises. The *Carnitas* Plate is an old Mexican delicacy, a massive platter of fried pork and potatoes, beans and rice. The pork was not overcooked and the seasoning was mild. It wasn't exactly a low cholesterol plate, but it was delicious. And now the oxymoron — the massive Mini Rafa's. The two-pound burrito was more than seven inches long and five inches wide. It was stuffed with beans, rice, lettuce, tomato, onions, cheese and your choice of meat. We vied for the Chili Colorado, a chunky spicy beef, and while we would have preferred more *kick*, the entire package was all rather carnal. The Mini, frankly, is meal enough for two, and as we walked out with doggy bag in hand, we thought of a full Rafa's Especial and shuddered.

TENGU
Manager: Nobo Eguchi.
795-9753.
8235 Old Redwood Hwy.,
   Cotati.
Closed: Monday.
Price: Inexpensive.
Credit Cards: MC, V.
Cuisine: Japanese.
Serving. D.
Reservations: Not accepted.

There's a cozy cafe in downtown Cotati where they never overcook the fish, and for those who don't like sushi, this family-run Japanese restaurant offers a dynamite salmon *teriyaki*. It also passes a reliable test: Asians often outnumber Caucasians. A good sign. If you want something showy like Benihana, Tengu isn't the place for you. There are no fancy grill tables or cutlery shows. Tengu is Sonoma County at its funky best. Inside, the walls are knotty pine and decorated with a few Japanese lanterns and posters. Don't expect privacy, either. Tengu is intimate. The small wooden tables are a close fit in the dining room. Service is attentive when Tengu isn't busy, a touch neglectful when it is. We like beer with our sushi, so we began with a Kirin, a smooth lager that Tengu carries in two sizes. Suntory is also available, as is Miller and an imported plum wine.

We began with the *Ungai Kabayaki*, barbecued eel on a skewer. An interesting taste, with an exotic appeal, but we didn't finish it. We followed with the *Nabeyaki Udon*, a hearty noodle soup served in a heavy black pot and accompanied by *tempura* shrimp and vegetables. Wonderful. Actully, you might not feel the need for appetizers at Tengu, because dinners include a bowl of brothy *miso* soup and a sliced cucumber dish with vinaigrette called *sunomono*. Both are light and refreshing beginnings.

For entrees, Tengu's version of Sushi 101, is the *Nigiri* dinner, a delectable assortment that demonstrates chef Nobo Eguchi's obsession with fresh fish. Included is salmon, yellowtail tuna, Japanese mackerel and our favorite — octopus. There's also a California roll, rice and vegetables wrapped in sea-weed, Japanese mustard and a volcanic pink horseradish. We also tried two of Tengu's four combination dinners, which allow diners the best of both the raw and the cooked. The *tempura* and *sashimi* combo included crisp prawns and vegetables lightly coated in a delicate batter. If you're like us and don't care to make a meal out of just sushi, the Tengu Super Combination is the way to go. It's a choice of *tempura* or *teriyaki* tuna, chicken or beef, with two large skewers of *yakitori* of barbecued chicken and a few sizable slabs of tuna *sashimi*. Fabulous and filling.

Healdsburg

LITTLE DARLIN'S ROCK 'N' ROLL DINER
Manger: Lola Hundley.
431-8181.
109 Plaza St., Healdsburg.
Price: Inexpensive.
Credit Cards: MC, V.
Cuisine: American.
Serving: B, L, D.
Reservations: Accepted.

The food won't knock your bobby socks off, but this '50s-style soda fountain is a whole lotta fun. Little Darlin's Rock 'N' Roll Diner is right on the Healdsburg Plaza. It's a good place to fuel up before or after a Wine Country foray. The joint was known for many years as Forty Karrots Cafe, and regulars will be glad to know that the menu and the decor haven't changed. Milkshakes, burgers and dogs are still the restaurant's mainstays. For the health conscious, there's still a wide range of salads including the charbroiled chicken salad and Hunza Veggie, a salad topped with tomato, mushrooms, onions, cukes, olives, carrots and cheese. If you decide to stop in for breakfast with a *San Francisco Chronicle* under your arm, there's quite a collection of Little Darlin's specials to consider. To name two, Cheezie Eggs, scrambled with Parmesan and cream cheese; and Biscuits 'N' Gravy, buttermilk biscuits floating in a soupy, sausage gravy. Mexican appetizers — such as the Super Duper Chili Nachos — are available for lunch and dinner.

Little Darlin's decor is still done up in bright yellow and black with chrome hubcap light fixtures and a lively montage of movie star posters. There's James Dean, Marilyn Monroe, Clark Gable, and yes, the immortal Elvis who seems to watch with envy as you order up a pie à la mode. The wine list is modest, petering out at about $14. Beers seem to be the way to go here. The diner has the usual American suds as well as an excellent local, Red Tail Ale from Hopland, just north of Sonoma County.

We ordered the Chili Size Burger, an open-faced hamburger with a smattering of chili, and it was satisfactory although a bit too tame for our tastes. The hamburger and fries were nothing special, but the espresso milkshake was amazing, a taste of heaven in a stainless steel fountain cup. The meat loaf special was a hefty portion smothered in a dark brown gravy that tasted like it was no stranger to the inside of a can or a box. The side order of zucchini and carrots, however, was crispy and fresh, and the sauteed red potatoes, hot and hearty.

The service was friendly but soon after we plopped down at our table the diner got crowded and the waitress was hopping, running around in what looked like a harried jitterbug. Little Darlin's festive atmosphere is the draw.

MADRONA MANOR
Manager: Jim Connell.
433-4231.
1001 Westside Rd.,
 Healdsburg.
Price: Moderate.
Credit Cards: MC, V, AE,
 D, CB.
Cuisine: California.
Serving: SB, D.
Reservations: Required.

If you want to feel privileged and pampered on a lazy Sunday morning, Madrona Manor is your best bet. Some Sunday brunches elsewhere are nothing more than a swarm of people stuffing themselves at a steam table buffet. But at the Manor, the entrees are fresh and inventive. Perhaps most pleasing is the genteel service that makes you feel like the master of this Victorian home and its lush gardens — for an hour anyway. The wine cellar includes both California and imported wines to complement the menu. The dinner menu is more varied than the Sunday brunch menu but we definitely favor the brunch. Strolling through the garden is part of the dining experience and it's best to see it in full daylight. The flowers are in bloom and you can spy the orchard and the herb/vegetable garden on which the chef relies.

Toasting the day with a glass of champagne is first on the agenda at the Sunday brunch. We were served a tasty, but inexpensive sparkler followed by a round of freshly baked breads, muffins, fruits and imported cheeses. The herb brie was especially delicious and the fruit plate — festooned with kiwi, strawberries and cantaloupe — was delicious. Eggs Benedict with a champagne Hollandaise sauce was also a delight. Tomato slices atop the grilled ham and the champagne sauce gave this traditional dish a hearty, fresh flavor. The smoked salmon tossed with vegetables and penne pasta in a fish stock, however, was too understated. But the mesquite grilled chicken breast with garden vegetables and herbs was savory. The vegetables and herbs played off each other wonderfully. No one really had room for dessert but that didn't stop us, not with something as alluring as Chocolate Velvet with raspberry sauce on the menu. It was outrageous, incredibly rich, an order that should be served with at least two forks, one for your salivating tablemate. The apple crisp served with vanilla ice cream was ordinary but the strawberry sorbet won high marks — every bite was an explosion of fruit.

TRE SCALINI
Managers: Cynthia and
  Fernando Urroz.
433-1772.
241 Healdsburg Ave.,
  Healdsburg.
Closed: Tues.
Price: Expensive.
Credit Cards: MC, V.
Cuisine: Italian, California.
Serving: D.
Reservations: Required.
Special features: Live music
  on occasion.

From the outside Tre Scalini promises little. Small and refined, the restaurant seems pleasant enough, but by the time you're sipping your coffee, you know the food is both ambitious and extraordinary. As for the wine list, it has a solid selection of Italian and California wines, many served by the glass. As we lingered over the menu, a mélange of tempting smells emerged from the kitchen, olive oil, garlic and prosciutto, a sneak preview. It was nearly an impossible feat to decide. Luckily we were able to nibble on tasty pencil-thin buttery breadsticks.

The menu is explicit and gives a sense of each entree, while your imagination fills in the blanks. For instance, *Taglierini dal Cielo Tre Scalini* is described as "our fresh egg pasta in a deliciously rich Roquefort, sour cream and pistachio sauce." And then there is *Carpaccio alla Fiorentina*, "paper-thin slices of raw beef laced with extra virgin olive oil, garnished with capers, onions, sharp Romano cheese, and sundried tomatoes." But the most appealing in print was the *Cappellini con Langosta e Tartufo Nero*, "fresh angel hair pasta served with sauteed lobster medallions and fresh mussels in a black truffle, cognac sauce." It proved to be the Cadillac of pasta, a dish so rich we couldn't help but savor every bite. The glaze gave the dish a sweet, subtle flavor and extra dimension. It was especially good with a bottle of 1988 Ferrari-Carano Chardonnay. This combination, we decided, is what they must serve in heaven to those who have meticulously paid their parking tickets over the years. The *Lasagna di Pesce al sugo di Langosta*, layers of fresh shitake mushrooms, sea scallops, steelhead salmon, sea bass and homemade pasta finished with a velvety crayfish sauce, was also first-rate. It was light in flavor and yet filling. A red baby crayfish was added strictly for presentation. This would probably offend animal rights activists. It was an arty touch, if a bit discomforting as it watched us eat. The swordfish, gently grilled and served in a smoky tart and peppery sauce, was a bit too fiery for our tastes, but interesting all the same.

We couldn't resist dessert, a deceptively-named *Spumoni*. It was an inch-thick bittersweet chocolate layered over a caramel and hazelnut flavored base that sat in a creamy white glaze marbleized with raspberry sauce. For presentation's sake, the edge of the plate was dusted with powered sugar. As lovely as it was, the flavor was deadened by the fact that it was still too frozen.

Overall there were no major problems with the food or the table service, just a minor irritation with seating. We had reservations and were promised a table in the front room if we were willing to wait. We did — for nearly 30 minutes — and still sat in the back room.

Geyserville

CHATEAU SOUVERAIN
Manager: Patricia L.
  Windisch.
433-3141.
400 Souverain Rd.,
  Geyserville.
Closed: Mon. and Tues. for
  lunch, Sun. through
  Wed. for dinner.
Price: Very Expensive.
Credit Cards: AE, CD, MC,
  V.
Cuisine: California and
  French country.
Serving: SB, L, D.
Reservations: Required.
Special features: Fireplace;
  patio dining.

From the tall, French windows of Chateau Souverain, you can spy the graceful hills of Alexander Valley, a view homeowners dream about. The restaurant's interior is nearly as stunning with towering cathedral ceilings, a massive stone fireplace and flamboyant flower arrangements. The entrees also had a designer's touch and were, for the most part, flavorful and inventive. There was really just one major flaw: the check. The high price might have been tolerable if the service had been more courteous, but it bordered on aloof.

Chateau Souverain is one of the few premium California wineries to offer year-round gourmet dining. The only wine the restaurant serves by the glass is its own label. Chateau Souverain's wine list's possibilities nearly made ordering an impossible feat. The menu likewise. But we finally chose for appetizers Sauteed Crabcake with ginger and the Butternut Squash Raviolis. The crab had a wonderful texture but the taste left something to be desired. Its honey tangerine sauce competed with the texture rather than complementing it. The butternut squash raviolis, however, were wonderful, subtly sweet and rich without being heavy. Entrees were also a hit. The Lobster, Scallops & Salmon Boudin was light, flavorful and beautifully designed on the plate. The spicy Thai-Marinated Filet of Beef with shitake mushrooms, roasted peppers and fried onions was even better. It was rich, bold and cooked to perfection. An '87 Rafanelli Cabernet we selected after diligently studying the wine list was a natural with the beef.

The white chocolate mousse on the menu beckoned seductively. We weren't disappointed. It was subtle, delicate and beautifully garnished with fresh strawberries. The warm apple crisp with whipped cream was fairly typical but nothing to complain about. We wholeheartedly recommend the Chateau Souverain for people on unlimited budgets. But for those of limited means, the aftertaste that lingers on the palate is the price.

RESTAURANTS — SONOMA WEST COUNTY

On Bodega Bay, Lucas Wharf features a fireplace, cathedral ceiling and greenery along with fresh seafood.

Kris White

LUCAS WHARF
Manager: Michael
    Krawczyk.
875-3522.
595 Hwy. 1, Bodega Bay.
Price: Expensive.
Credit Cards: MC, V.
Cuisine: Seafood.
Serving: L, D.
Reservations: Not accepted.
Special features: Bay view;
    fireplace.

THE TIDES WHARF
Manager: Carlo Galazzo.
875-3652.
835 Hwy. 1, Bodega Bay.
Price: Expensive.
Credit Cards: AE, MC, V.
Cuisine: Seafood.
Serving: B, L, D.
Reservations:
    Recommended.
Special features: Bay view;
    fireplace.

Ask a group of locals the best place to eat seafood on the Sonoma Coast and you're liable to start an argument. The coast is not nearly as populated with restaurants as, say, Cape Cod — there are just a handful. Maybe that explains why folks are so adamant in their choices. The debate inevitably centers on two spots: Lucas Wharf and The Tides. In the interest of health and harmony — we have to live here — we recommend both.

We will admit one thing. We find ourselves at Lucas Wharf more often than not. It may be just a matter of flair, both in decor *and* food. Lucas Wharf is cozier, more romantic, with a fireplace, cathedral ceiling and greenery. Lucas Wharf also tends to be more fanciful with its sauces and food presentation. The Tides has a simpler approach, playing up the distinct flavors of the fish and playing down the atmosphere. Both reach out onto Bodega Bay on wooden piers. But both rely on the same fresh seafood: red snapper, swordfish, ling cod and Pacific oysters. Native Salmon in season — mid-May through September — is a good choice at either restaurant. Likewise Dungeness crab, from mid-November to June. Both are deft with seafood and have impeccable service. So it's really a matter of your style.

At Lucas Wharf, we prefer the salmon poached or baked, as opposed to grilled, which is too often dry and flaky. The seafood pasta offers a delectable mix of textures, smells and flavors, blending fettuccini with a creamy sauce, chunks of various fish, mussels and clams. A favorite comfort food of ours is the Fisherman's Stew, a brothy concoction of fish, mussels, clams and bay shrimp, but we always feel the chef is a bit too careful with the spices. It seems to call out for fresh ground pepper. For a Wine Country restaurant, the wine list here is too frugal. Almost as bad, no vintage dates. A Sonoma seafood restaurant with only two chardonnays — however well selected — is short-changing its customers. The wine-by-the-glass selection is even more limited. Lucas does offer one of the best all-time seafood matches in the Kenwood Sauvignon Blanc and the price isn't bad. Lucas Wharf is popular with locals and tourists alike, so be prepared to wait for a table on weekend evenings in particular. Luckily, the waiting area is a warm corner with a fireplace.

The Tides was immortalized by Alfred Hitchcock in *The Birds*, but you'll never recognize it. The original restaurant, which was attacked by vengeful gulls in a major scene, is long gone and a new eatery is in its place. But the unpretentious attitude remains and locals flock to it. The "catch of the day" is a rather voluminous list — much larger than Lucas Wharf's — that almost makes you forget the regular menu. A favorite of ours is the poached salmon with a simple Hollandaise sauce, and the Crab Cioppino, a zesty Italian stew, is a knockout. The wine list is heftier at the Tides, offering eight chardonnays and even a few imported wines. Red wines are a definite weak link.

RUSSIAN RIVER VINEYARDS RESTAURANT

Manager: Jerry Topolos.
887-1562.
5700 Gravenstein Hwy. N., Forestville.
Closed: Mon. and Tues. in winter.
Price: Expensive.
Credit Cards: AE, MC, V.
Cuisine: Greek.
Serving: SB, L, D.
Reservations: Recommended.
Special features: Outdoor dining.

If you like Greek food, this is the best choice in Wine Country. That it is part of a fetching old Russian Orthodox-hop kiln winery and offers one of Sonoma County's most pleasurable outdoor dining experiences, only adds to the appeal. Only careless service and a few near-misses on the menu detracted from the evening. Russian River Vineyards is secreted away in a small shady valley. If the wooden winery with its distinctive towers wasn't such an unusual sight, it would be easy to miss. The restaurant and tasting room are in a restored farm house. Out back is the patio, where the view takes in the green Russian River Valley.

Problems, unfortunately, began as soon as we were seated. Our server dutifully explained the specials and disappeared for 15 minutes without leaving a menu. We also had to ask for bread and butter and continually begged for water refills.

With a menu finally snared, we found a limited list of entrees and a handful of first courses. Greek specialties were limited mostly to the lamb dish, *souvlaki*, and to *spanakopita*, spinach and feta cheese in a flaky filo pastry. Both were well-prepared renditions of Greek classics. American fare such as steak and roast baby rack of lamb fill out the menu.

We tried an appetizer of Prawns in Pesto Sauce, which were delicious as the rich tangy green sauce played off the crisp moist prawns. We followed with the Meze Plate, a rather stingy and overpriced assortment of Greek delights, including *doma*, feta cheese, olives and the like. The Greek salad, however, was fantastic, and beautifully presented with a tomato stuffed with zucchini, summer squash and rice. We also sampled two non-Greek entrees, including a spectacular Swordfish Steak grilled with garlic and ginger sauce. The New York Steak with green peppercorn sauce, however, was a flop all around. The steak was bland and the peppercorn sauce too mild. Russian River Vineyards wines are served exclusively at the restaurant. We would prefer a wider selection, though the winery makes a competent Zinfandel. A 1988 Cabernet Sauvignon paired well with the steak. The dessert plate had four offerings: chocolate mousse, chocolate cake, cheesecake and of course *baklava*. All were standard commercial quality, nothing special.

TRUFFLES
Managers: Rick Rozet and
  Charles Holmes.
823-8448.
234 S. Main St., Sebastopol.
Closed: Mon. and Tues.
Price: Expensive.
Credit Cards: MC, V.
Cuisine: California.
Serving: SB, L, D.
Reservations:
  Recommended.
Special features: Live music
  on occasion.

"Tonight's Calamari Salad is scallops," was the unintentional laugh our efficient waitress granted while explaining the specials of the day. A hint perhaps of a continuing comedy of errors? Luckily, no. Truffles' reputation was well established when Rick Rozet bought it in August 1990, and although he can't quite reach the high marks of the previous owners, Truffles remains one of West County's finer eating establishments. There is an air, here, of subtle refinement, a decor of soft shades of pink and black highlighted by paintings in the Southwestern style. The brief menu emphasizes duck, quail and the like, rather than fish. The small but carefully selected wine list offers the best of Sonoma County at a low mark-up. At $22, the superb Gary Farrell 1989 Pinot Noir is — relatively — a steal. Each wine is available by glass.

We began with two appetizers. The *Satay* of the Day, skewers of chicken with spicy peanut sauce, was delightful, but the Eggplant and Goat Cheese Terrine was all wrong: the egg plant terribly bland, the cheese overpowering. The Charred Pork Tenderloin with honey, dates and ginger was beautifully prepared — visually, the entire dinner was stunning — but its honey coating was cloyingly sweet. The Pan Roasted Duck Breast with wild mushrooms, zucchini noodle cake and cabernet sauce was fine but uninspired. We ended the evening with a fabulous Croissant Bread Pudding, which alone makes a return trip to Truffles something to anticipate.

FOOD PURVEYORS

A restaurant isn't the only place to feast. From fish markets brimming with the harvest of the Sonoma Coast, to chic bakeries and gourmet shops, Napa and Sonoma have food shops aplenty. Old family delis, with lingering irresistible smells of smoked meats and cheese, are a Wine Country tradition. A new coffee house seems to open in Napa or Sonoma every month, cozy places for sipping espresso and chatting the morning away. The San Francisco Bay Area is the capital of America's booming brewpub industry, and Wine Country has four of these popular nightspots that make their own beer. As you might expect, Napa and Sonoma have some of the finest wine shops in America, stocking both great bargains and rare finds. Donuts no longer rule the bakeries here, as croissants, bagels and even elaborate and decadent tortes and tarts tempt from behind glass counters. And how can we forget the old faithful: pizza.

BAKERIES

People drive for miles for bread from the Sonoma French Bakery.

Chris Alderman

Napa County

Napa County has two bakeries that cry out to you in the morning. OK, so they cry out in the afternoon, too, but that's beside the point. *The Model Bakery* (963-8192; 1357 Main St., St. Helena) is a tempting stop while shopping. Everything here is baked in a big brick oven. Sweet or sour baguettes are stacked like kindling in tall wicker baskets, and scones, muffins and croissants compete for shelf space. Behind the counter are burly loaves of rye, powdered white on top. One or two sandwiches are also available, as well as funky offerings such as a Chili & Jack Croissant. *The Yountville Pastry Shop* (944-2138; Vintage 1870) is hidden away in the rear courtyard of this popular shopping complex. Tortes, muffins and danishes are specialties, all available for the nibbling on a warm outside deck.

Sonoma County

In Sonoma County, there's no better breakfast-in-a-bag to begin a day of wine tasting than at *Cafe Des Croissants* (Three Santa Rosa locations: 1226 Fourth St., 2444 Lomitas Ave., 1791 Marlow Rd.). Whether you prefer the classic simplicity of a plain croissant or one stuffed with chocolate or berries, they make some of Wine Country's best. The secret is starting to get out about the *Downtown Bakery and Creamery* (431-2714; 308 Center St., Healdsburg). Its tortes and cakes taste like something you'd have at a four-star restaurant, and for good reason. Owners Kathleen Stewart and Lindsey and Therese Shere have all worked at Berkeley's famed Chez Panisse. Lindsey, in fact, is still pastry chef there and comes north on weekends.

People drive for miles for bread from *Sonoma French Bakery* (996-2691; 468 First St. E., Sonoma), a busy little storefront on Sonoma Plaza. Locals know where to go and every morning they swarm to *The Grateful Bagel* (404 Mendocino Ave. and 2700 Yulupa Ave. in Santa Rosa; 200 S. Main St., Sebastopol). Yes, great bagels in California. They're light yet meaty, as good as you'll find east of Queens. Super challah bread, too. As for *Mom's Apple Pie* (4550 Gravenstein Hwy. N., Forestville), well the name says it all. These fat pies are better than most mom's, served in tin pans or by the slice. Apple, of course, is the specialty and it's a killer. The coconut cream is also to die for. It's worth going out of your way. Try the fried chicken, too.

BREWPUBS

Courtesy Sonoma County Museum

Hop kilns were a common sight in Sonoma County when hops were harvested regularly to produce fine local beers.

Watch out wine connoisseurs, beer lovers are getting serious, too. Brewpubs — restaurants and clubs that make their own beer — have become the thing recently. It's a return to the old days when any city of size had a brewery or two, bottling suds for the local area. It also harkens to England and Germany where beers still have character. The San Francisco area is the undisputed American leader in brewpubs, though brewpubs are cropping up all over the country. Wine Country alone has four.

Napa County

There are two brewpubs just a few blocks apart in downtown Napa. *Brown Street Brewery* (255-6392; 1040 Clinton St.) is a cozy spot with wooden booths and all sorts of ales and lagers on tap. The kitchen also features the popular Papa Joe's Pizza as well as a full menu of seafood and pub food. Down the street in a colorful old art deco storefront is the more fashionable *Willett's Brewing Co.* (258-2337; 902 Main St.). Home to the smooth Willett's Lager and the rich Old Magnolia Stout, Willett's has a small bar area with a patio along the Napa River. Walk to the back, past the brewing equipment and you'll find the restaurant. The menu features everything from buffalo wings and bockwurst to a concoction named Drunken Black Beans, beans in a black ale with bacon, cilantro and tortillas.

To the north is one of our favorite Napa Valley destinations, *The Calistoga Inn* (942-4104; 1250 Lincoln Ave.). There's nothing more soothing on a scorching day than sitting in the Inn's shady green beer garden and sipping a Calistoga Pale Lager. It's light but still has personality. The garden, with flowering trees and bushes, is surrounded by a white picket fence and borders a gentle stream. If you want to eat, move from the beer garden picnic tables to the more formal outdoor patio or inside if weather warrants. The menu includes light fare — soups and salads — as well as heartier burgers and a grilled sausage plate with Calistoga Red Ale mustard. Fine.

The Biergarten at Calistoga Inn is within walking distance of the famous hot spring spas.

Chris Alderman

Sonoma County

There may be more people here, but there is only one brewpub — *Kelmer's Brew House* (544-4677; 458 B St., Santa Rosa). The atmosphere doesn't always suit us — it has a bit of the jock-fraternity-hangout feel about it, but the beer is fabulous. The Klassic is a knockout amber ale in the British tradition, and the crisp Krystal lager proves that light American-style beer doesn't have to be wimpy. The menu is also sizable and includes pizza, sandwiches and salads. Fish and chips are darned tasty here and the hamburgers are fat and juicy.

COFFEE HOUSES

Coffee drinkers come in two types. Most people sip it for a simple jump start; they're usually content with a homey coffee shop that serves up eggs, donuts and pie. Others prefer their coffee on a grander scale, savoring a cup of a rich exotic blend, freshly ground of course, in a smart cafe with classical or jazz music in the air and designer treats and savvy clientele to boot. That's the crowd we're concerned with here, people who unabashedly raise coffee drinking to an art.

Napa County

The *Caffe San Marco* (942-4671; 1336 Lincoln Ave., Calistoga) is a fun little hole in the wall with French attention to detail. Beans are ground for individual cups, then brewed through a fanciful French press. It's an uncompromising cup of coffee. Espresso, cappuccino and lattes are also elaborately prepared. *Java Express* (944-9700; Washington Sq. 6795) is an MTV-sort of coffee house — bright, bouncy and showy. Still, it makes a good espresso. It's a grab-and-go sort of place, with only a couple of tables and a counter. They also serve bagels, frozen yogurt and old fashioned sodas. The premier coffee house in the county is *Napa Valley Coffee Roasting Co.* (224-2233; 948 Main St., Napa). Inside a classic old downtown facade, the Roasting Co. is a popular hangout, with a handful of tables and a few benches. People crowd in, chat around the self-serve bar and sip Colombian Supremo or lattes and the like. Bags of raw greenish beans are open in the back — Ethiopian Sidamo and Sumatra Mandehling and other exotic types. To go with the brew, there are treats galore. The whole wheat scones are memorable.

Sonoma County

In Sonoma County, coffee houses are a boom industry. We selected a few favorites. *Aram's* (765-9775; 122 Kentucky St., Petaluma) has a Middle Eastern state of mind, a funky cafe with sidewalk tables and light food with Mediterranean tones. *Markey's Cafe* (763-7868; 8240 Old Redwood Hwy., Cotati) has a breezy atmosphere that encourages a warm mug over the morning paper. There are also hefty muffins, cinnamon rolls and light, mostly vegetarian, food. *A'Roma Roasters* (576-7765; 95 Fifth St., Santa Rosa) is the county's newest coffee house. Facing historic Railroad Square, A'Roma is a touch

Bohemian, with exposed rafters, copper counter top and a coffee bean roaster as a centerpiece to the table area. We've never tried its Lambada Blend but it's on out list. We have tried its blackberry pie and other tempters and rolled our eyes. Live music Wednesday through Sunday.

DELI & GOURMET SHOPS

Napa County

FELLION'S DELICATESSEN
942-6144.
1359 Lincoln Ave.,
Calistoga.

One of Napa Valley's biggest libraries of cold import beers makes this casual deli even more appealing. Whenever a place sells Pilsner Urquell by the bottle, it has our respect. There are more that 100 brands in all, a challenging quiz of your beer knowledge. We find ourselves selecting a sandwich to fit the beer we're craving. Let's see, a Samuel Adams with a Reuben, or a Fosters with a ham on onion roll, hold the mustard. A good choice for a grab and go winery lunch, or for low-key munching at the tables in the back. Besides the usual offerings of pastrami, salami and the like, Fellion's has *quesadillas*, chili, even a small salad bar. Breakfast rules in the mornings, with everything from French toast to lox and bagels. They also sell picnic supplies if you've forgotten a few items for the road trip.

GENOVA DELICATESSEN
253-8686.
1550 Trancas Ave., Napa.

You can almost smell Genova's from two blocks off, so rich is the bouquet of dried salami, roasting chicken, thick-crusted bread, *prosciutto* and garlic stalks. With a history that dates to 1926, Genova is called a deli but it's really a gourmet supermarket. In addition to lovely marbled and smoked cold cuts and thick cheeses, Genova has the usual glass case treasures: potato and egg salad, antipasto and olives. There's also fresh ravioli and other pastas, ready to eat or to take home and cook. One corner is stocked with Napa and Italian wine and across the aisle is a wine and espresso bar. Weight watchers would give up the ghost for Genova's chocolates and other desserts like Apple Cheese Tart. Takeout seems to be the usual, but Genova also has a handful of tables for those who want to savor lunch and *the smells* right here.

NAPA VALLEY OLIVE OIL MANUFACTURING CO.
963-4173.
835 McCorkle Ave., St. Helena.

Don't let the industrial name fool you. If you want to get an idea of what Napa Valley was like before the snazzy days of chic wineries, then venture from the beaten path to this faded white garage. Pull into the small gravel parking lot and you'll think: "Is this it?" If it weren't for the cola machine and picnic tables out front, you would think you were trespassing. Step inside and you realize you've stumbled onto a gem. This family-owned deli and olive oil company was founded in the 1920s when Napa Valley was a simple haven of Italian winemakers and farmers. St. Helena has been reborn but this deli remains in a charming time warp. You're as likely to hear Italian inside as English, and the deli counter looks like your (Neapolitan) grandmother's kitchen. Dried salami dangles from the ceiling and baskets of dried pastas, bags of polenta and other delights line the concrete floor. Then, of course, there are the jugs of thick olive oil, so green and dark they look like syrup.

The outside is deceptive; this is really a gourmet deli in disguise.

Chris Alderman

OAKVILLE GROCERY
944-8802.
7856 Hwy. 29, Oakville.

You'd think, from the outside, this was a plain, old country grocery, with its giant red Coca-Cola sign on the side and wooden screen doors with the colorful metal kick plates that read "Rainbo is Good Bread." Once inside, though, and you've been had. This is no ordinary grocery — it's a gourmet deli in disguise. Goodies include duck paté, cold cuts and even caviar. Unusual sandwich combos like sliced turkey with pesto are ready for your picnic. Nuts and spices are available in bulk and there's even a small produce section. Coffee is sold by the cup, to go along with macaroons and other bakery treats. A few remnants from the old days remain, particularly a hulking wooden walk-in cooler with thick glass doors where beer and cold drinks are chilled. There's also a fine offering of Napa wines and a particularly pleasing array of half bottles, perfect for a festive picnic.

Other Napa County delis worth noting: *V. Sattui Winery* (963-7774; Hwy. 29 at White Lane, St. Helena), which we detail in Chapter 6, *Wineries*. *Napa Valley Deli & Catering Co.* (963-7710; 1138 Main St., St. Helena) has a pleasant outside cafe. *Pometta's Deli* (944-2365; Hwy. 29 at Oakville Grade, Oakville) is a casual stop that specializes in barbecued chicken.

Sonoma County

DRY CREEK GENERAL STORE
433-4171.
3495 Dry Creek Rd.,
  Healdsburg.

For 110 years, this has been a gathering spot for rural families and farmers of Sonoma County. Sure, fancier trappings have been added over the years — a wine rack and a few gourmet goodies — but this perseveres as a landmark of Sonoma's rustic heritage. The floors are wooden and warped and out front under the carport is a tattered upright cola machine and a few benches. It's a perfect first stop if you're cruising toward the Dry Creek wineries. Sandwiches or sandwich fixings are at hand, as are cold drinks, wine and picnic supplies.

KOZLOWSKI FARMS
887-1587.
5566 Gravenstein Hwy. N,
  Forestville.

This orchard turned downhome gourmet enterprise is a Sonoma County treasure. Its jams and jellies, apple butter, raspberry and other vinegars are favorite Christmas gifts and can be found in stores throughout the region. Stopping by the orchard itself is a real treat, particularly in the fall when pumpkins line the drive and your yearly fix of apple cider is due.

THE PASTA SHOP
526-3600.
3080 Marlow Rd., Santa
  Rosa.

Great ravioli and pastas of all kinds, from spinach angel hair to black pepper fettuccine, can be found at this carry-out. And so fresh — made on the premises daily. The sauces are luxurious, from a marinara that's oil free and as healthy as it is spicy, to an outrageous creamy pesto. For picnics, try the ravioli salad, a tomato-based gut buster, or the Pasta Shop's big stuffed breads, lathered inside with pesto, cheeses and sun-dried tomatoes. If you haven't already trashed the diet, consider one of their bran muffins or better yet the huge moist macaroons coated on one half with dark chocolate. Gourmet vinegars and candies are also available to go, as is coffee by the cup.

**SONOMA CHEESE
    FACTORY**
996-1931.
2 W. Spain St., Sonoma.

Geez look at all the cheese! This supermarket-sized deli doubles as factory and tourist attraction. The Viviani family has made cheese in Sonoma since 1931, moving to their current locale on the bustling Sonoma Plaza in 1945. Sonoma Jack cheese is their specialty, but they produce a fantastic array: hot pepper, garlic, onion, cheddar, on and on. All, of course, are available for samples. In the rear is a large window where you can watch cheese in the making and there's also a film to reveal a more in-depth look. The Cheese Factory does a busy mail-order business, so you might keep those Christmas gifts in mind. There's also a large collection of wine for sale. Sandwiches to order are served up with every meat and cheese combo imaginable. There are a handful of tables inside, as well as a pleasant covered patio. If you crave even more elbow room, the shady Sonoma Plaza is across the street with wide lawns, handy picnic tables and a playground.

*Traverso's is a gourmet
deli and wine shop
with Italian roots.*

Chris Alderman

TRAVERSO'S
542-2530.
Third and B streets, Santa
    Rosa.

When Santa Rosa was just a small farm town, Traverso's was the heart of the proud Italian community. Now that Santa Rosa is a burgeoning city, Traverso's has evolved into the county's best gourmet deli and wine shop, never losing touch with its Italian roots. Dangling from the ceiling are flags of Italy, maps, salami and *prosciutto*. The deli case is a painting of salads, meats and other treats, from delicate pastries like a Chicken Apple Yoha and golden knishes, to hearty ravioli and tortellini. Sandwiches come on incredible and chewy hard rolls, and the meats are of excellent quality. There are also dried and fresh pastas, exotic vinegars and other jarred delights, as well as cold drinks and picnic supplies. Just two blocks east of Hwy. 101, it's also a convenient detour from your winery touring path.

FISH MARKETS

One of the joys of living on the Pacific Ocean is fresh seafood. Most prized locally are Dungeness crab and salmon. Crab season runs from mid-November to the end of May, but frozen crabs are available most of the year. Salmon is available year round, but local salmon season runs from mid-May to September. There are also a number of oyster farms just south on Tomales Bay and those beefy Pacific oysters are delicious. Large supermarkets in the area have fish counters that rival meat counters of the Midwest in size. Prices there are usually best, but quality is often higher in smaller specialty fish markets. Listed below are a few of those.

Johnson Oyster & Seafood Co. 763-4161; 253 N. McDowell Blvd., Petaluma.

Omega 3 Seafood Market 257-3474; 1740 Yajome St., Napa.

Lucas Wharf Deli 875-3562; 595 Hwy. 1, Bodega Bay.

St. Helena Fish Market 963-5331; 1232 Spring St., St. Helena.

Tides Wharf Fish Market 875-3554; 835 Hwy. 1, Bodega Bay.

PIZZERIAS

Pizza may not be the obsession here that it is in cities like Chicago, New York and Boston, but folks here do like their cheese pies. Chains like Pizza Hut, Domino's and Little Caesar's are a strong presence, but you're familiar with their pizzas. We've rounded up a sampling of the little guys — the independents and small chains.

If you like a bit of panache in your pizza, check out *Checkers* (942-9300; 1414 Lincoln Ave., Calistoga & 578-4000; 523 Fourth St., Santa Rosa). Purists will call Checkers "designer pizza," but who cares. The place is festive with abstract art and polished pine and black tile. The pizza is just as arty and fun, with a light crust and fresh toppings. There are traditional pies of sausage and pepperoni, of course, but there's also Thai Pizza, topped with marinated chicken, cilantro and peanuts. (Not something we'd want every week, but a great experiment.) Checkers also serves a wide list of salads, sandwiches and pastas, as well as frozen yogurt.

For those who demand New York style pizza, there's *La Vera* (575-1113; 629 Fourth St., Santa Rosa & 765-1113; 840 Petaluma Blvd., N., Petaluma). The cheese is thick and stretches for a city block and the meats are little explosions of pepperoni and sausage. The crust is that perfect unison of crunchy and chewy. The atmosphere is more formal that most pizza shacks, with polished brass and wood, but the prices are competitive. Pastas and calzones, salads, gelato and espresso also served.

Two other pizza parlors are more typically American. Both have several outlets and are family places. The better of the two is *La Prima Pizza* (963-

7909; 1010 Adams St., St. Helena & 942-6272; 1009 Foothill Blvd., Calistoga). It makes a pleasant pie, with a puffy crust that's crisp on the bottom. The toppings are generous and of good quality, but they seem piled on, not cooked in. La Prima also makes burgers and other sandwiches and barbecue. *Mary's Pizza Shack* (five locations in Sonoma and one in Napa) is fairly safe American pizza. The crust is a tad salty and the meat toppings rather bland, but the cheeses and veggies are top-rate. Mary's also serves salads and pastas. Look for gray-haired Mary waving at you from billboards.

Midwesterners crave the Chicago style of thick crusts and layered toppings, and the only fix they'll find hereabouts is *Old Chicago Pizza* (763-3897; 41 Petaluma Blvd., N., Petaluma). It's a small place and people line up to get inside. While the pie doesn't stack up to the best of the Windy City, it is fabulous. Old Chicago serves pizza on a pedestal plate/lazy susan, which is good because the slices are so heavy you need the downward momentum to guide it to your own plate. Excellent ingredients.

The Wine Exchange in Sonoma has the air of a big city book store.

Chris Alderman

WINE SHOPS

Even the best liquor stores around the country would be jealous of the wine selection available at any grocery store in Napa and Sonoma counties. Your typical Safeway carries perhaps 40 chardonnays. Some have more space devoted to wine than cereal; that's how common and everyday wine is here. The specialty wine shops, as you might imagine, are among the finest in the nation, offering a huge variety as well as hard-to-find treasures. You'll be surprised to learn that wine is seldom cheaper at the wineries than local retail shops, unless you catch a sale or buy by the case. So finding a good wine source will likely save you money. You run the risk, of course, of not being able to find a wine you loved at the winery. It's your gamble. Prices are often lower at grocery stores than wine specialty shops, but wine shops carry harder to find wines. (See also, Chapter Six, Wineries.)

Napa County

St. Helena Bottle Shop (963-3092; 1321 Main St., St. Helena). One of Napa's oldest, dating to 1953, this shop believes in the notion of "Only the Best." It has a small but extremely select offering of current Napa and Sonoma wines. Most shops beg for bottles of Spottswoode and Dunn cabernets, then sell them them only to preferred customers. They're stacked up in this shop. (At a price, of course.) There's also a superb cellar in the back devoted to older vintages, with vertical vintages of Silver Oak and Heitz Martha's Vineyard and the like and scarcities like a magnum of Caymus 1985 Special Selection Cabernet Sauvignon. Also, a fine line-up of cold imported beers.

Calistoga Wine Stop (942-5556; 1458 Lincoln Ave., Calistoga). Housed in an 1866-vintage Central Pacific railroad car, this shop is the centerpiece of Depot Railroad Station, a mini-mall of shops. A solid line-up of current Napa wines, with the best of Sonoma. A few older vintages. Prices are the going rate; few bargains.

Liquor Barn (257-1734; 1833 Lincoln Ave., Napa). Gigantic selection at generally low prices. Not much in the way of decor, but it *does* have a supermarket length aisle devoted entirely to cabernet sauvignon, for example. We counted 40 different merlots. Doesn't carry many California rarities, but has a handful of older vintages and French wines. Also has a vast selection of beer, liquor and picnic supplies.

St. Helena Wine Merchants (963-7888; 699 Hwy. 29, St. Helena). Has the same fantastic collection as the Bottle Shop just up the road, but goes one farther with a giant selection. No bargains here, but it does carry most current releases of California and France. Also a notable assortment of older wines and larger bottles. Want a matching set of all three Diamond Creek cabernets in 3-liter bottles? No problem.

Sonoma County

Tip Top Liquor Warehouse (431-0841; 900 Dry Creek Rd., Healdsburg). Not nearly as industrial as its sounds, Tip Top has an assortment of wine that lives up to its name. There's a heavy emphasis on Sonoma County wines, particularly from wineries around Healdsburg. Prices are usually a dollar or two below most and there's an emphasis on good quality bargain wines from California and Australia. Also some older and French wines, as well as imported beer and liquor.

Traverso's (542-2430; Third and B streets, Santa Rosa) Recently named one of the best wine shops in California by noted wine author Anthony Dias Blue, Traverso's has a special place in the hearts of winery owners and wine lovers around the county. This old Italian deli doesn't carry a huge selection of wine, only the best quality in all price ranges. Bill Traverso knows wine but is so unpretentious about it that you don't have to pretend *you do*. Traverso's has the best stock of Italian wines in the region, as well as a respectable list of French Bordeaux and Burgundy.

The Wine Exchange of Sonoma (938-0969; 452 First St., E., Sonoma). This shop reminds us of those chic big city bookstores. There's an air of restrained refinement, with sounds of Vivaldi playing faintly in the background as you browse. Somehow the Wine Exchange pulls it off without being hoity-toity. Don't expect many discounts, but do look for the best current releases and a few vintage wines. There's also an *enormous* selection of imported beers. We could spend hours scanning those. Another plus is the wine and beer tasting bar in the back.

OTHER WINE SHOPS

All Seasons Cafe 942-6828; 1400 Lincoln Ave., Calistoga.
Bottle Barn 528-1161; 3331 Industrial Dr., Santa Rosa.
Chateau du Vin 257-7121; 1886 El Centro Ave., Napa.
Groezinger's 944-2331; 6528 Washington St., Yountville.
Sonoma Wine Shop 996-1230; 412 First St., E., Sonoma.

CHAPTER SIX
Vintage Harvest
WINERIES

1986

Napa Valley

CABERNET SAUVIGNON

ALCOHOL 12.5% BY VOLUME

PRODUCED AND BOTTLED BY

ROBERT MONDAVI WINERY

OAKVILLE, CALIFORNIA

It's amazing how things change. As recently as the 1960s, a tasting room was simply a few tables and some crystal tucked into a corner of a winery. Loyal customers would stop by casually, often bringing their own jugs and bottles to get a fill-up from the barrel. But as Napa and Sonoma have gained prominence in the wine world, so has their appeal as vacation meccas. More than 2 million tourists come to Napa County each year; about 1 million visit Sonoma County. Winery hopping has become an avid pastime, and tasting rooms have evolved into bustling centerpieces, sometimes rustic, sometimes chic, but always inviting and fun.

Wineries, like the wines they make, come in different styles and qualities. You can even use the same words to describe them. Is it a sweet or sour experience? Subtle or bold? Is it friendly from the first or does it have to grow on you? In compiling our list of wineries, we asked ourselves: "What makes a winery worth visiting?" Is it the wine? A pilgrimage to the source of your favorite chardonnay has great appeal. Is it the fame? "Wow! There's Robert Mondavi — we *have* to stop there." Is it the winery itself? Or maybe glamour is more your speed, whether it's the old palaces of Beringer and Inglenook or the fashionable edifices such as Sterling and Domaine Carneros. There's also the tour to consider, and the tasting room staff — are they friendly, helpful? Is there a fee? Can you picnic? And so on.

Fall is the favorite touring season for many: the vineyards resplendent in rich golds and reds and the wineries and fields hectic with the harvest or "crush" as it's called. Our favorite time is spring, when the mountains and fields are lush and green, the vines and trees are budding, and the fields are covered with the yellows of wild mustard. Winter, too, has its charms: in the fog and rain, wineries are cozy stops. But summer remains king: toasty days followed by cool evenings, the vines thick with leaves and with grapes beginning to bulge.

When visiting a winery, be yourself — ask questions, don't try to impress, and above all, have fun. While tastings remain free at all but a handful of Sonoma County wineries, most Napa Valley wineries charge from $2 to $5. Usually a souvenir glass is thrown in, and the fee may be waived if you buy wine. We concentrated on wineries with set touring hours and those that permit drop-in visits. Many other wineries are open by appointment only. These are often smaller wineries that want to discourage visitors. Also, many new wineries, restricted by zoning laws, are not permitted to have open house policies. Either way, don't let the "By appointment only" scare you off.

As for tours, most wineries offer them and you'll be bored quickly if you take them all. We suggest trying two tours of different kinds: at some wineries, like Mondavi, Domaine Mumm and Simi, the tours emphasize *chemistry* or *technology* while at others, for instance, Clos Pegase, Charles Krug, Beringer or Buena Vista, the stress is on *history, art* or *ambience*. Still others, like Rutherford Hill and Glen Ellen, highlight the *subjective experience of tasting*.

Other tidbits of advice: Take notes. They don't have to be voluminous, just a brief note like "1987 Simi Cabernet — great" to jog your memory when you visit the liquor store at home. While touring, we recommend taking along crackers, cheese and a cooler with bottled water or soda. It helps to cleanse your palate between wineries, and besides, just because you're sipping wine all afternoon doesn't mean you won't get thirsty. Finally, don't feel that you have to try *every* wine. Many wineries are generous and you can feel the effects more quickly than you expect. If you're making several stops, limit yourself to one or two samples, or merely take a sip and pour out the rest. No one will mind.

We've included some general touring maps of the Napa and Sonoma wineries. For those who want more detailed atlases (there are over 300 of them), we can suggest a few. *Wine Country Tour Map* (Graphic Concepts), is one of our favorites: a simple paper fold-out available at most wineries for a few dollars. Another good map can be found in the *California Visitors Review*, a free weekly newspaper available everywhere in Wine Country.

Winery descriptions are organized here by region, beginning first in Napa, then Sonoma. So browse away and plan your route.

SPECIAL REMINDER

If your party is driving its own car, be **sure** to appoint someone as the designated **sober** driver.

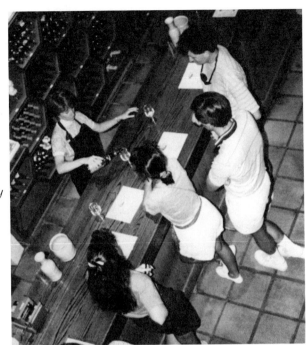

Visitors taste the current vintage in Buena Vista Winery tasting room, Sonoma.

SVVB

Wine Lingo

The world of wine tasting is both a fine place for casual fun among amateurs and a serious professional business. As in any professional craft, such as cooking or a sport, specialized language abounds. Bear in mind that to have a good time and to learn more about wines you do not need an expert's vocabulary. At the end of this chapter we provide a glossary of some technical and trendy wine terms (see Wine Glossary, page 216) to help beginners, but plain English works well in Wine Country, too. We recommend that you keep your sense of humor handy so you'll be ready to debunk or dismiss any so-called wine experts who can't (or won't . . .) discuss their subject in laymen's terms. If you say a wine you've just tasted has "a long-lasting aroma" and a wine expert says it's "long in the nose" or has a "profound bouquet," you're in the same ballpark. And the expert is really not being any clearer about what is, after all, a judgment call.

NAPA COUNTY WINERIES

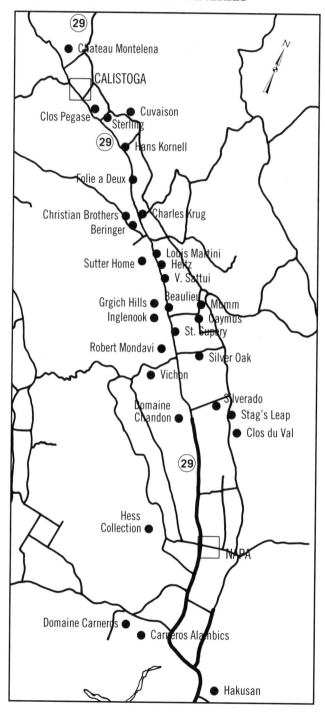

- Chateau Montelena
- **CALISTOGA**
- Clos Pegase
- Cuvaison
- Sterling
- Hans Kornell
- Folie a Deux
- Christian Brothers
- Charles Krug
- Beringer
- Louis Martini
- Sutter Home
- Heitz
- V. Sattui
- Beaulieu
- Mumm
- Grgich Hills
- Caymus
- Inglenook
- St. Supery
- Robert Mondavi
- Silver Oak
- Vichon
- Silverado
- Domaine Chandon
- Stag's Leap
- Clos du Val
- Hess Collection
- NAPA
- Domaine Carneros
- Carneros Alambics
- Hakusan

SONOMA COUNTY WINERIES

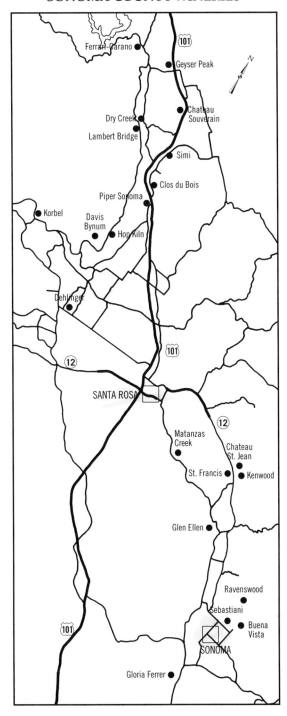

The Art of Tasting
Four Ss and a P

"I know how to taste wine," you say. "Put the glass to your lips and swallow, right?" We can't argue with that method. While there is an intricate tasting process that experts use, there's no need for the casual taster to be so *correct*. We would like to offer a few tips, however, that will help even novices savor wine more fully. First, understand that palates and preferences are different, but you can distinguish chardonnay from chenin blanc in much the same way you can differentiate pork from beef.

Sight:

Hold the glass up and consider the color. Red wines, for example, don't look the same. Pinot noir can be a soft shade of strawberry, while zinfandel is often as dense as blackberry jam.

Swirl:

There's a good reason wineries only pour a small amount — aside from the fear of going broke, that is. You can't swirl a full glass without making a puddle. Lightly swirl the glass for a moment and you'll be surprised how the wine changes. When infused with air, wine releases its aroma.

Sniff:

Take a whiff. Your nose is a key player in wine tasting. First, ask yourself is the aroma pleasant or not? Some wines have very subtle bouquets, while others will rush your nostrils like linebackers. One is not necessarily better than the other. Wines have characteristic smells. Sauvignon blanc, for example, may smell like freshly-mown grass.

Sip:

Don't take a big gulp. Swish it around your mouth, adding more air and exposing all your taste buds. Is it sweet or dry? Bitter or sour? A cabernet sauvignon, for example, might make you pucker. Those are tannins, which help the wine age. Try to sort out the sensations on your tongue. Chardonnay may have an almost buttery taste and pinot noir may taste lightly of cherry, with a lingering silky sensation.

Pour:

We couldn't think of another S-word. Expert tasters always Spit — if they didn't, they'd be passed out on the floor. You don't need to do that, but we would encourage you to only take a sip or two and then pour out the rest. Tasting rooms don't mind at all; in fact, they provide special buckets for this purpose. Also, remember you don't have to try *every* wine, particularly if you're stopping at a lot of wineries.

WINERIES — NAPA VALLEY

Napa & Carneros

CARNEROS ALAMBICS DISTILLERY
Brandy master: Erica Hiller Levy.
253-9055.
1250 Cuttings Wharf Rd., 1 mi. S. of Hwy. 12/121, Napa.
Tours: By appt., 10:30 and 2:30 Mon. to Fri.; 9 to 4 Sat.
Tasting: None.
Fee: None.

If drinking a cognac in front of a glowing fire is your idea of ecstasy, then Carneros Alambics will reveal the secrets behind your fantasy. OK, so Carneros Alambics' Blue Heron Brandy isn't technically cognac — cognac comes only from the Cognac region of France. The proud cognac house, Remy Martin, is behind Carneros Alambics, and the process and even the copper stills are imported from France. It's about as close as you'll ever get to seeing cognac made in this country.

Visitors driving through the sturdy stone archway are greeted by an expanse of vineyards. The operation is really rather small; three tile-roofed buildings that encompass the visitors' center, distillery and aging cellar. The comfortable visitors' center has a fireplace and displays that explain how brandy is made and evolves as it ages. The distillery, though, is where the fun is; an airy building with high wooden rafters, tile floor and eight red and copper stills that look like oversized Arabian tea pots. Guides detail how the stills work, explaining that five wines — French colombard, pinot noir, chenin blanc, palomino and muscat — are distilled and aged separately, then blended.

The final stop is the aging cellar, a large building half-buried in the ground. There's an extraordinary smell here — they call it "Angel's Share" — which comes from the alcohol evaporating from the aging brandy. It's like standing in a huge brandy snifter. Once your eyes adjust to the dark, you'll be able to see stacked some of the 4,000 French Limousin oak barrels in which the brandy ages for at least five years.

Sorry, Carneros Alambics doesn't offer tastings — it's against the law. But to give you some notion of what they are producing, they do offer *sniffs*. Don't laugh. It's rather fun. First you smell each of the five distilled wines, then the final product. It gives you some idea of how a fine brandy is carefully crafted.

DOMAINE CARNEROS
Winemaker: Eileen Crane.
257-0101.
Off Hwy. 12/121 at Duhig Rd., 3 mi. W. of Napa.
Tours and tasting: Winter, 10:30 to 4:30 daily; summer 10:30 to 5:30.
Fee: Wine sold by the glass.

The Domaine Carneros winery is an exclamation point along Hwy. 12/121, towering above a hilltop and surrounded by a sea of vineyards. Built in the style of an 18th-century French chateau, Domaine Carneros is no everyday winery. But then champagne — oops, sparkling wine — isn't your everyday libation. Owned by French champagne giant, Taittinger, Domaine Carneros is

Domaine Carneros' 18th-century French chateau and its mèthode champenoise *underscores its French heritage.*

Courtesy Domaine Carneros

a $14 million extravaganza designed to make a statement about its French heritage and the sumptuousness of sparkling wine.

As you ascend the 70 steps, you can pause on the terrace to view the cream and terra cotta mansion, as well as the lovely rolling hills of the Carneros district. Inside, you may appreciate the marble floors, the maple interior crowned with ornate chandeliers and the sound of baroque music in the background. Behind the stylish front is a state-of-the-art winery that released its first wine in the fall of 1990. Domaine Carneros is the only sparkling winery to use *all* Carneros grapes. This region is known for a long, cool growing season; a climate similar to that found in the Champagne region in France.

Tours introduce visitors to the complete French *mèthode champenoise* process of making sparkling wine and end in the tasting salon, where Domaine Carneros' only wine, a non-vintage Brut, is sold by the glass. It's a light, elegant sparkler, a melding of French and American tastes. An hors d'oeuvre, by the way, comes with it, and if weather permits, you can take your bubbly out to the terrace and enjoy its gorgeous view.

HAKUSAN SAKE GARDENS
Brewmaster: Takao Nihei. 258-6160.
Hwy. 12/29 at Jameson Canyon Rd., 4 mi. S. of Napa.
Tours: Self-guided 9 to 6 daily.
Tasting: 9 to 6 daily.
Fee: None.
Special features: Japanese garden.

You're driving along a Napa back road, admiring the scenery: wide skies, stately mountains, eminent wineries and field upon field of — RICE? Grapes aren't the only source of wine, you know. Sake, a rice wine, is the traditional wine of Japan, and while rice isn't *really* grown in Wine Country (they use rice from Sacramento Valley), Hakusan has been making sake just outside of the city of Napa since 1989. If all the chardonnays are starting to taste the same, try Hakusan Sake Gardens for something different.

Now you're probably wondering what a sake brewery — that's the proper term — is doing in Napa. Kohnan Inc., the firm behind Hakusan, originally wanted to build in Japan, but its high-tech plans clashed with certain Japanese traditions, and California was chosen instead. The visitors' center and gardens were opened in 1990.

Don't expect the tranquility you can find at San Francisco's Japanese

Gardens. Hakusan's garden is mostly for show, particularly with the sounds of Hwy. 29 nearby. But the visitors' center is a pleasant spot. You're greeted at the door, occasionally by a kimono-clad hostess, and encouraged to sit and watch a short video while you sip a fruity cold sake and partake of a sushi snack. The video describes the history of sake, which dates back to 710 B.C., and explains how it is made at Hakusan. When you've finished, a warm sample is brought to the table, and it is interesting to see how heat brings out the nuttiness. After tasting, you can follow a self-guided tour along the outside of the brewery, viewing the process through large windows.

THE HESS COLLECTION
Winemaker: Randle
   Johnson.
255-1144.
4411 Redwood Rd., 5 mi.
   west of Hwy. 29, Napa.
Tours: Self-guided 10 to 4
   daily.
Tasting: 10 to 4 daily.
Fee: $2.50.
Special features: Art
   gallery.

Along the rugged slopes of Mount Veeder is the most impressive art collection north of San Francisco. The Hess Collection is both a winery and a museum of modern art. Donald Hess, a Swiss mineral magnate, transformed the old Mont La Salle Winery into a showcase for his two great passions.

Wend through the thick glades of Mount Veeder and you'll find a majestic stone building among the vines. Covered in ivy, the winery dates from 1903. It was the first Napa Valley home of Christian Brothers before Hess renovated it and opened it to the public in 1989. Don't be put off by the chic atmosphere. Hess honestly wants to share his art and the staff encourages you to roam.

Inside, a towering three-story atrium with an elevator and staircase leads to two floors of painting and sculpture by artists such as Francis Bacon and Robert Motherwell. A self-guided tour allows you to view both art and winery — a porthole next to one painting, for example, provides views of the bottling line. Don't miss the Barrel Chai, a dark, cool cellar where wine ages in barrels for up to 22 months. For a more in-depth look at the winery, you can watch a brief video.

Before leaving, stop in the tasting room, a large hall of rich, dark wood, where another barrel aging room can be seen through a window. Hess concentrates on two wines: cabernet sauvignon and chardonnay. The chardonnay is stylish and oaky; the cabernet is fabulous and one of Napa Valley's best. There's something about mountain vineyards that make a rich, intense cabernet, but then that's no secret. Many of Napa cult cabernets — Diamond Creek, Dunn — come from the mountains.

Other Napa & Carneros Wineries

CHIMNEY ROCK WINERY (257-2641; 5350 Silverado Trail). Tasting 10 to 4 daily; tours 11 and 2 daily; one of Napa Valley's newest wineries, specializing in chardonnay and sauvignon blanc; tasting with $2.50 souvenir glass.

MONTICELLO CELLARS (253-2802; 4242 Big Ranch Rd.). Tasting 10 to 4:30 daily; tours 10:30, 12:30 and 2:30 daily; paying tribute to one of America's first winemakers, Thomas Jefferson, the hospitality center is a replica of Monticello; cabernet sauvignon a specialty.

MONT ST. JOHN CELLARS (255-8864; Old Sonoma Rd. and Hwy 12/121). Tasting 10 to 5 daily; tours by appt.; one of Napa's oldest, specializing in pinot noir and chardonnay; creekside picnic area.

TREFETHEN VINEYARDS (255-7700; 1160 Oak Knoll Ave.). Tasting 10 to 4 daily; tours by appt.; beautiful old three-story winery dates from 1886; one of Napa's most popular chardonnay producers.

Yountville & Stag's Leap

CLOS DU VAL
Winemaker: Bernard Portet.
252-6711.
5330 Silverado Trail, Napa.
Tours: By appt.
Tasting: 10 to 4 daily.
Fee: None.
Special features: Picnic area.

Bernard Portet was brought up among the casks and vines of Chateau Lafite–Rothschild, where his father was cellarmaster. The Bordeaux influence is strong here, both in the wines and the winery. An elegant and understated building surrounded by vineyards, Clos du Val evokes a small country winery, with red roses marking the end of each vine row, in typical French fashion. Even inside, Portet's distinctly French hand is clear.

Established in 1972, Clos du Val helped pioneer the notion that cabernet sauvignons didn't have to be muscular monsters to age well. Though anyone who has ever tasted a Lafite-Rothschild can tell you this is no secret, it wasn't the established thinking in Napa Valley at the time. Clos du Val's cabernets are in the Bordeaux style, soft and supple, helped by the generous blending of merlot. That they have proven worthy agers is often demonstrated by the older vintages poured in the tasting room. Cabernet, however, isn't the only specialty. Clos du Val's zinfandel has strapping gobs of fruit and the merlot considerable finesse. The pinot noirs have been uneven over the years, as have the chardonnays. If they're pouring their semillon, don't pass it up. Spicy and lean, it's always one of the best.

The tasting room is a cordial spot with a vaulted ceiling and a talkative staff. Much of the operation can be viewed through nearby windows, and for a touch of humor, Ronald Searle's wine cartoons decorate the walls.

DOMAINE CHANDON
Winemaker: Dawnine
   Dyer.
944-2280.
California Drive, Off Hwy.
   29, Yountville.
Closed: Mon. and Tues.,
   Nov. through Apr.
Tours: 11 to 5 daily.
Tasting: 11 to 6 daily.
Fee: Wine sold by the glass.
Special features:
   Restaurant.

The turning point for California sparkling wine came in 1973 when Moet-Hennessy built this ultra-modern winery in the hills west of Yountville. If that famed French champagne house believed in Napa's potential, then California winemaking had come of age. Thus began the rush of European sparkling wine firms to Northern California.

This may be the most unassuming sparkling winery in all of Wine Country. Driving along Hwy. 29, you'd hardly notice the glass, concrete and native-stone bunker built into an oak-covered knoll.

Not that Domaine Chandon lacks style. To enter, you cross a small wooden bridge that spans a pond busy with ducks and filled with flowering plants. Just inside is an intriguing museum, replete with displays of artifacts and explanations of everything from the classic French *mèthode champenoise* to how corks are made. Domaine Chandon's tour is thorough, and takes visitors past the large stainless steel fermentation tanks, the mechanized riddling racks and even the bottling line.

Domaine Chandon makes only two sparkling wines: a toasty salmon-colored Blanc de Noir and a round, complex Brut. Both are available by the glass in the stylish tasting salon, where on warm days, you can sit on the sun-drenched terrace to enjoy your cool glass of bubbly. The restaurant, considered one of Napa Valley's best *and most expensive*, serves — of course — French cuisine, prepared with a glass of sparking wine in mind. (See Chapter Five, *Restaurants and Food Purveyors*.)

SILVERADO VINEYARDS

Winemaker: Jack Stuart.
944-1770.
6121 Silverado Trail, Napa.
Tours: By appt.
Tasting: 11 to 4 daily.
Fee: None.

Face it, most wineries are lucky to make one, *maybe* two good wines. Rare is the winery that shines with cabernet sauvignon *and* chardonnay. Add the challenge of merlot and sauvignon blanc and the odds are impossibly stacked. Somehow, Silverado pulls it off, regularly producing outstanding examples of each. Best of all, this rising star seems to lack ego; all its wines remain reasonably priced.

Built by the Walt Disney family in 1976, Silverado offers a dramatic view from its perch atop a Silverado Trail knoll. Wind your way to the top of a drive and to discover this the Spanish-style winery of stone and stained glass. (Look closely, one window features Mickey Mouse.) A lovely flower-filled courtyard and fountain welcome visitors as they enter the denlike, handsome tasting room, with its large wooden counter.

The vineyards around Silverado produce some of the finest, most intense fruit in the valley. Pair that with Stuart's winemaking gift — he has, you might say, a purple thumb — and you will understand why Silverado's wines are among the best and keep getting better. The winery first made its name with cabernet, a lush and ripe wine with raspberry fruit; a recently-introduced reserve cabernet is a knockout. Silverado's merlot is big and vivid, still a baby. As for the whites, the sauvignon blanc is agile and fruity and the lush yet subtle chardonnay is fast becoming one of our favorites. Silverado doesn't pour all their wines but no matter what's offered, there's no going wrong.

STAG'S LEAP WINE CELLARS

Winemaker: Warren
  Winiarski.
944-2020.
5766 Silverado Trail, Napa.
Tours: By appt.
Tasting: 10 to 4 daily.
Fee: $2, includes souvenir
  glass.

Stag's Leap Wine Cellars falls into the select pilgrimage category. In 1976, it achieved instant fame when its 1973 cabernet won the famous Paris tasting. This was the first blind tasting where French wine experts rated American wines over French classics such as Mouton–Rothschild, and it changed the way the world looked at California wine.

Hidden within an oak grove, Stag's Leap is an ever-growing village of buildings. Founded by the Winiarski family in 1972, the winery retains much of its unassuming charm, despite its fame. The tasting room is merely a table tucked among towering wooden casks in one of the aging cellars.

A handful of wines are offered for tasting every day. Don't expect to sample the winery's premier bottling, Cask 23, a cabernet blend with a $75 price tag that is ever so scarce. Stag's Leap Vineyard, a second-tier reserve cabernet rich with velvety fruit, is, however, often on the tasting list. Though Stag's Leap's regular Napa Valley cabernet lacks the complexity of its two reserves, it is also an exceptional wine. Don't pass up an opportunity to try their lean and crisp chardonnays; they're gaining quite a following. In addition, Stag's Leap dabbles with petite sirah and merlot. Hawk Crest, Stag's Leap bargain label, offers simple but well-made everyday cabernets and chardonnays.

Other Yountville & Stag's Leap Wineries

S. ANDERSON WINERY (944-8642; 1472 Yountville Crossroad). Tasting 10 to 4:30 daily; tours by appt.; the aging caves are the highlight of any visit to this winery; specializes in chardonnay and sparkling wine; $3 tasting fee.

CONSENTINO WINERY (944-1220; 7415 Hwy. 29). Tasting 10 to 5 daily; tours by appt.; a new location for this winery, which specializes in Bordeaux-style blends of cabernet sauvignon, merlot and cabernet franc; tasting with $2 souvenir glass.

PINE RIDGE WINERY (253-7500; 5901 Silverado Trail). Tasting 11 to 4 daily; tours by appt.; unassuming little winery with picnic tables and swings; excellent cabernet sauvignon, merlot and chenin blanc.

ROBERT SINSKEY VINEYARDS (944-9090; 6320 Silverado Trail). Tasting 10 to 4:30 daily; tours by appt.; new winery making a name for itself with pinot noir and merlot; tasting with $3 souvenir glass.

Oakville & Rutherford

BEAULIEU VINEYARDS
Winemaker: Thomas
  Selfridge.
963-2411.
1960 Hwy. 29, Rutherford.
Tours: 10 to 3 daily.
Tasting: 10 to 4 daily.
Fee: Reserve wines only.

If you could sum up Napa Valley winemaking with a single bottle of wine, it would be the Georges de Latour Private Reserve Cabernet by Beaulieu. Though not necessarily the best wine every year, it has been the yardstick against which all other cabernets are measured.

Pronounced *Bowl-You* or called BV for short, Beaulieu is one of Napa's most historic wineries dating from it founding in 1900 by a Frenchman named Georges de Latour. In 1938, Latour hired a young Russian immigrant, Andre Tchelistcheff, who went on to revolutionize California cabernet and become the grandfather of American winemakers. Private Reserves from the 1930s and '40s are still drinking well today. Although the Latour family and Tchelistcheff are gone, Beaulieu continues their rich tradition.

Built of brick and covered with ivy, the winery isn't particularly impressive, but a tour can be an eye-opener. A video in the visitors' center briefs guests on Beaulieu's past and present. Walk in here, and chances are that you will immediately be offered a sample of the winery's crisp sauvignon blanc. It's one of the best for the price. As you sip, browse through the museum of old bottles and memorabilia. Three or four other wines are eventually offered. After going through a slump, Beaulieu's chardonnay seems to be improving, although we've never been inspired by its pinot noir. While not nearly as impressive as the Private Reserve, Beaulieu's other two cabernets have significant charm at a fraction of the price. Tastings of the Private Reserve are sometimes offered for a fee — don't pass it up.

CAYMUS VINEYARDS
Winemaker: Chuck
   Wagner.
963-4204.
8700 Conn Creek Rd.,
   Rutherford.
Tours: None.
Tasting: 10 to 4 daily.
Fee: $2, includes souvenir
   glass.

No American wine is more highly regarded than the Caymus Special Selection Cabernet. Fini. Some might argue that Heitz Martha's Vineyard or Beaulieu Private Reserve cabernets compare, but no wine more consistently tops the "Best of..." lists of critics and wine lovers alike. When it is released every January, people crowd the winery for the honor of paying $60 for a bottle. (That's ONE bottle — the limit in 1991.) Caymus remains a low-frills family outfit and tampers little with its wines. The main 40-acre vineyard lies east of the Napa River in the heart of Napa Valley's cabernet country; a blessed location.

The tasting room is a *tiny* room in a plain house. Guests often waver at the gate, afraid of trespassing; but don't hesitate. Don't expect to taste the Special Selection, but you might be lucky enough to sample Caymus' second-tier cabernet, their Napa Valley Estate. Also remarkable, it has a more reasonable price and sells out quickly, as well. Caymus also makes a good sauvignon blanc and zinfandel, though the pinot noir struggles to keep up.

GRGICH HILLS
   CELLARS
Winemaker: Mike Grgich.
963-2784.
1829 Hwy. 29, Rutherford.
Tours: By appt.
Tasting: 9:30 to 4:30 daily.
Fee: $2, includes souvenir
   glass.

French wine lovers worship the land, but in California, the winemaker is king. Cult followings have a way of developing, as with Mike Grgich, one of Napa Valley's best-known characters. The scrappy immigrant from Yugoslavia became a star in 1976 when, as winemaker at Chateau Montelena, his 1973 chardonnay beat Burgundy's best whites in the famous Paris tasting. Later, Grgich joined with Austin Hills and opened this winery.

An ivy-covered stucco building with a red tile roof, Grgich's winery remains a house devoted to chardonnay. Elegant and rich, it's consistently among the best in California, also one of the more expensive. It's also one of the few chardonnays that improve with a few years in the bottle. Grgich also makes a graceful fumé blanc and has considerable luck with zinfandel. And if there's a rising star on the Grgich list it's the cabernet sauvignon, a soft and complex red that's usually underrated.

All this can be sampled in Grgich's modest tasting room where the smell of oak and wine float in from the barrel aging room nearby. You can see most of the winery from the tasting room and parking lot, so a tour is rather succinct. You might see a feisty little fellow with a black beret — that's Grgich. He's usually around.

Winemaker Mike Grgich enjoys a sip of cabernet sauvignon in the barrel room of Grgich Hills Cellars, Rutherford.

Chris Alderman

INGLENOOK NAPA VALLEY
Winemaker: John Richburg.
967-3359.
1991 Hwy. 29, Rutherford.
Tours and tasting: 10 to 5 daily.
Fee: None.

A lot of us have a romantic ideal of what a Napa Valley winery should look like: a sturdy stone castle, shrouded in ivy and enveloped by vineyards. That's Inglenook. No winery better sums up the history and romance of Napa Valley.

Visitors approach the winery through a long tree-lined driveway. Just inside the entry, a display that includes old photos and bottles helps bring Inglenook's history to life. Scottish for "Cozy Corner," Inglenook originated in 1879 when Finnish sea captain Gustave Niebaum came to Rutherford and spent some of the fortune he made in the fur trade on building this towering Gothic structure. The Captain's Room near the front entrance mimics a ship's cabin, complete with porthole windows and latched cupboards.

Following a brief video, the tour proceeds through the magnificent stone aging tunnels that house giant oval oak casks, the impressive work of 19th-century German craftsmen. You can also view one of the largest libraries of old wines in the country, as well as the newer aging cellars across the courtyard. Wines are poured back in the main building and a leisurely seminar on the art of tasting is offered. Free tastings are also open to visitors *not* taking the tour, a rarity in Napa Valley.

Inglenook made its name with cabernet sauvignon. During the 1950s and '60s, their wines helped set the standard, but quality dropped in the '70s. It has rebounded somewhat recently and more recent Reserve Cask cabernets have been super. Inglenook's merlot is also gaining ground and the obscure Italian varietal, charbono, has a small but fanatical following. The winery sports a full line of white wines, from chardonnay to gewurztraminer, mostly simple and fairly priced.

MUMM NAPA VALLEY
Winemaker: Greg Fowler.
963-3434.
8445 Silverado Trail,
   Rutherford.
Tours: Hourly between
   10:30 and 4:30.
Tasting: 10:30 to 6.
Fee: Wine sold by the glass.
Special features: Patio; gift
   shop.

Mumm Napa Valley may have a French parent, but it's a California child through and through. The winery is a long, low ranch barn with redwood siding and green slate roof. Mumm is more at home on the American Back 40 than the coifed fields of Champagne. Mumm is one French company that decided to *fit in* rather than stand out, a philosophy that actually runs deeper than the mere design of a winery. Rather than imitating Champagne, rather than forcing France on California, Mumm is blending the best of both. Traditional French *mèthode champenoise* meets the distinctive fruit of Napa Valley and the result is one of California's best sparkling wines.

Mumm Napa Valley, a joint venture between Mumm and Canadian-based Seagram, made its first wines at Sterling before moving to a new winery a few years later in 1988. The winery and visitors' center, however, opened in May 1990. The winery tour offers a detailed look at the French way of making sparkling wine. Guides first lead you inside a football field of a room housing giant tanks where the grape juice is fermented. Then they continue through long hallways allowing gallery views of the winemaker's lab, bottling plant, aging cellars, etc.

Mumm relies on grapes from all over Napa to make its four sparklers. Brut Prestige is the main release, a snappy blend of pinot noir and chardonnay, and Blanc de Noirs is a zesty rosé. Vintage Reserve is aged longer and made in small lots and only in select years. Its most respected wine is the extravagantly lush Winery Lake. No tastings are offered, but wines are sold by the glass in the visitors' center and the prices are fair. A flute of the Vintage Reserve, for example, is $4.50. The saloon is quaint and country, with sliding glass doors that allow easy views of the Rutherford countryside. There's also an outdoor patio when the day begs a seat in the sun.

ROBERT MONDAVI WINERY

Winemaker: Tim Mondavi.
963-9611.
7801 Hwy. 29, Oakville.
Tours: 9 to 5 daily
  (summer); 10 to 4:30
  (winter).
Tasting: Offered with tour.
Fee: For reserve wines
  only; available without
  tour.
Special features: Art
  gallery.

Robert Mondavi has been such an innovator, such a symbol of the "new" Napa Valley, that it's hard to believe the his winery was founded in 1966. Once considered too flamboyant for conservative Napa County, his Spanish mission-style winery along Hwy. 29 now seems as natural as the Mayacamas Mountains. Since first setting out on his own from family-owned Charles Krug, Mondavi has been the most outspoken advocate for California and its wines.

Few Napa wineries are busier on a summer day than Mondavi. The parking lot is brimming with cars and RVs, even though the winery offers free tastings only after its exhaustive one-hour tour, one of the most thorough in the Valley. Guides lead visitors into the vineyards for a lecture on how grapes are grown and harvested; then to the grape presses, fermentation tanks, the all-important aging barrels and a view of all the latest wine wizardry. If that's not complete enough, Mondavi also offers a marathon three to four-hour tour that often includes barrel tasting. The tour ends in the tasting room where a selection of wines are offered along with a mini-course on the proper way to taste wine.

Mondavi bottles one of the most extensive lists of wines in the valley. It originated the concept of fumé blanc, a drier version of sauvignon blanc, but continues to struggle with it. The chardonnays are creamy and the chenin blancs fruity and vibrant. Reds seem to be Mondavi's strong suit. The reserve cabernet sauvignons and pinot noirs become more magnificent every year — and so do the prices. Of course the regular bottlings are hardly slackers. On weekends and the occasional weekday, a table is set up near the vineyards and tastings of reserve wines are offered for a fee. It's delightful to sit among the vines, savor an old wine like the 1977 Reserve Cabernet and test how well Mondavi's wines hold up.

ST. SUPERY VINEYARD AND WINERY

Winemaker: Bob Broman.
963-4507.
8440 Hwy. 29, Rutherford.
Tours: Self-guided 10 to
  4:30 daily.
Tasting: 10 to 4:30 daily.
Fee: $2.50.
Special features: Hands-on
  wine museum, terrace.

Wineries, on the whole, aren't the best place to take kids. Swirling and sipping, prowling around cellars, driving from one tasting room to the next, will test the patience of any teen or tyke. St. Supery, however, is one winery that is fun for both young and old. This recently completed winery adds a touch of science museum adventure, with colorful displays, hands-on activities, modern winery gadgetry and Old Napa charm.

St. Supery was established in 1982, when French businessman Robert Skalli bought some land in

Pope Valley, a part of eastern Napa County where few grapes are grown. He also bought Edward St. Supery's old vineyard just south of Rutherford and built a state-of-the-art winery next door. St. Supery's original Queen Ann Victorian has been restored and is now part of the tour. Nearby is a small experimental vineyard plot, which visitors may also stroll through.

A second-floor gallery shows off the day-to-day activities. Windows reveal the bottling line, the barrel aging room and the like. You can have fun here. Our favorite is what we jokingly call the "smell station," where noses are educated on how to evaluate cabernet sauvignon and sauvignon blanc. Ever hear cabernet described as cedar or black cherry? Well, here you can find out what these terms mean. Hold your nose to one tube, press the button and catch a whiff. Another display gives you a peek under the soil to see what a grapevine looks like. After the tour, St. Supery offers tastings of its cabernet, chardonnay and the sweet Moscato; its lovely outdoor terrace is open for wines by the glass.

SILVER OAK CELLARS
Winemaker: Justin Meyer.
944-8808.
915 Oakville Crossroad,
    Oakville.
Tours: By appt.
Tasting: 9 to 4:30 Mon. to
    Fri.; 10 to 4:30 Sat.
Fee: $5.

Not many wineries can live off one wine, but then Silver Oak isn't *just* any winery. You won't find any white zinfandel here, only cabernet sauvignon that has been raised to an art form. Low profile by Napa Valley standards, Silver Oak is known to cabernet lovers around the country, and that's all that matters. Silver Oak makes three wines, all in matching silver labels, all cult favorites: Napa Valley, Alexander Valley and Bonny's Vineyard. The Alexander Valley is the most accessible, both on your palate *and* the shelves of your local wine shop. All three, however, typically are velvety and opulent, with tastes that linger. You will, of course, pay for the privilege.

Silver Oak was established in 1972 on the site of an old Oakville dairy. Some of the dairy buildings are still used, though a Gothic-style masonry winery became home in 1982. Out front, you'll notice the water tower that's prominent on the label. Inside is a tasting room paneled with redwood from old wine tanks. To one side, behind glass, you can see a temperature-controlled wine library stocked with Silver Oaks from every vintage. Tastings are offered of available wines, *if* available. Don't be put off by Silver Oak's reputation. This isn't a stuffy place. Fledgling wine lovers should particularly make the stop, if only to find out what all the fuss over cabernet is about.

VICHON WINERY

Winemaker: Michael Weis.
944-2811.
1595 Oakville Grade,
  Oakville.
Tours: By appt.
Tasting: 10 to 4:30 daily.
Fee: For reserve wines
  only.
Special features: Picnic
  area.

We don't mind admitting, we're saps for Vichon. Let the wine snobs roll their eyes — it's a great place to picnic. Teetering on the edge of the Oakville Grade, Vichon offers a stunning view of the valley as well as a shady spot to relax, nibble on cheese and sip wine. That Vichon's wines have considerable charm only makes a visit more pleasant.

You'll find Vichon off busy Hwy. 29, where the harrowing Oakville Grade road begins its assault on Mt. Veeder. Built in 1982, the nondescript winery is shaded by a thick of oak trees. The best panorama is just past the front entrance, where hillsides ribbed with vineyards fall away from the winery and patches of checkered green stretch out across the valley. A half dozen picnic tables are shaded by oak and those with the best view are claimed early.

The Mondavi family has owned Vichon since 1985 and its influence is beginning to show. The cabernet sauvignons have steadily improved, particularly the Stag's Leap District reserve, a soft and polished wine. The merlot is known for its explosive fruit and the chardonnay is tart and tasty. The Chevrignon, a blend of semillon and sauvignon blanc, has its admirers, but we're not among them. Tours are offered, but they're hardly needed. A trip to the restroom will take you past the fermentation tanks, bottling line, the works.

Other Oakville & Rutherford Wineries

CHATEAU POTELLE (255-9440; 3875 Mt. Veeder Rd., Oakville). Tasting and tours 12 to 5 Sat. and Sun., weekdays by appt.; recently-transplanted French winemakers bought the old Vose vineyards high atop Mount Veeder and aspire to Bordeaux-style cabernet sauvignon and Burgundian chardonnay.

CONN CREEK WINERY (963-9100; 8711 Silverado Trail, Rutherford). Tasting 10 to 4 daily; tours by appt.; modern winery that makes a bit of everything; cabernet sauvignon a specialty.

DeMOOR WINERY AND VINEYARDS (944-2565; 7481 Hwy. 29, Oakville). Tasting 10 to 5 daily; self-guided tour; look for the geodesic dome and you know you're at DeMoor — that's the tasting room; cabernet sauvignons and zinfandels are full-throttle; picnic area; tasting with $1.50 souvenir glass.

FRANCISCAN VINEYARDS (963-7111; 1178 Galleron Rd., at Hwy. 29, Rutherford). Tasting 10 to 5 daily; cabernet sauvignons and merlots often exceptional; second label Estancia may be California's best bargains in cabernet and chardonnay; $1.50 tasting fee on weekends only.

PEJU PROVINCE (963-3600; 3466 Hwy. 29, Rutherford). Tasting 10 to 5 daily; a new winery has just been added to this family-owned estate which produces a wide range of wines.

Rutherford Hill's stylish barn, tucked into a hillside, offers a shaded picnic area.

Courtesy Rutherford Hill

RUTHERFORD HILL WINERY (963-7194; 200 Rutherford Hill Rd., off Silverado Trail, Rutherford). Tasting 10 to 4:30 daily; tours (including the extensive, eerily beautiful cave) hourly between 11:30 and 3:30; large winery in a contemporary mansard-roofed barn; offers tasty and reasonably priced cabernet sauvignon and merlot, and a truly memorable robust syrah, among others; shaded picnic area under a lovely arbor with adjacent herb garden; tasting with $3 souvenir glass.

SEQUOIA GROVE WINERY (944-2945; 8338 Hwy. 29, Rutherford). Tasting 11 to 5 daily; tours by appt.; family-owned winery specializing in cabernet sauvignon and chardonnay; $3 fee for reserve wines only.

VILLA MT. EDEN (944-2414; 620 Oakville Crossroad, Oakville). Tasting 10 to 4 daily; tours by appt.; winery dates from 1881; specializing in cabernet sauvignon; chenin blanc is delightful.

St. Helena

BERINGER VINEYARDS
Winemaker: Ed Sbragia.
963-7115.
2000 Main St., St. Helena.
Tours: 10 to 5 daily.
Tasting: Offered with tour.
Fee: Reserve wines only;
   available without tour.

There's something almost regal about the Rhine House, the circa-1876 peak-roofed mansion that forms the centerpiece of Beringer Vineyards. Sitting amid manicured lawns, you can appreciate its elegance as you approach through a tall tunnel of ancient elms. Meticulously restored, the Rhine House suggests that Beringer doesn't take its past or its reputation lightly. This is one of the few wineries that has it all. A prime tourist attraction with a lively, historical tour, it is one of Napa's most popular makers of cabernet sauvignon.

The oldest continually-operated winery in Napa Valley, Beringer was founded by German immigrants, Jacob and Frederick Beringer. The tour offers a few juicy details about the early days. Jacob, for example, had the idea for a winery, but no money. Frederick, his older brother, as was traditional, had inherited all the family wealth. He agreed to finance Beringer as long as *he* was the boss. He even made Jacob move his house so he could take advantage of its prime location to build the Rhine House. Jacob's lesser mansion today sits some distance to the north.

The tour takes visitors through the original aging cellar, a stone and timber building built into the side of a hill along with 1,000 feet of tunnels, cleared by Chinese laborers. If you want to see a working winery, though, you'll be disappointed. The real action takes place across Hwy. 29 and isn't open to the public.

Tours end in the Rhine House tasting room, where a varying selection of regular wines are offered. Beringer bottles three, sometimes four, cabernets and several chardonnays under the Beringer label. (It also makes the bargain Napa Ridge label.) To try the good stuff, climb the staircase to the handsome reserve tasting room, where Beringer's Private Reserve cabernet and chardonnay, if available, are poured for a fee. The Reserve cabernet is stunning.

The old stone archway welcomes visitors to Greystone Cellars in St. Helena, currently home to Christian Brothers.

Tim Fish

CHRISTIAN BROTHERS
Winemaker: John White.
963-0765.
2555 Main St., St. Helena.
Tours: 10 to 4 daily.
Tasting: Offered with tour.
Fee: None with tour;
   special barrel tastings
   offered 1 to 4:30 daily for
   $5.
Special features: Gift shop.

Greystone Cellars has a medieval feel, only fitting for a winery that bears the name Christian Brothers. Housed in a grand stone castle, it reminds us of an Old World abbey. The Brothers, in reality, are gone. They sold the cellars and the new winery down the road to Heublein in 1989, which as we write, has placed Greystone on the market.

Greystone was built as a cooperative winery for local grape growers who were being gouged at the time by San Francisco winemakers. The estate has seen its share of owners. Built in 1888 by William Bowers Bourn, it was the largest stone cellar in the world, three stories high, with three acres of floor space and constructed out of hand-carved native volcanic stone. The Christian Brothers, a 300-year-old religious teaching order that had been making wine in America since 1882, bought Greystone in 1950. By 1984, structural consider- ations influenced the Brothers to move their winemaking to a new facility.

Reopened as a visitors' center in 1987, Greystone offers little insight into the modern winemaking process, but remains an historical treat. On display is former cellarmaster Brother Timothy's massive collection of corkscrews, from an 18th-century beauty to one shaped like a pair of dice. The tour ends with a tasting of four wines and an informative seminar on wine and the art of tast- ing, instructing tasters to swirl their wine to release its distinct bouquet. As our informative and humorous guide, Jim Flowers, commented, "In Napa Valley we swirl everything: orange juice, milk. But it's not called swirling any- more. Now it's volatilizing your esters."

FOLIE À DEUX WINERY
Winemaker: Rick Tracy.
963-1160.
3070 Hwy. 29, St. Helena.
Tours and tasting; 11 to 5 daily.
Fee: None.
Special features: Picnic area.

If two psychologists opened a winery, what would they put on the label? An ink blot, of course. No, that's not a joke, that's Folie à Deux, the brainchild of two psychologists with a love of wine and a sense of fun. Its name translates as "Folly for Two," a delusion shared by two people.

For Evie and Larry Dizmang, the shared fantasy began in 1974, when they bought a former sheep ranch and transformed its small house into a win- ery. Open since 1981, the yellow cottage sits on a knoll covered with vines, easily Napa Valley's most quaint winery. Dogs and cats roam around and may join you as you step through the doorway. Stepping inside this chic farmhouse feels as though you've come to visit a neighbor, not taste wine. The tasting room is the living room, where wines are displayed on the fireplace mantel and poured from atop an antique cabinet.

Chardonnay has made the winery's name and it's a honey with light, crisp fruit. The cabernet sauvignon improves every year and a velvety merlot has just been added. Our favorite is the dry chenin blanc, a fresh and melony bou- tique of spring flowers. It's one of the best and we prefer it over many of the snobbier, more expensive chardonnays out there.

A tour of Folie à Deux won't take long. Fermentation is done in a shed attached to the rear of the house. Barrel aging is in the cellar as well as in other out buildings. As with many of the smaller Wine Country wineries, there are no bottling facilities. A semi-trailer with a portable bottling line is brought in when needed.

HEITZ WINE CELLARS
Winemaker: David Heitz.
963-3542.
436 Hwy. 29, St. Helena.
Tours: By appt.
Tasting: 11 to 4 daily.
Fee: None.

Driving along Hwy. 29, you'd never know that a redwood shack on the outskirts of St. Helena is home to one of America's most coveted wines. But the wine faithful do and they line up every January to buy Heitz Martha's Vineyard Cabernet Sauvignon. Is it worth the fuss? We stood in line two hours to buy the 1985 and have never regretted it.

Curmudgeon and maverick, Joe Heitz worked at Beaulieu before going his own way in 1961. Within a few years, he refurbished a stone winery in the hills of the valley's east side, keeping the old winery on Hwy. 29 as a tasting room. The key to Heitz's success seems to lie in the vineyards. Martha's Vineyard is just west of Oakville and produces some of the valley's most distinctive grapes. Napa is known for its minty cabernets and none show that character more powerfully than the Martha's Vineyard. The wine is approachable on release but also ages well, something few California cabernets can equal.

The modest tasting room features a library of old wines for sale, and each day, two or three current wines are poured from a handsome wooden desk. Don't expect to sample the Martha's Vineyard without waiting in line, but occasionally the second cabernet, Bella Oaks, is offered and is nearly as dynamic. A third regular Napa Valley cabernet is widely available, and though its reputation is spottier, it's sometimes exceptional. Heitz also has a chardonnay and pinot noir that garners little notice, but its grignolino, an Italian rosé, has considerable charm.

HANNS KORNELL CHAMPAGNE CELLARS
Winemaker: Hanns J. Kornell.
963-1237.
1091 Larkmead Ln., St. Helena.
Tours: 10 to 4 daily.
Tasting: 10 to 4:30 daily.
Fee: None.

With so many new extravagant French palaces out there, it might be easy to overlook this old family champagne cellar. It would be your loss. To tour and taste wine at Hanns Kornell is to sample Napa circa 1960.

Son of a Jewish winemaker, Kornell escaped from a German concentration camp and fled to America in 1940, making his way slowly from New York to California. When he finally saved up enough money, he bought an aging winery, Larkmead, built in 1906 and now on the National Register of Historic Places. Here winemaking, using the French *mèthode champenoise*, is simple and traditional. Gadgetry is kept at a minimum and there's a distinct hands-on approach. Wines, for example, are still riddled by hand, a painstaking process that slowly removes all yeast and sediment from the sparklers.

The tasting room is inside a small house behind the winery. Kornell bottles the usual line of sparkling wine — Brut, Blanc de Blancs, Blanc de Noirs, etc. — but mixes in a few that aren't traditionally in champagne blends, such as

chenin blanc and semillon. Two more common offerings are a sparkling muscat alexandria and a German-style sparkling wine called Sehr Trocken. While
Kornell's sparkling wines are hardly our favorite, the winery is a pleasing and
offbeat stop along the busy Napa trail.

Tim Fish

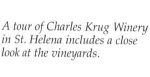

*A tour of Charles Krug Winery
in St. Helena includes a close
look at the vineyards.*

**CHARLES KRUG
    WINERY**
Winemaker: Peter
  Mondavi.
963-5057.
2800 Hwy. 29, St. Helena.
Tours: 10 to 4 daily.
Tasting: Offered with tour.
Fee: For reserve wines
  only; $3 with souvenir
  glass; available without
  tour.

Chardonnay with fish, cabernet with steak —
what sort of wine goes with history? Charles
Krug has it covered no matter what match you
choose. Napa's first winery, Krug bottles one of
the valley's most exhaustive menu of wines.

After working under Agoston Haraszthy in
Sonoma, Krug came to the Napa Valley and built
his own winery in 1861. His massive stone winery
was gutted by fire the day after it was finished but
he rebuilt. Today, this old winery is in disrepair, a
shadow of its former glory, but the wines are still
aged inside in immense redwood tanks. The rest
of the winemaking takes place in a modern facility
just behind. When the Mondavi family bought
Krug in 1943, another Napa dynasty began. Brothers Robert and Peter Mondavi ran the winery together until 1966 when a feud led Robert to open his
own winery.

Krug's 45-minute tour is one of the most thorough and educational in the
valley leading visitors into the vineyards and through the plant. "A hundred
years ago," one guide told us, "they used to filter wine through ox blood." A
varying selection of four wines are offered for tasting, along with a scholarly
seminar on drinking wine, from pulling the cork to the sniff, swirl and swallow. Krug's top cabernet sauvignon has recently regained its former stature
and is available during the tasting session for a $1 fee.

LOUIS MARTINI WINERY

Winemaker: Michael Martini.
963-2736.
253 Hwy. 29, St. Helena.
Tours and tasting: 10 to 4:30 daily.
Fee: Reserve wines only, $3.

Run by the third generation of Martinis, this large but unostentatious winery is one of Napa Valley's best known. That is, after all, one of the charms of visiting Wine Country. You know the label and like the wine, why not visit the source?

Martini is one of the Valley's great overachievers, producing a voluminous roster that includes several tiers of cabernet sauvignon, pinot noir and zinfandel, as well as petite sirah, merlot, chardonnay, barbera, Johannesberg riesling, even sherry and other dessert wines. Remarkably, they're all quite capable and good values. The top-of-the-line cabernet, Monte Rosso, once considered among the best, has recovered recently from a long slump to regain much of its glory.

Martini originated in Kingsburg, California in 1922; it moved to St. Helena is 1933. Napa's first post-Prohibition success story, Martini flourished 'when many of the older wineries lay in ruin. Founder Louis M. Martini, a dominating spark plug of a man, was one of the Valley's great characters. Son Louis P. Martini brought the winery into the modern era and today his children, Carolyn and Michael, run things. The winery, like the wine, is a no-frills notion. Rather industrial outside, the tasting room is warmed by a friendly staff and by displays that sum up the Martini sense of family.

V. SATTUI WINERY

Winemaker: Daryl Sattui.
963-7774.
Hwy. 29 and White Lane, St. Helena.
Tours: By appt.
Tasting: 9 to 6 daily.
Fee: None.
Special features: Deli; picnic area; gift shop.

Just about every winery has a picnic table tucked somewhere, but V. Sattui is Lawn Lunch Central. The tasting room doubles as a deli shop, offering some 200 cheeses, exotic salami, paté and salads. The front lawn — replete with wicker baskets and red and white tablecloths — is shaded by tall oaks and filled with frolicking kids. Picnickers won't find a heartier welcome in Napa Valley.

THE headquarters for Napa Valley picnicking, V. Sattui Winery in St. Helena.

Chris Alderman

While some wineries prefer simply to make wine and not deal with the public, V. Sattui is just the opposite. Its wines are available *only* at the winery. It's a busy place — selling an astonishing 500 loaves of bread a day, for example — yet the atmosphere is cordial, not frantic. Though only completed in 1985, the Italian Romanesque winery looks like an old monastery. Not only is it open for tours, but picnickers are welcome to use the cellar on rainy days.

V. Sattui is named for Vittorio Sattui, who founded a winery at a different location in 1885. It didn't survive Prohibition, but Vittorio's great-grandson, Daryl, revived the label in 1976. Eight varietals are offered; the most popular, a light and fruity Johannesberg riesling. Several sturdy and potent cabernets are also produced. Our favorite is a marvelous dry rosé named Gamay Rouge. In a distinctive slender bottle, it's a throwback to a time when rosé was more than liquid candy. And if there's a better picnic wine, we can't think of one.

SUTTER HOME WINERY
Winemaker: Steve
  Bertolucci.
963-3104.
277 Hwy.29, St. Helena.
Tours: None.
Tasting: 10 to 4:30 daily.
Fee: None.

Who'd have thought back in the '70s that a simple, sweet rosé would become the Grail — some would say *Unholy* Grail — of California wine. When white zinfandel became one of Wine Country's hottest commodities, even Sutter Home, its creator, was astounded. By the time the craze peaked in the late '80s, Sutter Home had grown from one of Napa Valley's smallest wineries to one of its biggest.

Tim Fish

Sutter Home's winery dates from 1874, though most of the action now takes place a few miles up the road in a factory built in the late 1980s. Swiss–German immigrant John Thomann built the original, but it was dubbed Sutter Home after John Sutter purchased it in 1906. Since 1946, it has been owned and operated by Italian immigrant brothers John and Mario Trinchero. In 1968, the winery pioneered the use of the vibrant zinfandel grapes from Amador County and until 1970, specialized in wine by the bulk. Then its well-known motto was: "If you can carry it or roll it through the front door, we'll fill it with wine."

In 1972, winemaker Bob Trinchero was exploring new uses for the plentiful Amador zinfandel when the idea of a blush zinfandel came to mind. Grape skins, you see, give red wine most of its color, so if the juice of a red grape is fermented away from the skin, a pink or blush wine is produced. No one had ever done that with zinfandel before. Originally dubbed *Oeil de Pedrix*, "Eye of the Partridge," then renamed white zinfandel, it grew so popular that other wineries started making it and it became the best-selling variety in America.

White zinfandel is, of course, popular in Sutter Home's new tasting room. Many visitors are surprised there is such a thing as *red* zinfandel, but that is poured as well and it's fruity and pleasant. A new addition for Sutter Home is chardonnay, and it's a lovely but simple little number at a bargain price. The chenin blanc is rather cloying, but the sauvignon blanc and cabernet sauvignon are winning.

Other St. Helena Wineries

CHATEAU NAPA-BEAUCANON (963-1886; 1695 Hwy. 29). Tasting 10 to 4:30 daily; tours by appt.; winery opened by the DeConinck family of France.

DOMAINE NAPA WINERY (963-1666; 1155 Mee Ln.). Tasting 10 to 5 daily; tours by appt.; this winery established in 1986 specializes in cabernet sauvignon and merlot.

FREEMARK ABBEY WINERY (963-9694; 3022 Hwy. 29). Tasting 10 to 4:30 daily; tour at 2 daily; top-of-the-line cabernet sauvignon called Cabernet Bosche traditionally among top in Napa Valley; Edelwein Gold sweet Johannesberg riesling one of California's top dessert wines; tasting with $5 souvenir glass.

Courtesy Freemark Abbey

MARKHAM WINERY (963-5292; 2812 Hwy. 29). Tasting 11 to 4 daily; tours Mon. through Fri. by appt.; an up-and-coming winery with super merlot, chardonnay and sauvignon blanc.

MERRYVALE VINEYARDS (963-0397; 1000 Main St.). Tasting 10 to 5:30 daily; tours by appt.; historic Sunny St. Helena Winery is home to this winery that features a top chardonnay; $3 tasting fee.

MILAT VINEYARDS (963-0758; 1091 Hwy. 29). Tasting 10 to 6 daily; roster includes white zinfandel, chenin blanc and cabernet sauvignon, sold only at the winery; tasting with $1.50 souvenir glass.

PRAGER WINERY AND PORT WORKS (973-3720; 1281 Lewelling Ln.). Tasting 10:30 to 4:30 daily; small family winery that produces port from cabernet sauvignon, as well as a line of regular wines; picnic area and bed and breakfast inn.

RAYMOND VINEYARD AND CELLARS (963-3141; 849 Zinfandel Ln.). Tasting 10 to 4 daily; tours by appt; outstanding cabernet sauvignon and chardonnay; $1.25 tasting fee for reserve wines.

SPRING MOUNTAIN VINEYARDS (963-5233; 2805 Spring Mountain Rd.). Tasting and tours 10:30 to 4 daily; home to the once-popular prime time TV soap "Falcon Crest"; grounds of 1885 Parrott mansion open for tours; $3 tasting fee.

WHITEHALL LANE (963-9454; 1563 Hwy. 29). Tasting 11 to 5 daily; a winery of modern angular design; cabernet sauvignon, merlot and pinot noir a specialty; tasting with $2 souvenir glass.

Calistoga

CHATEAU MONTELENA
Winemaker: Bo Barrett.
942-5105.
1429 Tubbs Ln., Calistoga.
Tours: By appt.
Tasting: 10 to 4 daily.
Fee: $5.
Special features: Picnic grounds.

"**N**ot bad for a kid from the sticks," was all Jim Barrett said when Chateau Montelena jolted the wine world by winning the legendary Paris tasting in 1976. A "Who's Who" of French wine cognoscenti selected Chateau Montelena's 1973 chardonnay in a blind tasting over the best of Burgundy. Chateau Montelena's star has been in orbit ever since.

No serious wine lover would think of leaving Chateau Montelena off his tour list. The wines are stunning and the winery is an elegant and secluded old estate at the foot of Mount St. Helena that includes the lovely Jade Lake. Alfred Tubbs founded the original Chateau Montelena in 1882; its French architect using the great chateaux of Bordeaux as inspiration. The approach isn't too impressive, but walk around to the true facade and you'll discover a dramatic stone castle.

During Prohibition, the winery fell into neglect, but in 1958, Chinese immigrant Yort Franks created the Chinese-style Jade Lake and the surrounding garden. Shaded by weeping willows, swans and geese, walkways, islands and brightly painted pavilions, it is Napa's most coveted picnic spot. Each day, the lake is reserved for *a single* group, and Saturdays and Sundays are booked months in advance.

In the handsomely panelled tasting room, three wines are typically poured; the selection varies. Most great Napa cabernet sauvignons need a few years in the cellar before they're ready, and Chateau Montelena is no exception. But Chateau Montelena *is* different in that it prefers to pour its older cabernets so that tasters can get a better idea of the wine in its prime. During a recent visit, the 1981 and 1983 cabernets were on the tasting list; exceptional, though they still needed a few years. The chardonnays and zinfandels are usually the current vintage, and the chardonnays continue to live up to their reputation as intense, oaky and lush.

The imposing entrance of Clos Pegase, designed by Princeton architect, Michael Graves.

Courtesy Clos Pegase

CLOS PEGASE
Winemaker: Bill Pease.
942-4981.
1060 Dunaweal Ln,
    Calistoga.
Tours: 10 weekdays, by
    appt.
Tasting: 10:30 to 4:30 daily.
Fee: $3, includes souvenir
    glass.
Special features: Art
    collection.

Clos Pegase is architecturally flamboyant, a postmodern throwback to the Babylonian temple; a shrine to the gods of art, wine and commerce. This commanding structure of tall pillars and archways, done in hues of yellow and tan, is the work of noted Princeton architect Michael Graves, winner of the 1984 design competition jointly sponsored by owner Jan Shrem and the San Francisco Museum of Modern Art. Unquestionably an eye-catcher, some locals call Clos Pegase "Hollywood's idea of Egypt."

The name, Clos Pegase, derives from Pegasus, the winged horse that according to the Greeks gave birth to art and wine. Shrem is an avid art collector. Redon's 1890 painting "Pegasus," featured on the wine label, is the centerpiece of his large collection, several pieces of which are displayed in the tasting room.

Clos Pegase's five wines are all made with great style and appeal. The cabernet sauvignon is ripe and spicy, and the two chardonnays are refined but with plenty of forward fruit. They're also one of the few wineries that produce both a fumé and sauvignon blanc — two slightly different wines from the same grape. The fumé, as is the norm, is the drier of the two, yet both are lovely, crisp and grassy.

CUVAISON WINERY
Winemaker: John Thacher.
942-6266.
4550 Silverado Trail,
  Calistoga.
Tours: By appt.
Tasting: 10 to 5 daily.
Fee: $2.50, includes
  souvenir glass.
Special features: Picnic
  area; gift shop.

At Cuvaison, the wine impresses with every sip. Just when you think the wine you've just tasted can't be topped, they pour another that proves you wrong. Cuvaison has been around since 1970 but has come into its own only recently. Currently, it is producing some of the best chardonnays, cabernet sauvignons and merlots in the business, and its zinfandel is no wimp, either.

A white mission-style building with a red-tiled roof, Cuvaison is bounded by vineyards and a splendid landscaped picnic area. The tasting room is busy but retains a friendly tone, as the staff chatter comfortably about wine and the winery. Tasting begins with the chardonnay, a remarkable and elegant wine with rich fruit; the cabernet is equally vibrant, intense and berrylike. Watch out, the merlot sells out so quickly you'll be lucky to try it.

STERLING VINEYARDS
Winemaker: Bill Dyer.
942-3344.
1111 Dunaweal Ln.,
  Calistoga.
Tours: Self-guided 10:30 to
  4:30 daily.
Tasting: 10:30 to 4:30 daily.
Fee: $5.
Special features: Access by
  aerial tramway; gift
  shop.

Sterling isn't a just winery, it's an experience. A modern white villa perched atop a tall knoll, it just may be Napa Valley's most dramatic visual statement. Seen from the distance, it looks like a bleached white castle along a jagged Mediterranean coastline. Sure, there's a touch of Disneyland — you ascend on an aerial tramway — but that's Sterling's appeal. From the top, the view is unsurpassed, and the fact that Sterling makes superior wine only adds to the attraction.

Sterling retains such a contemporary look that it's hard to believe it was built in 1969. A well-marked self-guided tour allows a leisurely glimpse of the winery's workings and finally leads you to one of Napa's most relaxing tasting rooms. After picking up a glass at the counter — usually a sample of sauvignon blanc — visitors can rest their feet at one of the tables inside or on the balcony. Once seated, the wines come to you. A varying selection of three wines are poured

*The aerial tram at
Sterling Vineyards in
Calistoga.*

Courtesy Sterling Vineyards

and even though Sterling seldom offers its best, none will disappoint. There
are four cabernet sauvignons; the best is the Monumental Reserve, but even
the simple Napa Valley bottling has great appeal. The Winery Lake chardonnay is a big brawling wine with touch of finesse, and the Napa Valley
chardonnay is lemony and fun. We also favor Sterling's merlot and pinot noir,
though they're hardly the best of their kind.

Other Calistoga Wineries

STONEGATE WINERY (942-6500; 1183 Dunaweal Ln.). Tasting 10:40 to 4:30
daily; tours by appt.; small family-owned winery known for its lush merlot
and a good cabernet sauvignon; tastings free weekdays, $1.25 with souvenir
glass Sat. and Sun.

WINERIES — SONOMA VALLEY

BUENA VISTA WINERY
Winemaker: Jill Davis.
252-7117.
18000 Old Winery Rd.,
  Sonoma.
Tours: Mon. to Fri. at 2; Sat.
  and Sun. 11:30 and 2.
Tasting: 10 to 5 daily.
Fee: Reserve wines only.
Special features: Picnic
  area; art gallery.

This is where it all began, California's oldest
premium winery. Buena Vista is where Agoston Haraszthy, known as the "father of California
wine," began his experiments in 1857. Though others had made wine in Sonoma before this, they
had used only the coarse Mission variety grapes,
brought north by Spanish missionaries for Mass
wine. Haraszthy was the first to believe that the
noble grapes of Bordeaux and Burgundy could
thrive in California. Just think, you might be sipping White Mission now if he hadn't.

Visitors to Buena Vista can stroll down a gentle

quarter-mile path, past thick blackberry bushes and tall eucalyptus trees to the tasting room, set inside the thick stone Press House, built in 1863. The self-guided tour is a gentle history lesson in disguise. The original winery was built in 1857, although the wine is now made a few miles away.

Buena Vista's reputation faded some over the years but rebounded during the 1980s. Its cabernet sauvignons are gaining a great reputation, and its chardonnay, merlot and pinot noir have a growing list of admirers. Prices remain moderate. In the Press House, you can taste a selection of new releases; some older vintages can be sampled for a small fee. As you sample your wine, check out the gallery in the upstairs loft. During the summer, Buena Vista has an artist-in-residence program, so you might actually get to see the artist at work.

CHATEAU ST. JEAN
Winemakers: Don Van
  Staaveren and Pete
  Downs (sparkling).
833-4134.
8555 Hwy. 12, Kenwood.
Tours: Self-guided, 10 to
  4:30 daily.
Tasting: 10 to 4:30 daily.
Fee: None.
Special features: Picnic
  area.

With Sugarloaf Ridge in the distance and a surround of thick lawns and tall trees, Chateau St. Jean is a visual treat. Your palate won't feel the least slighted, however, since the wines, here, are equally delightful.

Chateau St. Jean is one of Sonoma County's most prestigious wineries, specializing in vineyard-select chardonnays and sparkling wines. The Robert Young Vineyard chardonnay helped set the standard, and remains today one of the best. Other stars include a fumé blanc with great finesse and gewurztraminer. And for a warm summer picnic, we can hardly imagine anything better than Chateau St. Jean's melony Johannesberg riesling. Since the winery offers one of Sonoma's lushest picnic grounds, you might want to bring lunch and buy a cold bottle.

The denlike tasting room is located in a 1920s-era Mediterranean-style chateau. It's crowded on weekends, and the staff can get a bit harried, but they will pour four wines, plus a sparkler. Reserve wines are offered for a fee.

Behind the mansion is the winery, a modern version of a Medieval French castle, complete with a tower. A self-guided tour offers a complete look at the works — sparkling wine, however, is made at another facility — and ends in the tower where visitors can look out over the lawns and vineyards.

GLEN ELLEN WINERY
Winemaker: Mike
  Benziger.
935-3000.
1883 London Ranch Rd.,
  Glen Ellen.
Tours: Self-guided, 10 to
  4:30 daily.

Someone else may have written the original book on making good, cheap wine, but Glen Ellen has certainly made a fortune on the revised edition. Sonoma County's second-largest winery, Glen Ellen struck gold in the mid-1980s with their low-priced Proprietor's Reserve wines. They won't change the world but they're not bad for a casual dinner.

Tasting: 10 to 4:30 daily.
Fee: None.
Special features: Picnic
   area.

Glen Ellen is hidden among the dense hills and thick trees of Sonoma Mountain, not far from Jack London's old home. Lovingly restored by the clannish Benziger family, the ranch dates from 1860. Along the narrow driveway, you can see a tall vineyard knoll on the right topped with what looks like a Roman ruin, while on the left, a redwood grove shades a hillside picnic area. Past an old farmhouse and down the hill is the wooden ranch barn that serves as aging cellar and tasting room.

Glen Ellen is a friendly place and the tasting room is always crowded. A vast array of wines are offered, including the winery's second bargain label, M.G. Vallejo. The Proprietor's Reserve sauvignon blanc is actually not bad, considering the $5 price tag, and depending on the vintage, the merlot and gamay beaujolais have appeal. But you can taste those wines on the cheap at home. What you shouldn't miss are Glen Ellen's premium wines, bottled under the Benziger label. Harder to find, they are sometimes worth a search. The cabernet sauvignon can be a knockout in a good vintage, and the Benziger merlot is starting to make a name for itself.

Here, there, and everywhere: Road signs lead the way to Sonoma County's many wineries.

Bob Martin; courtesy SCCVB

**GLORIA FERRER
   CHAMPAGNE CAVES**
Winemaker: Bob Iantosca.
996-7256.
23555 Hwy. 121, Sonoma
Tours: 11 to 4 daily.
Tasting: Wines sold by the
   glass.
Special features: Caves;
   terrace with a great
   view.

If you've had the pleasure of paying a mere $5 for Cordon Negro, the simple but tasty little sparkling wine in the ink-black bottles, then you already know something about the people behind Gloria Ferrer. Freixenet of Spain is the world's largest producer of sparkling wine, and like the French champagne makers before it, it was drawn to the great promise of California. But instead of the hectic Napa Valley, Freixenet selected the peaceful undulating hills of Carneros in southern Sonoma County.

Gloria Ferrer, named after the wife of Freixenet's president, has greater ambitions than producing a reasonable sparkler at a low price. It competes easily with its French–American rivals, rating consistently among the top domestic bubbly in the $12 to $15 range. Three wines are made in the traditional *méthode champenoise* process: Brut, Royal Cuvee and Carneros Cuvee, each with a slightly different style and appeal.

The Carneros location places Gloria Ferrer off the high-traffic areas of Sonoma but it's an appealing place and worth the slight detour. Placed dramatically on a gentle slope of a hill, the winery is a bit of Barcelona done in warm tones of brown and red. The walls are stucco and the windows tall and arched. The fireplace glows in the winter, and during the summer the terrace doors are pushed open to the cool breezes from San Pablo Bay to the south. Take a glass of wine outside for a spectacular view, and you might even catch stunt planes in action from the nearby Schellville Airport. Gloria Ferrer's tour also has great appeal, particularly the man-made caves carved from the hillside where the sparkling wine ages underneath the winery.

KENWOOD VINEYARDS
Winemaker: Michael Lee.
833-5891.
9592 Hwy. 12, Kenwood.
Tours: By appt.
Tasting: 10 to 4:30 daily.
Fee: None.
Special features: Gift shop.

Don't let Kenwood Vineyards fool you. The tasting room might be in a rustic little barn, but behind the simple charm is a large, savvy winery; one of Sonoma County's masters of cabernet sauvignon. Here's a homey and relaxed winery with wines that will please everyone in your group. Built by the Pagani Brothers in 1906, the current owners, Marty and Michael Lee and John Sheela, bought the place in 1970. Substantially refurbished, a touch of the old Pagani style is also in evidence.

Kenwood doesn't really have a specialty. White or reds, they have good luck with all sorts of wines. There's no better wine with fresh oysters than Kenwood's lemony sauvignon blanc. Both zinfandels — the Sonoma and Jack London Ranch — have great style. But none of those compare to Kenwood's success with cabernet. It makes three, actually. The first is pleasant and inexpensive. A notch above is the Jack London cabernet, a stylish plum of a wine, followed by the expensive but outstanding Artist Series. It's a big, silky cabernet with great aging potential, and the label each year features the work of a different artist. On occasional weekends, Kenwood matches a wine with a particular food, hoping to promote food and wine as partners. A recent match of the Jack London cabernet with thin slices of beef roast on sourdough made us long for a full-course dinner.

MATANZAS CREEK WINERY
Winemakers: Susan Reed and Bill Parker.
528-6464.
6097 Bennett Valley Rd., Santa Rosa.
Tours and tasting: 10 to 4, Mon to Sat., 12 to 4 Sun.
Fee: None.
Special features: Art gallery.

If you forego the beaten path for this winery, you won't regret it. And if you're lucky enough to sample its merlot before it sells out — and it always sells out — all the better. Matanzas Creek is the only winery in Bennett Valley, a quiet, untouched fold of green, west of Kenwood.

The first wines were made in 1978 in a converted dairy barn, but these days, if you continue down the long driveway to the foot of the Sonoma Mountains, you'll find a state-of-the art facility. There are rarely crowds of visitors so you are likely to have the office-size tasting room all to yourself. But the staff is friendly, never making you feel on the spot. As an added treat, you can look at the lovely pastel landscapes by artist-in-residence, Mary Silverwood.

Matanzas Creek makes only three wines, each among the best in California, each inspired by their French counterparts. The chardonnay has the delicate finesse of a white Burgundy and the sauvignon blanc is fragrant and flavorful.

"Whale Song," woven wire sculpture by Sebastopol artist Peter Busby at Matanzas Creek Winery, Santa Rosa.

Chris Alderman

But the star here is the merlot, a lush, velvety ode to the classic Bordeaux of the Pomerol region. More than a few have compared it to Petrus, among the world's most coveted wines. Having only seen Petrus from the other side of a glass case, we wouldn't know, but the Matanzas Creek merlot is superb. Unfortunately, its price is also inspired by Petrus, making it the most expensive American merlot on the market.

The striking design created for Ravenswood's label.

RAVENSWOOD WINERY
Winemaker: Joel Peterson.
938-1960.
18701 Gehricke Rd.,
   Sonoma.
Tours: 11 and 2 daily.
Tasting: 10 to 4:30 daily.
Fee: None.
Special features: Picnic
   area.

Cabernet sauvignon may be a passion, but zinfandel is an obsession. Cursed with a shady reputation by its evil twin, white zinfandel, red zinfandel is often considered a second-class citizen. But zin fans know better. At its best, zinfandel is luscious and jammy, equal to cabernet in most ways and at half the price. Now zin lovers have access for the first time to one of the wine's great proponents: Ravenswood. Zin lovers have long been wise to Ravenswood, but spring 1991 brought a new treat. Ravenswood moved out of its old garage and into a larger facility, Haywood's old winery north of Sonoma Plaza. (Haywood has moved to Buena Vista).

Ravenswood's new location, an unassuming stone winery built into the side of a hill, fits the classic image of a circle of ravens that graces its label. The tasting room staff is jovial and offers a wide selection of wines. The view outside the large wooden doors is lovely.

Ravenswood makes not *one* zinfandel, but four. And not one is *white*. The Vintner's Blend is the most approachable, soft, lovely and a bargain. The other three are characters with distinct personalities. Ravenswood also makes a solid cabernet sauvignon and is increasingly handy with merlot. The new Vintner's Blend merlot is especially tasty. There's also a chardonnay but you get the feeling Ravenswood only makes it for the record.

ST. FRANCIS WINERY AND VINEYARD

Winemaker: Tom Mackey.
833-4666.
8450 Hwy. 12, Kenwood.
Tours: By appt.
Tasting: 10 to 4:30 daily.
Fee: $1 a taste for reserve wines, others free.
Special features: Fireplace; picnic area; gourmet foods.

Merlot is the current popular flavor, and St. Francis makes two of the best, a regular and a reserve. Both are gorgeous and full-bodied, with enough muscle to age a few years. Critics love them. Vines have been planted on the property since 1910, though managing partner, Joe Martin, bought the vineyard in 1972 and replanted. He experimented with this grape and that and in 1980 marketed his first vintage.

Another fine success with St. Francis is its chardonnay, a rich butterscotch style with great fruit. Its cabernet sauvignon is a recent addition that has its admirers and a lightly sweet Johannesberg riesling is one of our favorite picnic wines.

You can picnic on the quiet green patio outside St. Francis' tasting room that is located in a small house near the winery. While the patio is nice for summer days, St. Francis really comes into its own near Christmas. The outside is decorated for Kenwood's festival of lights and the inside is fire-warmed and cheery.

SEBASTIANI VINEYARDS

Winemaker: Doug Davis.
938-5532.
389 Fourth St., Sonoma.
Tours: 10:15 to 4:20 daily.
Tasting: 10 to 5 daily.
Fee: None.
Special features: Picnic area.

For many people, Sebastiani is another way to spell Sonoma. It's the epitome of the county's wine tradition — an unpretentious family winery, big, old and *Italian*. Sonoma County's largest winery, Sebastiani is also one of its most popular tourist attractions, especially on weekends and summer days.

The winery dates from 1896, when Samuele Sebastiani crushed his first grapes — zinfandel to be precise. The now-antique press is still on display in the tasting room. Samuele's son August, a man with an affinity for bib overalls and stout, simple wines, built the winery's reputation on inexpensive jug wines, using the plentiful grapes of the Central Valley. Since August's death in 1980, the family has down-played the jug wines somewhat — though yearly production remains close to 4 million gallons — and has added vintage wines.

Visitors can taste Sebastiani's wide range of wines, from the inexpensive Swan label to vineyard select-cabernet sauvignon such as Cherry Block. The spacious tasting room is warm and wooden, partly crafted from old wine tanks. Tours offer a thorough peek behind the scenes, from the wine presses to the aging tanks. The highlight is the winery's collection of intricately hand-carved wine casks believed to be the largest in the country.

Other Sonoma Valley Wineries

ARROWOOD VINEYARDS AND WINERY (938-5179; 14347 Hwy. 12, Glen Ellen). Tasting and tours by appt.; small lovely winery overlooking the Valley of the Moon; makes only two wines, cabernet sauvignon and chardonnay, both considered among California's best; don't let "by appointment" scare you off — they like visitors but call ahead.

GRAND CRU VINEYARDS (833-2325; 8600 Hwy. 12, Kenwood). Pleasant tasting room, located a few miles from the winery, and a roster of good wines; white zinfandel always among the best.

GUNDLACH-BUNDSCHU WINERY (938-5277; 2000 Denmark St., Sonoma). Tours and tasting 11 to 4:30 daily; a family tradition dating from 1858; merlot, zinfandel and pinot noir are highly recommended.

HACIENDA WINERY (938-3220; 1000 Vineyard Ln., Sonoma). Tasting 10 to 5 daily; tours by appt.; once part of historic Buena Vista vineyards; don't miss the dry chenin blanc.

LANDMARK VINEYARDS (833-0053; 101 Adobe Canyon Rd., Kenwood). Tasting 10 to 4:30 daily; tours by appt.; recently relocated to Kenwood, this winery does one thing and does it well — chardonnay.

ROCHE WINERY (935-7115; 28700 Hwy. 121, Sonoma). Tastings 10 to 6 May to Sept., 10 to 5 Oct. to Apr.; tours by appt.; one of the newest wineries, Roche specializes in chardonnay and pinot noir; $1.50 fee for tasting limited release wines.

SMOTHERS BROTHERS WINES (833-1010; 9575 Hwy. 12, Kenwood). Tasting 10 to 4:30 daily; jovial comedian-musician Tommy Smothers is one of Sonoma County's most familiar faces; his home and vineyard is just west of Kenwood; you might even chance upon him in the tasting room.

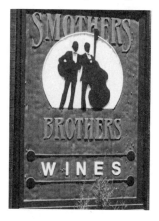

VALLEY OF THE MOON WINERY (996-6941; 777 Madrone Rd., Glen Ellen). Tasting 10 to 5 daily; this family-owned winery, one of California's oldest, dates from 1857.

VIANSA WINERY (935-4700; 25200 Hwy. 121, Sonoma). Wine and food tasting 10 to 5 daily; tours by appt.; Sam and Vicki Sebastiani split from the family dynasty and started their own winery a few years ago.

Russian River Area

CLOS DU BOIS
Winemaker: Margret
   Davenport.
433-8268.
5 Fitch St., Healdsburg.
Tours: By appt.
Tasting: 10 to 5 daily.
Fee: None.

This winery in downtown Healdsburg may not inspire a snapshot — it's pretty much a prefab warehouse — but who cares. The tasting room is warm and friendly and the wines are excellent. Clos du Bois, one of Sonoma's largest and most prominent wineries, seems to do *everything* well and a few things superbly. They may not produce big flashy wines but they're seldom disappointing, which is surprising considering the roster.

Clos du Bois has equal success with reds and whites, as the results of any major wine competition confirm. The key to this success are the vineyards, some 1,000 prime acres in Alexander and Dry Creek valleys. A whopping *three* cabernet sauvignons and three chardonnays are produced. Two are distinctive reserve wines, the third, an inexpensive regular bottling. The reserve chardonnays — Calcaire and Flintwood — are lush and steely, though we prefer the unassuming character of the regular chardonnay. Of the cabernets, the full-bodied fruit of the Briarcrest reserve impresses us most. Clos du Bois' pinot noir and merlots are also contenders, and even the sauvignon blanc and gewurztraminer have simple merits.

Clos du Bois pours a wide range of its current wine every day, and occasionally offers samples of its older library. These are also on sale in the tasting room. The staff is knowledgeable yet never rolls an eye at novice questions. If you're looking for an easy place to start your first day of wine tasting, there's no better spot than Clos du Bois.

DAVIS BYNUM WINERY
Winemaker: Gary Farrell.
433-5852.
8075 Westside Rd.,
   Healdsburg.
Tours: 10 to 5 daily.
Tasting: 10 to 5 daily.
Fee: None.

This unpretentious winery makes a bit of everything — merlot, pinot noir, chardonnay, gewurztraminer — and does it all surprisingly well. Situated amid tall cool redwoods, Bynum relies on the characteristically restrained grapes of the region. These are subtle wines, not overly oaked, yet strong in varietal character. Winemaker Gary Farrell is particularly gifted with pinot noir, creating rich, velvety wines that crave a dark night and a warm fire. The pinot bottled under Farrell's own label is one of our favorites. Bynum's merlot and sauvignon blanc also have a growing lists of admirers. Best of all — the prices remain reasonable.

Gliding peaceably along shady Westside Road, watch for Davis Bynum's small sign. It may seem like you're driving up someone's private lane, but continue up the hill. Bynum began making wine in Albany in 1965, moving to his present home in 1973. The building and tasting room are simple, but a cordial staff is always ready to talk about wine. Davis Bynum is among the growing list of wineries to offer futures. These are wines that aren't quite ready for release — sometimes they're still aging in barrel — but are sold in advance at a bargain price.

DEHLINGER WINERY
Winemaker: Tom
  Dehlinger.
823-2378.
6300 Guerneville Rd.,
  Sebastopol.
Tours: By appt.
Tasting: 10 to 5 daily.
Fee: None.

This country charmer of a winery is such a low-key affair that you might get the feeling that you're imposing when you visit. Not to worry. Certainly, if it's crush time, you might have to step around a portable grape press or a hose or two to get inside. But that's part of Dehlinger's appeal. Tom Dehlinger emphasizes wine first, to the great pleasure of the winery's devoted following.

As you might expect, Dehlinger has a limited production; it uses only its own grapes, producing about 10,000 cases a year. It's not easy to find, even in nearby Santa Rosa, so a stop at the winery is highly recommended. As you drive east on Guerneville Road, you will see Dehlinger's unusual octagonal house perched atop a vineyard knoll. Follow the winding gravel road and you'll come to the low-lying redwood winery. Inside, you'll taste at a wooden bar, surrounded by barrels and aging tanks.

Dehlinger has a knack with the grapes of Burgundy: chardonnay and pinot noir, two varieties that thrive particularly in this region. The chardonnays are crisp and buttery and the pinots are snappy and berrylike. Merlot is California's "hot" wine these days, and Dehlinger makes a good one. There's also a cabernet sauvignon and the more obscure (in America) cabernet franc, but neither are particularly good examples of the type. Dehlinger offers a library of its older wines as well as futures.

HOP KILN WINERY
Winemaker: Steve Strobl.
433-6491.
6050 Westside Rd.,
  Healdsburg.
Tours: By appt.
Tasting: 10 to 5 daily.
Fee: None.
Special features: Picnic
  area; lake.

Hop Kiln began life as an ode to beer, not wine — beer hops were a major crop along Sonoma County's Russian River at the turn of the century. It is one of the few remnants from that era. Built in 1905, the unusual stone barn is topped with three pyramid towers, used originally to dry the hops. Dr. Martin Griffin bought and restored the barn and began making wine in 1975.

Rounding a bend as you drive north on Westside Road, you might wonder if you've returned

Hop Kiln Winery is a remnant of Sonoma County's days as a major center of beer hops. Where hops were once dried, grapes are now crushed.

Kris White

to the Old Country. The tasting room inside is rustic but pleasant, warm with wood and history. There are historical displays, as well as a rotating exhibit of local art.

Tasters can choose from any number of wines. Zinfandel is a specialty and Hop Kiln makes a bold old style zin that packs in the fruit. Its petite sirah also has its devotees. Its two generic wines are great bargains: A Thousand Flowers (white) and Marty Griffin's Big Red. Both are delightful, especially for a picnic.

A picnic, by the way, is something you might want to plan for at Hop Kiln. There is a lovely small lake, bordered by a sunny patch of tables — be prepared to share with the ducks. There are also tables in a lovely grove of trees for those who crave shade. Westside Road makes a lovely route for a bike ride, and, as you might expect, Hop Kiln is a favorite stop for two-wheelers.

KORBEL CHAMPAGNE CELLARS

Winemaker: Robert M. Stashak.
887-2294.
13250 River Rd., Guerneville; 12 miles west of Highway 101.
Tours: May to Sept. 9:45 to 3:45; Oct. to Apr. 10 to 3.
Tasting: May to Sept. 9 to 5; Oct. to Apr. 9 to 4:30
Fee: None.
Special features: Picnic area and garden.

As you drive through the gorgeous redwood forests of the Russian River area, you'll see this century-old, ivy-covered stone wine cellar rising nobly from a hillside. Korbel is one of our favorite Wine Country stops, but we're hardly alone. It can't be beat for romance, history and beauty.

In the summer, to avoid the crowds, arrive early in the morning or late in the afternoon. The half-hour tour is great fun and full of information. The Korbel brothers, it seems, came from Czechoslovakia to Guerneville for its trees which were perfect for cigar boxes. Once the trees had been harvested, they turned to planting grapes and to producing wine using the traditional French *mèthode champenoise*. You'll get to poke your nose into the large wood aging tanks and learn the mystery of the riddling room where sediment is slowly tapped from each bottle.

Korbel's tasting room is among the friendliest you'll find. One of few remaining champagne houses in Wine Country that doesn't charge for tastings, it will pour any or all of its dependable sparklers, from the popular Brut to the deliciously dry Natural. There is also a pleasant picnic area. You might want to buy a cold bottle in the tasting room and split it with friends over cheese and sandwiches. In the summer, Korbel's prized antique garden is open for tour.

PIPER SONOMA
CELLARS
Winemaker: Chris Markell.
433-8843.
11447 Old Redwood Hwy.,
   Windsor.
Tours: By appt.
Tasting: 10 to 5 daily.
Fee: $3.50.
Features: Art gallery.

Don't call it champagne! It's sparkling wine, please. The French get rather touchy about this. To French vintners like Piper-Heidsieck, owners of Piper Sonoma, champagne can *only* come from the Champagne region of France. Yet even the French see the potential in California or they wouldn't be flocking here. And it's great fun comparing this "French" version with the nearby, made-in-America, Korbel.

Piper–Heidsieck is the first French firm to settle in Sonoma. Housed in a sleek concrete and glass structure, this ultra-modern winery opened in 1982. Contemporary art decorates the lobby and the tasting room has the feel of a stylish cafe. Piper Sonoma, of course, uses the classic French technique of making sparkling wine called *méthode champenoise*. Guests are encouraged to sit while they sample three of Piper Sonoma's sparklers: Brut, Blanc de Noir and Brut reserve. Wine is also available for $3 to $5 per glass.

As for its tour, well, what Piper Sonoma lacks in intimacy, it tries to make up for by offering a more penetrating look at the sparkling process. Visitors travel along a concrete catwalk through the entire production process, from the aging tanks to the bottling plant. You *do* get to see more of the winery than other sparkling houses allow, but there is a rather stand-offish feel to the whole thing. If you would prefer to tarry among the giant tanks, you might be disappointed. Nonetheless, you might enjoy Piper Sonoma's innovative approach.

Other Russian River Area Wineries

BELVEDERE WINERY (433-8236; 4035 Westside Rd., Healdsburg). Tasting 10 to 4:30 daily; tour by appt.; cabernet sauvignon and merlots from Robert Young Vineyards are often winners and inexpensive "Discovery Series" wines a good value.

CHATEAU DE BAUN (571-7500; 5007 Fulton Rd., Fulton). Tasting and sales 10 to 5 daily; specializes in wine made with new Symphony grape; impressive chateau-style visitors' center a local favorite for weddings.

DE LOACH VINEYARDS (526-9111; 1791 Olivet Rd., Santa Rosa). Tasting 10 to 4:30 daily; tours 2 p.m. Mon. to Fri., 11 and 2 Sat. and Sun.; intense fruity chardonnays, one of Sonoma's best; zinfandel and pinot noir also specialties; intimate country winery.

FOPPIANO VINEYARDS (433-7272; 12707 Old Redwood Hwy., Healdsburg). Tasting 10 to 4:30 daily; tours by appt.; old Italian family winery with tradition, founded in 1896; petite sirah always a favorite.

IRON HORSE VINEYARDS (887-2913; 9786 Ross Station Rd., Sebastopol). Among California's most prestigious sparkling wines; winery a chic update of classic old Sonoma barn.

MARK WEST VINEYARDS (544-4813; 7000 Healdsburg-Trenton Rd., Forestville). Tasting 10 to 5 daily; tours by appt.; solid pinot noir and chardonnay; winery offers warm views of rolling hillside vineyards.

ROCHIOLI VINEYARDS & WINERY (433-2305; 6192 Westside Rd., Healdsburg). Tasting 10 to 5 daily; tours by appt.; pinot noir in great demand, chardonnays also popular; charges fee for reserve wines.

RODNEY STRONG VINEYARDS (433-6511; 11455 Old Redwood Hwy., Windsor). Tasting 10 to 5 daily; tours daily, every half hour, 11:30 to 3:30; dramatically designed modern winery with intriguing views of winery process; fine selection of wines.

TOPOLOS AT RUSSIAN RIVER VINEYARDS (887-1575; 5700 Gravenstein Hwy. N., Forestville). Tasting 11 to 5 Wed. to Sun.; tours by appt.; winery an eclectic mix of Greek Orthodox and old hop kiln; restaurant specializes in Greek food.

WHITE OAK VINEYARDS (433-8429; 208 Haydon St., Healdsburg). Tasting 10 to 4, Fri. to Sun.; chardonnay and chenin blanc are super; small winery within walking distance of Healdsburg square.

WINDSOR VINEYARDS (800-862-4910; 239A Center St., Healdsburg). Tasting 10 to 5 daily; specializes in direct marketing; personalizes labels; makes a bit of everything and does it all well.

Alexander Valley Area

CHATEAU SOUVERAIN
Winemaker: Tom Peterson.
433-8281.
Hwy. 101 at Independence Lane, Geyserville.
Tours: By appt.
Tasting: 11 to 4 Tues to Thurs., 11 to 9:30 Fri. and Sat., 10 to 4 Sun.
Fee: $2.50.
Special features: Restaurant.

This dramatic chalet was inspired by the old hop kilns that once dotted the Russian River Valley. As you climb the stairs and look out beyond the wide courtyard with its huge fountain, you will be treated to a mesmerizing view of Alexander Valley. Not only is the building impressive, but there's a chic restaurant inside that's considered among the best in Wine Country. It's also one of the few Sonoma County wineries that charge for wine tasting. Unfortunately, the wines are nothing special, just competent, low priced, everyday wines, hardly worth the accompanying fuss.

Built in 1973, the winery is a natural for tours. An elevated walkway allows access to the entire process, from huge stainless steel tanks to the bottling line. The tasting room in the lower level of the east tower has recently been transformed into a cafe and wine bar. You'll be best off sampling Chateau Souverain's gentle chardonnay and one of the better, good-value merlots. The cafe serves food (for a review, see Chapter Five, *Restaurants & Food Purveyors*).

GEYSER PEAK WINERY
Winemaker: Daryl Groom.
433-6585.22281 Chianti Rd.,
   Geyserville.
Tours: None.
Tasting: 10 to 5 daily.
Special features: Picnic
   area.

Though Geyser Peak isn't *charming* in the sense of small — owned by Penfolds, the Australian conglomerate, with production of more than 400,000 cases a year — this is a charming place that makes charming wines. Its fine mid-priced wines retain much of the rich Sonoma County tradition that Augustus Quitzow originated in 1880.

On the northernmost edge of Wine Country, Geyser Peak is a noble complex of old and new set on a hillside overlooking Hwy. 101. In the days it was owned by the Bagnani family, drivers along the highway were comically welcomed with a sign warning them that Geyser Peak wines were not for sale because the owners drank it all. Those folksy days are gone, of course. Climb the steps to the expansive courtyard and you're now welcomed by an elegant fountain and a lovely old stone and wood winery.

The tasting room, constructed of old redwood tanks, exudes sophistication, with a staff pouring selections from Geyser Peak's large repertoire. Don't miss the soft Johannesberg riesling, which is ripe with lovely peachy fruit. The top-of-the-line cabernet sauvignon, Reserve Alexandre, is regaining some of its former stature after a considerable slump.

SIMI WINERY
Winemaker: Paul Hobbs.
433-6981.
16275 Healdsburg Ave.,
   Healdsburg.
Tours: 11, 1 and 3 daily.
Tasting: 10 to 4:30 daily.
Fee: Reserve wines only.

If we had to choose only a single winery to visit — akin to limiting yourself to *one* glass of champagne on New Year's Eve — it would be a tough call. What to do? We vote for Simi, an alluring combination of history with hi-tech. You never feel like you're being herded through a factory here, even though the winery is quite large. The staff knows wine but doesn't lord it over you. And, best of all, the wines are exceptional.

Hidden in a grove of trees on the northern outskirts of Healdsburg, Simi has had a history as shaky as it is long. Italian immigrants Pietro and Guiseppe Simi built the original stone winery in 1890 and called it Montepulciano. They prospered, producing bold wines in the Old World style. Wines produced during the 1930s and '40s — particularly the zinfandel — were considered masterful, and were still drinking well decades later. Over the years, changes in ownership brought good times and bad, until French champagne and cognac giant Moet–Hennessy bought Simi in 1981. Simi has since regained its former glory, becoming one of the most respected wineries in California.

The lovely old stone building remains but the inside is thoroughly updated. Simi's tour is among the best, offering peeks at everything from the newly finished oak barrel aging room to the bottling line. Guides tell you *just* enough, never burdening you with too many details. The same holds true in the tasting room, where Simi's array of wines are offered in an easy atmosphere. It's usually a good idea to limit yourself to just a few wines, but that's hard at Simi because all its offerings are tempting. The chenin and sauvignon blancs are delightful, and the chardonnays — particularly the reserve — are rich and buttery. Even more impressive are the cabernet sauvignons. Again, the reserve is considered among the best.

Other Alexander Valley Area Wineries

ALEXANDER VALLEY VINEYARDS (433-7209; 8644 Hwy. 128, Healdsburg). Tasting 10 to 5 daily, tours by appt.; once the estate of Cyrus Alexander, from whom the valley is named; makes a wide range of wines.

FIELD STONE WINERY (433-7266; 10075 Hwy. 128, Healdsburg). Tasting daily 10 to 5; tours by appt.; this unique winery is built into the side of a hill surrounded by oak trees and picnic tables; cabernet sauvignon and petite sirah worth noting.

JOHNSON'S ALEXANDER VALLEY WINES (433-2319; 8333 Hwy. 128, Healdsburg). Tasting 10 to 5 daily; tours by appt.; see a small family winery in action; delightful little spot.

MURPHY-GOODE ESTATE WINERY (431-7644; 4001 Hwy. 128, Healdsburg). Tasting 10:30 to 4:30 daily; tours by appt.; winning fumé blanc, chardonnay and more recently cabernet sauvignon.

PAT PAULSEN VINEYARDS (849-3197; 25510 River Rd., Cloverdale). Tasting 10 to 5;30 daily; deadpan comedian Paulsen is also a wine buff; when he's not on the road you might find him pouring his wines.

J. PEDRONCELLI WINERY (857-3531; 1220 Canyon Rd., Geyserville). Tasting 10 to 5 daily; tours by appt.; family winery offers some of the best values in California; makes a bit of everything and does it all well, particularly for the price; casual tasting room.

SAUSAL WINERY (433-2285; 7370 Hwy. 128, Healdsburg). Tasting 10 to 4 daily; makes a fabulous zinfandel at a fair price; tasting room offers a soothing view of Alexander Valley.

Dry Creek Valley

**DRY CREEK
    VINEYARDS**
Winemaker: David Stare.
433-1000.
3770 Lambert Bridge Rd.,
    Healdsburg.
Tours: By appt.
Tasting: 10 to 4:30 daily.
Fee: None.
Special features: Picnic
    area.

Dry Creek Valley, we've always imagined, is what Napa Valley used to be: small, quiet, unaffected. Driving or pedaling along the peaceful roads is a true pleasure. One of the best stops is this winery. Reminiscent of the small country wineries of France, Dry Creek looks like a simple country chapel, ivy-covered, with a pitched roof and rough stone walls. A lawn with flowers, shady trees and picnic tables are welcome sights on a dusty day. (And *Dry* Creek Valley *does* get dusty.)

It only adds to the pleasure that Dry Creek's wines are consistently fine and occasionally exceptional. The atmosphere in the tasting room is laid back and the staff is chatty. You might pause for a quick, succinct tour of the winery.

Visitors can choose four samples from the winery's impressive list. Not an easy task. Dry Creek has made its name with fumé blanc, a marvelous, crisp wine that dominates the winery's production. The chenin blanc is so fruity and distinctive that we prefer it over many chardonnays and it's one third the price. That's not to slight Dry Creek's always reliable chardonnay. As for reds, the zinfandel is always one of the best and the cabernet sauvignon has fine character and can be exceptional in a good vintage. We've never been impressed with Dry Creek's merlot, but good luck trying to find it anyway.

**FERRARI-CARANO
    VINEYARDS AND
    WINERY**
Winemaker: George
    Bursick.
433-6700.
8761 Dry Creek Rd.,
    Healdsburg.
Tours: By appt.
Tasting 10 to 5 daily.
Fee: None.

Most chardonnays have been called trunk agers — driving home in the trunk, they've aged long enough. Well, Ferrari–Carano's chardonnay is one of the few California whites that benefit from a few years on its side. Ferrari–Carano surprised everyone when it entered the scene in the mid-1980s, and its star has been rising ever since. Chardonnay, of course, is its flagship, a big, lush, complex wine as well as one of the more expensive. The fumé blanc is impressive in its own right, yet the cabernet sauvignons have trouble rising to the challenge of the whites. The merlot is snatched up rather quickly, but then most merlots are. We have to admit, though, we're rather fond of it.

Situated in northern Dry Creek Valley, the winery is surrounded by lawns, flowers and vineyards. Don and Rhonda Carano own the Eldorado Hotel and Casino in Reno and have ambitious plans for the winery they opened in 1981. An enormous underground cellar has been completed that will house 1,500 aging barrels. A culinary center is also on the drawing board.

Tours permit a look behind the scenes, but Ferrari–Carano's tasting room provides enough insight for most visitors. Tall windows have views of the above-ground barrel aging room, as well as of the large fermentation tanks. Ferrari–Carano seldom pours its merlot, though its other wines are available.

Lambert Bridge Winery, west of Healdsburg, is one of Sonoma County's most intimate winery stops.

Chris Alderman

**LAMBERT BRIDGE
WINERY AND
VINEYARDS**
Winemaker: Edward
   Killian.
433-5855.
4085 W. Dry Creek Rd.,
   Healdsburg.
Tours: By appt.
Tasting: 10 to 4:30 daily.
Fee: None.
Special features: Fireplace;
   picnic area.

"**Q**uaint" is a woefully overused word, but we can't think of a better way to describe Lambert Bridge. This romantic little winery, with redwood siding and a slate roof, fits comfortably among the oak trees and vines that cover the hillsides overlooking Dry Creek. Pause a moment beneath the wisteria vines that shade the full-length porch, or have a seat at the wide, round picnic table inside the gazebo. Few picnic spots offer a more soothing view.

Inside the winery, you'll be enveloped in darkness and cool air as you find yourself inside a cavernous room, lined with redwood and stacked to its pitched ceiling with oak barrels. Chandeliers echo the soft glow produced by the wood burning in the stone fireplace, and the sounds of a Mozart violin concerto waft through the air. In this cozy corner of the aging room, Lambert Bridge has set up its "tasting room." What better place to sip?

Open since 1969, Lambert Bridge has maintained a low profile. Not exactly tiny, it produces 25,000 cases a year, with chardonnay its specialty: a rich, juicy style with considerable oak. We've always been partial to Lambert Bridge's crisp fumé blanc, though we always found the cabernet sauvignon rather blunt and harsh. Lambert Bridge makes a fine merlot, although it usually sells out quickly. The staff enjoys talking about wine — and the best thing about visiting a small winery is taking the time to chat and learn.

Other Dry Creek Valley Wineries

ALDERBROOK VINEYARDS & WINERY (433-9154; 2306 Magnolia Dr., Healdsburg). Tasting 10 to 5 daily; tours by appt.; pleasant winery specializing in white wines at good prices; try its semillon for a change of pace.

LAKE SONOMA WINERY (431-1550; 9990 Dry Creek Rd., Healdsburg). Tasting 10 to 5 daily; tours by appt.; tiny winery specializing in cabernet sauvignon and zinfandel; offers a panoramic hillside view.

LYTTON SPRINGS WINERY (433-7721; 650 Lytton Springs Rd., Healdsburg). Tasting 10 to 4 daily; tours by appt.; if you like zinfandel, you must visit this winery; muscular, bold and jammy, the zin is always a top award-winner; winery not much to look at though.

MAZZOCCO VINEYARDS (433-9035; 1400 Lytton Springs Rd., Healdsburg). Tasting and tours 10 to 4 daily; a low-profile winery that makes excellent chardonnay.

MILL CREEK VINEYARDS (431-2121; 1401 Westside Rd., Healdsburg). Tasting 10 to 4:30 daily, closed Tues. to Thurs. Dec. through March; tours by appt.; quaint small winery with working paddle wheel; merlot a bargain.

A. RAFANELLI WINERY (433-1385; 4685 W. Dry Creek Rd., Healdsburg). Tasting and tours by appt.; this small family-owned winery is one of our favorites; housed in a folksy old barn, it's the epitome of Sonoma County wineries; the zinfandel may be the best in the business and the cabernet sauvignon is nearly as good, a wine to look for, if you can find it; we'd write more, but frankly don't want to let the secret out.

PRESTON VINEYARDS (433-3372; 9282 W. Dry Creek Rd., Healdsburg). Tasting 11 to 3 Mon. to Fri. and 11 to 4 Sat. and Sun.; tours by appt.; a bit out of the way, but a pleasant stop; zinfandels are usually winners and the sauvignon blancs, particularly the inexpensive Cuvée de Fumé, are delightful.

ROBERT STEMMLER WINERY (433-6334; 3805 Lambert Bridge Rd., Healdsburg). Tasting 10:30 to 4:30 daily; pinot noir is the specialty here.

WINE GLOSSARY

No one expects you to be an expert when you're wine tasting, but it doesn't hurt to know some of the language. Here's a quick course in the words of wine, how to pronounce them and what they mean.

Blanc de Blanc (*blonc deh blonc*) — A sparkling wine made from white grapes, usually chardonnay. Delicate and dry.

Blanc de Noirs (*blonc deh nwahr*) — A sparkling wine made from red grapes, usually pinot noir. Sometimes faintly pink. Fruity but dry.

Blush — A pink- or salmon-colored wine made from red grapes. Juice from red grapes is actually white. Red wine derives its color from juice left in contact with the grape skin. The longer the contact, the darker the wine.

Brut (*broot*) — The most popular style of sparkling wine. A blend of chardonnay and pinot noir. Dry.

Cabernet Franc (*cab-er*-nay *fronc*) — Red wine of Bordeaux, similar to cabernet sauvignon but lighter in color and body.

Cabernet Sauvignon (*cab-er*-nay *so-vin*-yon) — Red, fragrant and full-bodied grape of Bordeaux. Dry and usually tannic. Can age in the bottle five to 10 years.

Chardonnay (*shar-do*-nay) — California's most popular white wine, famed in France as white burgundy. Fruity, with hints of citrus or butter.

Chenin Blanc (shen-*nin blonc*) — White wine that's more delicate and less complex than chardonnay. Slightly sweet.

Crush — Harvest and pressing of grapes. The beginning of the winemaking process.

Estate bottled — Wines made from vineyards owned or controlled by the winery.

Fermentation — The conversion of grape juice into wine, using yeast to change sugar into alcohol.

Fumé Blanc (fu-*may blonc*) — Same as sauvignon blanc. Usually slightly more dry. Fumé means smoky.

Futures — Wines sold at a discount before release for later delivery.

Gewurztraminer (*geh*-vurz-*trah-me-ner*) — White wine that's medium-bodied, semi-sweet and lightly spicy.

Johannisberg Riesling (*jo*-hahn-*is-berg* rees-*ling*) — Delicate white wine, medium-bodied, semi-sweet, with a melony fruit taste.

Late harvest — Sweet dessert wine made from grapes left on the vine longer than usual. *Botrytis cinerea* mold forms, dehydrating the grapes and intensifying the sugar content.

Merlot (*mer*-lo) — Popular red grape from Bordeaux. Similar to cabernet sauvignon, but softer and more opulent.

Mèthode champenoise (*meh*-thowd *sham*-pen-*nwas)* — Traditional French champagne-making process. Still wine is placed with sugar and yeast into a bottle and then sealed. The yeast eats the sugar, producing carbon dioxide bubbles. The wine then "sits on the yeast," or ages, in the bottle several years. Finally, the yeast is extracted and the sparkling wine — never once removed from its original bottle — is ready to drink.

GRGICH HILLS

Napa Valley
CHARDONNAY
1988

PRODUCED AND BOTTLED BY GRGICH HILLS CELLAR
RUTHERFORD, CA   ALC.13.4% BY VOL. • CONTAINS SULFITES

Oak — Wine aged in oak barrels picks up some of the smell and taste of the wood. Also contributes to tannins and long aging. Example: "That chardonnay has too much oak for my taste."

Petite Sirah (*peh*-teet *syr*-awh) — Dark, rich, intense red wine.

Pinot Noir (*pe*-no-*nwahr*) — Silky, fruity, dry red wine that makes the great Burgundys of France.

Reserve — A term traditionally used to mean wine held back or reserved for the winery owners, but the meaning has become vague. It is now sometimes used to mean better quality grapes, or wine aged longer in oak barrels.

Residual sugar — Unfermented sugar that remains in the wine. Wine is considered sweet if it contains more than half a percent, by weight.

Riddling — A laborious process used to extract yeast from sparkling wine. Yeast deposits are slowly shaken to the neck of the bottle, where they can be removed without disturbing the wine.

Sauvignon Blanc (*so*-*vin-yon blonc*) A crisp, light white wine with hints of grass and apples.

Sparkling wine — Generic term for champagne. Technically, real champagne can only come from the Champagne region of France.

Syrah (*syr*-awh) — Ruby-colored grape of the Rhone region in France. Smooth, yet with rich and massive fruit.

Tannic — The puckery sensation caused by some wines, particularly young reds. Comes from the skin and stalk of the grapes, as well as oak barrels. Usually allows for long aging.

Varietal — A wine named after the grape variety from which it's made. Example: chardonnay is a varietal, Bordeaux is not. (A region in France, Bordeaux wine can contain a number of varietals: cabernet sauvignon, merlot, etc.)

Vintage — The year the grapes for a particular wine are harvested. Non-vintage wines can be blends of different years.

Viticultural area — A wine-producing region. Russian River Valley is one such area within Sonoma County, for example.

Zinfandel (zin-*fan-dell*) — A spicy and jamlike red wine. A California specialty. Used also to make a blush wine called white zinfandel.

CHAPTER SEVEN
On The Run
RECREATION

Courtesy SCCVB

Russian River, a favorite spot for canoeing, swimming, fishing.

Wine Country is such a beautiful place that a leisurely drive is activity enough for most vacationers. Rolling hills, fertile valleys, a spectacular coastline, a mild climate — no wonder so many people are drawn to Napa and Sonoma. In the words of horticulturist Luther Burbank, " . . . this is the chosen spot of all the Earth as far as nature is concerned." But there's more than wine and landscapes. If you crave activity, you'll keep busy. From long hikes through gentle wilderness to rides above it in hot air balloons, there are recreational activities to fit every style, taste and budget.

We have created a special section at the end of this chapter, headed "The Coast" (see page 252), which points out some of the more unusual and delightful activities available along Sonoma County's 62-mile coastline. The Sonoma Coast offers spectacular views, beaches, tidepools and year-round scuba diving. There is hiking along coastal trails in Salt Point State Park, whale-watching from the Bodega Headlands, and even horseback riding along the 18-mile Sonoma Coast.

220

AUTO RACING

Yes, racing in Wine Country. It's our version of the Indianapolis 500, where you can experience the thrill of watching the fastest cars in the world. The internationally known Sears Point Raceway presents plenty of action in its year-round schedule, which includes races for the hottest factory-backed sports cars, warp speed dragsters, motorcycles and even vintage cars. **Sears Point International Raceway** (938-8448; in California 800-338-SPIR; at junction of Hwys. 37 and 121, Sonoma).

BALLOONING

Ballooning: ready to ride the skies at dawn.

Ernest Lewin; courtesy SCCVB

Sailing silently above the vineyards and rolling hills of the Wine Country in a hot air balloon is an experience you will never forget. Rides start early in the day, before surface winds interfere with the launch, and each ride is unique, dependent on the whim of the winds.

Some balloon companies provide pickup at your lodging, most offer continental breakfast and a champagne brunch following the ride. Prices vary, but expect to spend about $155 per person. Reservations are necessary.

For a real balloon extravaganza, you should check out Sonoma County's *Hot Air Balloon Classic*. Each June, 50 or more balloons fill the sky over the vineyards in Windsor. (See "Seasonal Events" in Chapter Four, *Culture*.)

Napa County

Above the West (800-627-2759; Yountville). Pickup from San Francisco and Napa Valley hotels; champagne breakfast; family owned & operated.

Up, Up and Away!

It's 6 a.m. A group of early risers fends off the chilly dawn air with cups of coffee, eagerly anticipating their ballooning adventure. Pilots and helpers unroll expanses of magnificent colored fabrics onto the open field. Before long, giant fans are blowing air into the flat balloons, held open by the pilots. They grow slowly, looking like earthbound whales trapped above the water's surface. Only when the pilot lights his propane burner and begins to heat the trapped air do they begin to rise.

The heated air gradually lifts the weight of the fire-proofed nylon fabric, and within 15 minutes one balloon is inflated, standing on the open field—enormous, beautiful. Six or seven passengers hop into the basket along with the pilot and the lines are released.

Slowly, perspectives change as the balloon heads skyward. The passengers can see the other balloons below them on the field, then the surrounding buildings, then hills in the distance. There is no sensation of movement since the balloon moves with the wind nor is there sound except for an occasional "whoosh" from the burner keeping the air heated.

The balloon moves effortlessly with the wind, drifting as the pilot "finds" different currents to ride. Like a canoe on a river, the balloon's direction can't be changed at will. The pilot can turn a circle by opening flaps with pulleys, but he can't choose his landing place.

After about an hour's flight, the pilot lets the air cool, and the balloon slowly descends. Expertly maneuvering to avoid trees, the pilot finds a field and lands ever so gently. Usually passengers only feel a slight bump, though occasionally, they are treated to an undignified tumble on their return to earth. The company's vans or trucks have followed the balloon from below and are immediately on hand to secure it and give everyone a ride back.

The disappointment of returning to earth is diminished by a glass or two of champagne and a gourmet brunch designed to complete a memorable experience. It's as good as any trip to Oz.

Adventures Aloft (255-8688; Yountville.) Champagne flights daily; Napa Valley's oldest balloon company; seen on "Falcon Crest."

Balloon Aviation of Napa Valley (252-7067; Napa). Flights daily; champagne and brunch flights also available.

Napa Valley Balloons (253-2224; Yountville). Launches from Domaine Chandon winery; fleet of 14 balloons; catered picnic brunch; champagne flights daily; hotel packages.

Napa's Great Balloon Escape (253-0860; Napa). Upper Valley winery launch sites; daily flights; champagne brunch.

Once In a Lifetime (800-722-6665; Calistoga). Flights daily; gourmet champagne brunch; walking distance from Calistoga spas; hotel packages.

Sonoma County

Air Flambouyant (800-456-4711; Santa Rosa). Operating since 1974; complimentary champagne; brunches.

Airborn of Sonoma County (800-339-8133; Healdsburg). Operating since 1978; champagne flights; champagne picnics.

Sonoma Thunder Wine Country Balloon Safaris (800-759-5638; Santa Rosa). Romance flights for two; champagne; custom videos.

BICYCLING

What better way could there be to enjoy the rural countryside of Wine Country than on a bicycle? With terrain that varies from meandering valleys to steep mountains and a spectacular coastline, there are enough roads and trails to satisfy everyone, from the most leisurely sightseer to the bicycling fanatic. In fact, the United States's professional bicycle team, "7-11," which competes in the Tour de France, has been returning each winter to train on Sonoma County roads (and probably to enjoy its wines with dinner after a long day).

Mountain bicycling, which started in Marin County just to the south, is extremely popular in the Wine Country. Annadel State Park probably has more bikes than runners on its trails and Austin Creek is another favorite Sonoma County spot. Mountain cyclists in Napa County head for Skyline Park (Napa) and Mount St. Helena.

Serious enthusiasts can race in a number of events held annually, including the *Cherry Pie Race* (a 15-year Napa tradition) and the *Terrible Two* (a grueling 208-mile course in Sonoma County). Charity races are popular in both counties. Most bike shops have information about upcoming events.

Many local parks have extensive bike trails, including *John F. Kennedy Park* (257-9529; Napa), *Skyline Wilderness Park* (252-0481; Napa), *Ragle Regional Park* (527-2041; Sebastopol), *Spring Lake County Park* (539-8092; Santa Rosa).

Bicyclists of every level are welcome to join the *Santa Rosa Cycling Club*'s weekend jaunts. The club meets every Saturday and Sunday (weather permitting) at 9 a.m. at the Santa Rosa High School parking lot. Specific ride info can be picked up at local bike shops.

So, rent a bicycle, pack a picnic lunch and explore a park; or point toward the nearest country road and enjoy the scenery you would miss from behind the wheel of your car. Two excellent guides for specific trails are *Sonoma County Bike Trails* and *Rides In and Around the Napa Valley*.

*Bicycling through Wine
Country.*

Bob Martin; courtesy SCCVB

BIKE RENTALS

Napa County

Bryan's Napa Valley Cyclery (255-3377; 4080 Byway East, Napa).
Jules Culver (942-0421; 1227 Lincoln Ave., Calistoga).
Palisades Mountain Sport (942-9687; 1330 B Gerrard, Calistoga).
St. Helena Cyclery (963-7736; 1156 Main, St. Helena).

Sonoma County

Rincon Cyclery (538-0868; 4927 Sonoma Hwy., Santa Rosa).
Spoke Folk Cyclery (433-7171; 249 Center St., Healdsburg).

BOATING AND WATERSPORTS

The dry summer season, though key to helping wine grapes reach perfection, means that Napa and Sonoma aren't exactly wetlands. However, thanks to the wonder of modern engineering, dams have been built to create reservoirs, necessary for community water supplies and a delight for the avid watersport fan.

Napa County

The largest man-made lake in the area is *Lake Berryessa*, located about 15 miles east of Rutherford along Hwy. 128. Some 26 miles long, it's one of northern California's most popular water recreation areas. Berryessa features seven resorts offering complete facilities: full service marinas, boat rentals for fishermen, sailboats, waterski and jet ski equipment, overnight accommodations from tent and RV camping to top quality motels. Houseboats are available for rent at Markley's Cove for leisurely overnights on the water. Water ski instruction for beginners through competitive-level skiers is available at the *World Class Water Ski Center* (966-2441), run by German champion Willi Ellermeier, at the Steele Park Resort. For complete information about the area's offerings, call the *Lake Berryessa Chamber of Commerce*, 800-726-1256.

Lake Berryessa Marina Resort (966-2161). Boat launching, campsites, RV hookups, boat rental, jet skis.

Markley Cove Resort (966-2134). Boat launching, boat rental (including houseboats), water and jet ski rental; no camping.

Putah Creek Park (966-2116). Boat launching, campsites, RV hookups, boat rental, motel.

Rancho Monticello Resort (966-2188). Boat launching, campsites, RV hookups, boat rental.

South Shore Resort (966-2172). Boat launching, campsites, boat rentals.

Spanish Flat Resort (966-7700). Boat launching, campsites, boat rentals, water and jet ski rental.

Steele Park Resort (800-522-2123). Boat launching, campsites, RV hookups, boat rental, water ski rental, school, motel.

Waterskiing on Lake Berryessa; Willi Ellermeier, champion ski instructor at World Class Water Ski Center, Steele Park Resort.

World Class Water Ski Center

Sonoma County

Sonoma County's new **Lake Sonoma**, located 11 miles north of Healdsburg on Dry Creek Rd., offers 3,600 surface acres of scenic recreational waters. There are many secluded coves for the quiet boater or angler, while water and jet skiers are allowed in designated areas. Available are a public boat ramp, a full service marina, campsites, hiking trails, swimming areas as well as a visitor's center and fish hatchery near the Warm Springs Dam. **Lake Sonoma Visitors Center** (433-9483). Information. **Lake Sonoma Marina** (433-2200). Boat rental (including fishing, paddle, sail, ski, canoe, and jet ski).

Since the Pacific Ocean is rather chilly and the surf a bit rugged (see "The Sonoma Coast" in this chapter), the **Russian River** is Sonoma County's favorite waterway. During the hot summer, the riverside beaches are popular among families who enjoy swimming or canoeing in the refreshing water. Canoes and kayaks can be rented near Healdsburg or Guerneville for a leisurely trip, stopping to relax or swim along the way. Don't be surprised if you spot a few nude sunbathers. The county doesn't condone it but the freewheeling '60s still live in West County.

Burke's Russian River Canoe Trips (887-1222; River Road, 1 mile north of Forestville). Leisurely 10 mile trip to Guerneville; $27 per canoe, shuttle included. Closed in winter.

California Rivers and Kiwi Kayak Company (838-7787; 10070 Old Redwood Hwy., Windsor). One-person Kiwi kayaks are rented by the day ($18) or two days ($30). These kayaks are very portable and are more stable and easier to handle than many; they can be driven to any river or lake in Wine Country.

W.C. Trowbridge Canoe Trips (433-7247; 20 Healdsburg Ave., Healdsburg). Choice of 8 routes, from 5 to 16 miles; $32 per canoe; shuttle available. Also offers overnight trips on the Russian and Sacramento Rivers.

Canoeing at Spring Lake, Santa Rosa.

Kris White

Lake Ralphine (524-5115; Howarth Park, Santa Rosa). A popular spot for water activities, from sailboating to duck feeding. Stocked with fish, this small man-made lake has a city-run rental facility, where rowboats, canoes, paddleboats and sailboats (experienced sailors only) are available for a minimal fee. Sailing classes are held during the summer. Power boats are not permitted.

Spring Lake (539-8092, Off Montgomery Dr. in Santa Rosa). A lovely 75-acre lake open only to canoes, rowboats, and sailboats, all of which can be rented during the summer. Windsurfing and rafting are also allowed. There is a separate lagoon for swimming.

CROQUET

The difference between your casual back yard croquet and a world-class croquet tournament is the difference between a quick game of checkers and tournament-level chess. Each year the *Sonoma-Cutrer Winery* (528-1181; 4401 Slusser Rd., Windsor) is the host of the *Wine Country International Croquet Championship.* The tournament raises thousands of dollars for charities, and the entrance fee includes a courtside gourmet luncheon with the winery's finest offerings. Croquet in Napa County takes place at *Meadowood Resort* (963-3646; 900 Meadowood Ln., St. Helena), where two tournament courts are available for guests and members. A charity tournament takes place each summer, with pros and semi-pros dazzling the crowd with their finesse.

FISHING

For the expert or novice, Wine Country offers an unusual variety of fishing opportunities. Where else could you hook a giant salmon in the Pacific one day, then snag a trophy bass in one of California's largest man-made lakes the next?

Remember to pick up a fishing license through a local sporting supply or department store. See "Boating and Watersports" in this chapter for additional information.

Napa County

Lake Berryessa is a designated trophy lake, boasting trout, bass (both large mouth and black), crappie, bluegill, and catfish. With seven resorts, camping, and full service marinas, there are unlimited facilities for every type of fisherman. For more information, see "Boating and Watersports" in this chapter or call the *Lake Berryessa Chamber of Commerce* (800-726-1256).

Duncan Garrett

The Sonoma County country-side provides an idyllic backdrop for the Sonoma-Cutrer Winery's International Croquet Championships.

Lake Hennessey (located 4 mi. E. of Rutherford on Hwy. 128). The water supply for the city of Napa; fishing and boating are allowed, though the only facilities available are a car-top launch ramp and picnic grounds.

Napa River. Can be fished for stripers or sturgeon year-round. The *J. F. Kennedy Park* (257-9529; Streblow Dr., off Hwy. 121, Napa) provides a boat launch ramp and is a good spot for fishing off the river bank. The *Napa Sea Ranch* (252-2799; 3333 Cuttings Wharf Rd., Napa) also offers a boat launch ramp as well as a bait and tackle store and 1,800 feet of river frontage.

Smith's Mount St. Helena Trout Farm and Hatchery (987-3651; Western Mine Road., Middletown). A perfect opportunity for the novice angler. Bait and pole are provided, along with barbecue facilities.

Sonoma County

Lake Sonoma (11 mi. N. of Healdsburg on Dry Creek Rd.) offers 53 miles of shoreline and secluded coves for the angler as well as a boat launch ramp and a full-service marina for boat rentals. Fish include bass, Sacramento perch, channel catfish and blue catfish, though local fisherman aren't enthusiastic about the numbers. Of interest is the Fish Hatchery, where visitors can watch tankfuls of lively young salmon and steelhead, which are released into Dry Creek when they reach 6 to 7 inches long. *Visitors Center & Hatchery*, 433-9483; *Marina*, 433-2200.

Lake Ralphine and *Spring Lake* in Santa Rosa are popular destinations for families and those seeking low-key fishing expeditions. Both lakes are stocked with catfish, black bass, trout and bluegill and practically guarantee beginners a catch. Both lakes offer boat rentals.

The Russian River tempts fishermen with steelhead trout and salmon fishing from November through March. Ever wonder what makes a steelhead trout different from a rainbow trout? Easy. A steelhead leaves its freshwater birthplace to spend most of its adult life in the sea, since its home creek or

Waiting for the big one while sportfishing

Chris Alderman

river is faced with a shortage of water in the dry season. The Russian River can be fished from its banks or from canoes and other non-powered boats.

Bodega Bay is home port for sport fishing boats, offering all-day trips on the Pacific Ocean. Leaving daily (weather permitting), 55- and 65-ft. boats search out 200 species of rock and bottom fish and, between April and November, the prized salmon. The cost is about $40 a person, with equipment rental extra. Or you can take the ride just for fun.

Bodega Bay Sport Fishing Center (875-3344). Daily charter boats; equipment rentals; four 65-ft. boats available; sport fishing for many species of rock and bottom fish and salmon; whale watching tours.

Challenger Sport Fishing (875-2474). 55-foot boat, heated cabin; equipment rentals; sport fishing trips for ling cod, rock cod, salmon; whale watching and harbor tours.

Fly fishing enthusiasts will appreciate the fly-casting practice pond constructed in *Galvin Park* (Bennett Valley, Santa Rosa) by the city of Santa Rosa and the Russian River Flyfishers Club. Clinics are held the third Sunday of each month, with free lessons and equipment supplied. Call *Lyle's Tackle & Travel* (527-9887; 2690 Santa Rosa Ave., Santa Rosa) to reserve a place. For local fishing information call Lyle's or *King's Western Angler* (542-4432; 532 College Ave., Santa Rosa).

FLYING

Seeing the Wine Country from a bird's view is an experience you're not likely to forget. If you don't have the time or inclination for a leisurely balloon ride (see "Ballooning"), you can take a flying tour above vineyards and mountains, try aerobatics in a 1940 biplane or soar on thermal lifts in a motorless glider. Or if you'd like to go further afield, why not charter a plane for the day to explore nearby Mendocino or the giant redwoods near Eureka?

For those whose psyches crave an extra thrill, there's hang-gliding and paragliding by the cliffs near Jenner or Mount St. Helena; rentals can be arranged with **Airtime of San Francisco** (415-759-1177). Skydiving is about as close to being airborne on your own as it comes. **Skydance Skydiving** (800-752-3262; Yolo County Airport, Davis) has what you need, whether you're a first-time or a world-class jumper.

Napa County

Bridgeford Flying Service (224-0887; Napa County Airport, Napa). Specialty is scenic tours and charter flights. Their Napa Valley tour ($95 per person) lasts about an hour; the coastal tour ($200), about two hours. Three passengers per plane.

Calistoga Gliders Inc. (942-5000; 1546 Lincoln Ave., Calistoga). Ride the thermals like an eagle, when the tow-plane releases the glider at 3,000 feet. Twenty-minute flight for one person, $75; for two, $95; open year-round; call ahead for reservations on weekends.

Napa Valley Helicoptours (800-662-6886; Napa Airport). You can't get a tour any more personalized than this. Thirty-minute aerial tours of Napa Valley cost $125 a person, with a two-person minimum. A landing at a winery for a private tour and tasting costs $145. Less for groups.

Off to ride the thermals above Napa Valley. Glider rides are available at Calistoga Airport.

Penn; courtesy Calistoga Chamber of Commerce

Sonoma County

Aero Schellville (938-2444; Schellville Airport, 23982 Arnold Dr., Sonoma). Red Baron move over. Scenic tours of Sonoma Valley in vintage biplanes, meticulously restored. Aerobatic flights are also available, offering loops, rolls and `kamikaze' flights — not for the faint of heart.

Aeroventure (778-6767; Petaluma Airport). Scenic tours; $87 per hour (up to 560 lbs. weight); $97 per hour (up to 700 lbs.).

Dragonfly Aviation (800-677-9626; Sonoma County Airport, Santa Rosa). Scenic tours and charters; $76 per hour with up to three passengers; $410 per hour with up to six passengers; luxury twin-engine planes.

Let's Fly (546-9362; Sonoma County Airport, Santa Rosa). Scenic tours and charters; $110 per hour with up to three passengers.

Sonoma Airlink Limited (800-24-GO FLY; Sonoma Sky Park Airport, 21870 8th St. East. Sonoma). Aerial tours of Sonoma and Napa valleys, the coast and San Francisco Bay; also customized tours offered; $90 per hour for up to three passengers; open cockpit biplane also available.

GOLF

Golfing in Calistoga.

Penn; courtesy Meadowood

Golf courses cover the rich valleys and rolling hills of Wine Country as comfortably as vineyards. One of the region's favorite recreational activities, golf can be played year-round in this mild climate. Where to play? The visitor can stay at a premier resort with its own course, such as Silverado or Meadowood, or at accommodations with courses close at hand, such as Red Lion Hotel and Sonoma Mission Inn. Other visitors and residents are free to sample a variety of public and semi-private courses (private clubs that also allow the public to play). Many private clubs extend complimentary privileges to members of other clubs.

GOLF COURSES

Greens Fees, Price Code		
	Inexpensive	Under $10
	Moderate	$10 to $20
	Expensive	Over $20

Napa County

Aetna Springs (800-675-2115; 1600 Aetna Springs Rd., Pope Valley). 9 holes; par 35; public course established in the 1890s; driving range; pro; lessons; snack bar. Price: Inexpensive.

Chardonnay Club (257-8950; 2555 Jameson Canyon Rd., Napa). 27 championship holes; par 72; Scottish links style; semi-private course; driving range; 5 pros; shop; club house. Price: Expensive.

Chimney Rock Golf Course (255-3363; 5320 Silverado Trail, Napa). 9 holes; par 36; semi-private course; pro; shop; restaurant. Price: Moderate.

Napa Municipal Golf Course (255-4333; Napa-Vallejo Hwy., Napa). 18 holes; par 72; public course; driving range; instruction; cocktail lounge; reserve tee time 7 days in advance. Price: Moderate.

Meadowood Resort (963-3646; 900 Meadowood Ln., St. Helena). Private to members and guests; 9 holes; par 31; tree-lined narrow course. Price: Expensive.

Mount St. Helena Golf Course (942-9966; Napa County Fairground, Calistoga). 9 holes; par 34; public course; shop; snack bar. Price: Inexpensive.

Napa Valley Country Club (252-1111; 3385 Hagen Rd., Napa) Private; 18 holes; par 72; shop; pro; lessons open to public. Price: Expensive.

Silverado Country Club and Resort (257-0200; 1600 Atlas Peak Rd., Napa). Private to members and guests; 18 holes; par 72; pro; shop; host to annual Senior PGA tournament in Oct.; considered by many the best course in Northern California. Price: Expensive.

Sonoma County

Bennett Valley Golf Course (528-3673; 3330 Yulupa Ave., Santa Rosa). 18 holes; par 72; municipal course; 3 pros; shop; driving range; restaurant; bar; reserve a week ahead. Price: Inexpensive.

Putting around at Meadowood Country Club and Resort.

Courtesy Meadowood

NAPA AND SONOMA RECREATION SITES

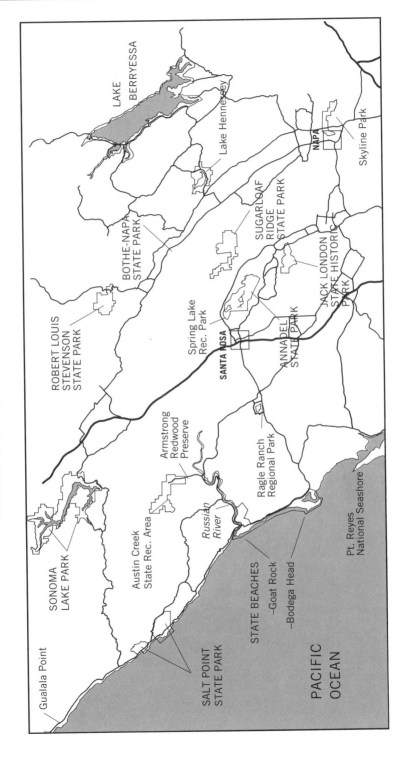

LAKE BERRYESSA

Lake Hennessey

NAPA

Skyline Park

SUGARLOAF RIDGE STATE PARK

BOTHE-NAPA STATE PARK

JACK LONDON STATE HISTORIC PARK

ROBERT LOUIS STEVENSON STATE PARK

Spring Lake Rec. Park

SANTA ROSA

ANNADEL STATE PARK

Armstrong Redwood Preserve

Ragle Ranch Regional Park

Austin Creek State Rec. Area

Russian River

SONOMA LAKE PARK

Gualala Point

STATE BEACHES
–Goat Rock
–Bodega Head

Pt. Reyes National Seashore

SALT POINT STATE PARK

PACIFIC OCEAN

Bodega Harbour Golf Links (875-3538; 21301 Heron Dr., Bodega Bay). 18 championship holes; par 70; designed by Robert Trent Jones; semi-private course; 2 pros; shop; lessons; restaurant and lounge; spectacular ocean view from all holes. Price: Expensive.

Fountaingrove Country Club (579-4653; 1525 Fountaingrove Pkwy., Santa Rosa). 18 championship holes; par 72; designed by Ted Robinson. Semi-private course; pro; shop; restaurant; tennis courts. Price: Expensive.

Healdsburg Municipal Golf Course (433-4275; 927 S. Fitch Mountain Rd., Healdsburg). 9 holes; par 35; public course; pro; shop; putting green; restaurant and lounge. Price: Inexpensive.

Mountain Shadows Golf Resort (584-7766; 100 Golf Course Dr., Rohnert Park). Two 18-hole championship courses; par 72; public course; pro; shop; practice range; restaurant and lounge. Price: Moderate to expensive.

Oakmont Golf Club (539-0415; 7025 Oakmont Dr., Santa Rosa). Two 18-hole championship courses; par 72 and 63; designed by Ted Robinson; public course; 4 pros; 2 shops; driving range; lessons; reservations suggested. Price: Moderate to expensive.

Sea Ranch Golf Links (785-2468; Sea Ranch). 9 holes; par 36; links style course designed by Robert Muir Graves; public course; pro; shop; driving range; lessons; snack bar; ocean view from every hole. Price: Moderate to expensive.

Sebastopol Golf Course (823-9852; 2881 Scott's Right-Of-Way, Sebastopol). 9 holes; par 31; public course; pro; shop; snack bar; picnic facilities. Price: Inexpensive.

Sonoma Golf Course (996-0300; 17700 Arnold Dr., Sonoma). 18 championship holes; par 72; public course; just completed $8.5-million renovation; driving range; putting green; restaurant. Price: Expensive.

Windsor Golf Club (838-7888; 6555 Skylane Blvd., Windsor). 18 holes; par 72; public course; driving range; shop; snack bar. Price: Moderate to expensive.

HIKING & PARKS

Choosing a trail through sand dunes or redwoods, grassy valleys or mountain forests, there is no better way to appreciate the natural beauty of Wine Country than to pack a snack and leave the roads behind. No matter the season, there are special things to enjoy: brilliant wild flowers in the spring, dry heat and golden grass in summer, colored fall foliage or cool breezes and green hills in winter. A number of state and county parks await you, whether you are introducing a baby to her first hike or ready for serious backpacking. For help with the details of your trip, see Bob Lorentzen's *The Hiker's Hip Pocket Guide to Sonoma County* (includes some hikes in Napa County).

POISON-OAK—*Rhus diversiloba.*

Margaret Warriner Buck

Watch out! Poison oak is plentiful in Napa and Sonoma counties.

Remember, though you might not be likely to find bears or mountain lions, rattlesnakes and ticks are not uncommon in the back country. Stay away from poison oak, and don't forget to take your own water on summer hikes.

Napa County

Bothe-Napa State Park (942-4575; 3801 Hwy. 29, 4 mi. N. of St. Helena). Originally home to the Wappo Indians, this land became a country retreat for the wealthy Hitchcock family in the 1870s. The History Trail passes a pioneer cemetery to Bale Grist Mill, a partially restored 1846 flour mill; 1,917 acres; day-use fee; 6 miles of hiking trails.

John F. Kennedy Park (257-9529; 2291 Streblow Dr. off Hwy. 121, Napa). This 340-acre park features hiking trails along the Napa River and plenty of undeveloped open space, as well as softball fields, playgrounds, and boat launch ramps.

Robert Louis Stevenson State Park (942-4575; 3801 Hwy. 29, 7 miles north of Calistoga). Composed of ancient lava, Mount St. Helena rises 4343 ft. to provide the highest landmark in Wine Country. In 1841, Russian settlers from Fort Ross scaled the peak, naming it for their Commandant's wife Elena. In 1880, Robert Louis Stevenson spent two months near here while recuperating from tuberculosis. It made a lasting impression on him, and he recalled it, renamed Spyglass Hill, in his famous "Treasure Island." 3,300 acres; 10-mile round trip to summit, past the once-prosperous Silverado Mine; undeveloped except for trails; open daily during daylight hours.

Skyline Wilderness Park (252-0481; 2201 West Imola Ave., Napa.) Wilderness close to downtown Napa, with 35 miles of hiking, mountain bike and horse trails. Its oak-wooded hills are ideal for hiking. On a clear day, there are spectacular views of San Francisco from the park's ridges. A small lake offers bass fishing; 850 acres; open daily year-round; day-use fee.

Armstrong Redwood Grove is home to some of California's tallest and oldest trees.

Chris Alderman

Westwood Hills Wilderness Park (Browns Valley Rd., Napa). City-owned park with hiking trails, native flora and fauna; 111 acres.

White Sulphur Springs (963-8588; 3100 White Sulphur Springs Rd., St. Helena). Secluded countryside 3 miles west of St. Helena, with hiking trails throughout; year-round creek and waterfalls. Day-use fee.

Sonoma County

Annadel State Park (539-3911; 6201 Channel Dr., off Montgomery Dr., Santa Rosa). Surrounded by an increasingly developed Santa Rosa, Annadel offers 5,000 acres of hills, creeks, woodlands and meadows reached by 40 miles of trails. In the summer, visitors are grateful for the small, centrally located lake created by the last owner, Joe Coney, and named after himself and his wife Ilsa as Lake Ilsanjo; day-use fee.

Armstrong Redwoods State Reserve (869-2015; 17000 Armstrong Woods Rd., Guerneville). In the late 1800s, Colonel James Armstrong sought to preserve this ancient grove of redwoods he had come to love. Because of his efforts and those of his family, Sonoma is fortunate to be able to enjoy this virgin stand of 1,000-year old trees stretching 300 ft. high — one of the largest of which is named after the Colonel. Walk among these giants, where, even on the hottest day, you will feel their cool serenity; 750 acres; day-use fee; hiking trails, picnic sites, outdoor theater; open year-round until sunset.

Austin Creek State Recreation Area (869-2015; 17000 Armstrong Woods Rd., Guerneville.) Adjacent to Armstrong Grove, this undeveloped park offers miles of trails for hikers and equestrians through canyons, enormous glades, and dark, cool forests; 4,200 acres; day-use fee; camping available.

Hood Mountain Regional Park (527-2041; Santa Rosa). Accessible by car from Alamos Road or by a four-hour hike from Sugarloaf Ridge State Park, Hood Mountain (elevation 2,730 ft.) commands an imposing view of the Mayacamas Range; day-use fee.

Lake Sonoma (433-9483; 3333 Skaggs Spring Rd. near Dry Creek Road, Healdsburg). Forty miles of trails wind through the redwood groves and oak woodlands surrounding Sonoma's newest man-made lake. Visitors' Center at base of the dam; 3,600 acres; camping, boating, swimming, fish hatchery.

Jack London State Historic Park (938-5216; 2400 London Ranch Rd., off Arnold Dr., Glen Ellen). Writer Jack London fell in love with the Valley of the Moon, and began buying land there in 1905. By the time he died in 1916, he was immersed in several innovative projects on his "Beauty Ranch." Visitors can see the remains of the London's Wolf House mansion; seven miles of trails as well as a scenic 3.5 mile climb with breathtaking views of the Valley of the Moon; 800 acres; day-use fee; open daily.

Ragle Ranch Regional Park (527-2041; Ragle Rd., off Bodega Hwy., Sebastopol). This former ranch offers trails through a rugged wilderness of oak woodlands and creeks; baseball fields, playgrounds, picnic areas; 156 acres.

Sugarloaf Ridge State Park (833-5712; 2605 Adobe Canyon Rd. off Hwy. 12, Santa Rosa). The Wappo Indians lived in this beautiful area before they were decimated by European diseases during the 1830s. Purchased by the state in 1920 as a site for a dam which was never built, Sugarloaf Ridge now offers 25 miles of trails through a varied landscape, including ridges surrounding Bald Mountain and meadows along Sonoma Creek. 2,700 acres; day-use fee; camping.

HORSEBACK RIDING

The Wine Country adamantly maintains its rural flavor, despite a growing population and world-wide tourist appeal. With an estimated 26,000 horses in Sonoma County alone, there is plenty of interest in horse breeding, competition and riding. Some 50 horse events take place annually at the

You might call these sea horses. In Bodega Bay, Sea Horse Stables is one horse rental facility that offers beach rides.

Edmond Bridant; courtesy SCCVB

Horseback riding at Annadel Park.

Sonoma County Fairgrounds, including top shows such as the *California State Horse Show* which attracts visitors from all over the West.

Like Jack London, described by one biographer the "sailor on horseback," many Wine Country residents and visitors take to the hills on horseback to explore the countryside. Bridle paths and trails can be found at *Annadel, Armstrong Redwoods, Austin Creek, Bothe-Napa Valley, Jack London, Salt Point, Skyline* and *Sugarloaf Ridge* parks. For those without their own steeds, the following stables rent horses for the day.

Napa County

Wild Horse Valley Ranch (224-0727; Wild Horse Valley Rd., Napa). Riding trips offered, with 3,000 acres of trails for every kind of rider, or bring your own horse to ride. The ranch also offers a race track, indoor arenas, polo, cross country courses, riding school, tack shop and horse boarding.

Sonoma County

Armstrong Woods Pack Station (579-1520; Armstrong Redwoods State Park, 17000 Armstrong Woods Rd., Guerneville). Rentals for trail rides through Armstrong Redwoods and Austin Creek parks; half-day or full day with gourmet lunch available.

Sea Horse Stables (875-2721; 2660 Hwy. 1, Bodega Bay). Scenic guided trail rides for riders of all levels; one- or two-hour treks on the ranch and dunes. Open year-round.

Sonoma Cattle Company (996-8566; Jack London State Park, 2400 London Ranch Rd., Glen Ellen). Rentals for Jack London and Sugarloaf Ridge state parks; guided tours for one- or two-hour tours (April through October); barbecue rides and day-trips available.

HORSE RACING

Horse racing fans converge each summer at the *Sonoma County Fair* (545-4200; 1350 Bennett Valley Rd., Santa Rosa) to watch California's fastest horses vie for a purse of nearly $2 million. During the rest of the year, the Fairground offers a "Watch and Wager" facility with simultaneous broadcasting of races at Golden Gate Fields and Los Alamitos.

RACQUETBALL

For the executive who needs stress relief or the athlete who loves fast action on an indoor court, racquetball is a lively game that demands focus and coordination and is increasingly popular among the health-conscious in Napa and Sonoma, especially during the rainy winter months when tennis is iffy. Private clubs with courts charge an annual or monthly fee; public courts charge by the hour. Most require advance registration.

Napa County

La Cancha Racquetball Health Center (252-8033; 1850 Soscol Ave., Napa) Private club; 6 courts; holds tournaments with other clubs.

Monoff Center (942-5188; Stevenson and Grant Sts., Calistoga). Public, city-run court.

Pay 'N Play Racquetball of America (257-2226; 875 Sousa Ln., Napa). Public; automated 24-hour racquetball and handball courts; equipment rental; 4 courts; leagues and tournaments; no reservations necessary.

Sonoma County

Anastasia's Athletic Club (544-9400; 1100 Piner Rd., Santa Rosa). Private; full health club; 5 courts; no tournaments.

The Parkpoint Club (578-1640; 1200 N. Dutton Ave., Santa Rosa). Private; full health club; 6 courts; tournaments.

Rohnert Park Sports Center (584-4800; 5405 Snyder Ln., Rohnert Park). Public, with yearly membership available; 2 courts; tournaments; equipment rental.

ROCK CLIMBING

For those who like to live on the edge, rock climbing has become a sport with built-in adventure, but it's important to do it right. *Sonoma Outfitters* (528-1920; 145 Third St., Santa Rosa) offers a complete selection of shoes and equipment plus a climbing wall (open weekend afternoons) for practice. Classes are also offered.

When you're ready for the real thing, favorite climbing spots in the area are *Sunset Boulder* at Goat Rock on the Sonoma Coast and *Mount St. Helena* in Napa. Check out the book *Bouldering in the Bay Area* for other possible challenges.

RUNNING

Joggers of all ages, sizes, and shapes, can be seen on park trails and roadsides in Sonoma and Napa Counties. The fresh air and countryside of the Wine Country, along with its mild climate, have made running an extremely popular year-round activity for the health conscious.

For serious runners, several competitions take place each year, including the *Napa Valley Marathon*, which is run from Calistoga to Napa on the second Sunday in March. Another demanding event is the *International Vineman Triathlon*, combining running, bicycling and swimming competitions. Many races in both counties benefit local causes, such as Napa's "Run for Literacy" and Sonoma's "Human Race." Get specific schedules from the *Sonoma County Convention and Visitors Bureau* (575-1191) or the *Napa Visitors Center* (226-7455).

SKATING

ICE SKATING

Famed cartoonist and ice skating buff Charles Schulz built the **Redwood Empire Ice Arena** (546-7147; 1667 West Steel Ln., Santa Rosa) in 1969, and it has become one of Sonoma County's most popular spots. The rink, surrounded by walls painted with Alpine scenes, is the site for recreational and would-be Olympic skaters, birthday parties (more than 8,000 to date) and holiday ice shows with professional figure skaters. A happy addition has been Snoopy's Gallery & Gift Shop (546-3385), filled with every conceivable item relating to Snoopy and the "Peanuts" gang, as well as skating gear including hi-tech Rollerblades.

ROLLER SKATING

Still a fun-time favorite with kids, teens and adults. After all, they say it's the best aerobic exercise around.

Cal Skate (585-0500; 6100 Commerce Blvd., Rohnert Park).

Star Skate World (544-7000; 2075 Occidental Road, Santa Rosa).

SOFTBALL

Softball is one of Napa and Sonoma's most popular sports for adults, as you can tell by all the would-be ball stars playing in parks throughout the Wine Country on summer weeknights and weekends. Santa Rosa alone has 265 men's, women's and mixed fastpitch and slowpitch teams, with more than 4,000 players on the field for three games a night all summer. Call the local recreation department for information about signing up.

Napa County

Napa (257-9529). 174 teams, sponsors American Softball district tournaments; host of state regional tournament in 1991.

St. Helena (963-5706). 30 teams.

Sonoma County

Healdsburg (431-3301). 59 teams.

Petaluma (778-4386). 70 teams.

Rohnert Park (584-4800). 83 teams.

Sebastopol (823-1511). Men's and coed teams; not city-run.

Santa Rosa (524-5116). 265 teams.

To watch a championship fastpitch softball team, catch the Guanella Brothers "Floormen" — one of the top five in the country — at the *Rohnert Park Stadium* (584-7357; La Bath Ave.) during the summer. Call for game schedule.

SPAS

Long before pioneers came to Northern California, Indians knew the locations of hot springs and used the steamy pools, volcanic mud and mineral waters to soak away aches and pains. After the Gold Rush, Sam Brannan — a pioneer who struck it rich in San Francisco real estate deals — became enchanted with the countryside in northern Napa Valley. He built an extravagant hotel-resort-spa around the area's hot springs and, in 1859, began to attract notables such as Leland Stanford to this beautiful valley backed by wooded hills. As the story goes, Brannan intended to proclaim his spa the "Saratoga of California" in his dedication speech, but his words came out as the "Calistoga of Sarafornia." It's been called Calistoga ever since.

Although Brannan's resort no longer stands, Calistoga still offers many facilities for mud and mineral baths and professional massage, and has made it big-time as a tourist destination town that combines small town American charm with old-country worldliness. Weekends are crowded with visitors who come to renew their bodies in the spa, and their spirits in the beauty of the Wine Country. For complete information, contact *Calistoga Chamber of Commerce*, (942-6333, 1458 Lincoln Ave. No. 4).

Getting a volcanic mud treatment at Doctor Wilkinson's Hot Springs spa in Calistoga

Penn; courtesy Calistoga Chamber of Commerce

Napa County

Dr. Wilkinson's Hot Springs (942-4102; 1507 Lincoln Ave., Calistoga). Mud and mineral baths; massage; swimming pools; lodging. One of the oldest, most popular and most publicized spas; only continually owned, family-operated spa in Calistoga.

Calistoga Spa Hot Springs (942-6269; 1006 Washington St). Mud and mineral baths; massage; steam baths; three outdoor mineral pools; lodging, with kitchenettes. One of the older spas, recently rebuilt into one of the most modern; pools are very popular; exercise room with aerobics classes; not quite as into "The Treatment" as other spas.

Calistoga Village Inn and Spa (800-543-1094; 1880 Lincoln Ave.). Mud and mineral baths; swimming pools; steam cabinets; massage; lodging; only spa with restaurant; landscaped grounds; old spa; lodgings not fancy.

Golden Haven Spa Hot Springs Resort (942-6793; 1713 Lake St., Calistoga). Mud and mineral baths; whirlpool; blanket wrap; massage and acupuncture; mud baths for couples; pleasant service.

Wine Country's Hot Spot

The Wine Country, along with all its other striking features, is blessed with a little extra something: geothermal activity. Some of this power has been harnessed by the only geothermal power plant in the United States, located on the lonely, winding Geysers Road between Geyserville and Cloverdale. This energy can be seen as Calistoga's Old Faithful Geyser shoots steam and vapor 60 feet into the air.

But the most popular signs of hot steam and bubbling mineral water are the "Spa" signs along Lincoln Avenue in downtown Calistoga, where salvation is offered to the body and soul in the form of mud and mineral baths.

What exactly is a mud bath treatment? First, you immerse in a thick, warm, black mass of volcanic ash power mixed with naturally heated mineral water. "It's like a warm cocoon enveloping you," explains Mary at Indians Springs Spa. "You have to learn to let go, to relax into a mud cushion."

After what seems like an eon of primordial bliss, you take a shower, a soak in warm mineral water, then open your pores in a eucalyptus-scented, geyser-heated steam room. Finish up with a cooling blanket wrap. Ahhhh. If you can handle additional pleasure, expert masseuses will work your body into a totally relaxed state. When you leave a spa you feel like a new person ready to take on the world again. After a steak and a nap, that is.

One hour mud treatments cost about $40; add about $30 for an additional half hour of massage, $50 for an hour. Other offerings at various spas include facials, skin glow rub, steam baths, herbal body wraps, whirlpool soaks, swimming pools. Enjoy!

Indian Springs (942-4913; 1712 Lincoln Ave., Calistoga). Mud, mineral, steam baths; massage; facials; olympic outdoor mineral pool; three active geysers; lodging (duplex cottages); set in 16 acres of gardens; site of original Sam Brannan resort; rebuilt and quite popular.

Nance's Hot Springs and Motel (942-6211; 1614 Lincoln Ave., Calistoga). One of the oldest spas; mud, steam and sulphur baths; indoor mineral pool; lodging, with kitchenettes; popular with folks who relish old-fashioned family atmosphere; co-owner Frank Hughes, in his 70s, still gives massages.

Roman Spa Motel (942-4441; 1300 Washington St., Calistoga). Two outdoor, one indoor hot mineral pools with whirlpool; sauna; massage; lodging; spa facilities at small, independently owned International Spa next door, which specializes in Japanese enzyme baths.

White Sulphur Springs (963-8588; 3100 White Sulphur Springs Rd., 3 miles

The Hot Spot — Geysers

Sonoma County Museum

west of St. Helena). Built in 1852, this is the first resort built in California. Its original owners were physicians who believed the sulphur springs helped relieve arthritis and rheumatism, and people have been coming ever since to soak away pains in the 95 degree natural sulphur pool; massage; a rugged get-away, rather than a full-service spa; 330 acres with picnic grounds, hiking trails; cottages and inn.

Sonoma County

Sonoma Mission Inn and Spa (800-862-4945; 18140 Sonoma Hwy., Boyes Hot Springs). No mineral baths, but whirlpools, sauna and steam rooms, two outside pools (one heated), fitness activities, more types of massage and body treatments than you've ever heard of. Day use open to the public except on weekends.

SWIMMING

Summer in the Wine Country brings day after day of blue skies, that is, after the sun breaks through the morning fog. What better way to dodge the heat than by packing a lunch and heading for a lake, river or pool for the day? Remember that the Pacific Ocean — with year-round temperatures around 50 degrees and dangerous undercurrents — is not a good place for a swim. For those whose want exercise more than fun, indoor pools with lap lanes are available year-round.

Napa County

Bothe-Napa Valley State Park (942-4575; Hwy. 29, 4 miles north of St. Helena). Swimming pool open mid-June through Labor Day; day-use fee.

Indian Springs (942-4913; 1712 Lincoln Ave., Calistoga). Largest pool in Napa Valley, Olympic size; mineral pool naturally heated by geysers; open weather permitting; day-use fee.

Lake Berryessa (800-726-1256; West of St. Helena). Miles of clear blue water, with temperatures up to 75 degrees, make this an ideal destination in the summer. Several resorts, including Putah Creek, Spanish Flat and Steele Park, offer swimming area. (See "Boating" in this chapter for specific information on resorts.)

Napa Public Pools (226-7455). Open to the public when schools are not in session, include Napa Valley College, Redwood High School, Napa High School, Silverado Middle School.

St. Helena Community Pool (963-7946; 1401 Grayson Ave.). Open all summer.

Swimming at Lake Ilsanjo in Annadel Park near Santa Rosa is one of the best ways to cool off.

Chris Alderman

Sonoma County

Agua Caliente Springs (996-6822; 17350 Vailetti Dr., Sonoma). Originally opened in 1888; offers large outdoor warm mineral pool, cold water diving pool, wading pool; indoor pool with whirlpool; picnic and barbecue; open daily in summer; weekends summer and fall.

Lake Sonoma (433-2200; 11 mi. N. of Healdsburg on Dry Creek Rd.). Provides beaches at Lake Sonoma Marina and at Yorty Creek, along with picnic, hiking and boating facilities.

Morton's Warm Springs (833-5511; 1651 Warm Springs Rd., Kenwood). Two large pools, one wading pool; picnic grounds; volleyball and baseball. Open summer only. Perfect for group outings.

Petaluma Swim Center (778-4410; 900 E. Washington St., Petaluma). Summer only; lap swim; instruction.

Rohnert Park Public Pools (584-7357). Outdoor pools are open from Memorial Day to Labor Day at Alicia, Benecia, Ladybug and Honeybee parks; rent one for a private party; lap swim; instruction.

Russian River. Residents and visitors alike enjoy swimming in the slow-flowing, deep green river. Swimming areas are located at *Veterans Memorial Beach* in Healdsburg (433-1625; Old Redwood Hwy., Healdsburg), *Monte Rio Beach*, and at *Johnson's Beach* in Guerneville (869-2022), both just off River Road, where inner tubes and paddle boats can also be rented.

Santa Rosa Swim Center (524-5180; 433 Ridgeway Ave., Santa Rosa). Heated outdoor pool open year-round; lap swimming; instruction and youth swim summer only.

Sebastopol Swim Center (823-8693; 7400 Willow Ave., Sebastopol). Outdoor heated pool open year-round; lap swim; instruction and youth swim in summer only.

Spring Lake (539-8092; Off Summerfield Rd., Santa Rosa). The 72-acre swimming lagoon — separated from the lake's boating and fishing areas — is filled with kids and their families every hot day of summer. A gentle sandy shoreline, water floats to mark depth, rafts and tubes to rent and lifeguards help make this a great swimming experience for beginners.

Windsor Waterworks and Slide (838-7760; 8225 Conde Ln., Windsor). Outdoor pool, wading pool, picnic sites, and four roller-coaster waterslides make this a cool spot on a scorching summer day. One ride down the slide and you're hooked.

YMCA (545-9622; 1111 College Ave., Santa Rosa). The Y's indoor heated pool is open daily year-round for laps, exercise, instruction and family fun. For the swimmer who works full-time, weekday hours are from 5:30 a.m. to 9:30 p.m.

TENNIS

In an area where the climate is mild and it only rains during 6 months of the year, you would expect tennis to be an avid sport — is it ever! With a variety of public and private tennis courts offering instruction and competition, Wine Country gives the tennis enthusiast plenty of action.

The *Sonoma County Tennis Association* (585-3155), active since 1982, has been instrumental in organizing tournaments throughout the year for all levels of players from youth to A-division, singles and doubles. With 1100 members from Sonoma, Napa and Marin counties, the SCTA sponsors matches mainly at Sonoma State University in Rohnert Park and Galvin Park in Santa Rosa. The public is invited to watch.

Napa County

Calistoga Public Courts (942-5188; Stevenson and Grant Sts.). Available year-round; 4 courts; lighted; city-run instruction in summer.

Meadowood Resort (963-3646; 900 Meadowood Ln., St. Helena). Courts open to members and guests; pro.

Napa Public Courts (257-9529). Available during the summer at Napa Valley College (Vallejo Hwy., Napa), Vintage High School (1375 Trower Ave.), Napa High School (2475 Jefferson St.), Silverado Middle School (1133 Coombsville Rd.); city-run instruction.

There's usually a match on at the tennis courts in Santa Rosa's Howarth Park.

Kris White

Napa Valley Country Club (252-1111; 3385 Hagen Rd., Napa). Private; pro; lessons open to public; active spot.

St. Helena Public Courts (963-5706). Available at Robert Louis Stevenson School (1316 Hill View Pl.) and St. Helena High School (1401 Grayson Ave.); city-operated courts at Crane Park (off Crane Ave.); active women's city league program for A and B players.

Silverado Country Club and Resort (257-0200; 1600 Atlas Peak Rd., Napa). Open to members and guests; pro.

Sonoma County

Countryside Racquets Club (527-9948; 3950 Sebastopol Rd., Santa Rosa). Courts open to members and guests; pro; 8 lighted courts; leagues and tournaments; very active.

La Cantera Racquet and Swim Club (544-9494; 3737 Montgomery Dr., Santa Rosa). Courts open to members and guests; pro; 12 courts, 4 lighted; leagues and tournaments.

Montecito Heights Health and Racquet Club (526-0529; 2777 Fourth St., Santa Rosa). Courts open to members and guests; pro; 5 courts, none lighted; leagues and tournaments.

Rancho Arroyo Racquet Club (795-546l; 85 Corona Rd., Petaluma). Courts open to members and guests; pro; 7 courts, 2 lighted; leagues and tournaments.

Rohnert Park Public Courts (584-7357). Available at seven parks: Alicia (300 Arlen Dr.), Ladybug (8517 Liman Wy.), Dorotea, Eagle, Sunrise, Honeybee (1170 Golf Course Dr.) and Golis. The Recreation Department offers instruction and sponsors the Rohnert Park Tennis Club, a group that draws players from Sonoma, Napa and Marin counties.

Santa Rosa Public Courts (524-5115). Available at Howarth and Galvin parks, Burbank Playground, Santa Rosa Junior College, Santa Rosa and Montgomery high schools.

WHALE-WATCHING

One of the great attractions in California is the opportunity to watch gray whales in their annual round-trip migration between summer feeding grounds in the Bering Sea and their breeding and birthing waters off Baja California. From late May through October, the gray whales feed in the cold waters, building fat for their 12,000-mile pilgrimage. Then, beginning in late November, they head south, passing close enough to shore to navigate by sight, as well as to avoid killer whales in the deeper waters. Their return usually starts in late February and lasts until early June.

> ### *Point Reyes National Seashore*
>
> The *Point Reyes Lighthouse* (415-663-1200) at the tip of the Point Reyes National Seashore in Marin County, about a 1½ hour drive from Santa Rosa, offers one of the best vantage points in the state for whale watching. The Lighthouse is open from 10 to 4:30 daily except Tuesday and Wednesday, but parking is limited and extremely crowded on weekends. Call ahead to find out if there is any visibility, since the Lighthouse sits on the windiest and rainiest spot on the entire Pacific Coast.

Sonoma County offers other good whale-watching sites, including *Gualala Point, Stillwater Cove, Fort Ross* and *Bodega Head*. On a clear day you will have plenty of company to share sightings — all bundled against the sea breezes, toting binoculars and picnic lunches, ready to spend several hours watching for the tell-tale spouts shooting above the blue Pacific waters.

For a close-up view, reserve a place on a whale-watching boat out of Bodega Bay. Remember that it's typically 15 degrees colder on the water, so wear plenty of warm clothes. Law prohibits boaters from harassing whales, but the large mammals have little fear of man and often approach boats at sea. All boats leave from *Porta Bodega Marina* on Bay Flat Rd., off Hwy. 1; about $12 per person.

The Challenger (875-2474). Two-hour cruises, twice daily January through April, weather permitting.

Bodega Bay Sport Fishing Center (875-3344). Three-hour cruises, twice daily January through April, weather permitting.

FOR KIDS AND KIDS AT HEART

The Wine Country isn't just a playground for adults. Kids and kids at heart can find all sorts of fun, from pony rides and water slides to a planetarium show guaranteed to stretch the imagination. Also see "Swimming" and "Boating and Watersports" in this chapter for other family activity suggestions.

Napa County

Petrified Forest (942-6667; Petrified Forest Rd., 5 mi. W. of Calistoga). Remains of a redwood forest turned to stone by molten lava from the eruption of Mount St. Helena 3 million years ago. The Petrified Forest was discovered in 1870 and immortalized by Robert Louis Stevenson in "The Silverado Squatters"; picnic grounds; museum; open daily. Admission: $3 adults, $2 children.

Old Faithful Geyser (942-6463; 1299 Tubbs Ln., 1 mile north of Calistoga). One of just three regularly erupting geysers in the world, it shoots steam and vapor 60 ft. into the air for 3 min.; repeats every 40 min.. Open daily; picnic grounds. Admission: $3 adult, $2 children 6-12, free children under 6.

Sonoma County

Howarth Park (528-5115; Montgomery and Summerfield rds., Santa Rosa). Popular city-run park offers merry-go-round, pony rides, small railroad; play and picnic areas; paddle boats, canoes, rowboats to rent and ducks to feed on Lake Ralphine. Some activities summer only.

J's Amusements (869-3102; Guerneville). Go-carts, waterslide, rollercoaster, carnival rides, arcade.

Pet-A-Llama Ranch (823-9395; 5505 Lone Pine Rd., Sebastopol). Feed and pet llamas; wool spinning demonstration and hand woven goods. Nominal fee.

Planetarium (527-4371; Santa Rosa Junior College, 1501 Mendocino Ave., Santa Rosa). An excellent planetarium open to the public on weekends dur-

The train in Santa Rosa's Howarth Park offers a pint-size ride.

Chris Alderman

ing the school year. Shows at 7 and 8:30 p.m. Friday and Saturday; no reservations, so arrive early. No children under 5.

Scandia Family Fun Center (584-1361; 5301 S. Santa Rosa Ave., Rohnert Park). Little Indy Racers, miniature golf, baseball cages, game arcade. A favorite recreation center for kids and families. Packed on summer weekends. Separate fees for each activity.

Train Town (938-3912; 20264 Broadway, 1 mile south of Sonoma Plaza). Ride a scale-model steam train through 10 acres of beautifully landscaped park, through a 140-foot tunnel, across bridges, past replicas of historic building. Open daily mid-June until Labor Day; weekends the rest of the year. Admission: $2.50 adults, $1.80 children.

Winners Circle Ranch (762-1808; 5911 Lakeville Hwy., Petaluma). The only miniature horse farm west of the Mississippi open to the public. Miniature horses have a colorful history dating from the 16th century, when royal families bred them as pets. Tours; wagon rides; picnic area; open Wednesday to Sunday, May through Labor Day; showtimes at 11 and 2 daily. Admission: $6 adults, $4 children 12 and younger.

YA-KA-AMA Indian Education (887-1541; Eastside Rd., Forestville). Educational and fun activities for children of all ages, including crafts, pottery, animal track identification, storytelling. Last Saturday of every month.

MINIATURE GOLF

In addition to the Scandia Center mentioned above, there are other spots in Napa and Sonoma to putt one through a windmill.

The Club House Family Fun Center (996-3616; Sonoma Hwy. 12 near Verano Avenue, Sonoma). Course features scale models of historic Sonoma landmarks.

Fairplay Golf (255-6166; 640 Third St., Napa).

Windsor World (838-3377; 8801 Conde Ln., Windsor).

NEIGHBORS ALL AROUND

Marine World & Africa USA (643-ORCA; Marine World Parkway off Interstate 80, Vallejo). Not technically in Napa or Sonoma, but only a short drive away. 160-acre facility includes shows, animal rides and wild creatures in their natural habitat. Open Wed. through Sun. year-round.

THE COAST

Hiking a coastal trail in Salt Point State Park.

Richard Hensley; courtesy SCCVB

Sonoma County's 62-mile coastline has a wild beauty that has scarcely changed from the days when the Miwok and Pomo Indians were the only inhabitants. Not that the white man hasn't left his mark. Early Russians hunters and trappers decimated the sea otter population in the 1800s. Now under government protection, the sea otter is slowly making a comeback — much to the distress of abalone divers who compete for the otters' favorite food. The Americanization of California that accompanied the population surge after the Gold Rush created a need for timber, and the giant redwoods near the coast were heavily harvested. Towns, railroads and stage coach lines

Bodega Bay Harbor

The harbor offers protection from the rough Pacific surf and is home port for many commercial fishing boats. Famed as the setting of Alfred Hitchcock's *The Birds*, the town of Bodega Bay has become a well-known stopover and destination for area residents and visitors alike. Sportfishing, harbor cruises and whale watching trips can be arranged from *Porta Bodega Marina*, off Hwy. 1 on Bay Flat Rd. The gentle beaches on the west side of the harbor afford a perfect spot for windsurfing or sea kayaking.

flourished, providing housing for workers and transportation of the lumber to San Francisco.

Though few traces of this past remain today, visitors flock to the Sonoma Coast to enjoy some of the most spectacular views in all of California. The cliffs, continually battered by the wild Pacific Ocean, afford a setting of breathtaking beauty.

Thanks to the foresight of those who fought to preserve public access to the coast, there are many outlets from which to view the ocean along Hwy. 1. Particularly popular is the stretch between Bodega Bay and Jenner, where several beaches offer a variety of topography and vistas for hiking, picnicking, wet-suit diving, surfing, or just relaxing. Every summer, Sonoma County participants join in the *Coastwalk* (869-9009), a celebration of California's unique coastline. Hikers can join in for three or six days, led by a scout.

Whatever your activities, it is always important to remember that the Pacific Ocean can be dangerous. Every year there are deaths caused by unpredictable waves and the strong undertow. Beware.

BEACHES

Here are some of the beaches along the coast, listed from north to south. For detailed information, call the *Sonoma County Convention and Visitors Bureau*, 575-1191.

Salt Point State Park (847-3221; 25050 Hwy. 1, N. of Timber Cove). 4,114 acres along five miles of shore, offering picnicking, fishing, skin diving, hiking and horseback riding. More than 14 miles of trails wind through tall forests, windswept headlands, a stunted Pygmy Forest and grassy valleys along the San Andreas Fault. Camping is available. Adjacent to the Park is *Kruse Rhododendron State Reserve*. In May and June, the brilliant pink blossoms of native rhododendrons brighten the forest along the path.

Goat Rock Beach (875-3483; Off Hwy. 1, So. of Jenner). Named for the huge rock that bears a resemblance to the hunched back of a grazing goat. The beach extends from the sand bars along the mouth of the Russian River, where sea lions and their young haul out at certain times of the year. They're fun to watch, but please don't disturb them.

Sonoma Coast State Beach (875-3483; Salmon Creek, Bodega Bay). This is actually a chain of beaches along 18 miles of coastline, from Goat Rock to Bodega Head. Each has its own personality and invites different activities, whether it's tidepooling or a serious game of volleyball. Wildflowers brighten the cliffs in the spring. The coast is always cool in the summer, providing an escape from inland heat.

The Bodega Headlands (875-3483; at the end of Bay Flat Rd., off Hwy. 1, Bodega Bay). Stretching a curved arm out to sea, the Headlands were originally part of the Sierra Nevadas. For 40 million years they have ridden the Pacific Plate northward, out of step with land on the other side of the San Andreas fault. The cliffs provide a spectacular vista of ocean and coast and is a favorite spot to watch for whales in the winter and early spring. Bring binoculars and a jacket. Also of interest at the Headlands is the *Bodega Marine Lab* (875-2211), open to the public on Fridays from 2 to 4 p.m. Very educational and kids will love it.

Doran Regional Park (875-3540; Doran Beach Rd., off Hwy. 1, So. of Bodega Bay). A popular family spot because of its level sandy beach and overnight camping facilities. An annual sand castle competition is held every August. Day use fee.

SCUBA DIVING

Scuba diving is popular along the Sonoma Coast. The water temperatures range from 40 to 55 degrees so a full wet suit is a minimum requirement. Many divers prefer dry suits for added comfort. Diving is a year-round activity as long as the sea is calm. Even experienced divers have lost their lives when diving along this Coast during turbulent seas.

Abalone can be harvested from April to December (excluding July). Scuba equipment is not allowed while hunting these succulent creatures, and there is a limit of four per person.

The **Redwood Empire Dive Club** (539-DIVE) is available for divers of any ability interested in monthly club-sponsored dives along the Sonoma Coast and in other areas.

Diving Center of Santa Rosa (527-8527; 2696 Santa Rosa Ave.). Diving courses, rentals, equipment sales, diving trips.

The Pinnacles Dive Center (800-443-3483; 2112 Armory Dr., Santa Rosa). Diving courses, rentals, equipment sales, diving trips.

Rohnert Park Dive Center (584-2323; 5665 B Redwood Dr.). Instruction, rentals, sales, trips.

TIDEPOOLING

The Sonoma coastline has its own wildlife preserve — the tidepool. As the tide goes out twice daily, small oases are left among the rocks, shelters for starfish, snails, sea anemone and a multitude of other visible and barely visible lifeforms. Coast visitors can spend many fascinating hours exploring tide-

Rockhopping at Shell Beach,
Sonoma Coast

Chris Alderman

pools. For additional insight into the world of the tidepool, visit the **Bodega Marine Lab** (875-2211), open to the public on Fridays from 2 to 4 p.m. Please do not take anything from the pools; even empty shells can provide a hermit crab's mobile home.

CHAPTER EIGHT
An Embarrassment of Riches
SHOPPING

Chris Alderman

Manager Ray Tokareff exhibits his wares at Flying Carpets, Napa.

For some, shopping is a sport unto itself and for those trekking through Wine Country, there is a marathon of possibilities. Start with a shot of espresso, set your stop watch, slip on your walking shoes and sling a bulky shopping bag over your shoulder.

This chapter is your compass. It will guide you to the traditional and offbeat. Some stores will be within easy reach, others will be off the beaten path. At some of the antiques stores we've listed, you may feel like you're prowling someone's attic. There are old *Life* magazines to peruse, carousel horses, long-discarded dolls, glass-encased toy trucks and fine pine furniture that dates from the 1870s.

You could spend a day or two wandering through the bookstores. All are user-friendly, with beautiful books, classical music and—for the most part—helpful clerks. Our favorite is the Napa Book Co. It has a sign outside that puts adults in their place: "A Store for Children (and Parents too.)"

As for clothing stores, we include both the conservative and the chic. Indeed, if you visit all the stores we've listed, you will eventually come across a pair of silk boxer shorts priced at $85. Just when did it begin costing more to *undress* than to dress? And from our gift shop listings, you will discover where Santa and the Mrs. hang out during the off season. They obviously have a satellite office in Napa County at the S. Claus store; a year-round Christmas shop chock-full of holiday cheer that you won't want to miss— even in the heat of summer. Diamonds, gemstones and other jewels will be easy to unearth after browsing through the section on jewelry. You'll even find estate jewelry dating back to the 1920s as well as pocket watches at Mary Stage in Sonoma.

Finally, for those who don't have anything in particular on their shopping list, note the shopping areas. These are great destinations with a large variety of interesting stores that make for convenient one-stop shopping. So, hit an automated teller machine, harvest some cash and pick a city, any city: Calistoga, Yountville, Sonoma, Sebastopol or Healdsburg. They all have their own special charm. You'll find that Sonoma County stores tend to be funkier than their Napa counterparts. Artifax in Sonoma, for one, is a sensory experience not to be missed. And you don't even have to pay a cover charge.

ANTIQUES

Napa County

Antique Fair (Manager: Eli Baker; 944-8440; 6512 Washington St., Yountville; open 10 to 5 daily). When you step through the doors, you feel like you're walking into someone's estate. If you fancy huge French Walnut armoires, tables, bookcases, carved bed frames and more, the Antique Fair is for you. This is definitely an upper crust shop. Don't expect many knickknacks.

Bale Mill Country Pine (Manager: Barbara Dorough; 963-4595; 3431 Hwy. 29, St. Helena; open 11 to 5 Tues. through Sun.). Bale Mill sits on a curve tucked back from Hwy. 29 and could be overlooked by even the most discerning eye. But Bale Mill has its share of shoppers. The owners build nearly all their furniture from scratch in 18th-century style. They are partial to traditional French, English and American designs and create many big farm tables, as well as huge tasting tables for wineries. You can also find Italian and French iron furniture nestled among the pine.

The Irish Pedlar (Manager: Juanita Greene; 253-9091; 1988 Wise Drive, Napa; open 11 to 5 Tues. through Sun.). The shop specializes in primitive pine with its oldest piece dating back to the 1840s. Mostly Irish, there is German and English pine as well. Some antiques are in great shape while others look like they need a little restoration. This shop has a cozy, country flavor with antique linens in one room and, in another, antique cookware replete with grinders, beaters, cookie cutters and cookbooks. And you guessed it, knickknacks and quilts. Off the beaten path, but it's worth seeking out.

Red Hen Antiques (Manager: Brian Bergevin; 257-0822; 5091 Hwy. 29, Napa, open 10 to 5 daily). More like a museum than a shop, its 18,000 square feet make the Red Hen the largest antique store in Napa Valley. The building

Red Hen Antiques on Highway 29, north of Napa, is one shop you can't miss.

Chris Alderman

meanders, room after room, with rare finds in every corner. We saw at least five carousel horses, an elaborate Balinese door, porcelain dishes, *Life* and *Saturday Evening Post* magazines, player pianos, grandfather clocks and even a moose head. This antique collective, which houses some 40 dealers, is on the west side of Hwy. 29 between Napa and Yountville. Just look for the white rooster on a platform attached to the barnlike building.

The Silk Purse (Manager: Steve Snyder; 963-7377; 115 Main St., St. Helena; open 8 to 5 Mon. through Fri., 8 to noon on Sat.). Maybe "you can't make a silk purse out of a sow's ear," but the owners of the Silk Purse make remarkably fine furniture all the same. Next to the retail shop are windows through which you can watch them repairing, refinishing and crafting fur- niture. The store is fun to browse. It has a small display of rolltop desks, grandfather clocks and trunks. It even has an enormous iron bird cage. Polly want a bird cage?

Sonoma County

Auntie's Shanty (Manager: Louise Flodin; 577-8794; 206 Wilson St., Santa Rosa; open 10 to 5 Mon. to Sat., closed Tues., 11 to 5 Sun.). Tiffany-style new and antique lamps are the attraction here. If you're a traditionalist, you'll like the older lamps with beaded fringe or the ones fashioned to look like Wisteria vines. Shoppers with more modern taste will be fascinated by items such as a lamp with a pink-toned desert scene complete with palm trees and camels. Prices usually correspond to the age of the lamp. Expect to shell out a few hundred bucks for some of these antiques.

The Buffy (Manager: Annie Paynter; 996-5626; 103 West Napa St., Sonoma; open noon to 6 daily). Collectors of Staffordshire porcelain animals can come here for more finds. The focus is on genteel European antique furniture with many fine china cabinets and tables. But smaller purchases can be made. Tiny compacts and pill boxes with colorful inlays are a bit easier to take home in your suitcase than a dining room table. Look for delicate china tea sets here, as well.

Lone Pine Antiques (Manager: Darrell Parker; 823-6768; 3598 Gravenstein Hwy. So., Sebastopol; open 10 to 5 daily, closed Tues. and Thurs.). If you were to build a pub in your own home, this would be the place to shop for accessories. Darrell Parker says he stocks his store with "anything odd and unusual," but the store's specialties are toys and old advertising. Coca-Cola memorabilia collectors will find old grocery display cases, and beer buffs can buy brewers' neon signs. Serious antique enthusiasts might want to steer clear of the store's back rooms. They mostly house a jumble of junk.

Marianne's Antiques (Managers: Dave and Marianne Neufeld; 579-5749; 111 Third St., Santa Rosa; open 10 to 5:30 Mon. to Sat., 11 to 5 Sun.). This is a

Keepsakes are for sale at Marianne's Antiques, Santa Rosa.

Chris Alderman

store for the serious antique shopper. There are carefully chosen European armoires, tables, chairs and desks. Nothing low-grade here.

Ray's Trading Co. (Manager: Ray Burrows; 829-9726; 3570 Gravenstein Hwy. So., Sebastopol; open 10 to 5 Tues. through Sat.). An important resource for Bay Area people who are restoring their Victorian homes, Ray's is a salvage company, its bins full of antique door knobs, drawer pulls, even whole windows and doors. There is also a collection of old chandeliers and hanging lamps. The store occasionally gets old cast iron and potbelly stoves as well as kitchen sinks.

Vintage Antiques (Manager: Warren Davis; 433-7461; 328 Healdsburg Ave., Healdsburg; open 11 to 5:30 Mon. to Sat., 11 to 4 Sun.). Eight dealers are housed in this large shop. You'll need to be patient and tenacious to hunt out the bargains in this mix of disposables and genuine antiques, but if you're the type who likes to sift through odd pieces to find the real gems, give it a try. Much of the jewelry is easy on the budget, rhinestones and plastic pieces from the '40s and '50s. Chairs and tables of wicker and wood are abundant. What some call junk, others call funk.

BOOKS

Napa County

Bookends Book Store (Manager: Thomas M. Pieper; 224-1077; 1014 Coombs St., Napa; open 9:30 to 6 Mon. to Sat., 9:30 to 9 Thur. and 10 to 5 Sun.). Serious and smart, this general purpose bookstore has a varied inventory and the classical music in the background adds a nice touch. The shop does a great deal of special ordering for customers. Sleekly contemporary, the shop lacks warmth, but you'll find a great selection of books.

Calistoga Bookstore — a cozy, friendly place.

Chris Alderman

Calistoga Bookstore (Manager: L. Reece Baswell; 942-4123; 1343 Lincoln Ave., Calistoga; open 10 to 6 Sun. to Thurs., 10 to 9 Fri., Sat.). It's always a good sign when you see a tangerine cat napping in the front window. Calistoga Bookstore is cozy—brick walls, tall ceilings, and antique lamps with fringe, with a fairly small supply of books geared primarily to the general reader. But specialties include a Native American corner and a full room devoted to history, mythology and symbols.

Copperfield's (Manager: Ken Losey; 252-8002; 1005 First St., Napa; open 10 to 9 Mon. to Sat., noon to 6 Sun.). See Copperfield's entry under Sonoma County.

Main Street Books (Manager: Liza Russ; 963-1338; 1371 Main St., St. Helena, open 10 to 5:30 Mon. to Sat.). A small, quaint store with a couple of comfortable reading chairs that make this a fun place to browse. There is a children's corner but otherwise a relatively limited selection of books. Tour books, cookbooks and photography books are racked and easy to leaf through. It's a refreshing place to spend an hour or two.

Napa Book Co. (Managers: Tom & Susan Turbin; 224-3893; 1239 First St., Napa; open 10:30 to 5:30 Mon. to Sat.). This bookstore definitely caters to kids, though parents are welcome to tag along, as well. Manager Susan Turbin apparently knows how to reach them; she's been a teacher for 20 years. A display of classics—*Treasure Island, Pinocchio, Heidi,* among others—in one of the windows; sections on parenting and teaching. The store itself is set up almost like an open classroom with different stations. The infants and toddlers corner has wooden chairs and a table heaped with books. More than 1,600 kids under 16 are members of the store's Book Club. Now that's fervent loyalty. Members can pick out one free book under $5 after they purchase 10 books. A bribe or a teacher's wizardry? You decide.

Sonoma County

Copperfield's (Manager Dave Sjosted; 829-1286; 138 North Main St.; Sebastopol; open 8 to 9 Mon. to Sat., 9 to 6 Sun.; there are other stores in this small chain in Petaluma, Santa Rosa and Rohnert Park). There's nothing like starting a new novel while sipping a cup of cappuccino or having a light lunch. You can do this at the small cafe at the rear of the Sebastopol Copperfield. (It's the only Copperfield's with a cafe, although there are plans to bring food to some of the other stores.) The bookstore itself is mainly general interest, but this being Northern California, there's a big section on metaphysics and several shelves devoted to holistic health, massage and yoga. Browse through the magazine stand for titles such as *Yoga Journal* or *Vegetarian Times*.

Plaza Books (Manager: Boris Bruton; 996-8474; 40 West Spain St., Sonoma; open 11 to 6 daily). Shopping here is like browsing through your grandfather's library. All the books are old with some more than 100 years old and of museum-quality. You'll find some first editions, though most are

Rohnert Park residents can find what they're looking for at their local branch of Copperfield's Books.

Chris Alderman

merely used books. As inviting as the texts themselves, are the feel of old leather bindings and the musty smell of old paper. The store has a little bit of everything, but specializes in books about wine and Jack London.

Sonoma Books (Managers: Carole & Marj Aleo; 935-1944; 483 First Street West, Sonoma; open 10:30 to 5 Tues. to Sat.). The emphasis here is on local authors. But there is also large section on self-awareness/popular psychology (a "hot" subject for Northern Californians), and sizeable selections of cookbooks and children's books. In addition, Sonoma Books carries candles and aromatic oils, self-help and New Age music tapes and hand painted greeting cards.

Toyon Books (Managers: Chip & Martha Wendt; 433-9270; 107 Matheson St., Healdsburg; open 10 to 9 Mon. to Thurs., 10 to 9:30 Fri. and Sat., 10 to 6 Sun.). Visitors looking for more information about Sonoma Valley's wineries will find a large "Wines and Vineyards" section at the front of this bookstore. Also prominently displayed are many titles on self-help and spiritual awareness. A bonus for parents is a well-stocked children's section tucked away at the back of the store.

CLOTHING

Napa County

Bellissima (Managers: Sally Bruhns & Maureen Marquez; 963-0162; 1325 Main St., St. Helena, open 10 to 5 Mon. to Sat.). Bruhns calls her work "wearable art." She has a studio at home where she creates hand-knitted and hand-woven clothes. Bruhns and partner, Maureen Marquez, both design specialty clothing to order. Some are high styled, like those you find in chic Los Angeles, others more tailored. Bellissima and the Creative Needle (see below) are share space in the same store.

Creative Needle (Managers: Susanne Salvestrin & Barbara Borges; 963-7533; 1325 Main St., St. Helena; open 10 to 5 Mon. to Sat.). Near the cash register you spy knitting needles dangling from a soft heap of yarn—a mohair sweater in progress. Welcome to the Creative Needle, where craft-oriented people come for supplies. The shop sells fine yarns and fabrics, as well as patterns for quilts, needlework and cross stitch. There are even classes to help customers master their crafts.

Mario's, Great Clothes for Men (Manager: Doug Champaign; 963-1603; 1309 Main St., St. Helena; open 10 to 6 daily). Apparently people shop here to make a statement—an expensive statement. Charmeuse silk boxer shorts are priced at $85. Charmeuse silk pajamas run about $400. The shop carries clothes by Nicole Miller and Jhane Barnes. Everything in this nifty store has a designer-look—the ties, the suspenders, the leather pants and even the boxer shorts. The sophisticated shopper who see himself as a canvas and wants to clothe himself in art will adore this shop—even if it makes him a pauper.

Modern Eve (Manager: Barney Thompson; 257-2824; 1222 First St., Napa; open 10 to 6 Mon. to Fri., 10 to 5:30 Sat., 11:30 to 4:30 Sun.). For the most part, you'll find conservative women's clothes with just a few racks of high-styled evening gowns that glitter with gold. Customers range from thirtysomething to 80. And small women who deem themselves misfits will be pleased to see the Missy and Petite clothing sections. A full assortment of accessories are proffered that will jazz up any outfit.

Overland Sheepskin Co. (Manager: Wendy Vogel; 944-0778; 6515 Washington St., Yountville; open 10 to 6 daily). Where once people sipped whiskey, today they are buying moccasins and sheepskin rugs. Overland is located in what was the Old Whistle Stop Bar from 1958 until 1989, and before that was Yountville's Railroad Depot. Photographs lining a wall trace the shop's history. The store still has the structure of a rustic depot: hardwood floors and brick walls. It's the only shop in Napa devoted to fighting mother nature's harsh winters a world away from Wine Country. There are leather and fur coats, rustic rain gear and fur hats.

Sonoma County

Button Down (Manager: Scott Clayton; 996-8816; 403 First Street West, Sonoma; open 11 to 6 daily). No off-the-rack department store fare in this men's clothing store. Typical are handmade Italian sweaters and shirts in luxurious cottons you won't find anywhere else. The store carries many items under its own label. Styles are casual: jeans, cotton sweaters and shirts, all woven in natural fibers.

Champagne Taste (Manager: Anne Gillet; 938-0858; 497 First Street West, Sonoma; open 10 to 6 daily). When you step into this boutique, you can't

Fine clothing for women at Dramatica in Sonoma.

Chris Alderman

help but wonder if you've been beamed to Beverly Hills' chic Rodeo Drive—a minimalist decor and an eclectic selection of clothing from the latest hot designers such as Matsuda, Moschino, Henry Lehr and Joan Vass. Anne Gillet has built such a reputation that New York magazine editors attend fashion shows at her place. The men's shop in the back carries Matsuda for men, Paul Smith, and Katherine Hamnett, to name a few. Nicole Miller's amusing ties and suspenders can be found here, as well. Bring your credit cards. Chic isn't cheap.

Dramatica (Manager: Marie Albano; 939-1413; 461 First Street West, Sonoma; open 10 to 6 Mon.to Sat., 11 to 5 Sun.). This store takes the edge off the "power" business suit. Dramatica carries suits in floral patterns, as well as delicate chiffon and rayon dresses. The store is pricey, but a fun small purchase could be antique-looking buttons to dress up a dull shirt.

Fabrications (Manager: Nancy Tobener; 433-6243; 118 Matheson St., Healdsburg; open 10 to 5:30 Mon. to Sat.). Adventurous stichers will be inspired by this store's exotic collection of natural fabrics from Guatemala, Bali, Africa and other locales. Dark batiks and unusual silks are specialties. The store also caters to experienced quilt makers with books and accessories. If you're in town for a longer stay, you may want to ask about Fabrication's quilting classes. Don't miss the collection of antique buttons.

Hot Couture (Manager: Susan King; 528-7247; 101 Third St., Santa Rosa; open 10 to 6 Mon. to Sat., 1 to 5 Sun.). If you always wanted to dress like Jackie Kennedy before she became Jackie O. or Elvis before he got fat, you can find the required duds at this vintage clothing store. Owners John and Marta Koehne's stock ranges from the 1920s to the '60s, but they are willing to bring in their collection of turn-of-the-century Victorian clothes for serious buyers. If you're not quite that serious, then maybe a pair of white go-go boots or a pillbox hat will do.

Las Manos (Managers: Elva Zimmerman; 578-1649; 133 Fourth St., Santa Rosa; open 10 to 6, Mon. to Sat., 11 to 4). Somehow you don't expect to find Central American ethnic clothing and jewelry in the middle of Railroad Square, but it's a pleasure nonetheless. Las Manos owners, Bruce and Diana Barkley, make periodic forays to Guatemala where they own a clothing factory, and they import chunky knit sweaters and flowing rayon blouses and skirts in bright, primary colors. The store also sells embroidered T-shirts from Guatemala, as well as blouses and shirts from Indonesia. There are a few men's shirts, although the man in question would have to be very confident to sport an orange, black and yellow rayon shirt that borders on loud. On the other hand, just right for a beach party!

GIFTS

Napa County

Hurd Beeswax Candles & Gift Gourmet (Managers: Mary Sue Frediani & Ellen Read; 963-7211; 3020 Hwy. 29, St. Helena; open 10 to 5 daily). The sweet scent of honey makes you wonder if a horde of bees might be lurking. Hurd is a tourist trap to be sure, but it's fun all the same. There are more than 200 types of candles, all handcrafted from sheets of pure beeswax. (Demonstrations are given for groups of 25 or more as long as you call in

Manager Mary Sue Frediana lights a spiral candle at Hurd Beeswax Candles, St. Helena.

Chris Alderman

The home rules at Vanderbilt and Co. in St. Helena.

Chris Alderman

advance.) In the gift and gourmet section, you'll find kitchenware, cook-books, wine tasting guides, cork screws, champagne stoppers and party goods. All the tools you need for a good time in Wine Country.

Flying Carpets & Art Decor (Managers: Marsha & Ray Tokareff; 252-8757; 1238 First St., Napa; open 10 to 5 Mon. to Sat., 11 to 4 Sun.). If you're look-ing for gifts and a T-shirt just won't cut it, a silk wall hanging might. At any rate it's a good excuse to check out this interesting shop in downtown Napa. You'll find ever-changing displays of masks, pottery or art alongside rugs from 14 countries. Soon to be a staple are ethnic jewelry and art from China.

S. Claus (Manager: Edy Allen; 944-XMAS; 7331 Hwy. 29, Yountville; open 10 to 6 daily). Wondering where to spy St. Nick and the Mrs. in the off season? Slip into S. Claus, the year-round Christmas shop. The store is filled with holiday cheer and an abundance of Christmas trees dressed in tinsel. Orna-ments range from Big Bird to grapevines to Victorian dolls. There's a special area just for tourists called Grapevine Gifts stocked with T-shirts, wine glasses and more. If you get tuckered out from all your early Christmas shopping, you can sit in the cafe and eat a piece of pumpkin cheesecake or a lemon square. Go ahead. Just pretend it's Christmas and you won't mind splurging on the calories.

T's 'n Tops (Managers: Sandi & Mike Perlman; 253-7177; 1139 First St., Napa; open 10 to 5:30 Mon. to Sat., 10 to 8 Thurs., noon to 4 Sun.). "How can I cope with Life when I can't even program my VCR?" This is the kind of philosophical, soul-searching question we found emblazoned on one T's 'n Tops T-shirt. The shop is Napa Valley's largest store for custom T-shirts and sweat shirts. Tourists will naturally gravitate to the festive black shirts celebrating Wine Country with colorful images of vineyards, grapes, and hot air balloons. As for the natives, they're bound to become regulars of the sports corner, chock-full of athletic uniforms and plaques.

Vanderbilt & Company (Manager: Tracy Heniford; 963-1010; 1429 Main St.; St. Helena; open 9:30 to 5:30 daily). V&C is brimming with all the smart, artsy fare you'd find in a glossy home and garden catalog. From bedding to kitchenware to patio sets—there is everything you need to warm up your home up with a little touch of country or cool it off with contemporary sleek. It's a refreshing place to shop, to say the least, with in-store fountains guaranteed to sooth the most harried tourist winding down from a hectic day of spending.

Sonoma County

Artifax (Managers: Thomas Rubel & Candace Tisch; 996-9494; 148 East Napa St., Sonoma; open 11 to 5 daily). A true sensory experience. You'll see exotic textiles and carved masks, smell burning incense and hear evocative tapes

Gifts from around the world are yours at Artifax in Sonoma.

Chris Alderman

of African drums and other ethnic music. Artifax's owners import eastern ritual art and crafts. They try to buy products from artisans who agree to use their profits to contribute to orphanages, health care clinics or other enterprises that benefit their own communities. Carved masks and woven fabrics predominate, also authentic musical instruments and earrings crafted from beads or coins. Artifax has thousands of stone, metal and wooden beads, from Africa, China, Tibet and other countries, so you can create your own jewelry.

Bertie's Gallery (Manager: Roberta "Bertie" Rothel; 823-3841; 1382 Gravenstein Hwy. S.; open 10 to 5 daily). Bertie herself is as much on display here as her stock of collectible dolls. She's a character and will demand that you take a walk through her garden, which she insists is the county's most beautiful—indeed, it's worth a look. The store carries the best in collectible (and expensive) dolls. The few Barbie dolls are special edition models. Collectors will be familiar with the elaborately dressed dolls from Victoria Ashlea and Ginny. Shoppers who come in with little girls, be prepared. Bertie will cajole them to pick up the dolls and love them. How's that for an irresistible sales pitch?

Bits & Pieces (Manager: Betty Van Zante; 431-1829; 330 Healdsburg Ave., Healdsburg; open 10 to 5 Mon. to Sat., 11 to 4 Sun.). Like to wear your art on your sleeve? This small shop carries brightly colored shirts and jackets with bold graphic designs billed as "wearable art" by owner Betty Van Zante, all handmade by local artists. What you buy here won't be available in your local department store. Also for sale are unusual and elaborate ethnic jewelry, such as silver pins dripping with colorful beads from Peru and "coin" earrings from Thailand.

Evans Designs Gallery (Manager: Candace Meaney; 433-2502; 355 Healdsburg Ave., Healdsburg; open 10 to 5 daily). Fans of creative pottery will find big bargains at this shop, which features factory outlet seconds, discontinued items and test pieces created by artist Tony Evans and his assistants at Evans Designs. Fortunately for the harried shopper, this isn't your typically sterile factory outlet. The merchandise is attractively presented and customers can watch a video explaining the Japanese pottery firing method called *raku*. Prices range from 60-to-90 percent off retail. A large round vase with a mottled black design goes for $175 retail. In the outlet, it's $52.50. Lamp bases (you buy the shades elsewhere) that sell for $100 retail, can be purchased here for about $50.

Hearth Song (Manager: Karen Smith; 829-0944; 156 N. Main St., Sebastopol; open 10 to 5 Mon. to Sat., noon to 5 Sun.; another shop is located in Santa Rosa at Magowan Dr. and Farmers Lane; 578-4215). Children who dream of knights, princesses and castles can feed their fantasies at this store specializing in creative toys largely imported from Europe. The magic wands, crowns and elf caps are designed to stimulate the child's imagination . There are many craft sets and parents will appreciate the unbreakable doll

Kids play AND learn at Hearth Song in Santa Rosa.

Chris Alderman

houses and castles. This store is one of two retail outlets in Sonoma County for the mail order company of the same name. Pick up a copy of their catalog in the store if you're in a hurry.

Noah's Ark (Manager: Dave Siegle; 431-0144; 320 Healdsburg Ave., Healdsburg; open 10 to 5:30 Mon. and Wed. to Sat., 11 to 4:30 Sun.). True to its name, Noah's Ark is loaded with stuffed animals of every stripe: zebras, pigs, lions, tigers and parrots. There are also animal note cards, posters and jewelry for the grownups. If you have a lot of money to spend, consider a giant fiberglass cow with a flat top that can be used for a desk. Or perhaps a gigantic fiberglass hippopotamus that opens up to reveal a full size sofa. Adorable wooden ark sets (complete with paired-off Mom and Pop animals) are perfect for small children. Don't miss the mural (covering the back wall of the store) depicting Noah on his ark leading the animals across the seas.

Sweet Potato (Managers: Rick & Carol Mohar; 526-2777; Railroad Sq., 100 Fourth St., Santa Rosa; open 10 to 7 Mon. to Sat., 9 to 6 Sun.). Are you a prankster? Then this is the place to stock up on gag gifts. This store has nothing you really need (how refreshing!) but some playful items you may deeply want: fake barf, a rubber chicken or a video of "How to Strip for Your Man." There's also has a good selection of new wave and artsy magazines from San Francisco.

Wild Rose (Manager: Karen McCrystle; 433-7869; 308 B Center St.; Healdsburg; open 10 to 5:30 Mon. to Sat., noon to 4 on Sun.). Painted wooden deck chairs that resemble pigs and cows and a jaunty collection of straw hats are just some of the cornucopia of gift items in this pastel-hued shop. Lovers of brightly painted salad or pasta bowls should find nice additions to their collections here. Gardening buffs will like the wicker baskets and small terra

Wild Rose in Healdsburg is a treat for all the senses.

cotta animals. The store also carries some casual women's clothing, such as linen pants and shirts as well as fragrant soaps and bath salts.

Wine Country Living (Manager: Phyllis Sweeley; 996-3453; 407 First St. West; Sonoma; open 10 to 6 Mon. to Sat., noon to 5 Sun.). Here's the place to find unusual Wine Country gifts for friends back home (especially if you've already loaded them down with bottles of vino). You might consider a terra cotta wine cooler (a variation on the ice bucket) decorated with cherubs or a picture frame bordered with grapes and grape leaves. If you're here close to Christmastime, the store carries sets of zany tree light covers shaped like cows, cacti and pieces of "laundry." Is nothing sacred?

JEWELRY

Indulge your exotic tastes at the Artful Eye in Calistoga.

Chris Alderman

Napa County

The Artful Eye (Manager: Christine Picon; 942-4743; 1333 A Lincoln Ave., Calistoga; open 10 to 6 Sun. to Thurs., 10 to 7 Fri. & Sat.). Walking through the Artful Eye is like meandering through a museum. The handcrafted jewelry is produced by some 300 artists and some pieces look as though they come from ancient cultures. Materials run the gamut: glass, feathers, sterling silver, rope, fine gemstones and even diamonds. The jewelry ranges in price from $8 to $3,000, but most of the pieces are lower-end sterling silver.

David's (963-0239; 1339 Main St.; St. Helena; open 10 to 5:30 Tue. to Sat., closed Sun. & Mon.). Essentially a designer's showcase for jewelry, this shop has a smart, contemporary feel—much like the style of the jewelry itself. David, the owner, is one of several designers whose work is displayed. Virtually every piece is handcrafted with clean, straight lines, and unusual shapes that play up classic gemstones and diamonds.

Discoveries Unlimited (Managers: Pat & Burt Quiggle; 963-4206; 1269 Main St.; St. Helena; open 10 to 5:30 Mon. to Sat., 10 to 4 Sun.). "Fabulous fakes." That's how Burt Quiggle refers to his line of jewelry. It's a step up from costume, but only a step. Everything is gold-plated and crafted by artisans. You'll find a hodgepodge of jewelry that you won't have to lock away in a safe deposit box as well as a smattering of Japanese masks, lacquered boxes, lamps, baskets and antique furniture. The Quiggles used to live in the Orient and still travel there several times a year in search of unusual gifts.

Harlequin (Manager: Mark London; 255-2121; 3158 Jefferson St., Napa; open 10 to 6 Tues. to Sat. and by appointment). You can lose yourself in a time warp here. Harlequin's two or three designers have custom-designed jewelry to mimic many periods, including Victorian and art deco. The store also carries imported 18-karat gold Italian, German and Swiss pieces, but tends to play up the "Harlequin Ring" designed by Mark London. This 18-karat gold, solitaire diamond ring won first place in the Lazare Diamond Design Contest in 1990.

Harlequin, Jefferson Street in Napa, displays some of Wine Country's finest jewelry.

Chris Alderman

Sonoma County

Classic Copies (Manager: Ray Stanz; 996-7956; 491 First St. West, Sonoma; open 10 to 5 Mon. to Fri., 10 to 5:30 Sat. & Sun.). Do you dream of wearing Tiffany jewels on a dime store budget? Classic Copies sells fakes with synthetic stones that look just like the real thing. While most of the metal is gold tone, there are some 14-karat gold pieces. Ray Stanz says the store attracts wealthy women who are afraid to wear their real jewels in public, as well as dreamers who want to look like a million. Which are you?

Mary Stage (Manager: Mary Stage; 938-1818; 126 West Napa St., Sonoma; open 10 to 5 Tues. to Sat.). Mary Stage concentrates on estate-purchased jewelry and silver, with a heavy emphasis on 1920s items. Some of the prettiest finds are delicate women's watches with skinny rhinestone bands.

Men's pocket watches are also featured. There's a good selection of jewelry with semi-precious stones such as jade, coral and onyx.

Micaela's Wine Country Antiques (Manager: Wilson Dills; 829-0732; 2830 Gravenstein Hwy., Sebastopol; 11 to 4 Wed. to Sun.). A small room next to the main antique store holds a cache of old jewelry, including a wonderful selection of men's pocket watches dating back to the late 1800s. There are a few 1930s-era Bulova watches with art deco-style faces. Some timeless women's pieces are pendants and pins with precious stones.

Tribal Beginnings (Manager: Leilani Kurz; 829-2174; 6761 Sebastopol Ave. in Gravenstein Station, Sebastopol; open 11 to 5 Wed. to Sat., or by appointment). This is one of the few places in Napa and Sonoma where you can find authentic Native American antique jewelry and textiles from the Navaho and Zuni as well as the local tribes of Pomo and Hupa. Some of the most beautiful pieces are antique silver and turquoise jewelry. Expect to pay big bucks for the authentic goods. If you're looking for something for a smaller budget, the store has a few porcupine quill and bead earrings. (They're prettier than they sound.)

SHOPPING AREAS

Napa County

CALISTOGA

People come to Calistoga in droves for peace of mind, making a spa-pilgrimage of sorts. For those ready to shop, relaxed after their mud treatment and massage, the strip of stores on Lincoln Ave. awaits them. The shops are both quaint and cosmopolitan. Of course there are a few tourist traps worth avoiding, but for the most part it is terrific fun to shop here.

For a visual treat visit *The Artful Eye* (942-4743), a gallery that has beautiful displays of jewelry, sculpture, painting, masks and clothing produced by over 500 artists. *The Bird's Eye* (942-0827) specializes in wearable art for women, much of it hand crafted batik. Check out the kimonos and the rack of machine washable silks. The *Calistoga Bookstore* (942-4123) is a good place to browse for books in a relaxed setting. Be sure not to trip over the tangerine tabby. *L. Funke & Son* (942-6235) has beautiful Gotcha brand shirts. And don't forget to top off your shopping spree with a treat at the *Good N Airy Angel* (942-0714), the ice cream shop/candy store/pastry extravaganza.

YOUNTVILLE

Yountville is a pretty town nestled between Napa and St. Helena, a pleasant enough place to shop if you don't mind typical. You will have to go on a treasure hunt for anything very "original" in Yountville, but you will succeed if you are patient.

The 1892 Richie Block building, with its unique latticework and stained glass detailing, proudly dominates Main Street in downtown St. Helena.

Chris Alderman

The principal shopping area is Vintage 1870. This complex, once the Groezinger Winery, evokes the past with its stone flooring, brick walls and wooden rafters. There is a fair amount of kitsch, but a sprinkling of interesting shops as well. *Hansel & Gretel Clothes Loft* (944-2954) caters to the needs of infants and children, chock-full of clothing, books and terrific toys. *Wee Bit O' Wool* (944-8184) has a wonderful array of sweaters, ponchos and fedora hats. And you'll feel like royalty wandering through *A Little Romance* (944-1350), a bedding and bath shop. It must be all those trinkets and lace.

The best shopping in Yountville is off the beaten path. Of course, you have to be in the market for antiques or winter wear. See also "Antiques" and "Clothing" in this chapter.

Sonoma County

HEALDSBURG

Healdsburg's town square looks like a town from a Norman Rockwell print, a town that time forgot. You'll have to hunt for bargains, though they can be found. The plaza is lined with inviting, upscale specialty shops such as *Friends in the Country* (433-1615) which features a collection of fine American country furnishings and fabrics. Shoppers who aspire to urban sophistication shouldn't miss *Palladio* (433-4343), a modern furniture shop with pieces designed by the owner. Across the street is the *Evans Designs Gallery* (433-2502) with discounted pottery lamps and vases, and across the square is *Robinson & Co.*(433-7116), an elegant housewares store. Don't forget to explore the side streets. *Vintage Antiques* (433-7461) is the best place to find bargains in Healdsburg.

SEBASTOPOL

Wind along Gravenstein Hwy. S. and you'll find a cluster of antique shops housed in old barns and schoolhouses. No big city emporia with polished furniture and snooty salespeople—this is real country shopping with some good buys for the sharp-eyed buyer. Be careful, of course. True antiques can easily be intermixed with stuff you can't imagine anyone saving, much less buying. *School Bell Antiques* (823-2878), housed in a turn-of-the-century school, is worth a long visit. So is *Robert's Relics* (829-1019), a tiny shop brimming with trinkets. If you continue up Gravenstein Hwy. to the intersection of Hwy. 12, you will be able to explore Sebastopol's North Main Street shopping area. Be sure to stop at *Copperfield's* (829-1286), a book store that encourages browsing and where you can treat yourself to a muffin or lunch in the cafe at the back of the store.

SONOMA

This little winery town with its Old World-style plaza is quickly being gen-trified. Today it hosts high-style clothing stores, chic gift shops, gourmet food shops, a sophisticated wine merchant and stores that sell African masks and textiles. Most shops are right on the plaza, but be sure to walk a block or two off the square in each direction. Otherwise you'll miss the *Chairhouse* (938-0298) with its fine collection of folk art. Another find is *Artifax* (996-9494), a store with an exotic mix of third-world crafts and textiles. And for a special treat, be sure to stop at *Plaza Books* (996-8474), there are few bookstores left that are like it.

CHAPTER NINE
Just the Facts, Ma'am
INFORMATION

Courtesy Five Oaks Farm

Five Oaks Farm offers winery tours in a surrey with a fringe on top.

Think of this chapter as a cross between a first-aid kit and a survival guide. The information covers emergencies, as well as everyday practical matters. Forget lugging around the phone book; don't pester the local librarian, the topics listed below are at your fingertips. A little peace of mind goes a long way — especially when you want to savor Wine Country.

Ambulance, Fire, Police	277
Area Codes, Zip Codes, City Halls	277
Banks	278
Bibliography	
Books You Can Buy	279
Books You Can Borrow	280
Climate, Weather Reports	282
Day Care	283
Guided Tours	283
Handicapped Services	284
Hospitals	285
Late Night Food and Fuel	285

Media
    Magazines and Newspapers   285
    Radio Stations   286
    Television Stations   287
Real Estate   287
Religious Services and Organizations   287
Road Service   288
Schools   288
Visitors' Bureaus   289

AMBULANCE, FIRE, POLICE, COAST GUARD

Simply dial **911** in both Napa and Sonoma counties. You will reach an operator who will swiftly put you through to the right agency: fire and rescue, ambulance, local police, sheriff, California Highway Patrol or Coast Guard Search and Rescue.

To report rape and sexual assault: *Napa Emergency Women's Services* at (707) 255-6397 or *Sonoma County's Rape Crisis Center* at (707) 545-7273. For the *Poison Control Center* call 1-800-523-2222 or (415) 476-6600.

AREA CODES, ZIP CODES, CITY HALLS

AREA CODES

The *Area Code* for Napa and Sonoma counties is 707.

The *Area Code* for San Francisco is 415; Oakland and Berkeley, 510.

The *Area Codes* for adjacent counties are as follows.

    Marin — 415   Mendocino — 707

    Alameda and Contra Costa — 510   Lake County — 707

    Solano — 707   Yolo — 916

ZIP CODES, CITY HALLS

	Zip Code	City Hall
Napa County		
Calistoga	94515	942-5188
St. Helena	94574	963-2741
Yountville	94599	944-8851
Napa	94558	257-9503
	94559	
	94581	

	Zip Code	City Hall
Sonoma County		
Bodega Bay	94923	
Healdsburg	95448	431-3317
Sebastopol	95472	823-7863
Santa Rosa	95401–95407	524-5361
Sonoma	95476	938-3681
Petaluma	94952–94954	778-4345

BANKS

Listed below are a sampling of regional and national banks. Each branch office is equipped with at least one automated teller machine. Note the systems to which each bank is electronically linked.

Napa Valley Bank (226-9932 or 800-635-4331). Linked to the "Star," "Cirrus" and "Plus" systems.

> Locations: 1 Financial Plaza, Napa
> 1400 Clay St., Napa
> 1221 Imola Ave., Napa
> 6470 Washington St., Yountville
> 1000 Adams, St. Helena
> 1110 Washington St., Calistoga

Bank of America (542-4433 or 800-523-3259). Linked to "Plus," "Star" and "Interlink" systems.

> Locations: 1429 Lincoln Ave., Calistoga
> 2 Financial Plaza, Napa
> 1700 First St., Napa
> 1001 Adams, St. Helena
> 35 W. Napa St., Sonoma
> 502 Healdsburg Ave., Healdsburg
> 1155 W. Steele Lane, Santa Rosa
> 2420 Sonoma Ave., Santa Rosa
> 7185 Healdsburg Ave., Sebastopol

Wells Fargo Bank (431-1667 or 579-4248). Linked to "Star," "Cirrus" and "Plus" systems.

> Locations: 445 Center St., Healdsburg
> 2960 Cleveland Ave., Santa Rosa
> 200 B St., Santa Rosa
> 2405 Fourth St., Santa Rosa
> 480 W. Napa St., Sonoma

BIBLIOGRAPHY

Browse through our bookshelves. Wine Country is an intriguing place, what with the specter of ghost wineries and the mystique of winemaking. If you want more detail, consider, if you will, the two lists below. *Books You Can Buy* offers titles generally available in Sonoma and Napa bookstores. For more information on Napa and Sonoma booksellers, see "Bookstores" in Chapter Seven, *Shopping*. *Books You Can Borrow* are generally found in Napa and Sonoma local libraries and in most public libraries elsewhere. They are typically no longer for sale. For more information on book borrowing, see "Libraries" in Chapter Four, *Culture*.

Books You Can Buy

WINE

Bernstein, Leonard S. The Official Guide to Wine Snobbery. New York: Quill Press, 1982. 160 pp., illus., $4.95.

Broadbent, Michael. *Pocket Guide to Wine Tasting.* New York: Simon & Schuster, 1988. 130 pp., illus., glossary, index, $9.95.

Johnson, Hugh. *Hugh Johnson's Pocket Encyclopedia of Wine.* New York: Simon & Schuster, 1990. 200 pp., maps, $10.95.

Johnson, Hugh. *Vintage: The Story of Wine.* New York: Simon & Schuster, 1989. 464 pp., photos. illus, bibliog., index, $39.95.

Kramer, Matt. *Making Sense of Wine.* New York: William Morrow, 1989. 190 pp., bibliog, index, $16.95.

Laube, James. *California's Great Cabernets.* California: Wine Spectator Press, 1989. 320 pp., $29.95.

Laube, James. *California's Great Chardonnays.* California: Wine Spectator Press. 1990. 352 pp., $29.95.

Parker, Robert M. Jr. *Parker's Wine Buyer's Guide.* New York: Simon & Schuster, 1989 to 1990. 914 pp., charts, appendix, index, $16.95

Thompson, Bob. *Simon & Schuster's Pocket Guide to California Wines.* New York: Simon & Schuster, 1990. 217 pp., maps, $10.95.

LITERARY WORKS

London, Jack. *Call of the Wild and Selected Stories.* New York: Penguin Books, 1960. 176 pp., $2.50.

Stevenson, Robert Louis. *The Works of Robert Louis Stevenson.* London: Octopus Pub. Group, 1989. 687 pp., $7.98.

BIOGRAPHIES

Dreyer, Peter. *A Gardener Touched With Genius, The Life of Luther Burbank.* Berkeley, CA: Univ. of California Press, 1985. 230 pp., photos, index, $12.95.

London, Joan. *Jack London and His Daughters.* Berkeley, CA: Heyday Books, 1990. 179 pp., photos, $10.95.

LOCAL HISTORY

Conaway, James. *Napa, The Story of an American Eden.* Boston, MA: Houghton Mifflin, 1990. 506 pp., photos, $24.95.

Heintz, William F. *Wine Country: A History of Napa Valley, The Early Years 1838 to 1920.* Santa Barbara, CA: Capra Press, 1990. 326 pp., photos, illus., $29.95.

Mullen, Barbara. *Sonoma County Crossroads.* Mendocino, CA: Pacific Transcriptions, 1987. 48 pp., photos, maps, footnotes, $5.95.

Wilson, Simone. *Sonoma County: The River of Time.* Chatsworth, CA.: Windsor Publications 1990. 121 pp., photos, illus., index, $25.95.

PHOTOGRAPHIC STUDIES

A Day in the Life of California. San Francisco, CA: Collins Publishers, Inc., 1988. Photographed by 100 of the world's leading photo journalists on one day, April 29, 1988. 236 pp., illus., photos, $19.98.

Wolman, Baron. *California From The Air, The Golden Coast, Aerial Photography.* San Francisco, CA: Chronicle Books, 1981. 142 pp., photos, $16.95.

RECREATION

Emmery, Lena & Sally Taylor. *Grape Expeditions in California.* San Francisco, CA: Sally Taylor & Friends, 1987. 74 pp., illus., maps, $7.50.

Lorentzen, Bob. *The Hiker's Hip Pocket Guide to Sonoma County.* Mendocino, CA: Bored Feet Publications, 1990. 201 pp., illus., maps, bibliog., index, $11.95.

Powers, Peter. *Touring California's Wine Country by Bicycle.* Eugene, OR: Terragraphics, 1990. 171 pp., maps, illus., $10.95.

TRAVEL

Matson, Robert W. *Sonoma Coast, North of San Francisco, The Untameable Coast.* Santa Rosa, CA: Sea Wolf Publishing, 1991. 73 pp., photos., illus, maps, $4.95.

Sangwan, B. *The Complete Wine Country Guidebook, Discovering California's Napa and Sonoma Valleys.* Tahoe City, CA: Indian Chief Publishing House, 1990. 135 pp., wine glossary, index, $7.95.

Books You Can Borrow

Benson, Robert. *Great Winemakers of California.* Capra Press, 1977. 295 pp., photos, illus., glossary. Twenty-eight winemakers tell all — their secrets of producing wines that rival those of France and Germany.

A quiet garden vista through the wide windows of the Sonoma Library.

Chris Alderman

Dutton, Joan Parry. *They Left Their Mark: Famous Passages through the Wine Country*. Illuminations Press., 1983. 180 pp., photos, bibliog., index. An historic look at the famous people who traveled through Wine Country and the influence they had on the region.

Haughey, Homer L. & Connie Kale Johnson. *Jack London Ranch Album*. Heritage Publishing, 1985. 48 pp., photos, maps, charts, text. A photo album of Jack London's life at his ranch near Glen Ellen.

Haynes, Irene W. *Ghost Wineries of Napa Valley*. Sally Taylor & Friends Publishing, 1980. 73 pp., photos, index. Take an eerie tour of old and abandoned wineries, if you dare.

Heintz, William F. *Wine Country: A History of Napa Valley, The Early Years 1838 to 1920*. Capra Press, 1990. 326 pp., photos, illus. The book is a history of California winemakers and winemaking during the Gold Rush, the Indian Wars and the construction of railroads.

Issler, Anne Roller. *Stevenson at Silverado*. Caxton Printers, Ltd. 1939. 247 pp., photos. The yellowed and worn pages of this book trace Stevenson's travels through Napa Valley. The book gives insight into his work *The Silverado Squatters*.

Johnson, Rheta Grimsley. *Good Grief: The Story of Charles M. Schulz*. Pharos Books, 1989. 254 pp., drawings, cartoons, bibliography. An intimate portrait of Charles Schulz, the Santa Rosan who creates the cartoon strip "Peanuts."

King, Norton L. *Napa County: A Historical Overview*. Self published, 1967. 98 pp., photos, bibliog., index. Geographic, topographic and geologic origins of Wine Country.

Kraft, Ken and Pat. *Luther Burbank: The Wizard and the Man.* Meredith Press, 1967. 261 pp., bibliog., index. In his time, Burbank was as famous as Henry Ford and this book chronicles both his life and his experiments at his "magic garden" in Santa Rosa.

LeBaron, Gaye, Dee Blackman, Joann Mitchell and Harvey Hansen. *Santa Rosa: A Nineteenth Century Town.* Historia, Ltd. pp. 210, photos, sources and notes, index. A history of Santa Rosa and its settlers gives insight into the entire region of Northern California.

Lundquist, James. *Jack London: Adventures, Ideas & Fiction.* Ungar, 1987. 188 pp. bibliog., index. A biographical portrait and critical study of the man who wrote *The Sea Wolf* and *The Call of the Wild.*

Wilson, Simone. *Sonoma County: The River of Time.* Windsor Publications, 1990. 121 pp., photos, illus., index. The book chronicles Sonoma County's metamorphosis as immigrants discovered its fertile river valleys, resources and mild climate.

CLIMATE AND WEATHER REPORTS

CLIMATE

The moderate weather common in Napa and Sonoma is a blessing for those who have suffered Midwestern blizzards. Winter is cool, with temperatures dipping down to the 40s. Rainy season begins in late December and lingers until April. Of course, the droughts in recent years have made the season somewhat unpredictable and the locals presently welcome each rain drop that falls. Rain makes for a lush countryside and hillsides ribbed with vineyards.

TEMPERATURE AND PRECIPITATION

Average Temperatures

	Napa	Sonoma
October	63.5	64.1
January	46.8	47.8
April	60.4	61.0
July	69.2	71.7

Average Annual Total Precipitation (1989)

	Napa	Sonoma
rain	16.1	19.8
snow	0	0

WEATHER REPORTS

Napa County

Calistoga	942-5188
Napa	253-5235
St. Helena	963-3601
Yountville	944-2988

Sonoma County

Cloverdale	894-3545
Healdsburg	431-3362
Sonoma	938-1519

DAY CARE

Child care spells relief for those parents who might want to roam Wine Country without their teetotaling tots. For travelers and newcomers alike, here's a sampling of reputable, licensed child care centers. The following organizations make free child care referrals:

Community Resources For Children, Napa (253-0366).
Community Child Care Council of Sonoma County (544-3077).
Here are a few specific options:

Napa County

La Petite Academy (Napa, 257-7796).
Little Friends (Napa, 252-8899)
Silver Lining Child Care Center & Preschool (Napa, 226-KIDS).

Sonoma County

Healdsburg Montessori Children's House (Healdsburg, 431-1727).
Happy Time Christian Pre-School & Day Care (Santa Rosa, 527-9135).
Alphabet Soup Pre-School and Day Care Center (Sebastopol, 829-9460).

GUIDED TOURS

Looking for some packaged fun? Consider our list of tours. They will take you on a Wine Country adventure via minibus, taxi, helicopter or horse drawn carriage.

FROM SAN FRANCISCO

Great Pacific Tour Co. (518 Octavia, San Francisco, 415-626-4499). This tour provides door to door service, picking up wine connoisseurs at the major hotels in San Francisco and whisking them north to Wine Country in a comfortable minibus or van. The tour begins with Sonoma County wineries and moves on to Napa County wineries. Count on a picnic at a choice spot.

WITHIN WINE COUNTRY

Five Oaks Farm (15851 Chalk Hill Rd., Healdsburg, 433-2422). Giddyup. This tour of Wine Country is by horse-drawn carriage, a surrey with a fringe on top to be exact. The carriage will take you near the vineyards of Alexander Valley. There will be a lot of talk about grape growing and later you will have a chance to taste the fine wines at Johnson's Alexander Valley Wines, Sausal Winery and Alexander Valley Vineyards Winery. Morning and afternoon rides. Lunch or dinner follows at Johnson's winery.

Napa Valley Helicopter Tours (1475 Fourth Street, Napa, 255-0809). These aerial tours offer a bird's-eye-view of Wine Country. You'll see the house and vineyards of film director Francis Ford Coppola, among other wineries, during the 30-minute flight.

Taxi Cabernet Tours (461 Crystal Springs Rd., St. Helena, 963-2620). Billed as "Prestigious Sightseeing for the Discriminating Traveler," you can choose between a Champagne Tour, a Small Boutique Winery Tour, a Winery and Restaurant Tour and a Hot Air Balloon Ride and Wine Tour, among others.

Wine Country Wagons (P.O. Box 1069, Kenwood, 833-2724). A rustic tour of wineries in the Kenwood area of northern Sonoma Valley is offered on a wagon drawn by Belgian draft horses. A gourmet lunch is included. By reservation only from May to October.

HANDICAPPED SERVICES

Wine Country is accessible — even in a wheelchair. Napa and Sonoma offer a number of easy solutions to help anyone with a handicap get around. Handicapped hikers might especially want to take note of the *The Hiker's Hip Pocket Guide to Sonoma County*, Bored Feet Pub. There is a special section for the handicapped describing the accessibility and amenities of various scenic trails.

Bear Flag Express (255-7631). Offers a bus route in Yountville and a connecting route to Napa. All buses are wheelchair-accessible.

Dial-A-Ride-Services, Inter City Van-Go (Greater Napa Area, 252-2600; Upper Valley, 963-4222). All vans are wheelchair-accessible.

The VINE (255-7631). The Valley Intracity Neighborhood Express has five routes in the city of Napa. All buses are wheelchair-accessible.

Volunteer Wheels of Sonoma County (573-3377). Transportation for senior citizens and disabled riders.

HOSPITALS

Healdsburg General Hospital (1375 University Ave., Healdsburg, 433-4461). 24-hour emergency care. Physician on duty. Call the general number and ask for the emergency room.

Queen of the Valley Hospital (1000 Trancas St., Napa, 252-4411; Emergency Room, 257-4038). 24-hour emergency care.

St. Helena Hospital (650 Sanitarium Rd., Napa; Emergency Room, 963-6425) 24-hour emergency care.

Santa Rosa Memorial Hospital (1165 Montgomery Dr., Santa Rosa, 546-3210; Emergency Room, 525-5207). 24-hour emergency services. Physician on duty.

Sonoma Valley Hospital (347 Andrieux St., Sonoma, 938-4545; Emergency Room, 938-0258). 24-hour emergency care.

LATE NIGHT FOOD AND FUEL

Insomniac after too much gourmet food or wine? Perhaps you're just a late-night traveler looking for a place to gas up. Here are some options for nightbirds.

Napa County

Bel Aire Shell Service (1491 Trancas, Napa).

Lucky (1312 Trancas St., Napa).

Safeway (1026 Hunt Ave., St. Helena).

Sonoma County

Fred's Union Service (8600 Gravenstein Highway, Cotati).

Lucky (390 Coddingtown Mall, Santa Rosa).

Safeway (477 W. Napa St., Sonoma).

MEDIA: MAGAZINES, NEWSPAPERS, RADIO STATIONS, AND TELEVISION

MAGAZINES AND NEWSPAPERS

California Visitors Review (P.O. Box 92, El Verano, 938-0780; weekly). A great magazine for tourists and natives alike. Interesting articles on wine-makers and upscale Wine Country hotels. Helpful charts and maps included in each issue.

The Healdsburg Tribune (706 Healdsburg Ave., Healdsburg, 433-4451; Wed. & Fri.). Published since 1953, this paper still has a '50s flavor. One key feature is the "Field & Vine" page which focuses on Wine Country.

The Napa Register (1615 Second St., Napa, 226-3711; daily). Since it was established in 1960, this paper has provided consistently good local coverage.

The Press Democrat (427 Mendocino Ave., Santa Rosa, 546-2020; daily). Purchased by *The New York Times* in the mid 1980s, *The Press Democrat* is the largest newspaper in the North Bay. It emphasizes Sonoma County, with little news of Napa.

The San Francisco Chronicle (901 Mission St., San Francisco, 800-323-3200; daily). This metropolitan daily is not impressive to look at but is a good source for national and international news. There are often good Wine Country articles in the "Food" and "People" sections.

The San Francisco Examiner (110 Fifth St., San Francisco, 800-345-3926; daily). Much cleaner-looking and wittier than *The Chronicle*. Since it's an afternoon paper, however, too few people read it.

Sonoma Business (3559 Airway Drive, Santa Rosa, 575-8282; monthly). A solid magazine that covers business and industry in Sonoma County quite well. It delves into the "politics" of business.

Sonoma Style (452 B St., Santa Rosa, 579-8418; monthly). A glossy magazine that often plays up style over substance, it still provides a festive look at Sonoma County. The articles tend to be off-beat and amusing.

The Wine Spectator (415-673-2040; 601 Van Ness Ave., Suite 2014, San Francisco; monthly) the magazine carries news of the wine world, including Napa and Sonoma, and plenty of what-to-buy advice.

RADIO STATIONS

KHTT-FM 92.9 (Santa Rosa, 545-3313. Top 40 pop music.
KQED-FM 88.5 (San Francisco, 415-553-2215). National public radio.
KRPQ-FM 105 (Rohnert Park, 584-1058). Country music.
KSRO-AM 13.50 (Santa Rosa, 545-3313). News and talk.
KVON-AM 14.40 (Napa, 252-1440). News and talk.
KVYN-FM 99.3 (Napa, 252-1440). Adult contemporary.
KXFX-FM 101.7 (Santa Rosa, 523-1369). Rock.
KZST-FM 100 (Santa Rosa, 528-2424). Adult contemporary.

TELEVISION

There's only one local station in Wine Country, *KFTY, Channel 50* (533 Mendocino Ave., Santa Rosa, 526-5050). Depending on your location, San Francisco and Oakland stations are often within range as well.

Both counties have access to cable television that offers most Bay Area and Sacramento TV channels, as well as the usual cable fare such as CNN, HBO, USA Network. *Viacom* services both the city of Napa (255-0300) and Petaluma (763-9800). *Post-Newsweek* supplies cable to Santa Rosa (544-7337) and *Multivision* services the city of Sonoma (996-8482) and Sebastopol (584-4617). *ML Media* hooks into St. Helena (963-7121).

REAL ESTATE

Buying a piece of the American Dream is downright costly in California. For some, prices may seem nightmarish. But if you come to Wine Country and decide to stay, here is information that may help you.

Housing costs in Sonoma and Napa are among the highest in the country. The median price for a single-family house in Napa County, for instance, is $155,400. Prices continue to rise, despite recession, although not as fast as they did during the 1980s. Most natives won't dicker endlessly over prices. They know they're not just purchasing real estate, they are also buying (or selling) rights to an ocean within reach, steep mountains and beautiful vineyards: a rare countryside.

For information on real estate, consult the yellow pages of Napa and Sonoma phone books under "Real Estate Agents." You can also try the *Napa Chamber of Commerce* (226-7455) and the *Sonoma Valley Chamber of Commerce* (996-1033.). For current information and helpful statistics on the real estate market, call the **Napa County Board of Realtors** (255-1040) and the **Sonoma County Realtors Association** (542-1579.). Finally you can follow the local newspapers. *The Press Democrat*, for instance, has a complete "Real Estate" section published every Sunday. See "Media" in this chapter.

RELIGIOUS SERVICES AND ORGANIZATIONS

The best sources for information about church and synagogue services are the Saturday editions of *The Napa Register* and *The Press Democrat*. The Napa and Sonoma County telephone books have comprehensive lists of all mainstream religious organizations along with specific church and synagogue numbers. You may also want to consult pamphlets published by the Napa and Sonoma Visitor Bureaus. For non-traditional groups, keep an eye on community bulletin boards at colleges such as Sonoma State University and Napa Valley College.

ROAD SERVICE

Puncture your tire on a broken bottle of 1986 Jordan Cabernet? Stranger things are known to have happened. *AAA* (253-2082) provides emergency road service from anywhere in Napa or Sonoma counties. Listed below are other 24-hour emergency road services.

Napa County

Calistoga Auto Body (942-5665).
Napa Vintage Towing (226-3780).
St. Helena Towing (963-1869).

Sonoma County

Express Towing (Santa Rosa, 578-7154).
Pellegrini's Towing (Healdsburg, 433-1700).
Sebastopol Towing (823-1061).

SCHOOLS

PUBLIC SCHOOL DISTRICTS

Napa County

Calistoga Joint Unified School District (Calistoga, 942-4703).
Napa County School District (Napa, 253-6800).
St. Helena Unified School District (St. Helena, 963-2708).

Sonoma County

Cotati-Rohnert Park Unified School District (Cotati, 792-4700).
Healdsburg School District (Healdsburg, 431-3435).
Piner-Olivet Union School District (Santa Rosa, 575-7057).
Roseland School District (Santa Rosa, 545-0102).
Santa Rosa School District (Santa Rosa, 528-5373).
Sonoma Valley Unified School District (Sonoma, 935-6000).

PRIVATE AND RELIGIOUS SCHOOLS

Napa County

Highland, A Private School (Napa, 255-2273).
Kolbe Academy (Napa, 255-6412).
St. Helena Montessori School (St. Helena, 963-1527).
St. John The Baptist Catholic School (Napa, 224-8388).

Sonoma County

Montessori Pre-School & Elementary School (Santa Rosa, 539-7980).
Open Bible Christian Academy (Santa Rosa, 528-0546).

St. Luke Lutheran Preschool & Day Care Center (Santa Rosa, 545-0512).
Sebastopol Christian School (Sebastopol, 823-2754).
Ursuline High School (Santa Rosa, 542-2381).

COLLEGES

Napa County

Napa Valley College (Napa, 253-3000).

Sonoma County

Empire College, Business School and Law School (Santa Rosa, 546-4000).
Santa Rosa Junior College (Santa Rosa; 527-4011).
Sonoma State University (Rohnert Park, 664-2880).

VISITORS' BUREAUS

Napa County

Calistoga (1458 Lincoln Ave., 942-6333).
Napa (1556 First St, 226-7455).
St. Helena (1080 Main St., 963-4456).
Yountville (6795 Washington, 944-0904).
Napa Valley Vintners Association (900 Meadowood Ln., P.O. Box 141, St. Helena, 963-0148).

Sonoma County

Bodega Bay (850 Hwy. 1, 875-3422).
Healdsburg (217 Healdsburg Ave., 433-6935).
Sebastopol (265 S. Main St., 823-3032).
Santa Rosa (637 First St., 545-1414).
Sonoma (453 First St. E., 996-1090)

Index

A

Abbey, The, 126
Actors' Theater, 103
airlines, national & charter, 18
airports, automobile routes from, 18-19; shuttle buses from, 19-20
Alderbrook Vineyards, 215
Alexander Valley Vineyards, 213
All Seasons Cafe, 133
Altimira, Father Jose, 5, 6
Ambrose Bierce House, 41
Ambrose Heath, 123-24
ambulance, 277
Anderson Winery, 181
antiques, 257-60
Arbor Guest House, 30-31
architecture, 78-79
area codes, 277
Arrowood Vineyards, 206
art galleries, 82-87
ARTrails, 86-87
arts and entertainment events, listings, 78, 99
Auberge du Soleil, 40, 124-26
auto racing, 221
automobile rentals, 18, 20-21; routes, 15

B

bakeries, 157-58
Bale Grist Mill, 87-88
ballooning, 221-23
banks, 278
Baroque Sinfonia, 96
beaches, 253

Bear Flag Revolt, 7-8
Beaulieu Vineyards, 181-82
Beazley House, 31
Belle de Jour Inn, 61
Belvedere Winery, 210
Beringer Vineyards, 188-89
Berkeley, 24
Best Western Garden Inn, 71
Best Western Hillside Inn, 71
Best Western Inn Napa, 70
bibliography, 279-82
bicycle rentals, 224
bicycling, 223-24
boat rentals, 225-27
boating, 224-27
Bodega Bay Fisherman's Festival, 107
Bodega Bay Harbor, 252
Bodega Bay Lodge, Best Western, 65
Bodega Coast Inn, 73
Bodega Harbor Inn, 73
book stores, 260-62
Bordeaux House, 37
Bosko's Ristorante, 134-35
Brannan Cottage Inn, 42
Brannan's Loft, 48
Brannan, Sam, 9
Brava Terrace, 127
brewpubs, 158-60
Brookside Vineyard, 31
Buena Vista Winery, 199-200
Burbank, Luther, 9; home and garden, 89-90
Burgundy House, 37

bus service, national, 16; regional, local, 16, 21-22

C

Cafe Pacifico, 135
Caffe 1991, 113-14
Caffe Portofino, 140-41
California Cafe, 116-17
California Museum of Art, 84
California Thai, 141-42
Calistoga Beer & Sausage Tasting, 107
Calistoga Inn, 48
Calistoga Spa Hot Springs, 52
Calistoga spas, 52-53, 231-43
Calistoga Wine Stop, 167
Calistoga, shopping areas, 273
Camellia Inn, 61
Campbell Ranch Inn, 64-65
campgrounds, general information, 74
campgrounds, Napa Valley, 75; Sonoma County, 75-77
Candlelight Inn, 31
canoeing, 224-27
Carneros Alambics Distillery, 175
Cavanagh Inn, 69
Caymus Vineyards, 182
Celebrate Sonoma, 107
Chablis Motel, 70
Chateau de Baun, 210
Chateau Hotel, 70
Chateau Montelena, 196-97

Chateau Napa-Beau-canon, 195
Chateau Potelle, 187
Chateau Souverain, 153, 211-12
Chateau St. Jean, 200
Chestelson House, 41
child care, day care, 283
Chimney Rock Winery, 177-78
China Room, 142
Christian Brothers, 189-90
Churchill Manor, 32
cinemas, movies, 79-81
Cinnabar Theater, 103-04
Cinnamon Bear Inn, 42
city halls, telephone numbers, 277-78
Clarion Inn Napa Valley, 70
climate, 3, 282-83
Clos du Bois, 207
Clos du Val, 178-79
Clos Pegase, 197-98
clothing stores, 262-65
coastal recreation, 251-55
coffee houses, 160-61
colleges, 289
Comfort Inn Napa Valley North, 71
Compadres, 117-18
Conn Creek Winery, 187
Consentino Winery, 181
Country Garden Inn, 32
Country Meadow Inn, 60
croquet, 227
Cross Roads Inn, 32
Culver's Country Inn, 48
Cuvaison Winery, 198

D
dance, 81-82
Davis Bynum Winery, 207-08
Days Inn, 71
De Loach Vineyards, 211
Dehlinger Winery, 208
delicatessens, gourmet shops, 161-63
DeMoor Winery, 187
Diner, The, 118-19
distances, travel, 16-17
Domaine Carneros, 175-76

Domaine Chandon, 119-20, 179
Domaine Napa Winery, 195
Doubletree Hotel, 58
Dr. Wilkinson's Hot Springs, 52
Dry Creek General Store, 163
Dry Creek Inn, Best Western, 61-62
Dry Creek Vineyards, 214

E
Econo Lodge, 71-72
El Bonita Motel, 42
El Dorado Hotel, 54
El Pueblo Motel, 71
El Rancho Tropicana, 72
Elm House Inn, 33
emergency numbers, fire, 277; police, 277
Estate Inn, 65-66
Fairview Motel, 72

F
Farmhouse Inn, 66
Farmhouse, The, 42
Feed Store, The, 136
Fellion's Delicatessen, 161
Ferrari-Carano Vineyards and Winery, 214-15
Field Stone Winery, 213
fish markets, 165
fishing, 227-29
Flamingo Resort Hotel, 58
fly fishing, 229
flying, 229-31
Folie à Deux Winery, 190
food and fuel, late night, 285
food purveyors, 157-63
Foothill House, 49
Foppiano Vineyards, 211
Forest Manor, 42-43
Fort Ross, 5, 88-89
Fountaingrove Inn, 58-59
Fourth Wall Stage Company, 104
Frampton House, 62
Franciscan Vineyards, 187

Freemark Abbey Winery, 195
French Laundry, 120-21
French wine, comparisons to, 14-15

G
Gables, The, 59
Gaige House Inn, 54
Genova Delicatessen, 161
Geyser Peak Winery, 212
gift stores, 265-70
Glen Ellen Winery, 200-01
Glenelly Inn, 54
Gloria Ferrer Champagne Caves, 202
Golden Haven Hot Springs & Resort, 52
golf courses, 231-34
golf, miniature, 251
Grand Cru Vineyards, 208
Grape Leaf Inn, 62
Gravenstein Apple Fair, 107
Gravenstein Inn, 66-67
Grgich Hills Cellars, 182-83
Grille at Sonoma Mission Inn, 137
guided tours, 293-94
Gundlack-Bundschu Winery, 206

H
Hacienda Winery, 206
Hakusan Sake Gardens, 176-77
handicapped, services for, 284
hang gliding, 230
Haraszthy, Agoston, 8-9
Harvest Inn, 43
Haydon House, 62
Healdsburg Inn on the Plaza, 63
Healdsburg, shopping areas, 274
Health and Harmony Festival, 107
Heart's Desire Inn, 67
Heitz Wine Cellars, 191
Hennessey House, 33-34

Heritage Inn, 72
Hess Collection, 83, 177
Hidden Oak, 54
Hideaway Cottages, 49
hiking, 234-37
historic sites, 87-92
history, natural, 1-3; cultural, 3-13
Holiday Inn Sonoma County, 72
Hometown Harvest Festival, 107
Hop Kiln Winery, 208-09
Hope-Merrill House, 65
horse racing, 239
horse rentals, 238-39
horseback riding, 237-39
hospitals, 285
Hot Air Balloon Classic, 107
Hotel St. Helena, 43

I
Indian Springs Spa and Resort, 53
Inglenook Napa Valley, 183-84
Ink House B&B, 44
Inn at Napa Valley, 34
Inn at the Tides, 67
Iron Horse Vineyards, 211

J
Jack London Lodge, 55
Jessel Gallery, 83-84
jewelry, 271-73
John Ash & Co., 138-40
John Muir Inn, 34
Johnson's Alexander Valley Wines, 213

K
Kenwood Pillow Fights, 108
Kenwood Vineyards, 202-03
kids' entertainment, 249-53
Korbel Champagne Cellars, 209-10
Kornell, Hanns, Champage Cellars, 191
Kozlowski Farms, 163

Krug, Charles, Winery, 192

L
L&M Motel, 72-73
La Belle Epoque, 34
La Casa, 138
La Gare, 143-44
La Residence Country Inn, 35
Lake Sonoma Winery, 215
Lambert Bridge Winery and Vineyards, 215
Landmark Vineyards, 206
Larkmead Country Inn, 49
Liberty Theater, 79
limousine services, 23-24
Liquor Barn, 167
Lisa Hemenway's, 144
Little Darlin's Rock 'N' Roll Diner, 150-51
lodging, general information, 28-29; price codes, 28
lodging, Napa County, 30-53; Sonoma County, 54-74
London, Jack, 77, 91
London, Jack, State Historic Park, 91-92
Los Robles Lodge, 72
Lucas Wharf, 154-55
Lytton Springs Winery, 215

M
Madrona Manor, 63-64, 151
magazines, 285-86
Magliulo's Pensione, 55
Magnolia Hotel, 38
Maps, 300
Marin County, 24
Mark West Vineyards, 211
Markham Winery, 196
Martini, Louis, Winery, 193
Matanzas Creek Winery, 203-04
Matisse, 145-46

Mayacama Mountains, 1, 3
Mazzocco Vineyards, 215
Meadowood, 44
Melitta Station Inn, 59
Mendocino County, 25
Merryvale Vineyards, 196
Milat Vineyards, 196
Mill Creek Vineyards, 216
Mission San Francisco Solano, 77
Miwok Indians, 4
Mixx, 146-47
Mondavi, Robert, Winery, 185
Mont St. John Cellars, 178
Monticello Cellars, 178
Motel 6, Napa, 70; Santa Rosa, 72
motels, Napa County, 70-71; Sonoma County, 71-73
motels, price codes, 89
Mount View Hotel, 50
movie houses, 79-81
Mt. Saint Helena, 3
Mt. Veeder, 1
Mumm Napa Valley, 184
Murphy-Goode Estate Winery, 213
museums, 92-97
music, 96-99; series and festivals, 98-99
Mustards Grill, 121-22

N
Napa County Fair, 108
Napa Inn, 35
Napa Valley Lodge, Best Western, 38
Napa Valley Olive Oil Manufacturing Co., 161-62
Napa Valley Railway Inn, 38
Napa Valley Symphony, 96
Napa Valley Travelodge, 71
Napa Valley Wine Auction, 109
Napa Valley Wine Festival, 109

Napa Valley Wine Train, 115
newspapers, 285-86
nightlife, 99-102
Noblett Gallery, 84-85
North Coast Ballet, 82

O
Oak Knoll Inn, 38-39
Oakland, 24
Oakville Grocery, 162
Old Vic, 147
Oleander House B&B Inn, 39
Oliver House Country Inn, 45

P
Pacific Alliance Stage Company, 104-05
parks, state and county, 234-37
Pasta Shop, The, 163
Paulsen, Pat, Vineyards, 213
Pedroncelli, J., Winery, 213
Peju Province, 187
Petaluma Adobe, 90-91
Petaluma Butter & Egg Days, 108
Piatti Ristorante, 122-23
Piccola Festa Italiana, 108
Pine Ridge Winery, 181
Pine Street Inn & Eurospa, 53
Pink Mansion, 50
Piper Sonoma Cellars, 210
pizzarias, 165-66
Point Reyes National Seashore, 249
poison control and information, 277
Pomo Indians, 4
Prager Winery, 196
Preston Vineyards, 216
Prohibition, effects of, 11
Pygmalion House, 59

Q
Quail Mountain B&B, 50

R
racquetball, 239
radio stations, 286
Rafa's, 149-50
Rafanelli, A., Winery, 216
Raford House Inn, 64
rail service, national, 18
Rancho Caymus Inn, 41
rape crisis information, 277
Raven Movie House, 79
Ravenswood Winery, 204-05
Raymond Vineyard, 196
real estate, 287
recreation sites, map, 233
Red Lion Hotel, 57
Redwood Empire Ballet, 82
religious services, organization, 287
rental properties, 30
restaurants, Napa County, 113-35; Sonoma County, 136-56
restaurants, price codes, 113
Ridenhour Ranch House Inn, 68
Ripley's Memorial Museum, 93-94
Ripley, Robert L., 93
Rivers End, 73
road service, 288
Roche Winery, 206
Rochioli Vineyards, 211
rock climbing, 240
Rodger's Creek Fault, 3
Rohnert Park Symphony, 96-97
Roman Spa, 53
Rose Garden Inn, 45
Royal Oak at Silverado Country Club, 116
running, jogging, 240
Russian River Barrel Tasting, 109
Russian River Vineyards Restaurant, 155-56
Russian River Wine Festival, 109-10
Russian settlement, 5-6

Rutherford Hill Winery, 188
RV parks, 75-77

S
Sacramento, 24-25
Salt Point Lodge, 73
Salute to the Arts, 110
San Andreas Fault, 3
San Francisco earthquake, 1, 190
San Francisco, museums and events, 24, 110-11
Sandman Motel, 72
Santa Rosa Symphony, 98
Sattui, V., Winery, 193-94
Sausal Winery, 213
Schoolhouse Inn, 68
schools, private and religious, 288-289
schools, public, 288
scuba diving, 254
Sea Ranch Lodge, 69
seasonal events, 107-09
Sebastiani Winery, 205-06
Sebastopol, shopping areas, 274-75
Sebastopol Apple Blossom Festival, 108
Sequoia Grove Winery, 188
Seventh Street Inn, 70
Shady Oaks Country Inn, 46
Sharpsteen Museum, 92-93
shopping areas, 273-75
shopping, 256-75
Silver Oak Cellars, 186
Silver Rose Inn, 51
Silverado Country Club, 36
Silverado Motel, 71
Silverado Museum, 93
Silverado Vineyards, 180
Simi Winery, 212-13
Sinkey, Robert, Vineyards, 181
skating, ice, 240; roller, 241
sky diving, 230
Slug Fest, 108
Smothers Brothers Wines, 206

softball, 241
Sonoma Cheese Factory, 164
Sonoma County Fair, 108
Sonoma County Harvest Festival, 110
Sonoma County Museum, 94
Sonoma County Wine & Food Series, 110
Sonoma County Wine Auction, 110
Sonoma Film Institute, 81
Sonoma Hotel, 55
Sonoma Mission Inn & Spa, 56
Sonoma Valley Inn, Best Western, 56
Sonoma, shopping areas, 275
Spanish settlement, 4-5, 6-10
spas, 241-44
Spring Mountain Vineyards, 196
Spring Street Restaurant, 128
St. Francis Winery and Vineyards, 205
St. Helena Bottle Shop, 167
St. Helena Wine Merchants, 167
St. Supery Vineyard and Winery, 185-86
stables, 238-39
Stag's Leap Wine Cellars, 180-81
Stahlecker House, 37
Starmont at Meadowood, 129
Stemmler, Robert, Winery, 216
Sterling Vineyards, 198-99
Stevenson, Robert Louis, 9, 77
Stonegate Winery, 199

Strong, Rodney, Vineyards, 211
Summer Repertory Theater, 105-06
Super 8 Lodge, 72
Sutter Home Winery, 194-95
swimming lakes and pools, 244-46

T
Taj Mahal, 148
television stations, 287
Tengu, 149-50
tennis, 246-48
Terra, 130
theater, 102-06
Thistle Dew Inn, 56-57
tidepooling, 254-55
Tides Wharf, 154-55
television, cable, 287
Timber Cove Inn, 73
Timberhill Ranch, 69
Tip Top Liquor Warehouse, 167
Topolos at Russian River Vineyards, 211
tours, guided, 283-84
Tra Vigne, 130-31
train excursions, 22
Traverso's, 164-65, 167-68
Tre Scalini, 152
Trefethen Vineyards, 178
Trilogy, 132
Trojan Horse Inn, 57
Truffles, 156

U
Union Motel, 74

V
Vallejo, Gen. Mariano, 5, 7-8; home of, 91
Valley of the Moon Winery, 207
Viansa Winery, 207
Vichon Winery, 187
Villa Mt. Eden, 188
Village Inn & Spa, 53

Vineyard Inn, 57
Vintage Inn, 39-40
Vintage Towers, 64
Vintners Inn, 59-60
visitors' bureaus, 289-90
Vista Cinema, 79

W
Wappo Indians, 4
watersports, 224-27
weather information, 283
Webber Place, 40
whale watching, 248-49
White Oak Vineyards, 211
White Sulphur Springs Resort, 46
Whitehall Lane, 196
Windsor Vineyards, 211
Wine Country Film Festival, 79, 81
Wine Country Inn, 46
wine country, seasonal events, 109-10
Wine Exchange of Sonoma, 168
Wine Festival and Crafts Fair, 110
wine industry, history of, 8-13
wine shops, 166-68
wine tasting, techniques, 174
Wine Valley Lodge, 71
wine, glossary, 171, 216-19
wineries, architecture of, 77; maps of, 172, 173
winery tours, general information, 170

Y
Yount, George, 5, 7
Yountville, shopping areas, 273-74

Z
Zinfandel Inn, 46-47
zip codes, 277-78

LODGING BY PRICE — INNS, B&Bs

Price Codes

Inexpensive:	Up to $75
Moderate:	$75 to $125
Expensive:	$125 to $175
Very Expensive:	Over $175

Napa County

INEXPENSIVE
Calistoga Inn

**INEXPENSIVE--
   MODERATE**
Calistoga Spa Hot
   Springs
Dr. Wilkinson's Hot
   Springs
El Bonita Motel
Golden Haven Hot
   Springs & Resort
Pine Street Inn & Eurospa
Roman Spa
Webber Place
White Sulphur Springs
   Resort

**INEXPENSIVE--
   EXPENSIVE**
Hideaway Cottages
La Residence Country
   Inn
Mount View Hotel
Pink Mansion

**INEXPENSIVE--VERY
   EXPENSIVE**
Village Inn & Spa

MODERATE
Arbor Guest House
Bordeaux House
Brannan's Loft
Brookside Vineyard
Burgundy House
Chestelson House
Culver's Country Inn
Elm House Inn
Larkmead Country Inn
Napa Valley Railway Inn
Rose Garden Inn
Quail Mountain B&B
Shady Oaks Country Inn

**MODERATE--
   EXPENSIVE**
Ambrose Bierce House
Beazley House
Brannan Cottage Inn
Churchill Manor
Cinnamon Bear Inn
Country Garden Inn
Farmhouse, The
Forest Manor
Hotel St. Helena
Indian Springs Spa and
   Resort
Ink House B & B
John Muir Inn
La Belle Epoque
Magnolia Hotel
Napa Inn
Napa Valley Lodge, Best
   Western
Oleander House B&B Inn
Silver Rose Inn
Stahlecker House
Wine Country Inn
Zinfandel Inn

**MODERATE--VERY
   EXPENSIVE**
Foothill House
Harvest Inn
Oliver House Country
   Inn
Rancho Caymus Inn

EXPENSIVE
Candlelight Inn
Hennessey House
Inn at Napa Valley

**EXPENSIVE--VERY
   EXPENSIVE**
Cross Roads Inn
Oak Knoll Inn
Vintage Inn

VERY EXPENSIVE
Auberge du Soleil
Meadowood
Silverado Country Club

Sonoma County

INEXPENSIVE
Dry Creek Inn, Best
   Western
Jack London Lodge
Pygmalion House

**INEXPENSIVE--
   MODERATE**
Camellia Inn
Cavanagh Inn
Frampton House
Grape Leaf Inn
Gravenstein Inn
Magliulo's Pensione
Ridenhour Ranch House
   Inn
Schoolhouse Inn
Seventh Street Inn
Sonoma Hotel
Vintage Towers

**INEXPENSIVE-
   EXPENSIVE**
Flamingo Resort Hotel
Fountaingrove Inn
Vineyard Inn

MODERATE
Campbell Ranch Inn
Country Meadow Inn
Glenelly Inn
Hidden Oak
Hope-Merrill House
Super 8 Lodge
Melitta Station Inn
Raford House Inn
Thistle Dew Inn

**MODERATE--
   EXPENSIVE**
Belle de Jour Inn
Bodega Bay Lodge, Best
   Western
Doubletree Hotel
Estate Inn
Farmhouse Inn
Gables, The
Gaige House Inn
Haydon House
Heart's Desire Inn

Inn at the Tides
Sonoma Valley Inn, Best
    Western
Trojan Horse Inn

**MODERATE--VERY
    EXPENSIVE**
Red Lion Hotel

Vintners Inn

EXPENSIVE
El Dorado Hotel
Healdsburg Inn on the
    Plaza
Sea Ranch Lodge

**EXPENSIVE--VERY
    EXPENSIVE**
Madrona Manor

VERY EXPENSIVE
Sonoma Mission Inn &
    Spa
Timberhill Ranch

LODGING BY PRICE -- MOTELS

Price Codes
Inexpensive: Up to $50
Moderate: $50 to $75
Expensive: $75 to $100
Very Expensive: Over $100

Napa County
INEXPENSIVE
Motel 6, Napa
Silverado Motel

MODERATE
Napa Valley Travelodge

**MODERATE-
    EXPENSIVE**
Wine Valley Lodge

**EXPENSIVE--VERY
    EXPENSIVE**
Best Western Inn Napa
Chablis Motel

Chateau Hotel
Clarion Inn Napa Valley
Comfort Inn Napa Valley
    North

Sonoma County
INEXPENSIVE
Best Western Hillside Inn
Heritage Inn
L&M Motel
Motel 6, Santa Rosa
Sandman Motel
Union Motel

**INEXPENSIVE--
    MODERATE**
Bodega Harbor Inn
Fairview Motel

**INEXPENSIVE-
    EXPENSIVE**
Salt Point Lodge

MODERATE
Best Western Garden Inn
Econo Lodge
El Pueblo Motel
El Rancho Tropicana
Holiday Inn Sonoma
    County

**MODERATE--
    EXPENSIVE**
Los Robles Lodge

EXPENSIVE
Timber Cove Inn

**EXPENSIVE--VERY
    EXPENSIVE**
Days Inn
Rivers End

VERY EXPENSIVE
Bodega Coast Inn

RESTAURANTS BY PRICE

Price Codes
Inexpensive   up to $10
Moderate $10 - $20
Expensive $20 - $30
Very Expensive $30 or more

Napa County

MODERATE
Abbey, The
All Seasons Cafe
Ambrose Heath
Bosko's Ristorante

Cafe Pacifico
Compadres
Diner, The
Mustards Grill
Spring Street Restaurant

EXPENSIVE
Brava Terrace
Caffe 1991
California Cafe
Piatti Ristorante
Terra

Tra Vigne
Trilogy

PRIX--FIXE
French Laundry

VERY EXPENSIVE
Auberge du Soleil
Domaine Chandon
Napa Valley Wine Train
Royal Oak at Silverado
    Country Club
Starmont at Meadowood

Sonoma County
INEXPENSIVE
Little Darlin's Rock 'N'
  Roll Diner
Old Vic
Rafa's
Tengu

MODERATE
California Thai
China Room
Feed Store, The

La Casa
La Gare
Madrona Manor
Mixx

EXPENSIVE
Caffe Portofino
Lisa Hemenway's
Lucas Wharf
Russian River Vineyards
  Restaurant
Taj Mahal

Tides Wharf
Tre Scalini
Truffles

PRIX--FIXE
Matisse

VERY EXPENSIVE
Chateau Souverain
Grille at Sonoma Mission
  Inn
John Ash & Co.

RESTAURANTS BY CUISINE

Note: For your convenience, we list here restaurants serving specific ethnic cuisines. Restaurants featuring American, California and/or Continental cuisine are many in number, and their definitions of cooking styles are hard to pin down. See Chapter 5, *Restaurants*, under the town where you expect to dine.

Napa County
FRENCH
All Seasons Cafe
Brava Terrace
Domaine Chandon
Starmont at Meadowood
Trilogy

ITALIAN
Bosko's Ristorante
Piatti Ristorante
Tra Vigne

JAPANESE
Terra

MEXICAN
Cafe Pacifico

Compadres
Diner, The

Sonoma County
BRITISH
Old Vic

CHINESE:
China Room

FRENCH
Chateau Souverain
La Gare
Matisse

GREEK
Russian River Vineyards
  Restaurant

INDIAN
Taj Mahal

JAPANESE
Tengu

ITALIAN
Caffe Portofino
Tre Scalini

MEXICAN
La Casa
Rafa's

THAI
California Thai

NAPA AND SONOMA MAPS

Cities, population of, xiii
Topography, 2
Access, 16-17
Napa County Wineries,
  172

Sonoma County
  Wineries, 173
Recreational Sites, 233
Napa, (city), 300
Santa Rosa, 301

Sonoma (city), 302
Petaluma, 303
Cultural Sites, 304

About the Author

A transplanted Midwesterner from Indiana, Tim Fish has settled in Petaluma, California, and is the "Arts and Entertainment" critic for *The Press Democrat* in Santa Rosa. His circuitous journey has taken him through Kentucky, where he graduated from Western Kentucky University after winning *Rolling Stone* magazine's college journalism award; to New York City, where he interned with *Forbes* magazine; and to Illinois and Ohio, where he wrote news and feature articles for various newspapers. In addition to his many freelance writing credits is publication in *The Wine Spectator*. He admits to a serious avocation of wine tasting and collecting. He shares his enthusiastic commitment to northern California with his wife, Peg Melnik, who worked with him on this book, and with his daughter, Sophie.

The pages of this book were composed on Quark Express by Berkshire Publication Services, Gt. Barrington, Massachusetts. The typeface, Palatino, created in the mid-20th century by Hermann Zapf, is named for the famous 16th-century calligrapher, Giambattista Palatino. Design of original text for the Great Destination series was by Janice Lindstrom, Stockbridge, Massachusetts.

CITY OF NAPA

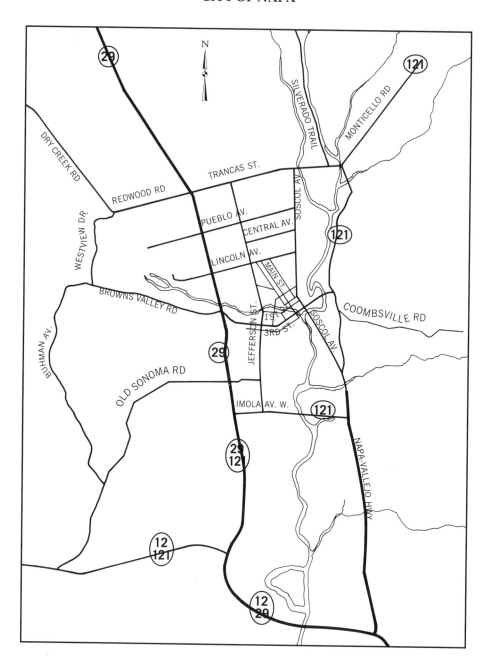

CITY OF SANTA ROSA

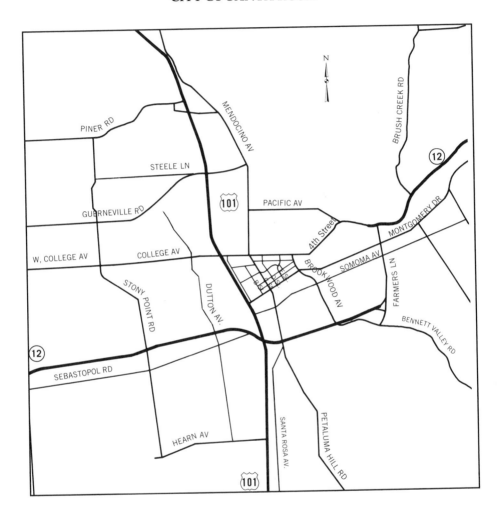

CITY OF SONOMA

City Map

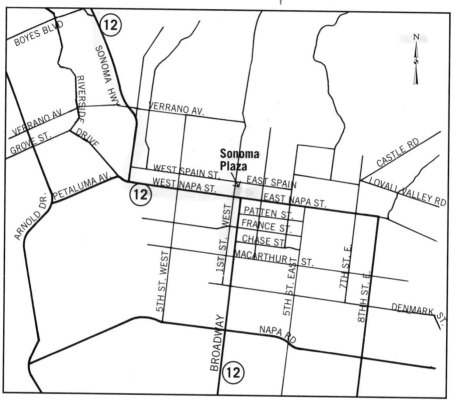

CITY OF PETALUMA

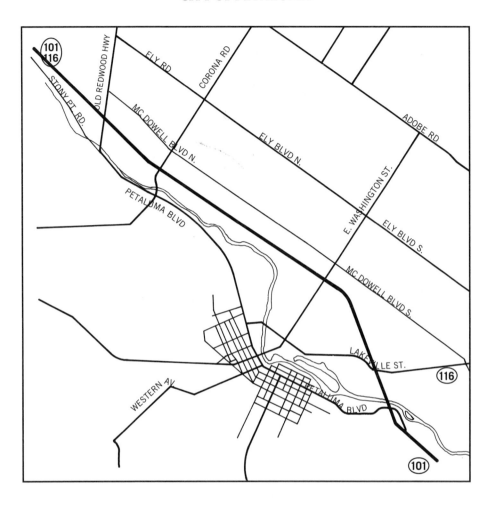

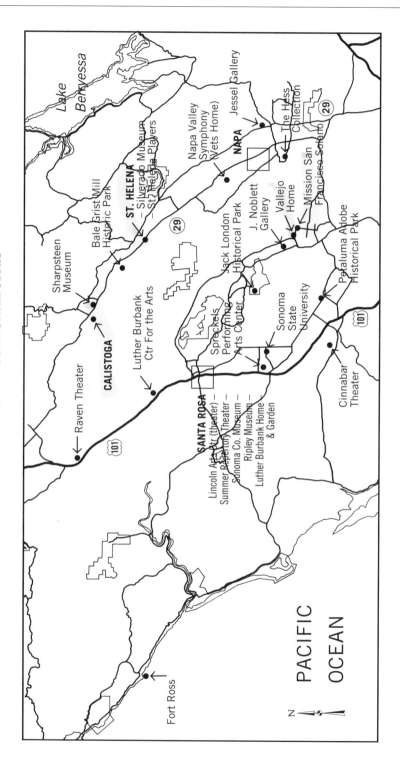

NAPA AND SONOMA CULTURAL SITES